M

Chinese Capitalists
in Japan's New Order

Chinese Capitalists in Japan's New Order

The Occupied Lower Yangzi,
1937–1945

Parks M. Coble

UNIVERSITY OF CALIFORNIA PRESS
Berkeley · Los Angeles · London

University of California Press
Berkeley and Los Angeles, California

University of California Press, Ltd.
London, England

Library of Congress Cataloging-in-Publication Data

Coble, Parks M., 1946–
    Chinese capitalists in Japan's new order : the
occupied lower Yangzi, 1937–1945 / Parks M. Coble.
        p.   cm.
    Includes bibliographical references and index.
    ISBN 0-520-23268-2 (cloth : alk. paper).
    1. Shanghai (China)—Economic conditions.
2. Shanghai (China)—Politics and government.
3. China—Foreign relations—Japan.   4. Japan—
Foreign relations—China.   5.   Sino-Japanese
Conflict, 1937–1945—Economic aspects—China—
Shanghai.   I. Title.
HC428.S5234 C635   2003
330.951'132042—dc21   2002012587

Manufactured in the United States of America
12   11   10   09   08   07   06   05   04   03
10   9   8   7   6   5   4   3   2   1

The paper used in this publication is both acid-free
and totally chlorine-free (TCF). It meets the minimum
requirements of ANSI/NISO Z39.48–1992 (R 1997)
(Permanence of Paper).

For Elizabeth, Lucy, Robert,
Parks, McLeod, and LaBorde

Contents

Tables

Acknowledgments

This study has benefited from grants from the Committee on Scholarly Communication with the People's Republic of China for research at the Shanghai Academy of Social Sciences, from two faculty development leaves from the University of Nebraska, and from a travel grant from the Stanford East Asia National Resource Center. The Shanghai Academy of Social Sciences was most helpful in two research visits. I would like to thank SASS's Resource Center for Chinese Business History as well as its Institute of History, Institute of Literature, and Institute of Economics. I am particularly grateful to Chen Mengxiong, Du Xuncheng, Huang Hanmin, Tang Zhenchang, Xu Xuejun, Shen Zuwei, Zhang Zhongli, and Zheng Qingsheng for their assistance in Shanghai. In addition I am deeply grateful to the Harvard-Yenching Library, the Fairbank Center for East Asian Research at Harvard, the East Asian Collection at the Hoover Institute, and the University of Nebraska–Love Library for access to collections. Most especially I thank the Fairbank Center, which has served as my "home away from home" as I worked on this study.

Many friends have provided assistance by reading or commenting on portions or all of the manuscript and by providing research materials and ideas. I must particularly thank Kai Yiu Chan, Sherman Cochran, Joshua Fogel, Po-shek Fu, Takeshi Hamashita, Christian Henriot, William Kirby, Elisabeth Köll, Chi-kong Lai, Pui-tak Lee, Sophia Lee, Andrea McElderry, Ramon Myers, Peter Schran, Keith Schoppa, Peter Seybolt,

Frederic Wakeman, Bernard Wasserstein, Wei Peh-t'i, Wong Siu-lun, and Wen-hsin Yeh for their assistance and suggestions. During my many visits to the Fairbank Center, James (Woody) Watson and Rubie Watson have been most helpful. I am grateful to many graduate students in my seminars at the University of Nebraska who were forced to read portions of the work in progress. They gave valuable feedback. Finally, I would like to thank Robert G. Root and Marilyn M. Root for always pressuring me to finish this project.

Two deceased colleagues were especially inspirational. In the early stages of this project, even though he was already seriously ill, my mentor and friend Lloyd E. Eastman provided encouragement and valuable suggestions for research, as he had always done. He is missed. Professor Benjamin Schwartz, whose breadth of knowledge and range of interest were legendary, was always a source of inspiration and insight. Ben was particularly helpful with this study, often delivering his advice over lunches at the Fairbank Center. Ben shared stories of his wartime experiences as an army officer in signal intelligence when he monitored Japanese secret radio traffic. He cautioned me to never consider "Japan" a monolithic entity when discussing the war. Japan had no single program or plan in China, he noted. He and his co-workers were constantly amazed at the disagreements among and within different Japanese groups operating in China, both military and civilian. I benefited greatly from Ben's advice, as well as that of many other friends and colleagues at the Fairbank Center.

My scholarly training was as a specialist in modern Chinese history. As my research interests in recent years have led me to deal with Sino-Japanese interactions, I found myself needing to learn more about Japan. During this process I have benefited from association with three groups. The Sino-Japanese Studies Group headed by Joshua Fogel has provided both direction and impetus to focus on the Japan side of things. For many years I have also been attending sessions of the Midwest Japan Seminar. Although the topics have varied from the Jomon to the Heisei eras, I have always found the seminar thought provoking and useful. I thank the many participants, leaders, and sponsors over the years. Finally, I benefited from participation in the Faculty and Curriculum Development Seminar on Japan sponsored by the Association of American Colleges and Universities. I thank the many colleagues who participated in and led the program, particularly Cameron Hurst and Jane Spalding.

Association with the Chinese Business History Group has also been fruitful. Participation in a conference at the University of Akron in October 1995 was instrumental in shaping the second half of this manuscript. Andrea McElderry, Robert Gardella, and Jane K. Leonard were particularly important in organizing both the conference and the group. Conferences sponsored by the Chinese Military History Society have been essential in fostering my understanding of war and conflict. Finally, my involvement with the Historical Society for Twentieth-Century China has been a source of pleasure and intellectual growth. I am grateful to Marilyn Levine, Ka-che Yip, David Barrett, Guido Samarani, Larry Shyu, and many other society members.

During the decade in which I worked on this project, I gave portions of the study at numerous conferences, including the annual meetings of the Association for Asian Studies, the American Historical Association, the Midwest Conference on Asian Affairs, Luce Seminars at Cornell and Berkeley, the Midwest China Seminar, and the Fairbank Center Seminar. Some portions of this text have been published in different formats as a result of participation in conferences. I thank Routledge for permission to reprint portions of an article, "Chinese Capitalists and the Japanese: Collaboration and Resistance in the Shanghai Area, 1937–45," which appeared in *Wartime Shanghai*, edited by Wen-hsin Yeh (1998, pp. 62–85). A portion of this manuscript is derived from "Japan's New Order and the Shanghai Capitalists: Conflict and Collaboration, 1937–45," in David P. Barrett and Larry N. Shyu, editors, *Chinese Collaboration with Japan, 1932–1945: The Limits of Accommodation* (Stanford, Calif.: Stanford University Press, 2000). Material from the earlier version is used here with the permission of Stanford University Press.

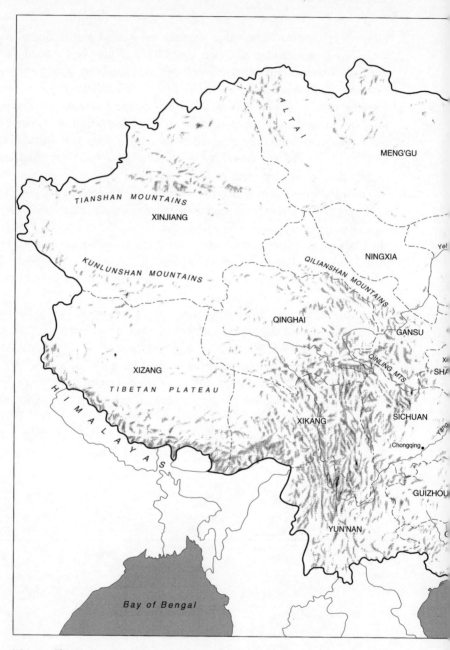

Map 1. China.
Source: Wen-hsin Yeh, *Provincial Passages: Culture, Space, and the Origins of Chinese Communism* (Berkeley: University of California Press, 1996).

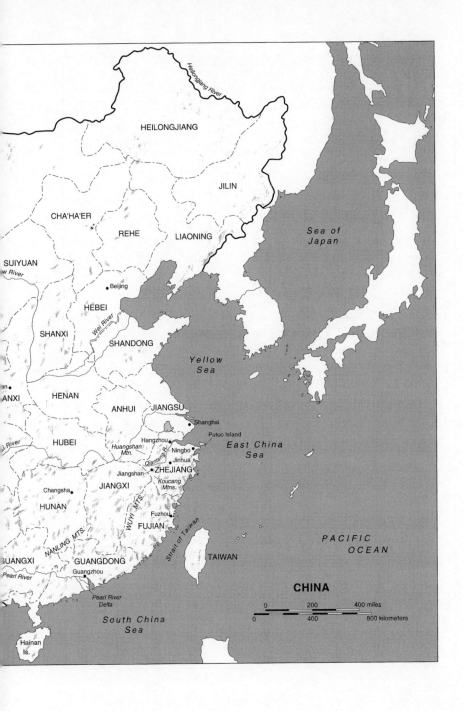

HEILONGJIANG

Heilongjiang River

JILIN

CHA'HA'ER

REHE   LIAONING

Sea of
Japan

SUIYUAN
w River

• Beijing

HEBEI

SHANXI

Wei River

SHANDONG

Yellow
Sea

ANXI   HENAN

ANHUI   JIANGSU

Shanghai

Putuo Island

Hangzhou•

Huangshan   Ningbo•
Mtn.

Qiantang R.   Jinhua•

Jiangshan•   ZHEJIANG

East China
Sea

i River   HUBEI

Changsha•   JIANGXI

Koucang
Mtns.

HUNAN

WUYI MTS.

Fuzhou•

NANLING MTS.   FUJIAN

Strait of Taiwan

PACIFIC
OCEAN

GUANGXI   GUANGDONG

Guangzhou•

TAIWAN

CHINA

Pearl River

Pearl River
Delta

South China
Sea

0   200   400 miles

0   400   800 kilometers

Hainan
Is.

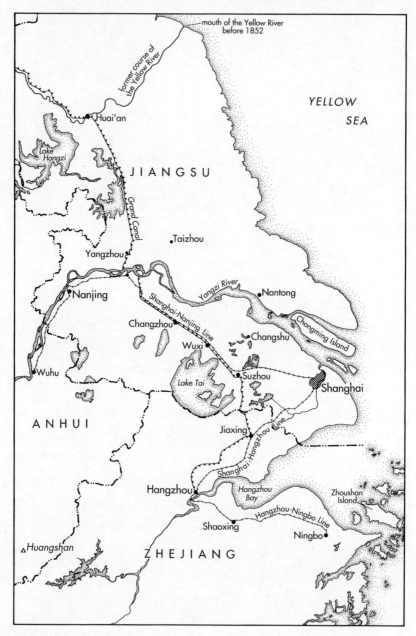

Map 2. The Lower Yangzi.
Source: Frederic Wakeman Jr., *Policing Shanghai, 1927–1937*
(Berkeley: University of California Press, 1995), p. 26.

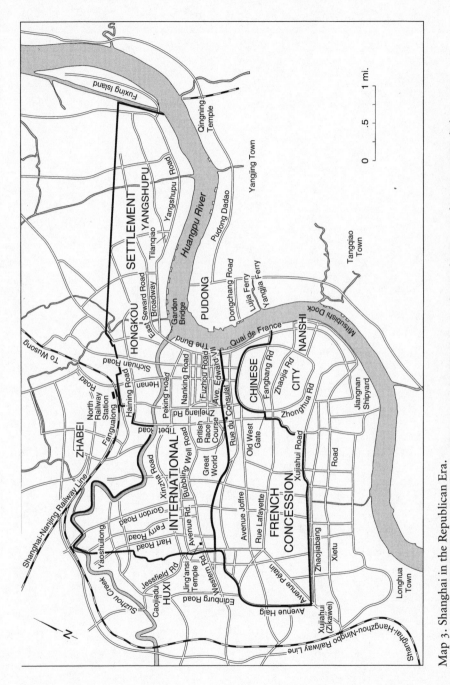

Map 3: Shanghai in the Republican Era.
Source: Hanchao Lu, *Beyond the Neon Lights: Everyday Shanghai in the Early Twentieth Century* (Berkeley: University of California Press, 1999), p. 41.

Introduction

Even in a century filled with war, revolution, and death, the eight years of the Sino-Japanese war stand out as a time of great violence and change. From the summer of 1937, when the Japanese swept through the economic and political heartland of China, cities and rural areas alike suffered devastation. The toll in human costs was staggering. Though exact figures will never be known, more than three million Chinese soldiers and probably eighteen million civilians perished. At least ninety-five million became refugees. Property losses are even harder to assess, but one recent estimate is more than US $100 billion.[1] Despite the enormity of this event, the war of resistance (as it is called in China) is probably the least studied and understood period of twentieth-century Chinese history. Within four years of the Japanese defeat, the Communists and Chairman Mao triumphed over Chiang Kaishek (Jiang Jieshi) and the Guomindang. This 1949 divide has nearly eclipsed the earlier war as a subject of scholarly interest. When Western scholarship has looked at the war era, notes Stephen MacKinnon, it "has focused not on the war itself but on the continuing political struggle for supremacy between the Communists and the Nationalists."[2]

Nor has the situation in China itself been better. For the first thirty-five years of the People's Republic, the war was largely ignored, save for commemorating the leadership of Chairman Mao and the Chinese Communist Party in China's resistance. The sacrifice of millions of soldiers in the Nationalist forces led by Chiang Kaishek was simply erased from public memory. Even the landscape of Beijing, notes Arthur Waldron, reflects this forgetting. "You will find no central war memorial: there is no cenotaph, no tomb of the unknown soldier, no elite honor guard, no eternal flame."[3] Of late, however, there has been an almost complete reversal, what Waldron labels a "new remembering," a sudden outpouring of works commemorating war heroes and detailing Japanese war atrocities. The genesis of this new remembering is a desire by the government to bolster a feeling of patriotism. Sensing the failure of communist ideology to generate loyalty to the Beijing government, China's leadership has turned to the war to weave the mythology of national struggle. "The new remembering of the Second World War in China," again quoting Waldron, "is part of a general recasting of Chinese history, culture, and memory, both popular and official, that attempts to cope with the failure of the communist state to create a culture and patriotism of its own."[4]

The "new remembering" in China has produced numerous studies of the war era and made possible scholarly work on this critical event. Yet the political agenda to which this work must conform prohibits a truly fresh examination of the war and its meaning for China. Thus neither Western nor Chinese scholarship has yet come to terms with a full understanding of the war. Only in Japan has the war been the focus of a vigorous academic debate. Yet the war certainly deserves a new examination by Western scholars. "The Sino-Japanese War transformed Chinese social, cultural, and political life in a fashion analogous to the impact of World War I on Europe," argues Stephen MacKinnon, "but the historian has yet to examine how."[5]

The purpose of this study is to analyze the war experience of a small but important group—Chinese capitalists in Shanghai and the lower Yangzi area. On the eve of the war, a small but dynamic and important modern sector flourished within China's economy. Following the lead of Western and Japanese businessmen in the treaty ports, Chinese entrepreneurs gradually moved into modern industry, transportation, and banking. The line between "traditional" and "modern" was often blurred. Modern industry might simply be advanced handicraft production using new energy sources. Yet the changes created a growing economic force, one heavily concentrated in Shanghai and the lower Yangzi. Indeed, more than half of the modern industry in China (excluding Manchuria) in 1937—measured in capital investment, number of workers, and value of output—was centered in greater Shanghai. Often in intense competition with Japanese and Western businessmen, the Chinese capitalists of the lower Yangzi were playing a key role in the transformation of at least part of China.

The outbreak of the Sino-Japanese war in 1937 and the horrendous fighting in the Shanghai area dealt a devastating blow to the fortunes of this group. Factories lay in ruins, warehouses burned, ships were sunk or commandeered, railways torn asunder. The accumulated physical plant from several decades of investment was destroyed. Yet by the end of 1937, Chinese Nationalist armies were forced into a long retreat, abandoning the lower Yangzi to the Japanese. In 1938, Wuhan and the key areas of the central Yangzi fell, as did the southern metropolis of Canton (Guangzhou). Although Chinese resistance continued from the interior and the Japanese hold on the occupied areas was never complete, millions of Chinese came to live under enemy occupation. Although some retreated with the Nationalists, by the end of 1938 nearly 46 percent of China's population lived in occupied areas.[6]

Yet that statistic actually understates the damage done to nascent Chinese capitalist entrepreneurs. Save for the foreign concessions in Shanghai and the British Crown Colony of Hong Kong, all of the key economic centers of coastal China would come under Japanese control by the end of 1938. Before the war, this occupied area had generated nearly 93 percent of China's textile production, 94 percent of flour milling, and 94 percent of China's international trade and contained almost 85 percent of China's railroads.[7] Nearly the entire modern sector of China's economy fell under enemy control.

But what of the experiences of the Chinese capitalists who had developed enterprises in this modern sector? Were they able to survive as businessmen during the war? Did they collaborate with the Japanese, join the resistance, or simply wait out the war? In fact there is little scholarly work that addresses the experiences of Chinese capitalists during the Japanese occupation. This is in part simply a result of the long neglect of the war of resistance by both Chinese and Western writers. Yet additional obstacles have inhibited such a study. With the Communist victory of 1949, many of China's most prominent businessmen left the new People's Republic. Few had any desire to recapitulate their wartime experiences. The question of collaboration during wartime is after all a sensitive issue in any culture. Many years elapsed after World War II before forthright accounts of the Vichy regime emerged in France. In memoir literature from occupied populations during the war, historical memory has generally emphasized resistance rather than collaboration. Those who lived in Vichy France have "remembered" their role in the underground far more readily than their acquiescence to the puppet authorities. To-day, more than half a century since the war, writings on "collaboration" and "war guilt" still raise passions in Europe. A similar construction of memory prevails among Chinese concerning the war years: people are far more likely to recount resistance than collaboration, or to say nothing at all.[8]

The 1949 divide is also an obstacle to dealing with the wartime activities of Chinese capitalists. Following the revolution, the writing of history in China fell under the Maoist approach in which Chinese capitalists were increasingly condemned as "class enemies." During the anti-rightist campaigns of the late 1950s and especially in the Cultural Revolution of the 1960s, Chinese businessmen who worked with the Guomindang or the Allied Powers during the war were often considered just as guilty of "crimes against the people" as those who collaborated with the Japanese. The term *hanjian* (traitor) was simply another in a long list of labels—comprador, bureaucratic capitalist, class enemy, running dog of imperialists—that were applied to pre-1949 businessmen.

Yet, just as the post-Mao era brought a "new remembering" of the war, there has been a sudden and even more dramatic turn in the treatment of capitalists by writers in China. Since 1978, the People's Republic has entered a reform era in which voluminous histories of Chinese capitalists and their enterprises have suddenly appeared. The portrayal of capitalists in these new studies is a complete reversal of the Maoist line. Now these historical capitalists are seen as progressive entrepreneurs who helped modernize China, struggling against countless obstacles such as technological backwardness and foreign competition. Indeed, the tone of much of the literature is so celebratory that it rivals the "captains of industry" approach that once dominated Western writing on business history. What accounts for this sudden reversal? This new "heroic capitalist" literature is clearly an attempt to support the reform policies. As Tim Wright has noted, "While on the surface [the new literature] deals with the historical record, its real intention is to support the current economic reforms. Such an 'activation of the propaganda potential' of historical or literary figures has been the central feature of most academic writing in China, whether in the Maoist period or since; indeed it was also common in Confucian historiography." This new writing therefore should be seen as reflecting, Wright argues, "the close link between the academic studies [on Chinese capitalists] and current policy concerns. . . . A judgement on their quality as historiography may well miss the point."[9]

The old Communist narrative of the capitalist as class enemy has thus given way to a new depiction of entrepreneurs as "patriotic capitalists," pioneers in the development of China's modern economy. The formulation *"aiguo shiye jia"* (patriotic industrialist) appears in the titles of numerous biographical articles.[10] This emphasis on patriotism is not accidental. Widespread disillusionment with communist ideology had created a vacuum in China. Just as the "new remembering" of the war of resistance is an effort by Beijing to promote nationalism as a glue to hold nation and party together, so too is the new depiction of "patriotic industrialist." As Wright has said, "One of the ironies of Maoist 'moral' incentives in industry was their failure to instill a corporate spirit among workers." The Chinese leadership has increasingly turned to an emphasis on patriotism to increase "enterprise spirit."[11]

The wartime record of the Chinese capitalists falls at the intersection of these two historiographical movements in China—the "new remembering" of the war of resistance and the recasting of capitalists as "patriotic entrepreneurs." Much of the new biographical writing on capitalists in China simply glosses over the war years, for reasons that this study will illuminate. When the war experiences are discussed, they typically follow a "resistance narrative." In this reconstruction, the heroic capitalist attempts at great odds and under difficult circumstances to move his factory or enterprise to the unoccupied interior. Under constant threat of enemy bombing, businessmen oversaw the loading of equipment on rickety boats to make this great journey.

This reconstructed patriotic narrative of the heroic capitalist was not entirely new. During the war itself, Chinese Nationalist propaganda celebrated the sacrifice of China's businessmen in their support of the war. The Chongqing government's English language publication, *China at War,* often ran articles lauding the contribution of those Chinese businesses that had relocated. In the summer of 1939, for instance, the journal praised the efforts involved in moving a Shanghai paper mill to the interior. "Ducking behind the machinery as shells from the Japanese shrieked and crashed," it recounted, "employees of a Shanghai paper mill saved their machines and sent them off on a perilous 1,500-mile river journey to west China. . . . 'We dismantled our machinery under fire,' the assistant manager told the reporter. 'Every employee jeopardized his own safety to save his machinery from bombs and planes.'" In another case, the journal reported in its November 1939 issue that Chiang Kaishek had given a special commendation to the general manager of the Baoyuan Coal Mining Company. In celebration of his support of refugees, Chiang presented him with a scroll reading, "peerless loyalty."[12]

This type of patriotic narrative was to be expected during the war years. Its sudden reemergence in China, following decades of denunciations of capitalists, is a bit startling. A new 1996 study edited by Shen Zuwei and Du Xuncheng of the Shanghai Academy of Social Sciences, for example, is entitled *Guonan zhong de Zhongguo qiye jia* (Chinese entrepreneurs during the period of national difficulty). It contains heroic accounts of twenty industrialists, including "Xiang Songmao: Diyi ge kangRi xunnan de qiye jia" (Xiang Songmao: The first entrepreneur martyred in the anti-Japanese war of resistance); "Fang Yexian: daozai diwei qiangtan xia" (Fang Yexian: Under enemy gunfire); "Rong Desheng: juebu yu diren 'hezuo'" (Rong Desheng: Who absolutely refused to cooperate with the enemy). Although these studies are well researched, all strongly emphasize the patriotic capitalist approach.[13]

Another new study by Sun Guoda, *Minzu gongye da qiantu—kangRi shiqi minying gongchang de neiqian* (The great removal of national industry: Chinese-owned industries move to the interior during the war of resistance period), likewise follows the heroic line. "On August 13, 1937, there is the sound of artillery fire at Wusong; the invasion of the Japanese bandits spreads through Jiangnan. . . . At this most serious moment of the national struggle for survival," queries Sun, "what of the national entrepreneurs?" They began the great advance inland in order to preserve their existence and "advanced the historically unprecedented anti-Japanese struggle."[14] This new literature thus blends the new heroic view of the war with a positive, patriotic look at Chinese entrepreneurs. Although valuable in opening up areas of research and publication, the new historiography is clearly grounded in contemporary policy concerns.

The wartime experiences of Chinese capitalists of the lower Yangzi area deserve a fresh look. That is precisely the aim of this study—to detail the wartime situation of Chinese entrepreneurs, to discuss how they survived or failed to survive the war, to analyze their relationships with the occupying forces, and to assess the impact of the war on the subsequent historical development of Chinese business. Among the themes I will develop is that, first, the war gravely weakened Chinese entrepreneurs. Not only did the war wreak enormous damage on the physical plants of Chinese businesses, but the war disrupted markets, devastated transportation, and reduced Chinese currency to worthless paper. Although some engaged in speculation and profiteering, the capitalists as a group suffered tremendous losses. A second observation will be that despite individual heroism, the experiences of most Chinese businessmen come closer to collaboration with the Japanese than to the heroic, nationalist narrative. Finally, I will argue that the war left a strong imprint on the organization and operation of Chinese business. The difficult conditions of wartime China favored certain features of Chinese business culture, which in turn were enhanced by the war experience. The legacy of these years thus continued after 1945. Many of the methods used to survive the war aided Chinese businessmen who chose to leave the People's Republic in 1949 and faced a new challenge of survival. By examining the wartime experiences of Chinese entrepreneurs from a fresh perspective, one not tied to particular policy concerns, I believe that we can enrich our understanding of modern Chinese history in general and the history of Chinese business and economic development in particular.

PART ONE

War

CHAPTER 1

Surviving the Fall of Shanghai

In the month immediately following the Marco Polo Bridge Incident of July 7, 1937, the fighting between China and Japan was confined to north China, and hope for a settlement seemed viable. The eruption of conflict in Shanghai on August 13, however, quickly brought the two countries into total war. Chiang Kaishek, leader of the Guomindang (Nationalist) Government, who had pursued a policy of appeasement since the Manchurian Incident of 1931, now decided that he could afford no further concessions. Feeling that he had a much better chance of holding the Japanese at Shanghai than in the north, Chiang rushed the core of his military into the new front. Eventually seventy-one Chinese divisions, totaling 500,000 men, would be sent to Shanghai, and the two Japanese divisions that began landing on August 13 would be joined by many more. Under the command of General Matsui Iwane, Japan's Shanghai Expeditionary Force would grow to 200,000 men. The bloody Battle of Shanghai would become the most intense conflict since Verdun in World War I. Although Japanese forces were much better equipped and led than were the Chinese, Chiang's troops did include divisions trained and aided by German advisers, including five artillery regiments that possessed substantial foreign weaponry.[1]

The ferocity of Chinese resistance shocked the Japanese, who held Chinese military prowess in contempt and expected the cakewalk they had enjoyed in Manchuria six years earlier. Japanese casualties would reach 50,000 by year's end, far exceeding anything they had anticipated. Despite all Chinese efforts though, the Battle of Shanghai would become a disastrous defeat. Japan quickly established complete dominance in the air and waters surrounding Shanghai; even the city's buildings provided little shelter from Japanese artillery and bombs. Matsui would slowly wear down the Chinese forces ringing Shanghai.

The turning point in the Battle of Shanghai occurred on November 5, when a Japanese force of 30,000 landed south of Shanghai at Hangzhou Bay in an amphibious landing that was virtually unopposed. Six days later, the Japanese 16th division landed farther up the Yangzi River, west of Wusong. Japanese troops now threatened to outflank the Chinese positions, forcing a general retreat. When Chiang's troops held their positions rather too long, an orderly withdrawal turned into a rout. One by one, key cities in the lower Yangzi fell. On November 19, a defensive line at Suzhou was hurriedly abandoned. On December 13, the Japanese entered Nanjing, and the infamous "Rape of Nanking" would begin. Chiang and his forces regrouped in the central Chinese city of Wuhan, but the losses had been devastating. An estimated 300,000 of his soldiers lay dead, his best German-trained divisions shattered and his elite Whampoa officers reduced to a fraction of their old strength.

This brutal fighting was also a disaster for the civilian population. For ninety days the two armies fought in one of the mostly densely inhabited and economically vital areas of China. Chiang deployed his major forces in a ring around central Shanghai, hoping to use urban fighting to negate Japanese advantages in weaponry and mobility. The foreign concessions—the International Settlement and the French Concession—largely escaped the devastation, though not entirely so. The most infamous incident occurred on August 14 when a Chinese pilot attempting to bomb a Japanese warship anchored in the Huangpu River dropped his bombs short of the target. Some landed in the midst of Nanjing Road, Shanghai's premier shopping street, others at the Great World Amusement Center. Nearly 2,000 civilians died in the carnage. Japanese forces also occupied the Hongkou section of the International Settlement, which lay north of the Suzhou Creek. Long considered the "Japan town" of the settlement, this area held one of the largest concentrations of Japanese residents in China. Overall, the remaining foreign concessions were an island of peace in the midst of bloody conflict; refugees poured into the area.[2]

All around the concessions, the destruction was extensive, particularly in the northern section of Shanghai. The Zhabei area, located just north of the International Settlement, was a major industrial center and residential area for working Chinese. The Battle of Shanghai actually began here on August 13; within days the neighborhood was essentially leveled. The battle lines extended east into the adjacent Hongkou area and beyond that to the Yangshupu waterfront sector, which stretched northeast on the west bank of the Huangpu River. Intensive fighting occurred all the way north to the town of Wusong, where the Huangpu met the Yangzi River, near its mouth at the Pacific Ocean. The many factories and warehouses in this battle zone suffered heavy damage. The fighting was somewhat less intense to the south and southwest of Shanghai, but Japanese forces overran the old walled city of Shanghai and the Nanshi section to its immediate south. The Longhua area (southwest of the French Concession) and the western Hongqiao area fell to the Japanese following extensive fighting.

DESTRUCTION OF BUSINESS PROPERTY

For Chinese capitalists in the lower Yangzi area, the Battle of Shanghai was a disaster. Industry, banking, and commerce suffered enormously because of the intense fighting, although the exact degree of damage is difficult to assess. Many factories, warehouses, and businesses caught fire or were heavily damaged by artillery. Those that survived were often commandeered for use by troops and frequently were looted in the process. During the battle, the Shanghai Chamber of Commerce attempted to provide frequent updates on the destruction of facilities. The numbers were reported to the Guomindang government as part of an effort to gain assistance. By the end of 1937, losses to industry in Shanghai were estimated at 560 million yuan.[3]

Although damage was substantial, it also varied from one area to the next. Indeed, the fortunes of war could be serendipitous. Even within one neighborhood a factory in one locale might be totally destroyed while a few blocks away another would escape with only minor damage. One estimate by a scholar in Chongqing suggested that as of 1943 within the greater Shanghai area (including the foreign concessions), 52 percent of industry was destroyed; in Nanjing, 80 percent was lost, in Wuxi 64 percent, and in Hangzhou only 28 percent. Variation within the city of Shanghai was also great. A recent estimate suggests that in Zhabei, 100 percent of factories were destroyed and in Hongkou and Yangshupu, around 70 percent. As noted above, the southern sectors of the city suffered less damage; the Nanshi (south city) neighborhood loss was about 30 percent. Of course, Chinese businesses were not the only ones to suffer. Although much foreign property was sheltered in the concessions, British, American, and Japanese losses were significant. Of thirty Japanese-owned textile mills in Shanghai, two were completely destroyed and twelve others were damaged.[4]

Nor were buildings the only loss; transportation was crippled as well. Business in the lower Yangzi depended heavily on river transport. Chinese merchant shipping companies, such as the China Merchants Steam Navigation Company (Zhaoshang ju), San Bei Navigation Company (Sanbei lunchuan gongsi), and Hong An had many ships sunk; others were commandeered by military forces, both Chinese and Japanese. China Merchants had 87,000 tons of commercial ships when the war erupted; 54,000 tons would be either sunk or captured. Another 23,000 tons were used to evacuate retreating Chinese soldiers. The company head, Cai Zengji, leased its wharves to an American firm and left for Hong Kong. Even after the battle abated the Japanese blockaded the Yangzi River for many months, effectively halting traffic between Shanghai and the interior. Foreign trade collapsed as well. In 1939 the tonnage of foreign trade passing through the port of Shanghai would be less than 25 percent of the level of 1936.[5]

Railway lines were in tatters—rails torn up, bridges destroyed, stations in shambles. Only 7 percent of prewar rolling stock remained operational. Months would pass before Japanese authorities could restore the key lines south to Hangzhou and west to Nanjing. Other sectors of the infrastructure suffered as well. Electricity production plummeted. A key power plant in Zhabei was destroyed and most power lines were down. Even the Shanghai Electric Company, whose location in the concessions offered protection, saw its sales for industrial use fall from a monthly average of 61 million kilowatt hours before the war to only 13 million in December 1937. Demand and delivery systems outside of the foreign concessions simply disappeared.[6]

By December 1937, the front had moved westward and a type of "normalcy" returned to the lower Yangzi area. Although guerilla warfare continued, positional battles in the area ceased. True, the Japanese did seize the foreign concessions in December 1941, and late in the war Allied bombing became a threat, but none of this reached the intensity of the opening six months of the war. For more than seven and a half years, the lower Yangzi would be a comparatively peaceful occupied zone. Yet recovery from the destruction of the Battle of Shanghai would be very slow. For reasons explored in Chapter 2, Japanese policy greatly inhibited the recovery. For months after the battle ended, Japan kept the Yangzi

River closed to commercial traffic. For security reasons, links between Hongkou, Pudong, Yangshupu, and the rest of Shanghai were severely limited. Even when conditions eased, the Japanese military so tightly controlled market connections between Shanghai and the interior that sales were made very difficult. Although Japanese forces curtailed looting, they reserved the right to confiscate raw materials, energy supplies, and scrap iron, often without compensation. One estimate was that nearly 10,000 tons of steel and iron commodities valued at US $1.5 million were seized from Shanghai area hardware stores. Even coins were taken and melted down for their copper content. Japan exported nearly 7 million yuan of copper coins from the occupied zone during the first year of the conflict. Shanghai residents began using postage stamps as substitutes until the government issued one- and five-fen notes.[7]

The Battle of Shanghai thus dealt a crippling blow to the Chinese capitalists of the lower Yangzi. Although the results were uneven, the level of destruction was extraordinary. Even for those businessmen lucky to survive the battle with little damage, market conditions were not favorable when the fighting stopped.

RESISTANCE

So what was the Chinese businessman to do when the fighting erupted at Shanghai? The "patriotic nationalist narrative" that has developed in recent historical writing on the topic in China suggests the proper course of action was to rush to support China's resistance. In fact, during the Battle of Shanghai most Chinese capitalists and their organizations, such as the Shanghai Chamber of Commerce, the Shanghai Bankers Association, and the Shanghai Native Bankers Association, did just that. The Nanjing government quickly announced that the government would issue 500 million yuan in "National Salvation bonds," and urged all patriotic citizens to purchase them. A special propaganda and promotion agency was established, headed by T. V. Soong (Song Ziwen), and included an assortment of leaders such as his sister Song Qingling (Madame Sun Yatsen), Guomindang leader Chen Lifu, and Shanghai Green Gang figure Du Yuesheng. The Shanghai General Chamber of Commerce promoted the campaign, and members of the banking associations agreed to handle sales of the bonds, as well as to subscribe themselves.[8]

The business groups also directed anti-Japanese boycott efforts. Pledging to sever all economic ties to Japan, the Shanghai Chamber of Commerce notified all member businesses to follow suit. In early October the chamber helped organize the Shanghai Citizens Commission for the Suspension of Economic Ties with Japan (Shanghai shi guomin duiRi jingji juejiao weiyuan hui). More than one hundred representatives of chambers of commerce, refugee relief groups, civic and educational associations, labor groups, and women's associations met to plot out strategy. Led by businessmen Wang Xiaolai and others, the group announced on October 13 a platform to suspend all relations with Japanese business and economic institutions, to urge all Chinese employees who worked for Japanese firms to quit, and to refuse to use Japanese currency. Any Japanese goods purchased before August 13 should be registered with the group. When the goods were sold, half of the proceeds should be used to purchase National Salvation bonds. Any Japanese goods purchased after August 13 were to be confiscated. The Shanghai Bankers Association and Shanghai Native Bankers Association pressured the six hundred Chinese who worked for Japanese banks in Shanghai to quit and provided economic assistance to those who did.[9]

Although these actions certainly aided China's efforts in the struggle against Japan, they play only a small part in the contemporary "patriotic nationalist narrative." In most contemporary accounts of patriotic capitalist activities, little is reported about the resistance in Shanghai. Instead, the ideal patriotic capitalist is described as having focused his efforts on relocating in the interior, away from the Japanese.

RELOCATION TO THE INTERIOR

In most current writing on the war, the patriotic capitalist is said to have made every effort against tremendous odds to move his factories and workers to the unoccupied interior of China where he could contribute to the war effort. The recent literature is filled with accounts of workers loading equipment onto boats in the midst of bombs and artillery fire; events even referred to as Chinese industry's "Dunkirk."[10] Yet how much of this actually occurred?

In fact, more than 600 factories, including nearly 110,000 tons of industrial material, were evacuated, and 418 of these plants were able to resume production in the unoccupied zone. Viewed from the perspective of the Chinese government in Chongqing, this move by Chinese capitalists was indeed a significant contribution to China's survival during the war. The interior provinces that would comprise Free China had virtually no industry when the war began. A mere 6 percent of China's industrial production had occurred in Sichuan, Hunan, Yunnan, Guangxi,

Shaanxi, Gansu, and Guizhou combined. Without the new factories from the coast, and the 42,000 workers who accompanied them, unoccupied China would have produced virtually nothing.[11] In the critical sector of weapons production, for instance, the government relocated fifteen major arsenals from Shanghai, Nanjing, and Jinan by mid-1938. Despite the isolation of the interior during the war, China's production of weapons was actually greater in 1945 than in 1936.[12]

The relocation effort thus looms large from the perspective of Chongqing. Yet viewed from Shanghai, the effort was minimal. Only a "negligible percentage of China's existing industry," in the words of William Kirby, was shipped to the interior. Of the factories in Shanghai on the eve of the war, only 5.6 percent would be evacuated. Few Shanghai area capitalists fulfilled the requirements of the "patriotic nationalist narrative" as it was later constructed.[13]

Why was more not done? First, few capitalists really had an ability to relocate. Japanese dominance of the Yangzi River and the skies over coastal China meant that the opportunity for moving equipment was very limited. As later sections of this study will demonstrate, many businessmen attempted to remove equipment from the battle zone, only to have it destroyed by enemy fire. Although hindsight makes it easy to see that the war was approaching, few were prepared to take action on August 13. Indeed, many of the factories that made it to the interior were from inland areas rather than Shanghai. Although Wuhan was much less significant than Shanghai as an industrial center in 1937, more than 160 of its existing factories made it to Sichuan by 1940, since local industrialists had both more time to prepare and more government assistance. Moreover, in Wuhan, factory owners were warned that any facilities not removed would be destroyed by the Chinese military rather than be left for the Japanese in keeping with its "scorched earth" policy.[14]

Even without the constant threat of Japanese attack, the logistics of moving Shanghai's industries would have been daunting. When the management of the Zhonghua copper foundry and rolling mill (Zhonghua niantong chang) tried to move the foundry's equipment from Shanghai to Wuhan, for example, they received government encouragement. Along with the materiel from several other factories, Zhonghua's equipment was loaded onto nine boats. When the ships reached Zhenjiang (about sixty-five kilometers east of Nanjing), they became mired because of low water levels in the Yangzi (as was normal in autumn) combined with the heavy nature of the loads. Local officials were not helpful, so only frantic negotiations with Nanjing to get assistance saved the material. The boats escaped just two days before the Japanese army reached the site. For every such success, however, there were more failures.[15]

Second, government assistance in moving industry was both tardy and inadequate. On August 10, just three days before the fighting erupted at Shanghai, Nanjing finally provided 560,000 yuan for the National Resources Commission to aid in relocation. The Shanghai Provisional Supervisory Commission for the Relocation of Industry (Shanghai gongchang qianyi lindu weiyuan hui) was charged with directing the effort. Yet in the chaos that ensued when the battle began, even this money was not fully utilized. "If the government had planned this industrial migration in advance," argued Lloyd E. Eastman, "the operation might have been carried out far more safely and extensively."[16]

Eventually the government entrusted the task to the Industry and Mining Adjustment Administration (Gongkuang diaozheng chu), which was far more effective in reestablishing factories in the interior. By that point, the Battle of Shanghai was long lost, so the agency's efforts were directed at moving plants from inland cities or further relocating facilities shipped to Wuhan. In the first wave of evacuations, many businesses were directed to that mid-Yangzi city, but it quickly became apparent that only more remote areas such as Sichuan offered any security.[17]

Moreover, in allocating shipping, the government quite naturally gave priority first to troop movements and then to the shipping of military arsenals and iron and steel foundries. China's private industrialists, who produced principally textiles, flour, matches, and other consumer goods, were mostly left to fend for themselves. The combination of war conditions and government inaction thus limited the effectiveness of the transfer program, even though some Chinese industrialists sincerely desired to contribute to the war effort and escape Japanese control. Perhaps the miracle is that any made it to Sichuan at all.[18]

Another factor may have slowed the evacuation program. Many Chinese businessmen may have been loath to place themselves entirely under the control of the Guomindang government. During the 1930s relations between some capitalists and Nanjing had been tense. For those at odds with Chiang Kaishek or his entourage, following the Guomindang to Wuhan or Chongqing must have been unappealing. Conversely, those enterprises with ties to Chiang's clique undoubtedly had first claims on government resources during the evacuation. In 1937, before the war erupted, T. V. Soong, Chiang's brother-in-law, had gained control of the Nanyang Brothers Tobacco Company, one of a number of firms in which he held an interest. Nanyang's plants in Shanghai and Wuhan both suf-

still sought to avoid conflict with the West. When the *Panay* Incident created a crisis with America, Japan acted with dispatch to defuse the situation. Thus despite the intensity of the Battle of Shanghai, Japan left the foreign concessions—the International Settlement (south of the Suzhou Creek) and French Concession—unoccupied. Surrounded by occupied territory, the foreign zones were labeled the "solitary island" (*gudao*) by observers. It was as if a foreign enemy seized the New York City area but left Manhattan a free, neutral zone.

The territory of this solitary island held little industry when the war began, for this real estate was simply too expensive. Most factories in the Shanghai area were either in the Chinese city or in the area north of the Suzhou Creek that Japan occupied. The unoccupied portion of the International Settlement was instead the center of commerce and banking. It included the famous Bund (waterfront area) with its impressive foreign buildings. Running west from the Bund, Nanjing Road contained China's most modern department stores, shops, restaurants, and hotels. In the midst of the concession lay the famous race course founded by the British, today's People's Park. The nearby French Concession contained shops, restaurants, and nightclubs but was best known for its elegant mansions, some belonging to Western residents but many owned by the Shanghai capitalists themselves.

In the weeks following the Marco Polo Bridge Incident of July 7, 1937, as the fighting in the north intensified, a few Shanghai businesses quietly moved material from factories, shops, and warehouses in the Chinese sectors of Shanghai into the foreign concessions. Most vividly remembered the intense fighting that had occurred in the winter of 1932, when the January 28th Incident left Zhabei in ruins. When full scale war developed after August 13, the trickle became a torrent. Even as tens of thousands of refugees poured into the foreign zone to escape the battle, businesses moved material and equipment as quickly as possible. The solitary island, a mere ten square miles, became one of the most densely inhabited spots on earth.

This strategy did not necessarily imply that these capitalists rejected the idea of moving their plants to the interior. No one knew for certain how long the battle would last, or that the Chinese army would eventually retreat, or that an armistice might not be arranged as had been done in 1932. Even businessmen who planned to relocate to Wuhan or Sichuan had to get equipment out of the battle zone if it were to survive. As the Chinese forces retreated, however, Shanghai capitalists were presented with a stark choice. They could personally follow the Chinese mil-

fered extensive damage during the fighting, but Soong was determined to rebuild in the interior. Although cigarette manufacturing was not a war industry, Soong directed through telegrams the efforts to relocate supplies and equipment to Chongqing. Soong's status was a clear advantage.[1]

H. H. Kung (Kong Xiangxi), another brother-in-law, was active in the economy of Free China. In 1938 in Chongqing he helped establish the Fuxing Company (Fuxing gongsi) with himself as chairman of the board of directors. The firm became a major trading organization through which were channeled many commodity transactions. Thus to operate successfully in Sichuan, many businessmen assumed that they must include Soong or Kung in ownership and management, a prospect that many found difficult and distasteful. One of the first businesses to produce light bulbs in China was the Yapu'er Factory (Yapu'er chang), established in 1923 with German technical assistance. (The company used a romanized foreign name because it was thought to appeal to Chinese consumers who might not trust a Chinese product of this type.) When the war broke out, the Yapu'er plant was occupied and stripped by the Japanese. Yapu'er's management moved some equipment to Chongqing and tried to reopen there; yet they never got the resources or funding to begin production in the interior. The management suspected that the key reason was that H. H. Kung owned a company that planned to manufacture light bulbs and did not want any competition. Whatever the truth of the situation, many Shanghai capitalists felt that relocating in Sichuan would take political ties they did not have.[20]

Ultimately, few capitalists followed the "patriotic nationalist narrative," because in 1937 none knew what this would entail. Few could imagine that the war would drag on for eight years or that China would ally with the United States and Great Britain to emerge on the victorious side. Many might have suspected that, despite the ferocity of the battle of Shanghai, Chiang might well negotiate a settlement with the Japanese. Rather than risk everything by attempting the dangerous journey upriver to an uncertain fate, most capitalists looked closer at hand—to unoccupied Shanghai.

RELOCATION TO THE INTERNATIONAL SETTLEMENT

Despite its ferocity, the war between China and Japan remained an undeclared war—the China Incident—until December 1941. Neither nation formally declared war because neither wanted to lose trade and contacts with neutral powers such as the United States. In July 1937, Japan

itary and attempt to reestablish in the unoccupied interior, thereby aiding in China's war effort and (unknowingly) fit the "heroic capitalist narrative" constructed by historians half a century later. Most would choose the alternative option—staying put in island Shanghai. Many already had homes in the city. Bankers, department store magnates, hoteliers, and shopkeepers had property in the foreign zone. A few lucky industrialists had factories in the island, while other rushed to reopen using the equipment they had salvaged. After the fall of Nanjing in December, the two most likely outcomes of the war would have seemed to be either a surrender by Chiang Kaishek or a negotiated settlement. Whichever transpired, most capitalists felt the option of staying in Shanghai was safer and more comfortable than an uncertain future in the interior.

And the trip to the interior was risky. Two of Shanghai's most prominent bankers, Xu Xinliu and Hu Bijiang, were killed on August 24, 1938, when their China Air plane from Hong Kong to Guilin was attacked by Japanese fighters and shot down. Both managed important private banks and were active in the Shanghai Bankers Association. That body held a special memorial service for the two on September 21. Five hundred people attended, a virtual who's who of the Shanghai business and banking community. The deaths of such prominent leaders drove home the risks of trying to leave island Shanghai to reach Free China.[21]

By the end of 1937, the solitary island was an odd place. Commercial shipping on the Yangzi remained closed for months. Japanese restricted movement from the island to surrounding neighborhoods of Chinese Shanghai. Even after these restrictions were eased, a Chinese pedestrian going from the Bund north to the Hongkou or Yangshupu area or a farmer bringing vegetables from Pudong or the western suburbs was subject to a frightening and humiliating search by the dreaded Japanese military police. The solitary island was thus sharply divorced from the surrounding city.

Yet at the same time, the waterfront remained open. Foreign flag ships regularly left the port of Shanghai for international waters. One could not easily get to Suzhou or Wuxi, but one could sail for Hong Kong, Manila, Haiphong, or Singapore. Commercial shipping between the solitary island and Southeast Asia could bring in raw materials, rice, and other commodities while carrying the products of Shanghai to their markets. Several Chinese ports along the southeast coast also remained unoccupied for months to come. Nearly ten foreign shipping companies with a combined fleet of eighty ships routinely sailed from Shanghai to Zhejiang, Fujian, Guangdong, Hong Kong, and even Tianjin. Particularly at

Wenzhou in Zhejiang, ships from Shanghai would bring commodities and people who could reach the unoccupied interior of China. Until the fall of Canton (Guangzhou) in October 1938, traffic from Shanghai could connect to Guiyang region via Hong Kong. A rail link existed from Hanoi into southwest China, and a road from British Burma stretched into the interior. Some estimates are that during the period from 1938 through 1940, as much as half of Shanghai's exports eventually arrived in interior China. A cotton shirt manufactured in Shanghai might thus reach markets in Rangoon, Saigon, or Chongqing more easily than nearby Jiading. The cotton that went into that shirt had likely been imported from overseas rather than from nearby cotton fields in China, as had been the case before the war.[22]

Under these anomalous conditions, most Shanghai businessmen chose to stay in the solitary island and reopen their enterprises there rather than in the interior. Manufacturing, which had been dispersed throughout the Chinese city and the suburbs, now concentrated in the foreign zones. Neighborhoods that had previously been considered residential, particularly the western areas, now contained bustling factories. In 1936, there had been only nine Chinese textile mills in the concessions with approximately 340,000 spindles and 1,700 looms. By 1940 there would be twenty-three Chinese-owned mills with 666,000 spindles and 5,500 looms, as many mill owners successfully relocated. These new mills relied almost entirely on imported, rather than domestic, cotton. Whereas in 1936 most cotton used in the Shanghai area came from China, and only 287,000 quintals was imported, in 1939, virtually all was imported—more than 2,138,000 quintals.[23]

Prior to the war, many Chinese industrialists had begun to establish cotton textile mills in smaller cities of the lower Yangzi, such as Wuxi and Nantong, taking advantage of better access to raw cotton and cheaper labor sources. Since the Japanese quickly overran these areas, many of these capitalists tried to rebuild in the solitary island, joined occasionally by refugees from north China. They often had to purchase equipment from overseas because they could salvage little from their original plants. Three new mills in island Shanghai, for instance, Baofeng, Changxing, and Guangqin, were established by refugees from Wuxi, while another new company, the Xinhe textile mill, was begun in December 1937 by two Chinese industrialists who fled Qingdao. A fifth company, Anda, was founded by a mill owner, Liu Guojun, whose plant in Changzhou had been captured (discussed in Chapter 7). The Xinhe mill (Xinhe shachang) was founded by Zhou Zhijun and Wu Boseng, who had fled Qingdao. Profits for the mills of island Shanghai were substantial. The price of raw cotton remained relatively stable until the outbreak of World War II in Europe, but wartime shortages in China drove up the market value of cotton thread and cloth at a rapid rate.[24]

Most silk filatures had previously been located in the countryside, but by October 1938 fourteen new ones suddenly appeared in Shanghai. Tanneries, cigarette factories, chemical plants, and even paper mills moved into the solitary island. Not everyone was pleased. The English-language *China Weekly Review* complained that the new plants used flimsy construction materials, did not reinforce their concrete buildings, were designed for short-term investment only, and increased noise, air, and water pollution. "Factories of various kinds have been springing up like mushrooms, spoiling what was once a peaceful, smoke free area, and causing depreciation in the value of costly residential properties," the journal complained. Such were the inconveniences of war.[25]

Not only factories moved into island Shanghai; capital poured in as well. The lower Yangzi area was the richest and most commercially developed in China. Foreign Shanghai was already the banking center of this region, but as the battle spread, China's wealthy transferred their money to this sanctuary. Many Shanghai banks showed rapid growth in both the number of depositors and the total savings during the weeks from July to November 1937.[26]

This concentration of capital was magnified as Shanghai banks closed their branches in the battle areas and consolidated deposits, and as regional banks moved their headquarters to Shanghai. One by one the banks of Suzhou, Wuxi, Yangzhou, Shaoxing, Nantong, Hangzhou, and then Nanjing moved to island Shanghai. The Nanjing Bankers Association relocated in Shanghai in the office of the Shanghai Bankers Association. Even the official government banks, such as the Bank of China and Bank of Communications, which moved their official headquarters with the Guomindang government, kept their Shanghai branches in operation. By the summer of 1938, banks even resumed making real estate loans in Shanghai, all of which had been suspended when the fighting began.[27]

Of course, most banks suffered tremendous losses in the process. Bank buildings outside of Shanghai not destroyed in the fighting were often occupied by the Japanese. Loans secured on property or merchandise in the occupied zone usually had to be written off. Several banks, such as the Jiading Bank and Wujin Commercial Bank of Changzhou, simply had to close.[28]

By fall of 1938, the solitary island had become a bustling center of
economic activity. Though surrounded by a war-scarred and devastated
hinterland, the Shanghai concessions experienced an economic flourishing fueled by the influx of capital and businesses. While total economic
activity in the lower Yangzi suffered, within island Shanghai a boom of
sorts occurred. Production levels in Shanghai in 1939 were equal or
greater than those in 1936 for cotton weaving, silk weaving, and flour
milling. Wool weaving, paper manufacture, and machinery production
actually experienced substantial increases. By the end of 1938, more than
4,700 factories in the island employed 237,000 workers.[29]

Because the war had reduced overall industrial capacity in China,
prices for industrial commodities soared. Those businessmen who were
lucky enough to be able to operate in the solitary island thus garnered
handsome profits. Moving to Chongqing became less and less appeal-
ing. Even the influx of refugees contributed to the flourishing. By 1940
an estimated 780,000 refugees remained in the island, swelling the population to more than 4 million. The dense population provided both a
cheap source of labor and a market for industrial goods. The number of
commercial shops increased, not only to meet the demands of the influx
of people, but also because many merchants had relocated.[30]

In the larger war, China's fate worsened. Wuhan fell in October 1938,
as did Canton. The small minority of businessmen who had moved westward with the Chiang government, together with soldiers, students, jour-
nalists, and myriad others, suffered great hardships as they pressed farther into China's remote interior. Those factories that did reopen in the
interior found themselves the frequent target of Japanese bombing; many
relocated in caves and used only human and animal power. The contrast
between their hardship and sacrifice in Free China and the "flourishing"
life in Shanghai became increasingly stark. As profits mounted, the
wealthy elite in Shanghai enjoyed the high life, at least in the imagination of those who had fled. Shanghai already possessed a reputation for
criminality, prostitution, drugs, and wild night life, activities that probably increased in wartime. Resentment of Shanghai became common. In
a radio address of May 1, 1939, Chiang Kaishek lashed out at Chinese
who lived in luxury in Shanghai (and Hong Kong) while patriotic Chinese were sacrificing to save China. Chiang's words were carefully
crafted, however; he hoped to lure capital and talent to the interior.[31]

The general press was less kind. As Poshek Fu has noted, "The anti-
Japanese press in unoccupied areas was filled with . . . veiled accusations
of people [in Shanghai] who, by choosing not to exile to the interior, were

seen as mostly weak-minded, selfish, hedonistic, and complicitous with the enemy."

The leftist press, particularly those journals associated with the National Salvation Movement, was even more direct. An article in *Zhiye shenghuo* (Professional life) in April 1939, for instance, accused the capitalists in Shanghai of hoarding funds in the illusory safety of the solitary island, while the interior desperately needed funds to develop industry and push China to victory. As Japanese bombs began raining down on Chongqing, those in Free China certainly felt they were the patriotic citizens, while the Shanghai and Hong Kong crowd hid behind the cloak of foreign imperialism.[32]

USE OF FOREIGN REGISTRY

The vast majority of Shanghai capitalists had thus chosen to stay in island Shanghai rather than risk the hardships of the interior. Seeking shelter in the foreign enclaves was hardly a new phenomenon in China. When the foreign settlements were created in the nineteenth century following the Opium War, they were originally intended for foreign residents. The upheavals of midcentury, such as the Taiping Rebellion, led to a massive influx of Chinese refugees. "Foreign Shanghai" became and would remain a city overwhelmingly Chinese in population. In the twentieth century, when revolution and civil war created unsettled conditions in China, Shanghai became a bastion of security for both money and people. All of the new Chinese modern banks in Shanghai opened headquarters in the foreign concessions; there, depositors were sheltered from the exactions of the frequently changing military governments. Capitalists were by no means the only group to avail themselves of the foreign sanctuaries. Sun Yatsen maintained a home in the French Concession that provided a haven when he was forced to leave his Guangdong base; the First Congress of the Communist Party met there in deepest secrecy. For bankers, businessmen, and industrialists, as well as political figures and intellectuals, the foreign concessions had long provided a safe haven. When businessmen in the Shanghai area rushed to the foreign settlements in August 1939, they were simply following a century-old tradition.

Many of the businessmen who stayed in Shanghai would take yet another step to insure their safety—one that removed them even further from the "patriotic nationalist narrative." They reinvented their businesses as foreign companies. This step allowed them to fly foreign flags over their property, something of a talisman to ward off the Japanese military. The process of doing this was relatively simple, given the some-what loose legal situation in Shanghai. Typically a Chinese company would arrange documents that implied that it had failed to pay a debt to a Western partner; the latter would then appear to assume control of the enterprise. Normally a Western name was added by the company, and sometimes a foreign "manager" was hired—usually just a front man who put in appearances as needed. These arrangements were fraudulent, of course; behind the scenes the Chinese management remained in place. The entire point was to protect the property against the Japanese.

One conspicuous example was the San Bei Navigation Company. In 1937, San Bei had nearly 90,000 tons of commercial shipping, about 13 percent of China's total. As noted earlier, it and other Chinese shipping firms were virtually shut down by the Battle of Shanghai. In San Bei's case nearly 30,000 tons was commandeered by Guomindang government and largely sunk. Another twenty ships totaling 20,000 tons were dis-abled by the war or trapped in Japanese blockades. Faced with a simi-lar situation, the management of the China Merchants Steam Naviga-tion Company had packed up for Hong Kong. San Bei, however, was led by the resourceful Yu Xiaqing, one of Shanghai's most prominent and best connected businessmen. A member of the Shanghai Municipal Coun-cil, Yu had excellent foreign contacts. Using a friendship with the Ital-ian consul in Shanghai, Yu reinvented San Bei as a joint enterprise, the Compania Italiano di Navigatione (ZhongYi lunchuan gongsi). San Bei held 88 percent of the stock in the new company; the Italians held the remaining 12 percent. San Bei still had nearly 40,000 tons of shipping, which now began to fly the Italian flag. This protection was substantial since Tokyo had relatively good relations with Rome, and Yu's contacts were solid. While the ships of its archrival, the China Merchants Com-pany, were largely confiscated or blockaded, Yu's vessels plied the wa-ters between Shanghai and overseas ports.

When business boomed in the flourishing island, Yu bought two Nor-wegian transport ships of about 20,000 tons in 1938, which flew the flags of Norway and Panama. The vessels made regular runs to Saigon and Rangoon to purchase rice, garnering Yu handsome profits. The refugee-swollen population of island Shanghai had driven up the price of rice, since little arrived from the surrounding countryside. In response to pub-lic criticism of profiteering, Yu donated substantial amounts of rice to refugee relief.[33]

Yu was hardly alone in pursuing this strategy. The Rong family, China's leading industrialist group, led by brothers Rong Zongjing and Rong

Desheng, held major textile and flour milling properties in the Shanghai area. Most were in the occupied zone and were either destroyed or confiscated (see Chapter 6), but the Rongs kept full control of their Shenxin #2 and #9 textile mills because both were located in the solitary island. In the turbulent war period, the Rongs decided that both mills needed foreign flag protection. The Rongs thus "leased" their two mills to foreign owners, in paper transactions, and reinvented them as foreign companies. The Shenxin #2, for instance, was ostensibly rented to an American company, Associated American Industries, Ltd., for a five-year period beginning on April 16, 1938. The American firm in turn obtained funds for this transaction from the Bank of China and Shanghai Bank, which then appointed a joint committee to operate the plant. This committee was composed, quite naturally, of the original management. Shenxin #9 underwent a similar transformation in May 1938 but used a British cover and also was registered in Hong Kong. The Rongs' Fuxin #7 flour mill was registered as British, as was their rival Fufeng flour milling company. This foreign protection reassured investors in Rong properties that their investments would be secure, regardless of the outcome of the war with Japan. At least five other Shanghai mills registered as British; four registered as American.[34]

Use of foreign cover was not restricted to industrialists. When Japan pressured the International Settlement authorities to shut down pro-resistance Chinese publishers in the solitary island, the solution was foreign registration. As Po-shek Fu has noted, this provided the only avenue for Chinese writers in Shanghai to promote nationalist rhetoric. The newspaper *Wenhui bao,* for instance, hired an Irishman, H. M. Cumine, as its manager, and became a major vehicle for Chinese writers. Cumine was even referred to as the "foreign bodyguard."[35]

Foreign flag protection was deemed particularly essential for properties outside of the solitary island, although the Japanese often ignored such arrangements. The Hengfeng textile mill (discussed in greater detail in Chapter 7) was located in the Yangshupu zone of Shanghai and was therefore blockaded by the Japanese for several months. In early 1938, the Japanese military permitted foreign firms in the zone to reopen while most Chinese industry remained closed. Hengfeng owners therefore tried to reinvent the firm as a British enterprise by leasing everything to a dummy group that financed the purchase through the Chinese National Commercial Bank. The latter would hold the stock as collateral and appoint the management team, as was done in the Rong case. After brief investigation, however, Japanese military authorities decided that the plan was fraudulent and formally confiscated the plant in May 1938, turning management over to a Japanese company, Daikō Textiles, which began operating the plant in October 1938.[36]

Leaders of the Dasheng mills of Nantong were a bit more creative. A legacy of the famous reformer Zhang Jian, the Dasheng mills suffered little damage in the fighting, but the city of Nantong was occupied in August 1938 (see Chapter 7). Anticipating this event, Chinese managers worked out a mortgage arrangement with a German bank and began using a German name for the plant, which was even draped with swastikas for a time. This ploy actually worked for a few months, until the Japanese determined it to be a ruse. The Japanese military occupied the plant by force in March 1939 and entrusted it to the Japanese Kanegafuchi Company.[37] As the battlefront moved westward, some industrialists believed that a foreign flag would offer protection from enemy attack, although that does not seem to have necessarily been the case. The owners of the Yuhua textile mill in Wuhan, for instance, paid about 60,000 yuan in expenses to gain the right to fly a Belgian flag over their facility. Although they followed the Guomindang to Sichuan, they continued to rely on foreign flag protection as they shipped material to Yichang.[38]

The most audacious firms even tried to re-register as Japanese. The Zhengtai Rubber factory (discussed in Chapter 9), located in the Hongkou section of Shanghai, was heavily damaged in the fighting and occupied by Japanese forces. In a process detailed later in this study, the Chinese owners, who fled to the solitary island, employed a Japanese businessman who visited their plant site and placed signs stating that the facility was a branch of a Japanese company for which he worked. The factory reopened with a Japanese name in July 1938, with the Japanese businessmen receiving a percentage of the earnings in exchange for providing protection.[39]

The vast majority of Shanghai businessmen not only stayed in Shanghai under foreign protection rather than evacuate to the interior, but many went even further, registering their companies as foreign flag concerns. Although most of these moves were merely paper transactions, they reveal the disjuncture between the actual experiences of businessmen during the war and the "patriotic nationalist narrative."

DECLINE OF THE SOLITARY ISLAND

In autumn 1940, the Japanese military decided to tighten its hold on Shanghai, including the unoccupied foreign zone. In particular they began to restrict the links between Shanghai and Free China, feeling that the trade helped the Chiang Kaishek forces survive. The fall of France and the creation of the Vichy regime gave Japan more leeway in dealing with French colonial possessions in Asia, including the French Concession. Agents of the puppet police force were allowed to operate in the concession, sharply reducing its sanctity from Japanese suasion. With Vichy cooperation, the Japanese military occupied northern Indochina, which broke the link between Hanoi and Guomindang China. To further tighten the noose, Japan began to prohibit third country shipping from landing in Zhejiang and Fujian ports, most of which had been occupied by the end of 1939. These restrictions drastically cut exports from the solitary island, particularly of textiles. Connections between Shanghai and the unoccupied interior grew more difficult.[40]

By 1941, island Shanghai's economy ceased to flourish. Cotton textile production in that year was only 63 percent of 1936, flour milling only 22 percent, and rubber production only 51 percent. A few sectors remained strong—particularly silk production, wool, and paper output. Overall, however, the economy weakened. Both the Chongqing and Nanjing governments began printing money, and inflation began to impact the economy. Price inflation, which had increased at modest but steady rates until mid-1939, suddenly began to soar. In 1941, prices in Shanghai increased 9.5 percent monthly. By the end of 1941, commodity prices were an average of 14.5 times those of June 1937. At these rates of inflation, many businessmen preferred to speculate by hoarding commodities. Future production of manufactured commodities was uncertain because of doubts concerning affordable raw materials.[41]

The end came on December 8, 1941, when Japan went to war against Britain, America, and Holland. Within hours of the bombing of Pearl Harbor and the attack on British Malaya, Japanese troops occupied the International Settlement and established effective control over the French Concession. Hong Kong succumbed within days. Now those Chinese capitalists who had stayed behind found themselves in occupied territory. The sanctuary of the foreign concessions, so alluring in August of 1937, now proved illusory. Yet in truth, most capitalists based in island Shanghai had already made significant compromises with the Japanese occupiers. In the last four years of the war, they would make more.[42]

PART TWO

Conquerors and Their Collaborators

CHAPTER 2

Japan's New Order

By early winter of 1938 Japan seemed triumphant in China. After weeks of bitter fighting, Chiang Kaishek's forces abandoned Wuhan and were in full retreat to Sichuan. The city of Canton (Guangzhou) fell in October with very little resistance. Now Hong Kong joined island Shanghai as a foreign enclave surrounded by Japanese-held territory. The coastal areas of China from Beijing-Tianjin to Shanghai to Canton, its richest and most economically advanced zones, were now in Japanese hands. But what did Japan plan to do with this new empire? Was it to be operated as a backward colony with no room for a Chinese business class? How was the economy of the occupied area to be meshed with that of the home islands, of Korea and Taiwan, and of the recently acquired Manchukuo (Manzhouguo)?

For months the Japanese seemed to have no concrete plan for China. Finally on November 3, 1938, Prince Konoe Fumimaro, Japan's prime minister, formally proclaimed the New Order in East Asia (Tōa shinchitsujo)—Japan's program for China. "Japan, China, and Manchukuo will be united by the common aim of establishing the New Order in East Asia and realizing the relationship of neighbourly amity, common defence against Communism, and economic cooperation." This vague formulation sounded a familiar note; it largely repeated the three principles issued by Hirota Kōki in 1935.[1] On the last issue, economic cooperation, Konoe was strikingly vague. "Japan does not intend to exercise an economic monopoly in China," the prime minister stated. "Japan only seeks to render effective the cooperation and collaboration between the two countries." "But," Konoe added, "in the light of the historical and economic relations between the two nations, China should extend to Japan facilities for the development of natural resources, especially in the regions of North China and Inner Mongolia."[2]

Konoe's formulation thus hinted at a comprehensive program of economic development, directed by Japan, focused on north China and Inner Mongolia. As to what might transpire in the lower Yangzi Valley and Shanghai itself, no clear answer emerged. But the "New Order" was hardly the last word from Tokyo. In August 1940 a new formulation, "The Greater East Asia Co-Prosperity Sphere" (Dai Tōa kyōeiken), was proclaimed, one that would eventually encompass the areas of Southeast Asia captured after Pearl Harbor. But the new "Co-Prosperity Sphere" seemed even more vague than the "New Order." The basic plan for the sphere stated that "those areas pertaining to the Pacific, Central Asia, and the Indian Oceans formed into one general union are to be established as an autonomous zone of peaceful living and common prosperity on behalf of the peoples of the nations of East Asia." This union would be created by eliminating the domination of this area by Western imperialism, a task that only Japan could accomplish. "The Japanese empire possesses a duty as the leader of the East Asiatic Union."[3]

The New Order and the Greater East Asia Co-Prosperity Sphere were plastic concepts whose scope altered with Japan's war successes and whose content changed with war needs. At their core, however, was the rhetoric of Japanese Pan-Asianism, a long-standing, somewhat romantic concept endorsed by many Japanese of all political stripes. Japan was seen as the last hope to prevent complete domination of Asia by the white race, burdened with the obligation to free Asia of this oppression and then direct its growth under Japanese tutelage. As one economist attached to the Shōwa Research Association wrote in January 1941, "East Asia has long suffered from the bane of Western Imperialistic capitalism with its watchword of exploitation. Whatever development has been carried about was set against a colonial or at best semi-colonial background."[4]

In its earlier forms, this Pan-Asian concept had drawn support in China. Indeed, Sun Yatsen himself adopted much of its rhetoric. But long years of Japanese aggression, particularly with the Manchurian Incident of 1931, had eroded support for the concept among Chinese. Few took Tokyo's pronouncements at face value; most Chinese had long assumed that the goal of Japan's policy was to convert China into a colony as Britain had with India or France had with Vietnam. In economic terms

Tokyo would "industrialize Japan, agriculturalize China" (*gongye Riben, nongye Zhongguo*). China would supply raw materials for modern industry that would be located in Japan. If factories were to be maintained in a Japan-dominated China, they would be owned and operated by Japanese zaibatsu.

This view strongly resembles what the Greater East Asia Co-Prosperity Sphere would actually become both in China and in Southeast Asia. As John Dower has noted:

> [T]he Japanese plan for the Co-Prosperity Sphere amounted to an almost perfect model of 'center-periphery' relationships, all designed to ensure the supremacy of the Japanese as a leading race. . . . Japan would be responsible for the production of high-quality manufactures and finished products in the heavy-industry sector. While Japan would provide capital and technical know-how for the development of light industry (generally for local consumption) throughout the Co-Prosperity Sphere, most countries would remain in their familiar roles as producers of raw material and semifinished goods.[5]

In this scheme, local capitalists in China would have only a marginal role.

Such was the broad design of the sphere; its implementation was never so orderly. "The Greater East Asia Co-Prosperity Sphere was not the result of careful planing," Peter Duus has noted, "but a series of improvisations shaped by local circumstances." There was never *one* plan for the sphere, there were many plans, "a surfeit of plans for developing Manchuria, occupied China, and the new conquered 'Southern Regions,' and for integration of these regions with the metropolitan economy." But the planners, Duus adds, "worked at cross-purposes with different ends in mind."[6]

Even within the Japanese military, major differences developed between the army and navy and within each branch. Civilian agencies in the Japanese government would clash with the military. Japanese capitalists often disagreed with the military and within their own community. Many right-wing militarists, for instance, were opposed to capitalism in general and saw the entire project in China as a way to purify not just China but more particularly Japan of the evils of this Western concept. When the puppet state in Manchuria had been created, the Japanese army had attempted to keep Japanese capitalists out of the development process. Honjō Shigeru, commander of the Guandong Army (Kantōgun), stated flatly that "we want to use Manchuria as the means to renovate (kaizō) Japan . . . and intend to absolutely exclude finance capital and the influence of political parties from Manchuria."[7]

When Japanese militarists developed their "Outline for Economic Construction in Manchukuo," announced on March 1, 1932, they noted that "in view of the evils of an uncontrolled capitalist economy, we will use whatever state power is necessary to control the economy."[8] The actual plans for Manchukuo announced in March 1933 called for intensive development of industry and economic infrastructure under state control. In a world of unlimited possibilities, therefore, Japanese military planners would have implemented a state-planned and state-controlled economic program in both Japan and China.[9]

The Japanese business community obviously opposed this program. Not only did Japanese capitalists want a strong role for private capital in Japan and on the mainland, but many sought to block any development of heavy industry in Manchukuo. According to Louise Young, the influential Japan Industry Club argued that "as much as possible Manchuria should be made into a supplier of materials. It is a mistake to encourage new industrial production that will compete with Japanese domestic industry . . . Manchurian tariffs should be kept as low as possible to encourage import of Japanese products. Industrial goods should be produced within Japan and exported to Manchuria."[10]

The disagreements over Manchuria were simply magnified when all of China was at issue, particularly the Shanghai area. Among Japanese groups favoring expansion on the mainland, attention had long been given to developing the resources of north China and Inner Mongolia, whose coal, iron ore, wheat, and cotton were seen as natural resources for Japan. Many military planners had assumed that Japan might well separate these areas from Nanjing without resort to serious war, as had been done in Manchuria. Less attention had been devoted to how central China might fit into a Japanese program. The fundamental problem with the lower Yangzi area was that its economy competed too closely with the metropole. Unlike such classic colonial matchups as Holland and the Dutch East Indies or Belgium and the Congo, in which the imperial country and the colony produced almost totally different products and maintained different levels of technological development, the economies of Japan and lower-Yangzi China were far more similar. Japan was certainly more advanced in heavy industry than China, but broad sectors of Japanese industry, such as textiles, might be viewed as in competition with coastal China.

Indeed, Japanese theorists, in constructing their ideal of the Co-Prosperity Sphere, realized that this might be a problem even in agriculture. One Japanese economic journal editorialized in April 1938 that

> The question of assisting in the technical improvement of agriculture on the continent requires special attention since there are many Chinese agricultural products which are also produced in Japan. Application of advanced Japanese methods to the production, for instance, of cotton and wool, which are not competitive with Japanese agricultural products, will raise no problem. But the utmost care will be needed in the case of similar technical assistance in the improvement of rice and cocoon production in the Central-South China region in view of their competitive nature with similar products raised in Japan.[11]

If improving production of rice and silk cocoons might create difficulties, allowing development of Chinese textile, chemical, and machine tool factories would create an even bigger problem.

Japan thus entered the China war with no one plan for integrating its conquests into the New Order. The disagreements between business and the military and among these communities simply deepened when the issue grew from including Manchuria to all of China. Furthermore, the architects of the New Order seemed far more comfortable with incorporating north China than the lower Yangzi. The former had been the subject of long planning and debate pertaining to its role under Japanese tutelage. The latter had not. Yet even if all of the Japanese actors had agreed on a uniform plan in 1937, it is not clear that it could have been implemented. When the war developed in ways unanticipated in Tokyo, wartime necessity, not grand theory, determined Japanese policy. As Peter Duus has noted, "Even the best-laid plans had to be adjusted to rapidly changing wartime conditions, and many were simply abandoned."[12]

"USING THE WAR TO SUSTAIN THE WAR"

The Japanese entered the war in July 1937 with no plans for an extended conflict. The Imperial Army assumed, according to Michael Barnhart, that "three divisions, three months, and 100 million yen would be sufficient to conclude the affair." By the spring of 1938, with China still fighting, the Japanese General Staff "found itself preparing new orders . . . Twenty new divisions were to be raised on an emergency basis; over 2.5 billion yen had been appropriated for long-term hostilities, with the promise of more levies to come."[13] The government's deficit financed by borrowing increased from 605 million yen in 1937 to 2,406 million in 1941. The strain of these burdensome debts came at the very time that Japan was attempting to build up its military and economic foundation for a

possible confrontation with the Soviet Union or the United States and
Britain.[14]

As a consequence, the army decreed a policy of extracting greater resources from China itself, adopting the phrase "*yizhan yangzhan*" (using the war to sustain the war). The Japanese military was expected to
squeeze as much income as possible from the area being conquered. In
the early months of the war, when military commanders still hoped for
a brief conflict, what often transpired was closer to plundering than a
program for developing a colonial economy. Factories were looted, and
equipment was collected for scrap iron. Markets were tightly controlled
so as to permit the Japanese to extract resources and income. Japanese
historian Hata Ikuhiko has described this policy as "ruthless plunder."
Japan compensated for its economic inadequacies, he states, by measures
that were

> reminiscent of early Spanish colonial policy. . . . on the Chinese mainland
> business and enterprises were confiscated; and Japanese forces fighting in
> China and later in the Pacific lived off the land. The army purchased daily
> necessities with excessive issues of unbacked military scrip that inevitably
> brought local inflation. In modern history there has been no other instance
> of a foreign expeditionary force's adopting a policy of local self-sufficiency
> from the very outset. It was a glaring demonstration of the enormous dis-
> parities between slogans and realities.[15]

As the contest became more protracted, however, Tokyo had to re-
think its approach. The economy of occupied China was devastated by
the fighting and paralyzed by Japanese policies. Far from meeting the resource needs of the Japanese fighting machine, the China war was straining the Japanese economy. Japanese dependence on imports from Anglo-
American areas actually worsened after July 1937. The outbreak of war
in Europe in 1939 meant that supplies of critical raw materials became
even more difficult to obtain. The great difficulty in relying on mainland
China for resources was its underdevelopment. Enormous capital out-
lays would be needed, capital that Japan could ill afford to send to China.
Japan's financial markets simply lacked the funding needed to develop
China's resources. Nor was capital the only item in short supply. In
Manchukuo, where Japan had a more established development program
that received priority in capital investment, economic growth fell short
of the targets of the Five Year Plan after 1937 because of underdeveloped technology and a shortage of skilled labor.[16]

As early as 1939, Japanese economists began to warn of the potential drain of resources on Japan. "The proposed establishment of a new

order in East Asia must, needless to say, be based upon the economic development of China," wrote Hon'iden Yoshio. Nonetheless, he noted, "it is obvious that no vast amount of Japanese capital will be available for industrial investments in China. Or rather, under the present circumstances, an excessive export of Japanese capital to China might affect unfavorably the expansion program now in full swing in Japan." The question raised, he wrote, was "whether Chinese domestic capital will be made available and mobilized for the development of China."[17]

In implementing the policy of "using the war to sustain the war," the Japanese thus faced significant constraints of capital and personnel, limitations that led to major changes in policy over time and place. The New Order/Co-Prosperity Sphere was a fluid construct that altered to fit changes created by war circumstances. The economic strains eventually forced the Japanese to seek greater participation of Chinese capital in the operation of the economy in the occupied area. The policy also varied by place, because available Japanese capital was channeled first to Manchukuo and north China, and lastly to central and south China. Japanese authorities felt the former areas were more strategic and the latter regions wealthier. They would become far more open to encouraging Chinese participation in the economy in the south than in the north.

Although continuities existed, Japanese policies can be roughly divided into three phases. In the first, from the outbreak of the war until November 1938, Japanese policy was characterized by destruction and chaotic attempts to control the economy. Levels of output dropped to one-half of the prewar level. In the second phase, from the proclamation of the "New Order" in November 1938 through the first year of the Pacific war, Tokyo made solid efforts to reinvigorate the economy of occupied China, creating large Japanese holding companies for that purpose. Agricultural production and mining output (mostly in north China) recovered to prewar levels or better, and Japanese forces extracted substantial raw materials for export to Japan. The final phase, from early 1943 until the Japanese surrender, was marked by a collapse of the policy. The desperate war situation led to a decline in transportation, raw materials, and economic activity. The economy of the Greater East Asia Co-Prosperity Sphere deteriorated in concert with Japan's military position.[18]

THE EARLY WAR: "SIMPLE PLUNDER"

In this first phase of the war, Japan crudely extracted resources from China to cover the escalating costs of the conflict, an approach that in-

hibited economic recovery. The simplest methods of extraction were im-
position of local tariffs (the equivalent of the likin), creation of local mo-
nopolies in key commodities, and forced procurement of commodities
at below market prices. Of these, the local tariff was the simplest to en-
act. The puppet Dadao government, which the Japanese established in
Shanghai, for instance, announced a 5 percent duty in March 1938 on
virtually all goods entering or leaving Chinese Shanghai. Many locales
in the interior followed suit.[19]

Japanese authorities tightly regulated links between urban and rural
areas, creating higher prices for agricultural products in the cities and
for manufactured products in the countryside. This lowered the procurement price paid by the Japanese military for foodstuffs and increased
the profits from selling Japanese goods. As Wang Ke-wen has written regarding wartime Shanghai, "During the early years of the occupation the
Japanese imposed a blockade on the city, and with the help of Japanese
merchants monopolized the exportation of industrial goods from Shanghai. This allowed them to trade these goods for the agricultural products
of the Lower Yangtze area that they badly needed."[20]

Economic controls were imposed on commodities such as sugar, oil,
salt, cloth, soap, matches, and medicines—the prices and movement of
which were regulated. Guards around cities such as Hangzhou searched
those in transit to regulate the movement of commodities and to maintain tight control over prices. In occupied Shanghai, a Central Market
and Central Marine Produce Market were created to control the prices
of virtually all agricultural and fish products in that city. The artificially
higher prices in the cities created an indirect tax on urban consumption
and an important source of revenue.[21]

Japan's procurement policy was designed to provide both a cheap supply of raw materials for the Japanese military in China and exports to
the home market in Japan. By keeping rural prices low and limiting access to urban Chinese markets, the controls reduced the costs of rice to
the Japanese military. The Japanese often forced Chinese producers to
accept military scrip, which was issued without a reserve fund by the
Shanghai branch of the Bank of Yokohama. Not convertible into yen,
the military scrip was not a desirable currency, yet Japanese troops gave
the Chinese no choice. The scrip, in the words of one Western observer,
provided "bayonets as security."[22] The policy was lucrative. Japanese authorities, for instance, purchased raw cotton in central China for 375
yuan per bale in autumn 1940, paid in military scrip. This cotton was

then sold in Shanghai to Japanese textile manufacturers for 540 yuan and on the open market for 750 yuan. The army pocketed the price differential as revenue, clearly "using the war to sustain the war."[23]

Japanese market controls were crucial for procurement for the home islands as well. Tokyo was particularly concerned with the so-called two whites (cotton and salt) and two blacks (iron and coal) in which Japan was deficient. Chinese cotton, for instance, could substitute for imports from Western countries such as the United States. When north China producers revealed a proclivity to export their cotton to central China and Manchukuo, where prices were kept high, Japanese authorities restricted such shipments, forcing export to Japan despite the lower prices there. The needs of the home country had priority.[24]

Japanese market controls could also serve secondary purposes. Western businessmen believed that Japanese authorities deliberately restricted transportation of Western goods into the occupied areas so as to give Japanese products a monopoly. American ambassador Joseph C. Grew eventually sent a letter of protest to the Japanese foreign minister complaining that Americans were being denied access to the lower Yangzi on the grounds that the area was not secure, while Japanese merchants and their families traveled freely in the area.[25] Some Japanese and puppet officials may also have used market controls for personal enrichment. Where military edicts created artificial barriers to trade, opportunities to get rich quickly soon followed. As F. C. Jones has written, "Japanese officers in China, like the Spartans abroad, soon yielded to the opportunities of peculation which their control of a puppet regime made possible."[26]

The policy of extraction provided immediate results in bringing in income for the military; yet in many ways the policy was counterproductive. Restrictions on trade and the flow of goods inhibited economic recovery in the occupied area, while the reduced purchasing power of the Chinese population limited the market for Japanese goods. Moreover, faced with unfavorable terms of trade for their agricultural produce, Chinese farmers had little incentive to market their commodities. When Japanese offered less than half the market value to north China wool producers in 1938, for example, Chinese shepherds simply held almost two-thirds of their product off the market. Cotton farmers responded to the Japanese procurement procedure by curtailing acreage. As a consequence, the Japanese began to modify the policy. In 1939, for instance, Japanese procurement of cotton in central China was 1,924,000 piculs, which represented 92.4 percent of the entire crop. By 1942 this figure would drop to 1,232,000 piculs while total production rebounded to 3,405,000. The procurement total was only 33 percent of the harvest in central China in the latter year. The "policy of plunder" had simply pro- vided too few incentives for producers in China. Japanese authorities modified the policy when they realized that the economy of the occupied area had to be revived.[27]

CONFISCATION OF CHINESE FACTORIES

The quest for quick income also informed Japan's policy toward the in- dustrial base in the lower Yangzi. With the surrender of Wuhan, virtu- ally all Chinese industry fell into Japanese hands save that in island Shang- hai and the small fraction evacuated to the interior. The Japanese quickly seized this property. Iron and coal mines, smelting plants, electric power plants, and machine-produced silk mills came under Japanese control, as did 90 percent of wheat milling facilities. Even in textiles, in which unoccupied Shanghai played a key role, the Japanese controlled 57.5 per- cent of the cotton textile spindles in central China by 1941, compared with less than 37 percent in 1936.[28]

Control of the facilities was but the first step. Chinese factories could make no contribution to the *yizhan yangzhan* policy unless they were in production. This was no easy task in 1938 and 1939. Not only had many plants been devastated by the fighting, but often the facilities had been used as barracks, stables, or hospitals. Restoring production was a daunt- ing task. Japanese authorities used two major approaches to resuscitat- ing Chinese industry. The first was to place the enterprise under direct military management (*jun guanli*). This approach was most common in north China and most often used for production related to the military needs. Mining enterprises, electrical plants, and iron foundries often fell into this category.[29]

The second method was to entrust (*weiren jingying*) the management and rehabilitation of the plant to a Japanese company. This method was more commonly used in central China and for light industries such as textile and flour mills, and cigarette and match factories. Altogether 137 factories came under this category, including 40 textile mills, 18 flour mills, 11 shipbuilding firms, 9 paper manufacturers, 9 rubber plants, and 8 cigarette plants. In addition to firms that were entrusted, or were di- rectly under military management, some firms were listed by the Japa- nese as being under joint Sino-Japanese management, although with the Chinese as junior partners. In 1943 nearly 70 were listed in this category, including 27 chemical plants and 10 machinery manufacturers. Another 31 were considered to be plants that were rented, and 20 were listed as having been purchased.[30]

As the war continued, however, military authorities increasingly brought Japanese merchant management even into those factories under direct military control. Army officers simply proved unequal to the task of managing manufacturing enterprises and had to rely on businessmen. The distinction between a factory under direct military control and one entrusted to a firm such as Toyoda nonetheless remained. The former was considered the property of the army or navy, with management serving at its pleasure; the latter was considered the property of the private Japanese firm. The output of the former was more likely to be strictly for military purposes; the latter sold on the open market.[31]

Entrusting Chinese factories to Japanese concerns not only extended Japanese control over the economy but was also considered partial compensation for losses suffered by Japanese companies during the China war. In the Shanghai area before July 1937, for instance, thirty of sixty-four textile mills were Japanese owned. During the fighting, two of these—the Toyoda #1 and #2 mills—were totally destroyed; seven others were heavily damaged. Five mills suffered light damage, and only sixteen escaped unharmed. Total losses by Japanese firms in Shanghai reached almost 228,000 spindles and 4,341 looms. Japanese losses were even more dramatic in Qingdao, where they had totally dominated prewar textile production. Retreating Chinese armies destroyed nine Japanese mills with more than 614,000 spindles and 11,544 looms. An additional Japanese mill in Wuhan with 24,800 spindles and 380 looms was seized by the Chinese army and used to make military uniforms. Later the plant was moved to Chongqing. In total, of more than 2,250,000 spindles held by Japanese mills when the war began, 887,000 were destroyed.[32]

Japanese mill owners were eager to recoup these losses and developed a plan to restore 422,000 spindles and 7,100 looms. Half of this target could be reached by bringing in idle equipment from Japan. For the rest, the mill owners clamored for restitution from the pool of confiscated Chinese mills.[33] The Kanegafuchi Company, which was part of the Mitsui group, had mills in Shanghai, Qingdao, Tianjin, and Jiaxing (in Zhejiang). It received four Chinese plants whose prewar spindles had totaled more than 190,000, including the large Dasheng #1 in Nantong and the Shenxin #7 in Shanghai. It actually operated five additional mills in north China that were under Japanese military control. Naigai Wata, headquartered in Osaka, had mills in Shanghai and Qingdao and received two plants that had had about 78,000 spindles. Dōkō bōseki took over the Dafeng and DaHua plants in Shanghai. Toyoda, the largest of the Japanese textile firms in China before the war, had suffered the greatest damage. It received five mills outright, including the Shanghai Yong'an #1 and Jiafeng mill in Jiading, and managed two more in the north under military control. The Shanhai bōseki company, which had been the first Japanese textile firm to invest in China, also received control of several large mills, including the Shanghai Shenxin #5 and #6 (which together had had 123,000 spindles on the eve of the war), as well as the Zhenxin mill in Wuxi. Dai Nippon (which used the name Daikō on its China facilities) received five mills that had had almost 200,000 spindles, including the Hengfeng mill in Shanghai and the Qingfeng mill in Wuxi. Finally, Yūhō bōseki took over six mills in the south, including the Yong'an #2 and #4, and managed three in the north for the Japanese military.[34]

Control of these factories was intended as compensation to the Japanese firms for losses suffered in the war, yet this was not a free gift. Most of these Chinese mills were heavily damaged; indeed some were mere heaps of rubble. Many of the Japanese companies had to make substantial investments merely to restore partial production at their new plants. Nonetheless, as the military front moved inland, Japanese textile firms were able to revive much of this property. By the end of 1939 in the Shanghai area, Japanese management had restored the formerly Chinese mills to more than 80 percent of prewar capacity. With both their original plants and those taken from the Chinese, the Japanese had control of 1,477,630 operating spindles, an increase of 12.5 percent over the number of Japanese controlled spindles in July 1937. By March of 1940, this number increased to 1,570,000 spindles. By contrast, the remaining Chinese and British controlled mills, operating in unoccupied Shanghai, retained only 510,000 and 260,000 spindles, respectively. The initial Japanese efforts to seize control of China and revive its industrial production under Japanese control had borne some fruit.[35]

Textiles were the most notable area of this activity, simply because it was the largest source of industrial activity. The Japanese military followed similar policies in other areas. The Yongni Cement Plant in Longhua, founded by Liu Hongsheng, was given to a Mitsui subsidiary to operate; the China Cement Company (Zhongguo shuini gongsi) in Longtan to Mitsubishi. Tōa Tobacco took over several Chinese tobacco mills, and Japan took control of many of the machine tool plants in

Shanghai. A number of the facilities were located in Zhabei and Pudong and had suffered extensive damage.[36]

CHINESE PARTICIPATION IN JAPANESE-CONTROLLED FIRMS

But where were the Chinese capitalists during this process? Were they offered any share in this restructuring? Apparently, even by the spring of 1938, Japanese authorities tried to induce major Chinese capitalists to return to their businesses and to agree to joint Sino-Japanese operations of their former enterprises. Those overtures were designed not only to give a greater sense of legality to the Japanese takeover but also to lure Chinese capital into the rehabilitation process. Many of the major Chinese industrialists of the lower Yangzi had relocated into unoccupied Shanghai. Their liquid capital remained in its banks.

These early offers were largely refused. In the aftermath of the bitter struggle of the early war period, few major capitalists were willing to risk life in the occupied zone. Further, initial Japanese offers were not generous. Chinese partners would have to accept junior status (at most 49 percent of the stock) with the Japanese firms to which their plants had been entrusted. Chinese capital would be required for rehabilitation; yet future profits would be shared, with the Japanese partners getting the larger portion. Finally, accepting a Japanese offer would require taking on the stigma of collaboration. Therefore, as the *Yinhang zhoubao* (Bankers' weekly) reported in April 1938, Chinese owners for the most part rejected the onerous Japanese terms.[37]

The only significant collaboration by Chinese capitalists early in the war was generally engaged in by smaller capitalists, particularly those away from Shanghai, who had few resources on which to fall back. Medium-scale capitalists or even workshop managers accepted Japanese offers as their only option. In the interior, Japanese control over commodity movements virtually dictated some cooperation with a Japanese partner or access to raw materials was impossible.[38] A typical case was that of the Wuhu, Anhui, Zhongyi Textile Mill, a small facility with 18,400 spindles (discussed in greater detail in Chapter 4). In May 1938 the Japanese military turned the mill over to the Yūhō bōseki company, which repaired the facility, part of which was being used as a military headquarters. In this case, the Japanese induced the Zhongyi managers to sign a cooperative agreement in April 1939, making them junior partners with the Japanese.[39] In 1938 and 1939, such agreements brought very limited benefits to Chinese manufacturers; profits were usually marginal. Later, when the Japanese modified their policies to make more generous offers to Chinese, some of these earlier agreements were useful to the Chinese capitalists, because they served as claims to regain control of their property.

Once Japanese companies assumed management of these firms, and especially after they had invested capital in the rehabilitation of the damaged plants, they were naturally quite reluctant to give up control. As Japanese economist Hon'iden Yoshio wrote in June 1939, concerning the confiscated plants:

> It appears obvious that their titles to these plants should be duly recognized when the legitimate Chinese proprietors come forward with their claims after the restoration of peace. Even so, there will remain the question how their claims should be reconciled with those of the Japanese entrepreneurs who have invested their own capital in repairs and improvements and are now actually operating the plants. A solution may be found through an agreement whereby the Japanese entrepreneurs will continue to direct actual operations while the Chinese proprietors will be assured of a certain share in the profits.[40]

Hon'iden's concerns represented an early recognition of the problem of reconciling the Japanese policy of seizure and entrustment with the conflicting policy of creating a genuine co-prosperity sphere.

Encouragement of Japanese emigration was another issue that emerged early in the war. It had long been a dream of Japanese expansionists that emigration would populate the mainland with substantial Japanese colonies. A key argument used by the expansionists to justify their program, in fact, was the alleged overcrowding of the home islands. In 1937 Tokyo established a two-billion-yen program to have one million Japanese households (totaling five million people) emigrate to Manchukuo over a twenty-year period. By November of 1939 the government enrolled 30,000 young volunteer emigrants from the Japanese countryside to move to northeast China.[41]

In the aftermath of Japanese conquest of the lower Yangzi, the immediate need, in the view of Japanese military leaders, was to encourage the immigration of Japanese entrepreneurs to assist in control and development of China's economy. Property confiscated from Chinese businessmen served as an inducement. As one eyewitness wrote:

> During 1938 and the first months of 1939, any Japanese merchant who came to Nanking was offered both a commercial and a residential property, which were taken from Chinese owners by the Special Services Organ of the

Army, or by the Gendarmerie. Often no compensation whatever was allowed; but in others a contract was drawn up and filed in Japanese offices.[42]

Once Japanese merchants or businessmen were established in China, they continued to be favored by Japanese authorities, whose tight controls over supplies, prices, and transportation made their help essential. Japanese Special Services also often pressured Chinese to accept Japanese partners in order to secure permits to operate.[43]

Generally, Japanese businessmen were more successful in taking over existing Chinese enterprises than in establishing totally new firms. As of February 1940, for instance, Japanese had established 65 new enterprises in Shanghai and restored 34 that had been damaged in the fighting. Meanwhile, Japanese took control of 90 enterprises that were formerly Chinese but were entrusted to Japanese management; another 113 were Chinese firms that agreed to either become joint Sino-Japanese ventures or to rent their facilities to Japanese. Clearly, squeezing Chinese capitalists was easier than building firms anew. Thus Japanese control of China's economy continued to grow. The number of Japanese firms in Shanghai expanded from 137 in 1936 (with capital of 83 million yen) to 342 in 1941 (with capital of 276 million yen). Total Japanese investment inside the Great Wall increased to 1.83 billion yen in 1938 from 1.11 billion in 1936. But controlling and rehabilitating a factory were not the same as operating it profitably.[44]

In the first phase of the war, from July 1937 to November 1938, the Japanese attempted to extract income from China as quickly and crudely as possible. The haphazard nature of Japanese policy led to serious problems, not just for Chinese businessmen but for the Japanese firms operating in China as well. Japanese commodity and fiscal control undermined the market. Farmers had less incentive to market commodities; urban factories, even those run by Japanese, often lacked raw materials as the procurement system gave priority to exports to Japan. The fifteen Japanese-controlled wheat mills in central China, for instance, operated at only 37.1 percent of capacity in 1940; the twenty-three such mills in north China did only somewhat better at 55 percent of capacity.[45]

From the perspective of Chinese capitalists, Japanese policy appeared to be pure looting. Their properties seized, most capitalists chose the safely of foreign concessions in Shanghai. Even later in the war when Japanese authorities attempted to attract Chinese business capital, the occupation never completely lost this coercive aspect. Local Japanese military commanders still felt that they could seize the property of Chinese firms, such as vehicles, furniture, and supplies, if they felt they needed it for the war effort. Valuable equipment would be taken in scrap iron drives. War was not an environment conducive to secure economic development.[46]

CHAPTER 3

Establishing Control

The North China and Central China
Development Companies

In the opening phase of the war from July 1937 until November 1938, Japanese forces had adhered to the policy of "using the war to sustain the war." While this often brought short-term gains, plundering and extractions did little to foster economic recovery. As economic and political problems in the occupied area mounted, Tokyo undertook a more systematic approach to the organization and development of its economy. In March 1938 the Japanese cabinet began planning for the establishment of large national development companies for China. Envisioned as broad-based holding companies, they were to channel and organize public and private Japanese capital to develop infrastructure and revive industry. From November 1938, when these were announced, through most of 1942, Japan succeeded in breathing new life into the economy of occupied China. North China in particular would make significant contributions to Japan's war effort during these months.[1]

On November 3, 1938, Japan's Prime Minister Konoe proclaimed the "New Order in East Asia." One week later the government inaugurated the North China Development Company (Kita Shina kaihatsu kabushiki kaisha), whose capital was set at 350 million yen, and the Central China Development Company (Naka Shina shinkō kabushiki kaisha), whose capital was set at 100 million yen. Half of the capital was to come from the Japanese government, half from the private sector. The concept of the development company was not new. The South Manchurian Railway Company (Mantetsu) served as a prototype, and in December 1935

it had organized a subsidiary, the Xingzhong (Kōchū) Company, to promote development of north China. Xingzhong directed Japanese capital
into coal and iron ore production, two areas in which the Japanese military was especially interested. It also set up several electric power companies in locales in Tianjin and east Hebei.[2]

The Japanese Imperial Army became dissatisfied with the South
Manchurian Railway (SMR) and its subsidiary Xingzhong and wrested
control of the economic development policy from the company. Many
large Japanese zaibatsu had also feared that they would be shut out by
SMR and worked with the army in organizing the new development companies in China. Businesses were stripped from the SMR and Xingzhong
Company and transferred to the North China Development Company
or to the Manchuria Industrial Development Company (Mangyō). The
latter was established in Manchuria in December 1937 under the leadership of Ayukawa Yoshisuke of the Nissan Company. The SMR was
left with its railway interests and little else; the Xingzhong Company was
dissolved in December 1941.[3]

The North China Development Company (NCDC) thus inherited the
electric power and mining interests of its Xingzhong predecessor, and it
began to control the enterprises that the Japanese military had seized,
including public utilities, transportation, and communications. The puppet governments established by the Japanese in the north signed over public property to the development company. The North China Company
also oversaw operations of those Chinese factories confiscated by the
Japanese and placed under military control but managed by Japanese
companies, such as Kanegafuchi and Toyoda. As the Japanese military
expanded its control, the North China Development Company would
follow. When Japan captured thirty-nine factories and mines in Shanxi,
for instance, the NCDC set up a subordinate firm, the Shanxi Production Company (Sansei sangyō kabushiki kaisha), to operate the concerns.[4]

By June 1942 the NCDC had numerous subsidiary companies, including four in transportation and communications, among them the North
China Shipping and North China Communications companies. The latter had been set up in February 1939 to operate and develop the railways of north China. Another five subsidiaries were involved in electric
power, ten were coal mining operations, eight iron ore mines, and two
salt production firms. Other members of the group were a telephone and
telegraph company, a chemical production firm, and a unit established
to increase production and export of cotton. In Zhangjiakou (Kalgan),
a wool manufacturing association was set up in conjunction with eight

Japanese firms; and in Shandong a flour milling company operated flour mills in Qingdao and Jinan that had been confiscated from the Chinese. At its peak the North China Development Company and its subsidiaries employed more than 600,000 personnel.[5]

Headed by Ōtani Son'yū, a former colonial minister, the firm had its headquarters in Tokyo and set up two branch headquarters in China. The first, in Beijing, coordinated with the puppet regime established there, the Provisional Government of the Republic of China (Zhonghua min-guo linshi zhengfu), initially under Wang Kemin; the second, in Zhang-jiakou, was to work with the Federated Autonomous Government of Mongolia (Mengjiang lianhe weiyuan hui), which the Japanese set up for Inner Mongolia. The NCDC operated under a nine-year development plan, which commenced in January 1938.[6]

The North China Development Company achieved considerable suc-cess in implementing the policy of "using the war to sustain the war." Total coal production in north China had declined to 10.09 million tons in 1938 from 16.73 million in 1936, but under the company's direction increased to 18.01 million tons in 1940 before peaking at 24.24 million in 1942. Pig iron production, which was 5,000 tons in 1936, reached 39,000 tons in 1939 and 90,000 in 1942. These successes were coupled with similar achievements in Manchuria, where coal production increased from 10.89 million tons in 1937 to 25.40 million in 1943. Pig iron pro-duction had been 430,000 tons in 1933; it reached 1,700,000 tons in 1943. This new production was geared toward the needs of the Japanese home islands. In 1943, for instance, 85 percent of the iron ore was ex-ported, mostly to Japan. China had supplied Japan with only 14 percent of its iron ore imports in 1937, but this rose to 49 percent in 1941.[7]

Even in textiles, progress was made in north China. The Japanese in-creased textile production in Tianjin, partially to offset losses in Qing-dao. Four new mills were built in the early war years, raising the number of spindles in that city in late 1938 to 462,000, an increase of 59 per-cent since the war began. The number of looms grew from 2,500 to 7,800 for the same period.[8] Under the domination of the Japanese military and with the assistance of Japanese capital, north China's economy was de-veloped to assist Japan's war machine.

The Chinese realized the threat that this economic program posed. In a 1939 publication in Chongqing entitled "How to Smash the Policy of the Japanese Bandits of Using the War to Sustain the War," Chen Zhengmo wrote of the Japanese plans to use the resources of the occu-pied area. Iron, coal, and foodstuffs would supply the Japanese war machine. Income from the control of cotton, wool, and rice provided capital for the investment program, which Japan would otherwise lack. How could China counter this? Chen urged the economic development of textiles and handicrafts in the unoccupied areas, which could serve as a lure for farmers to sell their produce there. Guerrillas and saboteurs could infiltrate the workforce at Japanese-controlled iron and coal mines, disrupting work. Transport lines from the mines to the coast were long and could be blown up.[9] Chen's arguments reveal a clear perception of the threat posed by Japan's economic thrust.

If the Pacific war had not erupted, Japan might well have continued to develop a colonial-style command economy in the north. For all of the problems posed by the China war and all of the strains on Japanese capital, the Japanese program made progress in the north; resources were developed to serve the Japanese war machine. Economic and fiscal controls were used to channel funds into Japan's projects; industry was organized under the control of the military in conjunction with Japanese zaibatsu. In such a scheme, Chinese capitalists had virtually no role to play. Only in the very last phase of the war, when economic conditions seriously deteriorated, would local officials in the north make significant changes in this policy.

DEVELOPMENT IN CENTRAL CHINA

From the beginning, however, Japanese policy toward central and south China differed from that toward the north. Japanese planners had long sought to integrate north China into an economic bloc with Manchukuo, Korea, and the home islands. Indeed, many Japanese leaders had assumed before July 7, 1937, that Japan could detach the five major provinces of north China under an "autonomy" scheme that would allow Japan to supervise the economic development of the area without having to fight a major war. Such had been the case with Manchuria. Not only did north China have the iron and coal resources Japan desired, but it could obviously be more easily integrated into existing projects in contiguous Japanese-controlled territory. Further, north China was viewed as critical to Japanese defense because of the potential for conflict with the Soviet Union.[10]

Japanese planners had not fully anticipated the spread of the conflict to central China after August 13, 1937. With limited funds available, Tokyo's investments in central China took a back seat to those in the north and in Manchuria. This was apparent in the capitalization levels for the two holding firms: 350 million for the northern and 100 million yen for the central company. Actual investment figures reflected this trend. Total Japanese investment in China (excluding Manchuria) in 1938 was 1.8 billion yen. Of this total 60 percent was invested in north China, 37 percent in central China, and the remainder in south China and elsewhere. For the entire war period, investment in north China, Inner Mongolia, and Xinjiang totaled 71 percent, central China only 22 percent, and south China 7 percent. Meanwhile, government investment in Manchukuo, which was 45 million yen in 1936, reached 112 million in 1938 and 255 million in 1941. Investment by the South Manchurian Railway Company was 134 million yen, 144 million, and 376 million for the same period.[11]

Faced with its lower priority for available capital, the Central China Development Company initiated fewer infrastructure projects than did its northern counterpart. Instead of beginning new enterprises from the ground up, it concentrated on rehabilitating and reorganizing existing companies. Central China certainly had more to work with than did the north, even with war damage. More than 75 percent of existing modern factories in the occupied zone (as of the end of 1938) were located in central China, compared to 15 percent in the north and just under 10 percent in the south and elsewhere. Funds were critically needed, however, to repair many of these facilities.[12]

Under these conditions, the participation of Chinese capital in the Co-Prosperity Sphere in central China would seem more promising and more necessary than in the north. As Itō Takeo, writing for the Japan Council of the Institute of Pacific Relations noted, "In Central China the situation in this regard is such that few economic policies can be regarded [as] sound and practical, unless the question of participation of native capital is fully taken into consideration."[13] A Japanese economics journal also editorialized in 1938, "The bourgeoisie of Central and South China differs from that of the North in that the former's . . . capital accumulation is incomparably larger than that of North China." As a result, the journal concluded, "participation by Japanese capital in the industrial development of these regions should be of only a supplementary character; the activities of the Japanese capitalists should be confined to giving assistance to the native Chinese capitalists so that the latter may better serve the interests of the bloc economy. . . . The basic policy of the East Asia economic bloc . . . must be more liberal . . . in Central and South China than in North China."[14]

Even in central China, however, Japanese authorities were not inclined to take so passive a role in 1938. While the subsidiary firms of the parent holding company were supposed to be joint Sino-Japanese ventures, most of the capital and actual control rested on the Japanese side. Of the thirteen largest subsidiaries of the Central China Development Corporation in March 1940, 73.6 percent of the capital actually invested in them came from Japanese sources—divided between the Tokyo government and zaibatsu. The remaining 26.4 percent of capital investment was listed as coming from Chinese partners, although this figure was devised by counting the value of confiscated property as part of the Chinese contribution.[15]

REHABILITATING THE INFRASTRUCTURE

Some of the most important subsidiaries of the Central China Development Company (CCDC) were transportation firms. War devastated commerce along the lower Yangzi, because of both the destruction of commercial ships and the Japanese military's decision to close the river to commercial traffic. The Shanghai Inland Navigation Company (Shanghai neihe lunchuan gufen youxian gongsi), established in August 1938 with headquarters in Shanghai, was given a virtual monopoly on inland river traffic. The CCDC eventually subscribed to 600,000 yen of the 2 million yen in capital. Using ships and docks from Chinese firms, including almost sixty taken from the China Merchants Steam Navigation Company, the company also received investment from Nisshin Kisen Kaisha. Although the tonnage shipped in inland rivers from Shanghai never recovered to prewar levels, the firm did achieve some success. In 1939, it shipped 580,000 tons; in 1941, 1,715,000 tons; in 1942, 1,656,000 tons; and in 1943, 1,729,000 tons. Only in 1944 did a serious decline set in; only 204,965 tons were shipped in the first six months of the year.[16]

Yet another shipping firm, the China Steamship Company (Zhonghua lunchuan gufen youxian gongsi), was established in February 1940 in Shanghai as a subsidiary of CCDC. This company, which was involved in transportation both on the Yangzi and along coastal areas, was capitalized at 17,094,000 yen, of which 3,063,000 came from the CCDC and 4,894,000 from the Japanese East Asian Sea Transport (Tōa kaiun kabushiki kaisha). The latter was a Japanese national policy corporation formed in Tokyo in August 1939 and designed to foster Japanese control of shipping in China. The Nanjing puppet government received credit as an investor in compensation for thirteen Chinese ships that were originally property of the China Merchants Steam Navigation Company. Although listed as a CCDC subsidiary, the firm actually answered to the Japanese partner, for Tōa kaiun increasingly controlled the China-Japan trade. The China Steamship Company shipped 252,000 tons in 1941, 600,000 in 1942, and 694,000 tons in 1943 before losing ground later in the war as American bombing and fuel shortages combined to restrict shipping.[17]

By creating these shipping concerns, Japanese authorities were able to regulate transport of commodities, a key to control of prices and commerce. At the same time, promoting a revival of shipping assisted in restoring economic vitality to the lower Yangzi. Similar concerns led to the creation of yet another subsidiary of CCDC, the Central China Railway Company (Huazhong tiedao gongsi). The Japanese military had initially assumed direct control of railway lines captured in the conflict. In April 1939 this new subsidiary was created with a substantial infusion of capital from the parent firm to rehabilitate the major lines in central China. In the first year of operation (May 1939-April 1940), the firm carried 6.46 million passengers and 1.78 million tons of freight. Although this was only 41 percent of the passenger traffic and 70 percent of the tonnage of 1935, it still represented a major recovery. In late April 1940 the company also reopened Shanghai's North Station, which had been virtually destroyed in 1937. Because of the importance of railways, a high percentage of the company's employees were Japanese—nearly 38 percent of the 14,000 employees in 1940.[18]

The railway company nonetheless faced major obstacles. Railway lines were particularly vulnerable to guerrilla attack. In 1941, for instance, there were 129 incidents of blockage of rail lines, including 31 on the Nanjing-Shanghai line and 34 on the Shanghai-Hangzhou line. Replacing cars destroyed in these attacks, which were sometimes caused by land mines, cost an estimated 1 million yen. Nonetheless, the company frequently announced grand schemes for new projects, such as a railway tunnel under the Yangzi at Nanjing and a link south from Nanjing to Hanoi.[19]

Other transportation units of CCDC included the Central China Urban Motor Transport Company (Huazhong dushi zidong che gufen youxian gongsi). This firm, originally just the Shanghai Motor Bus Company, was established in November 1938 with an authorized capital of 3 million yen. It took over the bus service in the major cities of the lower Yangzi, including Shanghai, Nanjing, Hangzhou, Suzhou, and Zhenjiang. Passenger traffic increased through 1942, then began a pronounced decline in 1944.[20] The final subsidiary of the CCDC in transportation was the Central China Transport Company (Huazhong yunshu gufen you-xian gongsi). Established in 1942, this company focused on smaller trans-port. Funded by the CCDC and the East Asian Sea Transport, it received investments in materials from the Central China Railway Company, China Steamship Company, and the Shanghai Inland Navigation Com-pany. The company used motor vehicles, small steamships, junks, and even horses.[21] These subsidiary companies thus gave the Japanese the abil-ity to control and develop transportation by rail, water, and land far more effectively than in the early months of the war.

Utilities were another target of CCDC. The Central China Telecom-munications Company (Huazhong dianqi tongxin gufen youxian gongsi), formed in July 1938, assumed control of telephone and telegraph ser-vice in the occupied area, including Shanghai, Nanking, and Hangzhou. Capitalized at 15 million yen, 6 million supplied by CCDC, it offered radiogram service from Shanghai to Japan, Hong Kong, and Dairen, and operated a radio station in Shanghai. The company faced the challenge of restoring telegraph service in the lower Yangzi, as most lines had been destroyed in the fighting.[22]

The Central China Water Works and Electric Power Company (Hua-zhong shuidian gufen youxian gongsi) took over the water and electric power systems in the lower Yangzi urban areas, including Nanjing, Zhen-jiang, Suzhou, and Hangzhou. In Shanghai the firm decided to merge the heretofore separate systems in Nanshi, Pudong, and Zhabei. CCDC sup-plied more than 16 million yen to the concern, whose capitalization was set at 43 million. The puppet regime was granted a substantial share in the enterprise based on the value of confiscated material. The Pudong electric company, for instance, had been a separate company in the pre-war period. Japanese troops occupied the plant in November 1937; it resumed operation the following March, and in June 1938 was trans-ferred to the new subsidiary. The value of its plant was fixed at 470,000 yen, so shares of this amount were given to the Ministry of Industry of the Reformed Government. A duplicate arrangement was made for the Chinese Electric Power Company located in Nanshi. Nanjing received shares valued at 1.7 million yen in exchange for its facilities.[23] A third utility company was the Greater Shanghai Gas Company (Da Shanghai wasi gufen youxian gongsi), established in December 1938 with a capi-tal of 3 million yen, 1.8 million of which was from CCDC. This enter-prise operated the natural gas business confiscated from the Shanghai Gas Company (Shanghai zilai huo gongsi).[24]

The utilities in the foreign concessions remained free of CCDC control until after Pearl Harbor, when the Japanese confiscated most of these on the grounds that they were enemy property. On March 29, 1942, the Japanese military then entrusted these telephone, electric, and water facilities to the CCDC system. Central China Electric Communications received the Shanghai Telephone Company, Central China Water Works picked up two new electric companies and one water plant, and Greater Shanghai Gas Company got the British and American Shanghai Gas Company. For the first time, utilities of the various segments of Shanghai were united, although under foreign control.[25]

The military basis of the CCDC program was particularly evident in the efforts to develop mining resources. Although north China was the clear focus of these investments, some effort was expended in central China. The Central China Mining Company (Huazhong kuangye gufen youxian gongsi) was established in April 1938 with a capital of 20 million yen, 4.5 million of which came from CCDC. Ten million yen was credited to the Nanjing regime as compensation for properties taken by the company. Huazhong's goal was development of iron ore sources in Anhui, Zhejiang, and Jiangsu. In particular, the firm hoped to revive the Taochong Mines, which had produced 280,000 tons of coal per year in the mid-1930s. The South Manchurian Railway Company, Japan Steel, and Asano Steel shared in the investment, and the Nanjing government was listed as a partner, credited with the value in kind of Chinese mines seized by the Japanese.[26] A companion firm, the Huainan Coal Mining Company, was established in June 1939, with capital of 15 million yen, more than 4 million of which came from CCDC. Major Japanese investors included both Mitsui Mining and Mitsubishi Mining companies.[27]

THE SEARCH FOR PROFITS

Original plans for the CCDC included control of strategic industries such as communications, transportation, and mining. Consumer goods such as textiles, tobacco, flour, and paper were not considered essential to its mission. However, chronic shortages of capital led the company into new areas, including light industry, marketing, and even real estate. The purpose of these new concerns was simply to make money; the links to military and strategic needs were not apparent. For instance, CCDC established a match manufacturing division in March 1942, later named the Central China Match Company (Huazhong huochai gufen youxian gongsi). It operated factories formerly held by the Great China Match Company (Da Zhonghua huochai gongsi), Meiguang Matches (Meiguang huochai gongsi), and several smaller firms. One of the most successful efforts was in marketing—the Central China Marine Products Company (Huazhong shuichan gufen youxian gongsi), established in November 1938. Tied to a central fish warehouse in Shanghai, the company controlled and licensed trawler fishing and fish wholesaling. Profits were said to benefit the Japanese navy, which was diligent in enforcing the monopoly. In March 1942 it acquired the facilities of an American cold storage company and later set up fish markets in Nanjing and Wuxi.[28]

Production and sale of salt had been a fiscal mainstay of government in China for a millennium, so this was a natural fit for the CCDC. In August 1938 the Central China Salt Industry Company (Huazhong yanye gufen youxian gongsi) was established with capital of 5 million yen, taking over property formerly operated by the Salt Gabelle, including the Huaibei Salt fields. CCDC invested 2 million yen, the Nanjing regime was given credit for 1,640,000 yen, and the Nippon Salt Company invested the remainder.[29]

The Shanghai Real Estate Company (Shanghai hengchan gufen youxian gongsi) was set up in September 1938 with the announced goal of rehabilitation of properties destroyed in the fighting. One half of the stock was to be held by the "reform" Nanjing government, 25 percent by CCDC, and 25 percent by private Japanese firms. Four textile companies, Kanegafuchi, Shanhai bōseki, Naigai wata, and Yuhō became the principal Japanese partners. The Chinese investment was compensation for municipal property formerly held by the Shanghai city government, including the government center at Jiangwan and wharves at Wusong, which was given to the new firm. Much of this property had been destroyed in the fighting and needed extensive restoration. In May 1942 the company got a further boost when the Japanese military entrusted it with more than twenty-five real estate firms that had been seized in the International Settlement after Pearl Harbor. These were mostly British and American concerns, which were considered enemy property.[30]

The activities of the company became a point of conflict between the Japanese and the puppet governments they created. Rather than invest in rehabilitating property, Shanghai Real Estate became involved in rentals and in market speculation, buying and selling properties. In the volatile real estate market of wartime Shanghai, these activities were very profitable. Chinese who had signed on with the Japanese-established regime felt that the company limited their ability to function as a municipal government because of both the control it had over property and the manner in which it operated. Except for the chair of the board of di-

rectors, all key personnel were Japanese. Chen Gongbo, whom Wang
Jingwei appointed mayor, particularly resented the company's control
of municipal property, because this had been signed away by an earlier,
rather ephemeral puppet regime (discussed below). Chen raised many of
these issues on February 13, 1941, when he met informally with representatives of the company, the Asian Development Board (Kōain), and
Japanese Special Services. Chen complained of the company's handling
of road and waterfront development. He also suggested somewhat
obliquely that the Japanese military ignored Chinese opinion when uti-
lizing some of the property. The case that Chen raised was the sudden
removal of graves from the Cantonese (Guangdong) cemetery in Shanghai because the Japanese military wanted to use the land. Chen's concerns were rebuffed by the representatives of Japanese Special Services
on the grounds that military needs had priority. The Chinese authorities
could do little to counter the speculation schemes of the company.[31]

These subsidiaries were established simply to earn income, since real
estate speculation, salt production, fish marketing, and match production were not fundamental to Japanese war plans. One subsidiary, however, found itself in a dilemma when trying to maximize profits. The Central China Sericultural Company (Huazhong cansi gufen youxian gongsi)
marketed a product—silk—in which China and Japan were competitors.
Founded in August 1938, the company eventually had capital set at 10
million yen, one-fifth of which was to come from CCDC. Although many
Chinese filatures had been destroyed or relocated to unoccupied Shanghai, the company confiscated the remaining from Chinese owners, who
were granted 30 percent of the stock in the new firm as compensation.
Japanese participants included Kanegafuchi, Mitsubishi, and Katakura
Silk Reeling Company. Central China Sericultural Company received a
monopoly on the sale of cocoons, silk worm cultivation, and silk manufacturing in Zhejiang, Jiangsu, and Anhui, which it enforced through
a licensing system. The export of silk products was also regulated, with
the Mitsui Company gaining control over most exports to Japan.[32]

All cocoons produced in this area had to be sold through agents of
the company. Procurement prices were low, and Japanese buyers sometimes paid in military scrip, which few producers wanted. Company authorities also restricted sales of silk to filatures in unoccupied Shanghai,
where many Chinese producers had relocated. The latter thus acquired
silk cocoons from unoccupied areas (such as portions of eastern Zhejiang, which escaped Japanese control for a time). These were slipped
down to unoccupied ports and sent to Shanghai on "foreign shipping."

The combination of wartime destruction and company policy hindered production and led to a decline in output. Mulberry acreage in Zhejiang, for instance, dropped 65 percent from 1937 to 1945; cocoon production in the same province fell 77 percent in that period.[33]

In April 1940, the subsidiary and CCDC decided that production was being curtailed too severely. The company's target for production (which had been set at 19,400 piculs in 1939) was set for 32,400 piculs annually for the years 1940 through 1942. Corporate leader Kodama Kenji announced that the Sericultural Company would extend loans to farm families to assist in production. But this policy was short-lived. When world silk prices fell in late 1940, Tokyo economic authorities decided that increasing Chinese silk output would be detrimental to Japanese producers and reversed CCDC's move. Tokyo ordered Chinese production curtailed anew. In December 1940 filatures in China were forced to reduce output by 20 to 50 percent. Actual production of raw silk, which had been 17,276 piculs in 1939 and 26,362 in 1940 fell to 15,928 in 1941. Profits remained strong, however, in part because of lower labor costs and the low cost of cocoons.[34]

Throughout the rest of the war, Japanese policy continued this pattern. Tokyo ordered Chinese production of silk decreased whenever the Japanese market was threatened, increased when more production was deemed useful. The loss of the American market with the severance of economic ties acutely effected central China. The ups and downs of the silk industry are reflected, for instance, in the history of the Dali Silk Company. Established in 1939 in the International Settlement by two silk industrialists whose original mills had been lost in the war, the firm had 240 looms and relied on cocoons purchased surreptitiously in the Ningbo area. When the Japanese occupied the "island" in 1941, the firm was not confiscated but virtually had to suspend operations because their cocoon supply was seized en route by the Japanese. The Dali mill was able to operate for only eighteen days in 1942. In 1943, however, Japan relaxed controls and allowed production by the Dali and other Chinese silk mills to grow, for a time, provided that they operated under the direction of Central China Sericulture.[35]

Tokyo's silk policy clearly indicated the fundamental nature of the Co-Prosperity Sphere. The interests of the home country came first, and policies in China had to reflect this reality. Economic development on the mainland ideally would fit Japanese needs, such as iron or coal production, or it might be complementary, such as salt or fish production. It could definitely not be competitive with Japan. The home economy was

too dependent on silk exports to allow excessive competition from occupied China. Ironically, cotton textiles, an area of potential conflict between China and Japan, largely escaped controversy. Because most of
the cotton mills in central China had been entrusted to Japanese firms,
the CCDC did not get directly involved. Japanese firms could coordinate
production between their Chinese units and those at home with less government involvement.

The problems with Tokyo's silk policy also reflect the divergent interests of groups involved in the planning of the CCDC. The creation of
this one general organization did not really eliminate conflict among
Japanese agents over how to handle occupied China; it simply created a
new arena of conflict. The lack of a clear vision for the New Order/
Greater East Asia Sphere meant that plans were patched together as the
war continued. When the Central China Sericultural Company was created, an operating plan for the firm was laid down in a planning meeting held on October 20, 1938, at the Mitsui Bank building in Shanghai.
Attending was Suzuki Kakusaburō, representing the company's board
of directors, but he was joined by Harada Kamakichi of the Special Services of the Japanese army, Nomura Michikuni of the Special Services of
the Japanese navy, and Hidaka Shin'rokurō of the Japanese consulate.
Coordinating policy among these groups was difficult. When business
and bureaucratic interests in Tokyo intervened, the result could be frequent changes in policy and disputes among Japanese agents.[36]

SINO-JAPANESE COOPERATION?

The creation of the North China and Central China Development corporations and their numerous subsidiaries did represent a more sophisticated approach by the Japanese to exploit the resources of China. The
simple expropriation policy followed in the early phase of the war had
not yielded sufficient results for the policy of "using the war to sustain
the war." The Japanese military had difficulty operating and rehabilitating enterprises such as the railways or commercial shipping of central
China. Establishment of the development companies was a method of
drawing Japanese capital and civilian businesses into a program to meet
Japan's military needs. In central China this meant restoring and controlling the transportation and communication networks and public utilities, developing natural resources for military use, and tapping obvious
sources of revenue such as salt production or real estate sales.

But what of Chinese participation in these schemes? Virtually all of the subsidiary firms were labeled "joint Sino-Japanese" ventures. Chinese served on the boards of directors and supervisors. Sometimes the nominal head of the firm was Chinese and the vice director Japanese. The chairman of the Central China Marine Products Company, for instance, was Zhou Jue, a Chinese who had been educated in Japan and who had served as an official in the Chinese Ministry of Foreign Affairs. The vice chair was Taguchi Chōjirō. The chair of the Central China Match Company was Chen Bofan, the vice chair Ueno Ryōsaku.[37] Despite this official setup, most observers felt that this was purely for show; Japanese were in charge. Nanjing insider Jin Xiongbai recalled that virtually all of the CCDC Chinese participants were followers of Zhou Fohai or Mei Siping, who were tied to the Wang Jingwei government. But Wang's regime could not get Japanese to accept its authority; it remained a puppet regime. When disputes developed, representatives of the Special Services of the Imperial Army and Navy seem to have set policy.[38]

ESTABLISHING CURRENCY CONTROL

Control of the currency in the occupied zone was an essential part of Japan's New Order in East Asia. The creation of the two large holding companies was paralleled by an effort to enforce use of Japanese bloc currencies. Success of this policy would have placed powerful fiscal tools in the hands of the Japanese and allowed them to dictate the terms of trade of the occupied area. Tokyo also felt that replacement of the Guomindang currency, fabi, or legal tender, would be a crippling blow to the Chiang Kaishek regime. Such dominance would not come easily; indeed, the struggle between Japanese-backed currency and fabi during the 1937 to 1941 period was often called a "currency war," one in which the Japanese were initially at a disadvantage. As with the war in general, Japan simply did not provide adequate funding to back the issuance of sound, secure currencies that would be widely accepted. The second major difficulty was that the banking centers of China remained unoccupied, being in neutral areas beyond the direct control of either the Guomindang or the Japanese. A free market for currencies persisted regardless of political edicts from Tokyo, Beijing, or Chongqing. The International Settlement of Shanghai was the primary financial center of China, containing all of the Chinese modern banks of Shanghai. Major foreign banks such as the British Hongkong and Shanghai Banking Corporation were centered on the Bund, and enjoyed the added protection of extraterritoriality. Even in north China the center of banking was not Beijing but the foreign concessions in Tianjin. A free market persisted in currencies and foreign exchange.

Because of these limitations, the Japanese made a strong delineation early in the war between north China and central China, much along the lines of the two development companies. In north China, the Japanese would try to establish currency tightly tied to the yen bloc, building on the base in Manchukuo and the east Hebei area. In central China the Japanese delayed such an effort until 1941. As Japanese scholar Naka-mura Takafusa has noted, "The Central China Area Army did not at-tempt to set up its own bank or currency. . . . Japan had decided to re-gard north China as an extension of the Japanese homeland but to treat central and southern China as a foreign territory like Hongkong."[39]

In north China, Japan already had an established tradition of incor-porating the area into the yen bloc. The Manchuria Central Bank, es-tablished in 1932, issued yuan denominated banknotes that were tied to the yen at parity in 1935. Japan introduced into wide circulation the notes of the Tianjin branch of the Bank of Chosen (Korea), particularly in east Hebei, where the Japanese established a puppet regime following the He-Umezu Agreement of 1935. When the Japanese military began opera-tions in north China after July 7, 1937, it initially used notes of the Bank of Chosen to pay its bills, so much so that the currency began to depre-ciate. After the Japanese North China Army established a puppet regime in Beijing, the "Provisional Government of the Chinese Republic" (dis-cussed in Chapter 4), it decided to issue a new currency. In March 1938, a new China Reserve Bank (Zhongguo lianhe zhunbei yinhang, some-times called the Federal Reserve Bank of China) was established as the state bank for the Beijing government. The Japanese began replacing the notes of the Bank of Chosen with those of the China Reserve Bank. Tight restrictions made it difficult to exchange the notes for foreign currency.[40]

The Japanese were eager to have the China Reserve notes totally re-place the use of Guomindang fabi as the legal currency, but this was slow to happen. In June 1938, the Beijing authorities decreed that all fabi notes be exchanged for China Reserve Bank notes within one year under penalty of law. Yet many were reluctant to accept the notes, which were issued in large quantity. They traded at a disadvantage against fabi in Tianjin and other open markets, often requiring a 30 percent discount. As John Hunter Boyle noted, "The currency, which had only nominal backing, fell in value as huge inflationary printings swelled the volume in circula-tion to higher and higher levels each month." Even Japanese business-men disliked the currency, since it was difficult to exchange it even for yen to remit to Japan. Large quantities of fabi were hoarded in Tianjin and widely used in areas outside of direct Japanese control.[41]

The fight between the Japanese-backed currency and the fabi was referred to as the "currency war," and was sometimes violent as both sides tried to block use of the other currency. While British interests continued to use fabi in their Tianjin concession, the Japanese demanded that notes of the China Reserve Bank be acceptable for payment of taxes and other debts there. In December 1938 the British Municipal Council yielded to Japanese pressure. In explaining to the British consul in Tianjin why the council caved in, A. E. Tipper, the chairman, wrote that "many electors believe that tension between the Municipality and the Japanese Military Authorities will be sensibly diminished by the course which has been taken."[42] The situation in Tianjin remained tense, however. Japan and Great Britain almost came to blows over control of silver reserves held in the Chinese Bank of Communications in the British concession in Tianjin, as well as continued use of fabi there. In June 1939 Japan even blockaded the concession until the two sides compromised in June 1940. The pressure of the European war led Britain to compromise.[43]

The vehemence of the currency war was driven by each side's contention that currency domination was the key to political control of territory. One strength of the fabi compared to China Reserve Bank notes was that it had been freely exchangeable for foreign currency, such as the British pound sterling or American dollar. When the war erupted, the Guomindang government felt it must adhere to this policy and would do so for the first eight months of the conflict. The Japanese took advantage and began to convert the large quantity of fabi collected by the China Reserve Bank in Beijing into foreign exchange at Shanghai. This put such great pressure on the Chinese yuan that on March 13, 1938, the Chiang Kaishek government announced very strict restrictions on foreign exchange. The Guomindang could not eliminate the trading of fabi by foreign banks in Shanghai, so a disparity developed between the legal exchange rate and trading rate of fabi. The Guomindang attempted to counter by providing additional funds for foreign exchange, even though much of this ended up in Japanese hands. Yet, ironically, even Japanese found holding fabi useful since it was a convertible currency while the Beijing notes were not.[44]

Nonetheless, in the currency war General Doihara Kenji was convinced that eliminating fabi was critical to Japanese success. In contrast, Chiang Kaishek was determined to maintain the prestige of the currency.

"Confidence in these currency issues," noted Lincoln Li, "was tied to the exchange rate of these currencies in the open market in Shanghai and Tientsin." That was certainly the view among most Chinese. The economist Ma Yinchu wrote in March 1939, "The enemy knows that if it wants to destroy our country, it must first destroy our fabi." As long as fabi was widely used in the occupied areas, Chongqing felt, the Japanese could not establish complete economic control. Whatever the wisdom of this policy in terms of the prestige and viability of fabi (and it remained more desirable than the puppet currencies for quite some time), it aided the Japanese in that they continued to cash in their fabi on the open market and build up valuable foreign reserves.[45]

The banking arrangements in north China were designed to serve the "using the war to sustain the war" approach. The Japanese military drew heavily on the income of the China Reserve Bank, which issued additional currency to cover these expenses. Its note issue expanded by 450 percent from 1938 to 1941, while its value in foreign exchange decreased. This in part generated the severe inflation that developed during this period. Ironically, the attempt to maintain the foreign exchange position of the fabi provided the major source of exchange to back the China Reserve Bank currency. But the fabi also lost value as China bled foreign exchange through Shanghai while continuing to print more currency. In early May 1940 Chongqing virtually abandoned an effort to hold the value of the yuan, after heavy purchases of foreign exchange by Japanese in the previous four months. Fundamentally, the Chongqing government simply did not have sufficient revenue to cover expenses and increasingly relied on printing paper currency to cover its debts. Despite the foreign exchange restrictions and some support from Britain, and to a lesser extent the United States, the exchange value of the fabi yuan fell from just over 29 cents in July 1937 to only 6 cents in December 1940. The flood of printed currencies created inflation in both occupied and free China, but by late 1940 the value of the China Reserve Bank notes surpassed that of fabi notes. During 1941 the notes of the Beijing regime "became the chief currency of occupied north China," noted Arthur N. Young, then a financial advisor to the Guomindang government.[46]

The most egregious use of unsupported currency was the military yen. In central and south China the Japanese military made no immediate attempt to establish a new bank or currency. Instead it frequently used military yen issued by the Bank of Japan or Yokohama Species Bank to cover expenses. This currency could not easily be remitted back to Japan and so for all intents and purposes was unsecured. As Frank Tamanga noted in his wartime study of China's financial situation, military yen "lacked the guarantee of a responsible financial institution and the coverage of a bullion and/or foreign exchange reserve." Yet it was difficult to refuse to accept the currency when proffered by the Japanese military, so circulation in China increased. In June 1940 official reports stated that more than 100 million military yen was in circulation in China; unofficial reports placed the total much higher—near 600 million yen.[47]

A first, half-hearted attempt was made to establish a puppet government bank in Nanjing, the Huaxing Commercial Bank (Huaxing shangye yinhang) in May 1939. Although it handled tax receipts for the puppet regime (the Reformed Government), which the Japanese set up in the old Guomindang capital, the bank did not have adequate reserves and its currency was little used. No effort was made to tie the currency to the yen; it was convertible into fabi. Only in January 1941, after the establishment of the Wang Jingwei regime would a substantial effort be made to create a new currency for central China.[48]

The Japanese efforts to gain control of currency in China paralleled but lagged behind the development companies. As in the case of the two umbrella companies, the Japanese distinguished between north China, thought to be more closely linked to Japan and Manchukuo, and central China, where Japan's presence was less dominant. In the currency realm, the strong role of "solitary Shanghai" was such that Japan was quite slow to set up a new structure.

Japanese policy during this second phase of the war, from November 1938 through most of 1942, appears to be the creation of a colonial regime. Japanese authorities strove to create an economy controlled by and complementary with the home islands. The role of Chinese capital was limited and subordinate. Only in the last phase of the war, after the Japanese suffered reversals on the battlefield and faced severe constraints on labor and capital, would this change. The Japanese would be forced to create more vital puppet regimes, breathing real life into Nanjing. In the economic sphere they would suddenly be eager to invite Chinese businessmen to participate in the economy under considerably more generous terms than had been offered earlier. True Sino-Japanese Cooperation really emerges only late in the war period, a time when strains of inflation and shortage of raw materials severely curtail economic production.

CHAPTER 4

Puppet Governments and Chinese Capitalists

Creation of client governments featured prominently in Japanese activities in China, dating from the establishment of Manchukuo. Pejoratively referred to as puppet governments, these regimes differed from purely colonial administrations (such as Korea and Taiwan) in that they were nominally independent entities. Why create such structures? Although the answer is complex, the simplest explanation is that such governments were thought to assist in controlling conquered territory by gaining the support or at least acquiescence of the population. The Japanese structures were marred by several major flaws, the most significant of which was the failure of the military to grant the "puppets" meaningful independence and authority. Their impotence both gutted their claims to be legitimate, autonomous governments and impeded the effort of the Japanese to get individuals of prestige to join their cause.

A second major failing of the Japanese undertaking was the haphazard and disorganized way in which the puppet governments were created in China, reflecting the lack of a clear plan or even vision for Japan's New Order. The Japanese established an array of these regimes, including the formation of governments in Inner Mongolia and north China and the Dadao government of Shanghai, not to mention the prototype, Manchukuo. These governments were initially established by local Japanese military units; none exercised meaningful authority during the early period. The Federated Autonomous Government of Inner Mongolia (headed by Prince Yun and Prince De) was the creation of the Japanese

Guandong (Kantō) Army, which controlled Manchukuo. Japan's North China Area Command, on the other hand, set up the "Provisional Government of the Chinese Republic" in Beijing on December 14, 1937, headed by Wang Kemin, a banker who had earlier served as a financial official in various warlord governments. With the strong support of Major-General Kita Seiichi, head of the Special Services Section of the North China Command, the Beijing regime launched the Xinmin Hui (People's Renovation Society), which was to be a rival to the Guomindang.

The Central China Army Command, meanwhile, established the Dadao (Great Way) Municipal Government in Shanghai on December 5, 1937, followed by a "Reformed Government of the Republic of China" in Nanjing in March 1938, headed by Liang Hongzhi, an old associate of Duan Qirui. The "Reformed Government" had nominal authority over Jiangsu, Zhejiang, Anhui, and the cities of Shanghai and Nanjing. The Dadao regime was then reorganized as a Special Municipality of Shanghai headed by mayor Fu Xiao'an. Creation of the "Reformed Government" was a veritable comedy, with the "leaders" hustled to Nanjing for the inauguration, then quickly returned to a New Asia Hotel in Shanghai.[1]

This plethora of regimes reflected division among Japanese military commands, each of which jealously guarded its sphere of influence and none of which was eager to replace its regional regime with a central government. Under such circumstances, the puppet governments had difficulty exercising meaningful authority. Even at the most basic level of finance, few of the governments had a meaningful revenue base. None were able to tax the agrarian sector effectively. Customs revenue, which had provided Chiang Kaishek's government with much of its revenue, was initially closed off when the Inspector General of Customs, Sir Frederick W. Maze, refused to surrender receipts. As a consequence, wrote John Hunter Boyle, the puppet regimes became "dependent on funds grudgingly supplied by Japan, extralegal income, currency manipulation, and squeeze. Japanese financial support was irregular at best."[2]

Without meaningful control of territory, lacking a secure source of income, and obliged to serve the needs of Japanese authorities, the early puppet governments exercised little real authority. They provided no more than a veneer over the Japanese occupation. Even the departure of Guomindang stalwart Wang Jingwei from Chongqing, and the inauguration of a new regime in Nanjing on March 30, 1940, brought little immediate change. In November 1940 Wang acquiesced to the continuation of separate councils at Beijing and in inner Mongolia that were only nominally under his authority. As W. G. Beasley has written, Wang's "administration was treated as little more than a device for maintaining order in Japanese-occupied areas. . . . Wang . . . never won the kind of independence from Japan that would have made it possible for him to compete with either nationalists or communists for Chinese popular support."[3]

Given the impotence of the client regimes, whether in Nanjing, Shanghai, or Beijing, they could do little to protect Chinese enterprises even though these represented a potential source of income. In the early months of the conflict, when Japanese activity emphasized extraction, the puppet governments were powerless. They could not intercede as the Japanese military expropriated Chinese factories and granted them to Japanese companies. In the next phase of the war, when Tokyo created the large holding companies, the client regimes actually aided in the process. When the North China Development Corporation and the Central China Development Corporation sought Chinese property, the Beijing and Nanjing governments signed away rights. In examining the formal structure of the subsidiaries of the NCDC and CCDC, the various puppet regimes appear as major participants because they were granted stock in the companies as compensation for confiscated property. The Nanjing Reformed Government, for instance, was credited with a paid investment of 8,775,000 yen in the China Steamship Company, 13,300,000 in the Central China Motor Bus Company, and 20,400,000 in the Central China Tele-Communications Company. None of this represented any financial investment by Nanjing but simply figures that the Japanese assigned as compensation.[4]

The "participation" by Chinese regimes in the NCDC and CCDC created the illusion that these were cooperative joint ventures. Indeed, one reason the Japanese established puppet regimes was to lend credence to the assertion that they were effecting genuine Sino-Japanese partnership, not simply confiscating Chinese property. As John Hunter Boyle noted, "From the standpoint of Japan, one of the principal ends served by the Reformed Government was validating schemes for Japanese control of industry, transportation, and communication in Central China. The sanction the Government lent to these schemes was . . . illustrative of the regime's puppet character."[5]

Chinese were not necessarily consulted in the process. Wang Kemin, leader of the Beijing government, learned of the creation of the NCDC after the fact and was reportedly very resentful. His Minister of Industries, Wang Yintai, apparently stated, "All economic matters have been placed under the jurisdiction of the Development Company, and in every locality there are special services agencies, new people's associations, cooperative organizations, and propaganda groups interfering without local administration. . . . Why should we even have a government?"[6] Meanwhile, Liang Hongzhi signed agreements with Japanese Special Services agents, granting rights to Chinese property to the CCDC. Although the Nanjing government was to be consulted about management of the enterprises, Japanese authorities could act first and inform the Chinese later when there was "unavoidable military necessity."[7]

Thus "participation," if one could call it that, by representatives of Chinese puppet regimes in creation of the national development firms did not really enhance the viability of these governments. Nor, at this stage of the war, did it provide any meaningful opportunity for Chinese capitalists to protect their interests in the occupied areas. Before Pearl Harbor, and indeed for some months after, when Japanese sought the economic participation of Chinese businessmen in the economy of occupied China, they did so only under terms unfavorable to Chinese interests. Industrialists could sometimes retain an interest in a factory, but as a junior partner of a Japanese firm. Businessmen could play a role as long as it assisted the Japanese in their control and procurement policies. As a consequence, most Chinese businessmen relocated to the solitary island in Shanghai, to Hong Kong, or to the interior.

RECRUITING CAPITALISTS: THE WAR OF TERROR

But if the Japanese were loath to grant economic power to their client regimes and unwilling to extend attractive terms to most Chinese capitalists in central China, they were eager to gain the political support of businessmen for the puppet governments. Indeed, in many occupied areas, capitalists were seen as local notables, individuals whose public identification with the regimes would lend them credibility. Wang Kemin, for example, had obtained some prominence as a banker as well as a government official. For the most part, however, the collaborators who joined the Japanese were political figures whom time had passed by, either former officials in the warlord regimes or, in the case of Wang Jingwei, a Guomindang figure whose political star had been eclipsed by Chiang Kaishek. The only major business figure who signed on in the early years was Fu Xiao'an, and he is perhaps a special case—a longtime, bitter enemy of Chiang Kaishek. Head of the Shanghai General Chamber of Commerce in 1927, Fu actually fled to Manchuria when the new Guomindang government issued an order for his arrest. Fu had been unwilling to help finance the new regime. He returned in the 1930s to lead the Commercial Bank of China, only to have it take over by the Nanjing government in the "banking coup" of 1935. His bitterness toward Chiang led him to embrace the Japanese.[8]

But Fu was the exception. Most major capitalists, taking refuge in the foreign concessions, refused to deal with the Japanese. Yet in luring capitalists into supporting their client regimes, the Japanese had both a carrot and a stick—the latter being most prominent. The "carrot" was restoring some control or income over property held in the occupied zone. For others who had lost most of their wealth, working with the Japanese might mean a job, an income, status and protection, a way to secure income for family members. The "stick" was the threat of arrest or worse for capitalists who rejected Japanese overtures. Use of these tools in combination brought some businessmen into the Japanese camp.

Even as the Dadao government was being formed in Shanghai in December 1937, Japanese pressed businessmen and bankers to join in its support. The Japanese Dōmei News Agency reported on December 31 that a Shanghai Citizens Association (Shanghai shi minxie hui) composed of twenty-one prominent citizens was being organized to assist the new regime. The list included Yao Mulian of the Nanshi Water Company; Rong Zongjing, the great textile and flour milling magnate; Wang Yuqing, a manager of Rong's Fuxin flour mills; Lu Bohong, manager of the Nanshi Electric Company; You Jusun of the ZhenHua textile mill; and Gu Xinyi chair of the Grain Merchants Association.[9]

But did these individuals voluntarily come forward to work with the Japanese? This was not at all clear. Many became extremely nervous when the Japanese publicized their names. Rong Zongjing, who had been listed as being on the board of directors of the new group, met with a reporter on December 31 to state that the new group was merely an association to assist refugees and was not a political organization connected with the Dadao government. The association, Rong argued, was no different from a chamber of commerce or charitable organization. Its function was to help refugees in part through restoring production in factories located in the war zone. Since this required direct negotiation with Japanese military authorities, few accepted Rong's contention. Pro-Guomindang publications decried the new body, suggesting that the participants were primarily interested in protecting their property held by the Japanese. Rong's Shenxin Textile Company had several mills controlled by the Japanese by that point.[10]

Attacks on these supposed collaborators quickly turned violent. Guo-mindang operatives in Shanghai under Dai Li began a campaign of as-sassination and terror, which the Japanese would match bullet for bul-let. Both sides sought to intimidate those who would cooperate with the other, and Chinese businessmen were caught in the cross fire. The open-ing shot came on the very day in which the association was announced. Lu Bohong, a member of the board of directors of the group, was gunned down on the night of December 31.[11]

Most of the businessmen bolted. Rong Zongjing suddenly left for Hong Kong. Wang Yuqing announced that he was too busy to join the association. Gu Xinyi stayed on and was felled by gunfire on June 19, 1938. You Jusun was wounded and one of his bodyguards killed in an attack. Of course businessmen were not necessarily Dai Li's key targets. Anyone who accepted direct political appointment in the puppet gov-ernments could become a victim. Ren Bao'an, land commissioner of the puppet government, and Chen Deming, head of its boats inspection office, were cut down in June 1938. Chen Lu, the Reform Government's for-eign minister, was shot in his own home on Yu Yuan Road in February 1939, and the mayor of Shanghai, Fu Xiao'an, the most well-known cap-italist to support the Japanese, was hacked to death in his own home in October 1940. Li Guojie, grandson of Li Hongzhang, who had joined the China Navigation Company of the CCDC, was another prominent victim.[12]

Chinese capitalists in Shanghai thus found themselves under intense pressure. Japanese authorities demanded that they support the puppet regimes. If they agreed (or even wavered), they could become targets of GMD terror. In Shanghai most had the luxury of staying in the solitary island. Outside of the city, those who did not flee found themselves at the mercy of the Japanese authorities. Throughout central China, agents of the Special Services of the Japanese military approached businessmen and bankers, as local notables, demanding that they publicly commit to the occupation authority. Euphemistically called "self-governing com-mittees," local groups were to implement Japanese policies, particularly in providing grain and supplies for the Japanese military. In Hangzhou, for instance, not long after Japanese troops occupied the city, a Japanese Special Service agent organized the Hangzhou City Self-Governing Com-mission (Hangzhou shi zizhi weiyuan hui). The head of the city cham-ber of commerce, Xie Hucheng, had remained behind when Chinese forces retreated. A Japanese military agent informed him that he would be the vice director of the society. Other merchants, such as the head of the rice guild, were told to join as well. Like it or not, Chinese merchants staying in the occupied zone were coerced into collaboration with the new regimes created by the Japanese.[13]

In the initial phase of the war, Dai Li and the pro-Guomindang forces seemed to be winning the war of assassination. To counter this influence, the Japanese established a puppet Chinese special service agency, recruiting many who defected from the communists or nationalists, as well as individuals who would best be described as criminals or psychopaths. Known simply as Number 76 because they set up a headquarters in July 1939 at that address on Jessfield Road in western Shanghai, this group quickly became notorious. Number 76 was feared as a torture chamber from which few escaped. Businessmen in Shanghai thus faced pressure from both sides. Cooperation with the Japanese brought threats of assassination by Dai Li's group; resistance might lead to kidnapping and removal to Number 76. Rumors spread that the puppet group kept a hit list of prominent locals who were considered anti-Japanese. The foreign concessions provided only limited security from Number 76, since plainclothes agents operated with impunity.[14]

Because of the prominence of criminal types and the lack of adequate funding for the puppet forces, the line between political kidnapping and sheer extortion was often blurred. The manager of the China General Machinery Corporation recalled being held at Number 76, handcuffed and chained. Eventually he bought his way out of jail with the help of Yu Xiaqing. In another instance, Zhou Zongliang, a prominent comprador for German interests in Shanghai, was targeted by the Japanese for having contacts with Chongqing and rejecting a request to support Wang Jingwei. Although he successfully hid in the French Concession, puppet police arrested his wife. A payment of 40,000 yuan gained her freedom. Contemporary scholar Lynn Pan recalls how her grandfather was kidnapped off the street on Avenue Joffre in 1942. Her uncle paid a bribe to Number 76 to secure his release. The prevalence of this activity gave Number 76 a reputation for extortion that was well deserved.[15]

The war of assassinations achieved what patriotic propaganda had not—it drove many prominent capitalists to finally depart island Shanghai for the interior. Yu Xiaqing, for instance, had remained in Shanghai in the face of pressures from both sides. Japanese agents tried to persuade Yu, who was a well-known Chinese businessman, to become mayor. Because he had traveled to Japan and had numerous Japanese business contacts, Yu was considered open to Japanese suasion. When he refused to join the puppet regime, Japanese agents turned to the less prominent Fu Xiao'an, only to renew their pressure following Fu's assassination. Fearful that Yu would eventually cave in, Chongqing urged him to move to Sichuan. Chiang Kaishek, who had long-standing ties with Yu, sent a personal message, and Yu's son-in-law, Jiang Yiping, who was already in Chongqing, sent numerous telegrams begging Yu to come westward. But Yu also received a threatening letter, containing a bullet, suggesting he leave Shanghai. Despite the pressures, Yu was loath to abandon the comfort of the great city. Not only was he well into his seventies, but Yu earned large profits from importing rice from southeast Asia with his San Bei Company, remade as a Sino-Italian joint venture. By the spring of 1941, however, even Yu could not withstand the tension and departed for Hong Kong. Eventually he reached Chongqing, where he worked with Wang Xiaolai to develop transportation (by ship and truck) in the interior. His eldest son managed most of his property in Shanghai, while his second son handled the shipping company.[16]

Yu Xiaqing was not the only capitalist to flee Shanghai under pressure. Yu Zuoting, a prominent native banker with interests in Ningbo and Shanghai, had spent the first years of the war in the solitary island pursuing his banking interests but avoiding any political activity. After Pearl Harbor, the Japanese and Wang Jingwei pressured Yu to chair the Nanjing government's central bank. Unwilling to support the puppet endeavor, Yu and his brother left Shanghai for Chongqing, via Hong Kong and Guiyang.[17]

BEYOND TERROR

The Japanese realized that terror had its limits. Although it led many to acquiesce to the occupation, terror did not create new bonds linking the puppet government to society at large. To effect genuine cooperation between the occupation and Chinese businessmen would require a more positive policy. With the formal creation of the Wang Jingwei government in the spring of 1940, and its much-delayed recognition by Tokyo in November 1940, there was discussion of a better deal for China. Indeed, the Wang government hoped that it would be given economic control of the lower Yangzi by the Japanese to strengthen its existence. Nanjing could then offer to Chinese capitalists who supported the regime the return of the confiscated plants and businesses. Nanjing also sought a true partnership role in the CCDC, not merely a paper presence. Such was not to be, at least in this stage of the war, but there were hints of a new policy. At the time of Wang's inauguration in March 1940, General

Nishio Toshizō, Commander-in-Chief of the China Expeditionary Force, suggested that some Chinese factories might be restored, but later statements from military headquarters emphasized that the "rightful owners . . . shall pledge loyal allegiance to the new regime and . . . recognize the new relations between China and Japan."[18]

Puppet leaders, in fact, found themselves unable to gain real authority from the Japanese and were forced to serve Japanese ends with no real quid pro quo. In a radio address on December 4, 1940, Mei Siping, Minister of Industry for Wang, admitted that the Sino-Japanese economic treaty did call for China to assist Japan in meeting its military needs, but Mei tried to argue that China's needs would come first. Japanese procurement policies, however, were unabated, so Wang's regime achieved little in this area until the war began to turn against Japan.[19]

Even many Japanese realized the problem. Itō Takeo, writing for the Japan Council of the Institute of Pacific Relations, noted that in the early war, "a period marked by the height of martial excitement, the Japanese authorities in China took various emergency steps. These included the military management of Chinese owned factories, the enforcement of control over the marketing of imported staple products, and the establishment of specially franchised Japanese companies." Itō concluded, however, that these policies would have to change if genuine Sino-Japanese cooperation was to occur under the new government. "We may assume that Japan, in view of the . . . new Chinese Central Government, should be ready to make drastic modifications in order to meet the wishes of the new regime and its capitalist supporters." But would this actually happen? Itō noted with hope that the Japanese High Command in China had announced on March 18, 1941, that they would return "to their original *bona fide* owners of those Chinese factories in occupied areas, which have been under temporary military management." Itō's comments were more a plea that this should be done than a statement of actual accomplishments.[20]

In fact, change came only as the circumstances of the war shifted. With Pearl Harbor and the outbreak of the Pacific war, the strains on Japanese manpower and capital grew exponentially. More than ever Japan needed participation of Chinese capitalists if the policy of "using the war to sustain the war" was to succeed. As Akira Iriye has noted, after Pearl Harbor Tojo "established four guidelines for the development of occupied areas: Japan must secure resources that were essential for the prosecution of the war, prevent natural resources from reaching the enemy, ensure self-sufficiency for its armed forces throughout Asia, and try to

get existing business enterprises to cooperate with the war effort."[21] In
the China theater, Japan had been weakest in implementing this final
point. Would occupation authorities make a real effort at partnership
with Chinese capitalists?

Pearl Harbor certainly brought a new environment for the Chinese
businessmen who had stayed in island Shanghai. Japan seized the International Settlement, haven for so many of China's capitalists, as well
as Hong Kong. The Japanese military could finally confiscate many of
the largest Chinese factories, which had heretofore used the protection
of the foreign concessions. Many of these were technically registered as
British or American firms and so now fell under the category of "enemy property." The former shield of foreign registration had now become an albatross. In 1937 when factories had been seized, most had
been entrusted to Japanese firms such as Mitsui, Mitsubishi, and Kanegafuchi. Yet now this option was less viable. The enormous strain of the
war meant Japanese firms lacked capital and personnel to expand their
operations in China. The Japanese now had both the incentive and the
means (complete control of Shanghai) to offer the Chinese capitalists a
new deal.[22]

Yet even after Pearl Harbor, the Japanese occupation changed only
slowly. Military commanders were distrustful of Chinese motives and
were loath to grant the puppet authorities real autonomy. When the Wang
government sought permission to declare war on the Allies and thus become a co-belligerent, this act was blocked for months by Tokyo, which
was fearful that such status could limit Japanese control in China. Japanese policy in China did not undergo a fundamental shift until late 1942,
when the war situation turned against Japan. Setbacks in the south-
western Pacific, writes Akira Iriye, forced the Japanese to alter their policy toward China. The defeats meant that "not enough supplies and foodstuffs from the south seas were available to the Japanese forces in China.
Moreover, increasing numbers of troops stationed in China had to be di-
verted to the Solomons."[23]

The exigencies of war did what no amount of propaganda about the
"New Order" could accomplish. Tokyo attempted to breathe life into
the moribund Wang Jingwei government. The regime had been unable
to attract meaningful support in part because Japanese authorities had
granted it so little authority. It could portray itself as nothing other than
a puppet regime. As Poshek Fu notes, "The Peace Movement made little headway in Shanghai between 1939 and 1941. It never outgrew the
political stigma of treason and terror."[24] Driven by defeats on the bat-

tlefield, Japan would make one last attempt to change its policy toward Nanjing and the Chinese businessmen of the lower Yangzi.

THE GREAT DEPARTURE

An Imperial Conference in Tokyo on December 21, 1942, delineated a major shift in Japan's China policy termed the "great departure." Japan would strengthen the Nanjing regime and permit it to declare war against the Allied Powers. The conference revisited the issue of competing claims among the Japanese client regimes in China. When the Wang Jingwei government had been created in 1940, it had sought and was promised status as the central government of China. In reality, pre-existing regimes in Beijing, Kalgan, and elsewhere retained most of their autonomy. Now a new pledge was made that Nanjing's status was to be paramount. Extraterritoriality and the unequal treaties were to be abolished, and Japan agreed to phase out the use of military scrip in China, relying instead on banknotes issued by Nanjing. The Special Service agencies were to be replaced by "Liaison Units," members of which were instructed to halt the use of harsh language toward Chinese government officials. In sum, the Wang government was to be given sufficient status and power to lay claim to be a viable political entity.[25]

Economic power was at the center of "the great departure." Both parties recognized that Nanjing needed greater authority over economic matters if it were to be taken seriously as a government. Moreover, the Japanese had never given the puppet regimes sufficient financing to operate independently. Even after they created the client regimes, the Japanese retained the strict system of market controls that aided procurement. The Japanese army, and to a lesser extent the navy, regulated movement of such items as rice and wheat from rural areas to the cities. Often controlled by regional military units, the income and supplies supported the Japanese military—a legacy of the policy of "using the war to sustain the war." In Shanghai and central China, for instance, Japan had formalized this control in March 1939 by establishing a Central China Commodity Control Association. This regulated the shipment and sales price of twelve types of products, such as rice, cotton, and coal, being shipped from rural central China to Shanghai or to north China and Manchuria. Nine categories of processed goods from Shanghai, including edible oils, cotton goods, soap, matches, and so on, were subject to similar controls when transported out of the Shanghai area. This control of commerce and marketing, combined with the dominant role of the development

companies, left little room for an autonomous Chinese regime to exercise authority over the economy. To gain such power, Wang Jingwei went
to Tokyo in late 1942, accompanied by Minister of Finance Zhou Fohai, Minister of Industry Mei Siping, and Vice Minister of Industry Yuan
Yuquan, to hammer out new arrangements. There they met with Japanese military and civilian leaders, including Minister of Industry and
Commerce Kishi Nobusuke.[26]

Disagreements plagued these talks. The Japanese military did not wish
to surrender its control over the procurement and commodity trading
system on which it had become even more dependent when the Pacific
war increased the need for foodstuffs and income from mainland China.
Long before Curtis Lemay's bombers threatened Japanese cities, Allied
submarines and planes played havoc with Japanese commercial shipping.
Although Japan had captured rich colonial empires from Burma to the
Dutch East Indies to the Philippines, it was unable to exploit these fully,
in large measure because it did not have secure transport. The resources
of China remained vital for the Japanese military on the mainland, and
it would brook no threat to this source.

Wang also sought the abolition of the Japanese holding companies,
notably the Central China Development Company and its subsidiaries.
He wanted these to be turned over to his government, which would obviously gain financially through these actions. Further, since the CCDC
controlled shipping, transportation, power production, and heavy industry, it clearly restricted the autonomy of any Chinese regime. During
the summer of 1940, Wang's government developed plans to reorganize
the major components of CCDC when they were returned. Finally, Wang
demanded the "enemy property" seized from American, Dutch, and
British subjects after December 8, 1941, which was being held by the
Japanese military. As a co-belligerent, the Wang regime felt that it should
control this property, which amounted to eighty-two enterprises and
fifteen banks. Much of this had already been given to Japanese firms.
The wharves in Shanghai belonging to American and British firms, for
instance, had been handed over to Mitsubishi, Osaka Mercantile, Nihon
Sokusen, and Yamashita Mining, among others.[27]

Both sides also agreed that they needed to promote participation of Chinese businessmen and their capital in economic activities. Wang sought the
power to grant rendition of factories and commercial property that had
been seized from Chinese businessmen, including those that had been entrusted to Japanese firms. By offering return of these factories, Wang felt
he could induce Chinese capitalists to join in supporting his regime.

The Tokyo summit left Wang disappointed. He fell well short of obtaining the concessions he had sought. The Japanese military was still
reluctant to abolish the national development companies; they were too
lucrative a source of income. Although vague promises were made to
handle the issue in the future, no resolution was achieved. Yuan Yuquan,
vice minister of industry in Nanjing, recalls several attempts, for instance,
to get the Japanese to abolish the monopoly of the Central China Marine Products Company over fish marketing in the lower Yangzi. But the
Imperial Navy had already grabbed this source of income and would not
divvy it up.[28]

Only very late in the war were even nominal changes made. In late
June of 1944, the Japanese military held an elaborate ceremony at the
Astor Hotel in Shanghai in which titles to six public utilities in Shanghai, including electricity, gas, waterworks, telephone, telegraph, and tram
service were transferred to the Nanjing Government. Zhang Sumin, chief
of the Shanghai office of enemy properties, accepted the titles in the presence of representatives from the Japanese consulate, the Japanese army
and navy, and the directors of the Central China Development Company.
The actual operations of the firms under CCDC direction, however, did
not change.[29]

COMMODITY CONTROL

Wang achieved greater concessions on the issue of commodity control.
Tokyo agreed to surrender power to the Chinese side so long as Japan's
needs were given top priority. Even here, Tokyo was cautious. Control
was to be given to committees that were to include Chinese businessmen.
Not only was Japan eager to gain the support (and capital and expertise)
of China's capitalists at this point, but also Japan apparently did not wish
the Wang regime to accumulate too much power. A second limitation was
that the commodity control committees would answer to an advisory
board (Wuzi tongzhi shenyi weiyuan hui; Materials Control Deliberation
Commission) with representatives from the Wang government, including
Minister of Industry Mei Siping and Yuan Yuquan, the Japanese consulate,
and the Japanese military. The board, which met monthly, would set the
general policy direction that the various commissions were to follow. A
permanent secretariat of the advisory group actually set most of the pricing decisions, which were then ratified by the monthly meeting.[30]

Because of the disagreements between Wang and the Japanese military, the commodity control talks dragged on until March 1943, when

a visit to China by Japanese Prime Minister Tojo Hideki himself helped
to resolve the issue. Tojo met with Japanese military leaders in Shanghai, who had been reluctant to transfer authority. His instructions—to
cooperate in the new venture—were published in the Japanese newspa-
pers in Shanghai, which provided the push needed. The National Commerce Control Commission (Quanguo shangye tongzhi weiyuan hui) was
created on March 15, 1943, in Shanghai. Subordinate commissions were
organized over the next few months to assume authority over cotton,
wheat, rice, edible oils, and general consumer goods. All were to have
Chinese business representation, all were to accept the guidelines of the
advisory board, and all were to recognize Japan's paramount interest in
maintaining its supply of resources. Japanese businessmen would participate in the subordinate commissions, not on the central commission.
Usually, a Chinese would chair a commission, and a Japanese would vice
chair.[31]

The new Commerce Control Commission and its constituent agencies
were to take over from the Japanese military the task of regulating transportation and sales of commodities in the lower Yangzi, specifically in
Zhejiang, Jiangsu, and Anhui. (Wang still had difficulty exercising power
outside of this area). The purpose the system remained unchanged—to
keep procurement costs of raw materials down and to create an indirect
tax on consumption in urban areas. Permissions now came from the new
boards rather than the Japanese military, as had been the case before
March 1943. Movement of primary products such as cotton, flour, rice,
and other grains into Shanghai and urban areas from the countryside
was to be tightly regulated so as to keep procurement prices low. The
twelve main groups of products continued to be included. Conversely,
the movement of manufactured products, such as cotton yarn, cloth, medicines, soap, matches, rubber, hardware, and even candles, from Shanghai to the surrounding area was controlled. In addition, special permission was required to move certain commodities out of the lower Yangzi
area, even to other parts of China. These included metals, rubber, wood,
iron, steel, cement, grains, wheat, rice, corn, vegetable oils, hemp, cotton, wool, leather, tobacco, foodstuffs, sugar, cloth, matches, soap, papers, vehicles, petroleum, and machinery.[32]

The new body was conceived as a broad-based umbrella organization,
taking over the functions of existing bodies. The commission was given
jurisdiction over all kinds of guilds and merchant associations (Chinese
and Japanese) that continued to play a role in the occupied zones. Often
Japanese military authorities had used the existing guild structures to en-

force the procurement policies. Now the commission would be expected to do the same. This in part is why the Japanese thought strong participation by Chinese businessmen was essential for the system to function.[33]

Wang appointed Tang Shoumin, formerly the general manager of the Bank of Communications, chair of the Commerce Control Commission. Wang's first choice, Zhou Zuomin, manager of the Jincheng Bank, had declined, although he eventually agreed to serve on the Board of Supervisors. Nanjing next turned to Wen Lanting, a longtime textile merchant and business leader. Despite several visits from Minister of Finance Zhou Fohai, Wen would agree to serve only on the supervisory board. This highlighted a problem faced by the Nanjing government. Tokyo had indicated a strong preference for having Chinese businessmen and bankers participate in the commissions; yet few were eager to identify too strongly with Nanjing, and none wanted a task that would place them so prominently serving Japanese needs. Nanjing finally persuaded Yuan Ludeng, then chair of the Shanghai Chamber of Commerce, to serve as head of the rice control commission. Lin Kanghou, a prominent banker, agreed to serve as secretary general of the commission. After much pressure, Wen Lanting would head the cotton control group. Yet many capitalists were evasive when approached. Textile magnates Rong Desheng and Guo Shun initially declined to participate.[34]

Nanjing could use various pressures to induce cooperation, including the threat from 76 Jessfield Road. After Japanese surrender, when Guomindang authorities arrested Tang, Lin, and Yuan, the arrestees argued (unsuccessfully) in their defense that they had been coerced into collaboration. Tang Shoumin, Zhou Zuomin, and Lin Kanghou had been in Hong Kong in December 1941. When the Japanese took the city, all were placed under house arrest by the Japanese. The Japanese consul suggested that they could return to Shanghai if they consented to work with the Japanese. Lin recounted that he had been held 104 days in Kowloon before suddenly being flown to Shanghai on the same plane with Zhou and Tang. Lin was then held in the Jin Jiang Hotel in Shanghai until he agreed to cooperate. Yuan Ludeng, who had stayed in Shanghai, emphasized that he was confined to his home by agents from Number 76 until he agreed. Obviously all of these individuals would stress the involuntary nature of their collaboration when facing jail sentences in postwar trials. In any case, intimidation was undoubtedly a factor in getting commitments of support from key leaders.[35]

The Chinese capitalists living in the occupied zone realized they had limited options. Nonetheless, Tokyo and Nanjing sought more volun-

tary cooperation and support from capitalists than could be obtained
from intimidation. Both realized that genuine cooperation by Chinese
businessmen was needed if the system were to work properly. They offered positive enticement to those who came forth.

RETURN OF PROPERTY TO CHINESE CAPITALISTS

The major carrot at Japan's disposal was the potential return of enterprises that had been confiscated earlier in the war. There had been discussion of returning these to their original Chinese owners for some time.
In his first talks with the Japanese in 1939, Wang had raised the issue of
nearly 200 industrial properties under Japanese control. The June 1940
treaty between Nanjing and Tokyo, formally signed on November 30,
1940, had stated that firms should be returned except for a few cases of
military necessity. Wang even established a committee under Yuan
Yuquan to negotiate with the Japanese and supervise the rendition. Yet
little had been achieved in this process by December 1941; only a dozen
or so small plants had been returned. Japanese military authorities resisted when large plants were involved and insisted on joint Sino-Japanese management. The problem, stated Yuan, "was a real headache."[36]

After Pearl Harbor, the Japanese had actually increased their holdings of Chinese properties. The large number of factories in the foreign
concessions, many of which had been registered as British or American
concerns, were confiscated as "enemy property." With the "great departure" these properties were now available as bargaining chips to elicit
active support for the Wang government and for the commodity control
program. Industrial magnate Rong Desheng, for instance, had been most
reluctant to cooperate. Yet he would seem to have had much to gain from
collaborating with the Japanese, for his family's cotton and flour mills
in Shanghai were under Japanese control. Five of his seven textile mills
in Shanghai had been seized in 1937 and given to Japanese firms. Two
others located in the International Settlement remained in Rong hands
until after Pearl Harbor. The Rongs had registered these latter properties as British and American firms during the solitary island period, so
these were seized as enemy property.[37]

In 1942 and 1943, however, the Japanese were ready to return these
plants to the Chinese owners. Not only could this carrot be used to en-
tice the Chinese entrepreneurs to come forth publicly to support Wang
Jingwei, but, as noted earlier, strains on Japanese manpower and capi-

tal made it difficult for the Japanese to absorb the new group of plants acquired in December 1941. Japanese companies that had been eager to take over plants in 1937 and 1938 now found themselves stretched thin, short of capital and personnel. Returning these plants to the Chinese owners could more easily get them back into production and keep the economy of the occupied areas functioning. Once they received their plants, Chinese industrialists would be forced to cooperate with the Commodity Control Commission if they were to have access to raw materials. The days of island Shanghai were now over.

Under these circumstances, the Japanese began to return properties to the Chinese owners. Seven mills that were taken in December 1941, including Shenxin #2 and #9 and Yong'an #3, were returned to their Chinese owners on May 22, 1942. And this was only the beginning. Over the course of 1942 and 1943, nearly 140 plants were returned, including many that had been held since 1937, such as Yong'an #1, #2 and #4, Shenxin, #1, #3, #5, #6, #7, and #8. Among flour mills, the Rongs' Fuxin #7 and the Fufeng, both of which had been seized as British property in 1941, were returned. The Japanese often made a great show of returning the plants to their Chinese owners. On July 25, 1943, for instance, a big ceremony was held in Shanghai to celebrate the rendition of twenty-four plants. Yong'an textile industrialist Guo Shun thanked the Japanese on behalf of the Chinese side. A similar wholesale return was undertaken in north China, which included electric power plants, cotton mills, flour mills, and a cement factory. This latter action was done to boost the Wang Kemin puppet regime (now technically the North China Political Affairs Commission).[38]

These "gifts" from the Japanese came with strings attached. In exchange, the industrialists had to agree to maintain close relations with the Japanese and to work with the Wang Jingwei government. And the process of return was also often fraught with obstacles. If a Japanese firm had invested in repairs, it often insisted that the Chinese owner accept a "joint venture" arrangement. The Zhongyi Mill in Wuhu, Anhui, for instance, was seized by the Japanese in June 1938. A small facility with 18,400 spindles, it suffered heavy damage; part of the plant was used as a military hospital. The Yūhō textile company took over and operated the plant, making a substantial investment in the process. When the Zhongyi owners petitioned for return of the property, Yūhō agreed only if Zhongyi would accept a cooperative, joint operation. Similarly, Yong'an #2 and #4 agreed to joint management with Yūhō, and the Zhenxin mill retained a partnership with Shanghai bōseki. In many cases of this type, the original Chinese owners simply accepted stock in the new firm as being "rendition."[39]

At other times, the Japanese military might block a return on the ground of "military necessity." The Japanese navy, for instance, delayed the return of Shenxin #7. The site of this mill was occupied by the navy, which hoped to convert the facility into a ship manufacturing plant. On April 16, 1943, the Rongs appealed to the Japanese consulate for assistance in getting the property released. The Imperial Navy, finally realizing that its plans could not be brought to fruition, returned control to the Rongs in July 1943.[40]

Most plants were eventually returned either completely or in partnership with a Japanese concern. The Chinese capitalists began the required cooperation with the Nanjing regime, joining the Commerce Control Commission and its subordinate agencies. Return of the plants would be pointless unless one had access to raw materials. Nanjing official Yuan Yuquan personally visited key businessmen to inform them that if they did not participate in the commodity commissions they would be cut off. When the Cotton Control Commission (Mianye tongzhi weiyuan hui) began work, for instance, it included participation by several Chinese industrialists, even those who had previously resisted Japanese overtures. Guo Shun himself represented the Yong'an mills, and Chen Baochu the Dasheng mills of Nantong. Still there were holdouts. Rong Desheng, the senior surviving figure among the Rongs, declined to serve; nor would he let his son Rong Er'ren or nephew Rong Hongyuan participate. Instead he dispatched managers not bearing the Rong surname. The Shenxin mills were represented by Tong Luqing, Wu Shihuai (from Shenxin #9), and Qin Defang (Shenxin #2).[41]

OPERATION OF THE COMMERCE CONTROL SYSTEM

By late 1943, most of the capitalists who had remained in the Shanghai area had made some accommodation with the Japanese and the Nanjing regime. In exchange for return of their property, most now participated in the economic control system that supported the Japanese military in China. Yet ironically, the capitalists received little real benefit from the new arrangement. With the deteriorating war situation for Japan, the pressure on China for supplies remained intense. Availability of raw materials (particularly petroleum) dried up; shipping became impossible, and allied bombing would threaten the lower Yangzi. The currency systems of both occupied and free China virtually collapsed, and the commodity control system became so stifling that economic activity either ceased or slipped into the underground economy. The Shanghai capitalists collaborated but gained little economic benefit in the final months of the war.

Two major issues plagued the system: continued Japanese needs and currency hyperinflation. Although Japanese fortunes were literally sinking throughout the Pacific, on the China mainland Japan continued to be dominant. Indeed, after months of only low-level activity on the China front, Japan would launch its largest military campaign of the entire war in 1944—Operation Ichigō. Designed to eliminate Allied air bases in China and to allow Japan to complete a rail link from Beijing to Wuhan to Guangzhou, Operation Ichigō contained two phases, in Henan and Hunan. The former saw 140,000 Japanese troops cross the Yellow River in mid-April 1944. Chinese Nationalist units collapsed; Luoyang fell to the Japanese on May 26. The Hunan phase saw the largest Japanese concentration of forces of the war, 360,000 soldiers, in a ferocious battle that finally led to the capture of Changsha on June 18, 1944. By November, Japanese units in Hunan, Guangxi, and Vietnam linked up; they came to within 100 kilometers of Guiyang by the end of the month. Operation Ichigō was a devastating defeat for Chiang Kaishek; for a time in early November it appeared that Japan might finally knock Chongqing out of the war. Meanwhile, in Wuhan in August 1944, the Central China Railway Company announced with (misplaced) confidence that the Beijing-Wuhan and Wuhan-Guangzhou Railways would shortly reopen and would eventually link Manchukuo with Hanoi, Saigon, and Bangkok.[42]

Operation Ichigō could not undo Japanese loses in the Pacific, however. Even as Japanese units threatened Guiyang, Allied forces were bombing the home islands from newly captured airfields in the Marianas. Yet Ichigō had a great impact on China. This large operation, involving 500,000 Japanese forces, could not easily be supplied from Japan or southeast Asia. The needs of the campaign had to be met by occupied China, greatly straining the commodity supply system.

The second great problem facing the commodity control system was hyperinflation (discussed below). Under the best of circumstances, price and market controls discourage production. Faced with artificially low prices for their goods, China's farmers either curtailed production or hoarded commodities. Similarly, producers were not eager to sell at low prices; hoarding and speculation were constant features of wartime China. The accelerating hyperinflation of the late war period, however,

made voluntary compliance with commodity control virtually nonexistent. By the end of 1943 the price of consumer goods in Shanghai was
forty-five times the level at the start of 1940. Prices set by the commodity control commissions were usually only a fraction of the black market price of commodities—and the percentage dropped daily. Under these
conditions, everyone attempted to hoard and use the black market.[43]

The problems are perhaps best illustrated by the operations of the Rice
Control Commission (Miliang tongzhi weiyuan hui). Established on October 1, 1943, it was headed by Shanghai Chamber of Commerce leader
Yuan Ludeng and included both Chinese and Japanese rice merchants.
The commission was to take over the rice procurement, pricing, and rationing system that had been operated by the Japanese military. It had
considerable authority; its permission was required for transport and sale
of rice. Nonetheless, the commission was given the impossible task of
meeting the requisition needs of the Japanese military while supplying
urban Shanghai. In theory this should have been feasible. According to
Wang Ke-wen, the Japanese forces consumed only 5 percent of the total rice production of the lower Yangzi. Yet, the control system so disrupted the market as to create major shortages. "In the first four years
of the war," notes Wang, "the average level of rice supply to the Lower
Yangtze markets was about half the prewar level." And with hyperinflation, most farmers tried to avoid official sales and deal with the black
market. In 1943 and 1944, according to Wang, the commission failed
to purchase even half of the target quantity. Of 254,000 tons of rice, the
commission did purchase in 1944, 220,000 were allocated for Japanese
forces.[44]

The commission could not, therefore, supply sufficient rice for the rationing system. According to Poshek Fu, between 1942 and 1945, the
total supply of rationed rice was less than was needed for one year's consumption. Seventy percent of rice in Shanghai was purchased on the black
market, despite severe penalties for such dealings.[45] Not only did peas-
ants attempt to smuggle rice into the city to sell outside of the control
system, but Japanese suspected that merchants on the commission itself
were hiding purchases and engaging in speculation and black market activity. With each Japanese setback in the war, confidence in the currency
of the Nanjing government weakened and black market prices escalated.[46]

Similar problems beset the Wheat Flour Control Commission (Fenmai tongzhi weiyuan hui), which controlled sales and shipment of wheat,
flour, and bran. From the start the Japanese could not get Wang Yuqing,
general manager of the Fuxin mills, to head the group. (He and Shi Fuhou

did agree to represent Fuxin on the commission.) Sun Zhongli, general manager of the Fufeng Mill finally agreed to be chair. Half of the technical personnel were Japanese and half Chinese, with most of the latter coming from the Fufeng or Fuxin mills. Mitsui and Mitsubishi, who had directed purchases for the Japanese military before the new commission was formed, were among the Japanese firms with representatives on the group. Altogether the commission had more than 400 members and employees. Designated representatives were established in rural areas to handle purchases of wheat.[47]

Despite enormous pressure from the Japanese, the commission could simply not acquire sufficient supplies. In 1943, it purchased only 44 percent of its target of wheat. And as with the rice group, the wheat commission was ordered to supply a large requisition for Japanese military needs or for export to north China and Japan. Chinese mills received only 10 percent of the total allocation and, as a consequence, operated at far less than capacity. Fuxin #2, #7, and #8, Huafeng, and Fengfu mills had a capacity to produce 24 million bags of flour annually, but struggled to produce only 2 million in 1943. Overall Chinese mills in Shanghai operated at only 9.71 percent of capacity during the final 26 months of the war. Even Japanese mills in Shanghai suffered, operating at less than 19 percent of capacity for the same period.[48]

The Cotton Control Commission (Mianhua tongzhi weiyuan hui) was headed by Wen Lanting and included as Chinese representatives Jiang Shangda of Minfeng mills, Tong Luqing of Shenxin, Chen Baochu of Dasheng, and Guo Shun of Yong'an. Japanese firms participating included Yūhō bōseki, Dai Nippon, Nikka, Shanhai bōseki, and Naigai wata. The Cotton Control Commission was to regulate both the supply of raw material and the sale of yarn and cloth. It faced two major challenges, hoarding of processed cotton goods and maintaining adequate supplies of raw cotton. In an era of hyperinflation, cotton yarn and cloth were hoarded in lieu of increasingly worthless cash. One estimate was that in 1943 sixty percent of the floating capital in Shanghai was held in cotton speculation. The commission was charged with eliminating this practice and acquiring sufficient textiles to meet Japanese needs.[49]

To solve this problem, the commission decreed in July 1943 a forcible purchase of nearly all yarn and cloth in Shanghai at a price level of spring 1943. Failure to sell to the authority would result in stiff penalties. This buy-up from August to September 1943 was done at about one-fourth of the black market price. The action further stifled the production of cotton goods since few producers wanted to sell at that level. Japanese manufacturers suffered as well, being paid in Japanese bonds for their product.[50]

Maintaining a supply of raw cotton at low, regulated prices was also a challenge. The commission set both prices and quotas for sale of cotton but strictly regulated all shipments. The Japanese prohibited all trade with the unoccupied areas. The commission faced chronic shortages of cotton, since farmers were unwilling to sell at the regulated price. The Japanese military had set the procurement price per picul of raw cotton at only 714 yuan in 1942, a level the cotton commission tried to maintain. By the spring of 1943, however, this was less than half of the black market price of cotton, so most farmers tried to avoid the system. The dearth of raw cotton hit Chinese mills in Shanghai particularly hard because the imported cotton on which Shanghai had relied before December 1941 was cut off by the Pacific war. Further, when the commission did purchase raw cotton, the distribution plan was for 60 percent to be used to meet the needs of the Japanese military or for export to Japan, and 40 percent to supply mills in China. Japanese-controlled mills grabbed the lion's share (three-fourths) of the latter, creating a chronic shortage of legal cotton for Chinese mills.[51]

Chinese industrialists responded in a number of ways. Most simply curtailed or closed production; they had no choice. In 1943 Chinese textile mills in Shanghai produced only 4.3 percent of the cotton yarn output of 1936 and only 5.8 percent of the cotton cloth. Some industrialists sneaked equipment into cotton-producing areas, where they set up small-scale handicraft-style production. The latter had been exempted from control by the commission, so this quickly developed as a loophole in the regulations. Many of these facilities would have only 1,000 to 2,000 spindles. They purchased cotton at black market rates and sometimes bribed puppet police or military officials to overlook their activities. The large difference between the regulated price and the black market price was a strong incentive for suppliers to evade the regulators. Flour milling underwent a similar process, with a number of very small scale and dispersed mills being developed in the rural areas where wheat was grown. Many actually used old stone grinders, with daily production of twenty to forty bags. This small scale was successful because it often escaped Japanese attention.[52]

As more cotton and textile production slipped into the "black market" economy, Japanese authorities became upset that procurement needs were not being met. Japanese officials from the Greater East Asia Ministry put together a conference in early 1944 with officials from central and north China in an attempt to improve the situation. At one point, the commission even began to offer special gifts to farmers, such as matches, candles, and sugar, if they would sell the cotton at the fixed prices.[53]

The Commerce Control Commission failed to meet both Chinese and Japanese expectations. The Chinese businessmen who joined in had hoped to receive sufficient raw materials to maintain production. Instead, few were able to operate their factories at anything more than a fraction of capacity. Japanese had hoped to maintain a steady source of supply for the military procurement system. Here too was disappointment. As the war situation became more desperate, Japan intensified pressure on the China market, which did not produce. For the Chinese capitalists, many of whom finally collaborated with the Japanese in 1943–1944 after holding out earlier, the results were also disappointing. Although most got their properties back, the collapse of the economy and the absence of raw materials, energy, and transportation meant idle facilities. These capitalists earned the stigma of collaborator but with little gain.

THE COLLAPSE OF THE ECONOMY

Tokyo's "great departure" had signaled a new deal for the Wang Jingwei government, and indeed, many changes were made on paper. Nanjing appeared to take over the commodity control system of the Japanese military. Industrial properties of Chinese capitalists were returned to a great extent, in exchange for which they began to work publicly with the Nanjing regime. Yet the crumbling of the Japanese empire across the Pacific led to desperation. The pressure on the procurement system in China increased, and little was left for the Chinese businessmen. Ultimately the currency became worthless, the energy and transportation system became nonexistent, and the economy went almost entirely underground.

The most obvious sign of failure was the inability of the agencies of the Commerce Control Commission to procure sufficient resources. Whether rice, wheat, or cotton, none met its quota. The Japanese began to routinely ignore the Wang authorities, desperate for raw materials and unwilling to share strained resources with Chinese. When the subordinate commissions met, real power rested with the Japanese merchants, who had the backing of their authorities when disputes with the Chinese developed. In May 1944 Tang Shoumin resigned as head of the CCC under pressure from Tokyo and Nanjing. Wen Lanting took over the job, but the black market had clearly triumphed over the control system.[54]

The dominance of the black market became entirely clear when the Rice Control Commission quit even trying to regulate the sales market in Shanghai. Shortly after Wen took over the commission, the price restrictions were lifted. The commission had not been able to supply sufficient rice to provide rations at fixed prices. Rice riots followed in the spring of 1945 as prices soared. The amount of grain available in the rationing system in Shanghai, which had averaged 0.56 dou of husked rice per month per capita during the last six months of 1942, dropped to only 0.304 in 1944 and 0.019 in the first eight months of 1945. Ration grain was increasingly adulterated with dirt to expand the volume. Not only were groups dropped from the rationing system entirely (children under eight and adults over sixty), but the length of time between distribution was increased. Eventually, full rations were available only to the privileged among the Chinese population—government officials, police, and educational and health personnel.[55]

A key to this economic collapse was the lack of energy to run the factories. By 1943, industrial use of electric power was only 40 percent of the prewar level in Shanghai; by the end of 1944, it was only 20 percent. Even water supply was only at 30 percent of that level. Most public transport in Shanghai came to a halt, so even had plants been in operation, workers would have had difficulty reaching them. Railways stopped as well. In June 1944 the Central China Railway Company announced conversion of passenger trains to freight, deemed more critical to the war effort. Nanjing even started a project in 1944 to reopen the Grand Canal to link Hangzhou to Beijing. A total of 640,000 laborers were to repair the long damaged waterway, use of which was to be more feasible than rail transport.[56]

Japanese authorities became so desperate in the last months of the war that they began confiscating equipment from factories for use as scrap iron. Although damaged equipment had been taken as such in the early phase of the war, now Japanese authorities began seizing usable but idle equipment. The Japanese army and navy, in conjunction with the Japanese consul general, announced that factories, banks, hotels, and restaurants would be investigated for articles that would be reclaimed for iron, copper, and other metal content. Chao Kang estimates that in the final years of the war, more than one million spindles and 4,500 looms in textile mills in China were taken as scrap iron for military production in Japan. In eastern Hubei, when the owners of the Lihua coal mine

(Lihua meikuang) returned after the war, they discovered that all of the steel cables and even metal supports had been stripped from the mine in the closing months of the war, making it virtually impossible to resume production.[57]

HYPERINFLATION

One of the gravest problems affecting all sections of China during the later war years was hyperinflation. Both the fabi of Free China and the currencies of occupied China had become virtually worthless by 1945. In the early years of the war, Japan had attempted to incorporate north China into the yen bloc by establishing the China Reserve Bank as the official bank of its north China regime under Wang Kemin. Japan had fought to replace use of fabi in the north with the new currency and by 1941 had largely succeeded. In central and south China Japan had been slow to challenge the fabi. The Japanese military had widely used military yen to pay its bills, but the lack of convertibility (even to regular yen) and the unsecured nature of the currency limited its appeal in areas not directly controlled by the Japanese military. Yet even fabi became less desirable. The rapid growth in the supply of fabi, as Chongqing's revenues fell far behind its expenses, and the loss of foreign exchange at Shanghai undermined its value.

When the Wang Jingwei government was formed, it was eager to establish its own central bank. As with other aspects of economic policy, the Nanjing authorities felt that creation of a viable currency was essential to its credibility as a legitimate government. Yet the previous experiment at Nanjing, the Huaxing Bank, had failed in this attempt. After the long struggle to establish the China Reserve Bank in Beijing, the Japanese were slow to back Wang Jingwei's efforts. The Japanese military, moreover, did not wish to give up its reliance on the military yen to pay its bills in the south. Ironically, the drop in value of the fabi in late 1940 slowed down the efforts to open the new bank, since Nanjing had accumulated reserves in fabi to secure the new currency.[58]

Finally on January 6, 1941, the Central Reserve Bank (Zhongyang chubei yinhang) was established in Nanjing with Zhou Fohai as director. The Nanjing authorities had also taken possession of the abandoned building of Chiang Kaishek's Central Bank of China on the Bund on November 9, 1940, and established a Shanghai branch there. Eventually forty branches with a total of 1,600 employees would be created. As was the case with most institutions established in the occupied zone, the bank had Japanese advisers. More than forty "assisted" the bank's operation, headed by Kimura Masutarō. Throughout the first eleven months of the bank's existence, until Pearl Harbor, Nanjing would engage in a "currency war" with the fabi, which at times was a violent, bloody conflict.[59]

Nanjing's move in establishing a new currency was a sharp challenge to Chongqing, whose fabi had dropped in value in late 1940. The Chiang government was determined to retain control of the banking center of the island Shanghai and informally told Chinese bankers there that acceptance of the new currency would be considered treason. The Japanese and Wang authorities thus applied pressure to get bankers to support the new bank. Even before the bank opened its doors, the terror began. When banker Zhu Boquan rejected a request from Zhou Fohai to serve on its board, he found himself grabbed and held at Number 76 Jessfield Road on November 29, 1940. Zhu was released after ten days and later served as an official of the Central Reserve Bank.[60]

The currency war quickly became a war of terror in Shanghai, as Frederic Wakeman has detailed. Chongqing fired the opening shot on February 20, 1941, when its agents attacked the Central Reserve Bank building on the Bund with guns and homemade bombs. On two other occasions in March, Chongqing agents made assassination attempts (one successful) against officials of Wang's bank. Nanjing responded with even greater terror. On March 21, 1941, its agents attacked three pro-Chongqing banks in Shanghai with hand grenades. Six gunmen entered the Jiangsu Farmers Bank building, killing five and wounding six. The following day, the pro-Wang police raided the (Chongqing-controlled) Bank of China compound in the western section of Shanghai and arrested 128 employees, who were held as hostages. Eventually three senior accountants of the bank would be executed at 76 Jessfield Road. Perhaps the most spectacular incident was the dynamiting of the Central Bank of China branch in the French Concession. Seven were killed and twenty-one wounded.[61]

These attacks struck fear and panic into the Shanghai banking community. Most Shanghai bankers had bowed to Chongqing's wishes and refused to accept the new Central Reserve currency, so 76 Jessfield Road developed a hit list. The violence therefore set off a wave of panic. Some fled. Li Ming, one of the most prominent Shanghai bankers, was tipped off that he was near the top of the list so left for the United States in March 1941. Most finally acceded to Nanjing's demands.[62]

At one level therefore Nanjing won—Shanghai banks began to accept the currency of the Wang regime. Yet as long as island Shanghai existed in any form, the Nanjing currency remained unpopular. At the end of 1941, according to Arthur Young, nearly sixty times as much fabi circulated in China, as did notes of the new Nanjing bank. Nonetheless, the war of terror deeply scared the banking world of Shanghai, further weakening the financial and currency system of China. The hollowness of Nanjing's triumph became clear after Pearl Harbor. The end of the solitary island meant that Nanjing no longer had to contend with quasi-independent banking in its midst. The Wang government decided therefore to move from a policy of using fabi to one of eliminating fabi. In late March 1942, the Wang government decreed that after June 1, 1942, fabi would no longer be considered legal tender in Zhejiang, Jiangsu, and Anhui, including the cities of Nanjing and Shanghai. All fabi must be exchange for Central Reserve notes by that point.[63]

The Central Reserve Notes had originally been set at a par with the fabi notes. When the government issued its order mandating exchange, however, it set a two-to-one ratio in favor of the Central Reserve notes. Suddenly all of the fabi being held in the occupied area, including Shanghai, lost half its value. Most merchants responded by simply keeping the posted prices the same, in effect doubling the price when measured in the old fabi. Although inflation had been a persistent problem throughout the war, this act quickened the arrival of the hyperinflation of the late war period. Even Zhou Fohai later expressed deep regrets at this action, which he acknowledged eventually caused enormous losses to the population of the lower Yangzi, most of whom still held fabi.[64]

The fight to establish the new currency of the Wang Jingwei regime was aimed not only at Chongqing's fabi, however. Nanjing had to battle the China Reserve Bank in Beijing and the military yen. The former was attached to the Wang Kemin government and backed by the Japanese army in the north. The Wang Jingwei regime fought a long, hard, and losing battle to assert its authority over north China. The Japanese military in the north considered the Beijing authorities "their" puppets and were unwilling to have them curtailed. In the currency realm, moreover, the Beijing currency was already well established and was tied to the yen. Nanjing could do little more than declare a truce. In effect the two regions became two different currency zones—north China in the yen bloc and central China using the yuan. Travelers between the two zones could exchange money at a rate set in 1943 as 100 yuan (Nanjing) to 18 yen (Beijing). Nanjing had difficult maintaining this rate and eventually in March 1944 prohibited all exchange between the two currencies except at eleven official banks, including the Yokohama Bank, Bank

of Chosen, Bank of China, and Bank of Communications. Travelers to
north China could legally carry only 5,000 yuan in Nanjing notes, although this restriction was eventually lifted under Japanese pressure.[65]

Within its own realm, Nanjing tried to challenge the use of military
yen. Largely unsecured, this currency could not be remitted to Japan
without permission but was a great convenience to the Japanese military, which forced people to accept the currency. Nanjing felt it had to
limit the use of this scrip in order to establish its authority. Nonetheless,
the Japanese were originally unwilling to budge, so the Central Reserve
Bank had to accept military yen as a major rival currency. Even minor
concessions were hard for Nanjing to negotiate. Earlier, Japanese authorities had decreed that all railway, bus, and steamship tickets and all
utility bills owed to firms in the Central China Development Company
group had to be paid in military yen, not fabi. This was done to encourage
circulation of the unpopular currency. Yet after the Wang government
opened its new bank, the Japanese did not want to bend this rule. Only
on June 20, 1942, did Japanese authorities permit people to buy tickets
or pay utility bills in either military scrip or notes of the Central Reserve
Bank. When the Wang government was finally allowed to declare war
on America and Britain in January 1943 and thus became a co-belligerent,
it asked Tokyo to eliminate the military yen in recognition of Nanjing's
new status. In April 1943 the Japanese agreed to withdraw gradually
the military yen and replace it with Nanjing's notes, at a ratio of five
yuan per one military yen. But the process was very slow. In reality the
amount of military yen circulating in China increased from 248 million yen in 1940 to 407 million in 1943 to 671 million at the end of
1944, although in terms of real value this represented a shrinkage of
its use.[66]

In addition to these major currencies there were a host of smaller issues. Despite the great departure proclaimed by Tokyo, most Japanese
military commanders in China were still distrustful of creating a strong
Wang Jingwei regime and actually followed a policy of localization. Not
only was there a central currency in north China, but also notes of the
Mengjiang Bank at Kalgan were used in Inner Mongolia. In Guangdong,
a local puppet-sponsored bank issued notes in the Canton area, and Bank
of Taiwan notes circulated throughout south China as well. Nanjing's
currency never penetrated very far from the lower Yangzi.[67]

Ultimately everyone lost the currency war. In effect, four authorities
were issuing vast quantities of paper money to cover debts for which there
was insufficient revenue—the Chongqing regime and its fabi; the Nan-

TABLE I. WHOLESALE PRICES
IN SHANGHAI, 1937–1945*

1937	January to June	100
1939	June	164
	December	318
1940	June	451
	December	523
1941	June	803
	December	1,560
1942	June	2,940
	December	4,470
1943	June	10,400
	December	21,400
1944	June	56,000
	December	249,000
1945	June	2,130,000
	August	8,520,000

SOURCE: Adapted from Arthur N. Young, *China's Wartime Finance and Inflation, 1937–1945* (Cambridge, Mass.: Harvard University Press, 1965), p. 152.
*Base = 100

jing government and its Central Reserve Bank notes; the Beijing regime and its China Reserve Bank; and the Japanese military and its special military yen. All four of these competed as currencies (not to mention smaller issues). The flooding of the market with so much unsecured paper caused a sharp drop in the value of all; hyperinflation reached throughout China, free and occupied. Even the communist base areas suffered the effects of this plague. The price level in Shanghai (based on 1937, January to June, equal to 100) had reached approximately 451 by the June of 1940 and almost 523 by the end of the year, inflationary but not extraordinary given the circumstances of war. But then things worsened rapidly. By December 1941 it reached 1,560 and by June 1942 a staggering 2,940. At that point the Wang government decreed its two-for-one exchange of the old fabi for the Central Reserve notes and by December it reached 4,470. Under these conditions, normal commerce was virtually impossible. Hoarding and speculation became ways of life; barter replaced monetary transactions. And conditions only worsened. In 1944 Shanghai prices rose twelvefold and by June of 1945 the price index reached a ludicrous 2,130,000. Paper currency was essentially worthless (see table 1).[68] The price index in Free China was not quite as extreme but still reflected an extraordinary increase (see table 2).

The final months of the war thus brought nearly a complete halt to

TABLE 2. WHOLESALE PRICES
IN FREE CHINA, 1937–1945*

1937	January to June	100
1939	June	226
	December	323
1940	June	487
	December	724
1941	June	1,050
	December	1,980
1942	June	3,590
	December	6,620
1943	June	13,200
	December	22,800
1944	June	46,600
	December	75,500
1945	June	216,700
	August	264,700

SOURCE: Adapted from Arthur N. Young, *China's Wartime Finance and Inflation, 1937-1945* (Cambridge, Mass.: Harvard University Press, 1965), p. 152.
*Base = 100

"normal" economic activity. Even if manufacturers had had raw materials and energy supplies, few would have chosen regular production. Sales of textile products or refined flour at the price levels set by the control commissions would have meant significant losses. Most businessmen hoarded commodities and waited out conditions at the end of the war. Economic activity took place in the black market.

Indeed as factories and shops in Shanghai remained idle, much of the economic activity took place in the outskirts of the city. As Japanese control over the countryside weakened, unregulated black market trading increased. Indeed, without such activity the population of Shanghai and Nanjing would have starved.

THE FAILURE OF COLLABORATION

Most of the Chinese capitalists who stayed behind in island Shanghai in November 1937 thus found themselves drawn into a web of collaboration. In exchange for return of their property and the promise of access to raw material, they were expected to work with the Wang Jingwei government. Not all did; some left for the interior, such as Yu Xiaqing, or went overseas, such as the banker Li Ming. But the increased Japanese control after Pearl Harbor and the use of terror by Number 76 limited their options. The list of capitalists who worked with Wang's commerce control commissions was long.

Yet at war's end these capitalists had little to show for their compromises. Normal economic activity had come to a virtual halt. Factories sat idle and were sometimes stripped of their machinery. Although the Axis had been losing the war worldwide, the sudden collapse of Japanese power in 1945 left many Chinese in the occupied zone surprised. With Japan's success in the Ichigō campaign in China, many businessmen (and many in the puppet government) assumed that they would have more time to reestablish connections to the Chongqing authorities to salvage some reputation as patriots. But when the war ended suddenly in August 1945, most had to face the stigma of being labeled collaborators.

After the war the GMD set up an Enemy Property Commission, which operated in Jiangsu, Anhui, and Zhejiang to seize property held by the Japanese and their collaborators when the war ended. Many even found themselves being put on trial for treason. Banker Lin Kanghou, in defending himself for serving on the Commerce Control Commission, claimed he did so only to help the common people get through the war. The court found, however, that the association really served the Japanese military. Like so many other businessmen who stayed in Shanghai, Lin found himself tainted with the label "traitor."[69]

The irony was that few of the Chinese businessmen and industrialists had been eager to join the Greater East Asia Co-Prosperity Sphere. Most had relocated in unoccupied Shanghai if they had the ability to do so. When trapped there or in Hong Kong in December 1941, their options were limited. For most the lure of regaining their enterprises was irresistible, the alternative unappealing. With great reluctance in some cases, they began to work with the Japanese and the Wang Jingwei government. Unfortunately for them, many found their enterprises confiscated anew at war's end when returning Guomindang forces labeled them "enemy property."

PART THREE

Chinese Capitalists

Survival and Collaboration

CHAPTER 5

Individual Firms
and the War Experience

Chinese capitalists did not experience the war as a class; they did so as individuals. Each businessperson made his (rarely her) own decisions based on circumstances, opportunities, and personal views. That so many chose to act in the same way—in moving to the foreign settlements in 1937, for instance—suggests that the background of the individuals and the circumstances they faced were similar. Yet the fortunes of war could often vary quite widely. Factories just a few blocks apart often suffered strikingly different degrees of damage. Some businessmen had better luck, better connections, and better timing in moving material out of the war zone. Luck played a major role in the fate of those who chose to move to the interior. Some got their equipment shipped successfully; others lost everything when the Japanese sank their shipments in the Yangzi.

Personal choice also played a role. A few capitalists, a minority perhaps, were determined to follow the nationalist forces to the interior and contribute to the war effort. The majority did not follow this path, but put survival of their enterprises first. For the most part they took the easier approach of moving to island Shanghai. Yet here as well, individual choice mattered. Some capitalists operated only in the island, and contributed to war relief and the resistance movement. At some risk, they obeyed instructions from Chongqing and refused to deal with the Nanjing regime or use its currency. When pressure to work with Japan became too great, they finally left Shanghai. Others were less nationalistic, often trying to reopen facilities in the occupied zone even if that meant dealing with the Japanese. The limits on their collaboration were more a result of the unattractive offers made by the Japanese rather than by nationalistic sentiment. What accounts for the different approaches by these individuals? In this chapter, we examine the individual experiences of businessmen and attempt to understand the war situation that each faced and why individual responses varied.

Unmasking the motivations of individual capitalists is often very difficult. Unlike intellectuals and politicians, few businessmen wrote or published widely. Many, in fact, shrouded their activities in secrecy, their public statements limited to a few platitudes. Much of the biographical data used in this study comes from personal histories written in the People's Republic under rather unfavorable circumstances, essentially confessions. These have to be used with caution, especially when assessing motives for actions taken under very different circumstances. The very nature of the source material makes it more difficult to understand "the why" of the actions of China's capitalists.

THE AMBIGUITIES OF THE WAR EXPERIENCE

Perhaps the key difficulty in understanding wartime experience lies in its ambiguities. Few entered the war with a clear conception of what they wished to do. Events were sudden and dramatic; no one knew what the next few days, let alone months, would hold. In other words, the Shanghai capitalists for the most part simply reacted to unexpected events. It is difficult to attach clear labels of "collaborative," "resistant," "patriotic," or "traitorous" to most of their behavior—the record is simply too ambiguous.

In 1989 the popular Chinese journal *Renwu* (Personalities) published a brief article on a minor Chinese industrialist in the Republican period. Entitled "Zhongguo huaxue boli gongye xianqu—Wang Xinsheng" (China's vanguard in the chemical glass industry—Wang Xinsheng), this article was part of a new body of literature appearing in the 1980s that gave a very positive interpretation of Chinese industrialists. As noted earlier, this historiographical trend was tied to the pro-reform agenda in China rather than simply to historical research. Yet a quick reading of the historical narrative the authors present about Wang Xinsheng reveals how difficult explaining wartime behavior can be.

Wang's enterprise was the Central Chemical Glass Factory (Zhongyang huaxue boli chang), which he established in the Yangshupu district of Shanghai in July 1934. The firm manufactured high-quality, specialty glass implements and was the first Chinese company to produce glass beakers of sufficient strength to withstand the high temperatures of chemical and medical work. Wang was born in Kobe, Japan, of a Japanese mother and Chinese father and had been educated in both countries. He attended college in Japan, where, the 1989 article assures us, he read several works by Marx and Engels. When the Manchurian Incident occurred, Wang was deeply moved by the plight of his native country (*zuguo*) and was determined to return home to help in China's development. Although he took a job as a technician in a Shanghai factory when he returned, he quickly sought his own opportunity. A major Japanese-owned glass factory had been destroyed in the January 28 Incident of 1932, creating a market niche, so several Chinese manufacturers began producing glass products, including thermoses and light bulbs. None of them could manufacture glass of sufficient quality for chemical work, however.[1]

Supported by his father, Wang opened his small factory with an initial capital of only 15,000 yuan. His training and Japanese connections were key to his success. He had taken advanced work in chemistry, and he hired several Japanese technicians to direct the manufacturing process. Because Cai Yuanpei, then head of Academia Sinica (Zhongyang yanjiu yuan), encouraged Wang, he named his factory the "Central" (Zhongyang) chemical glass plant. Despite his mixed background, Wang's first reaction when war erupted was to move the factory to Chinese-held territory, first to Changsha and later to Chongqing. Unfortunately, Wang lost virtually all of the material and equipment shipped. Sixty tons went down to Japanese bombing in transit from Shanghai, and a second shipment was lost in a shipwreck en route to Chongqing.

Having failed to establish production in the interior, Wang tried to reopen in Shanghai. Wang's factory, however, was located in the Japanese-held Yangshupu area. Japanese authorities had confiscated the plant and placed it under military management using the pretext that the name "Zhongyang" (Central) denoted Guomindang ownership. At this point Wang utilized his Japanese ties. He had his mother, whose Japanese name was Kinoshita, write the Japanese consulate in Shanghai, claiming that the factory was Japanese property and that it should be protected. The company then reopened with the name Kinoshita Factory.

Despite Wang's seeming new identity as a Japanese, the 1989 *Renwu* article stresses the patriotic nature of Wang's wartime operations. Undaunted by the risks involved, Wang's plant sold materials to unoccupied China. Flasks and beakers from the plant, for instance, were used at universities in Kunming, thus contributing to the survival of chemical research in Free China. Perhaps because of this, Japanese and puppet authorities suspected that the plant promoted anti-Japanese activity. In May 1943, when Wang had prepared seventy boxes of glass instruments for transshipment through Wenzhou to unoccupied areas, puppet authorities visited the plant, and Wang fell under increased scrutiny. Japanese consular officials routinely monitored shipments from the plant.

When the war ended, Wang's plant was temporarily confiscated by Guomindang agents as enemy property. Classified as a traitor by a Shanghai court, Wang departed for Hong Kong, where he began anew. The authors of the 1989 article, however, have no difficulty in reading Wang's narrative in a heroic way, because the article is part of a historiographical approach that stresses the patriotic nationalist narrative. Yet a close analysis of the events surrounding Wang's wartime record suggests that many other readings are equally plausible. The very identity of Wang as a "Chinese" capitalist is subject to question. He was of mixed ethnic background; he used his mother's name when it was expedient to do so. His return to China could easily have been seen from an economic viewpoint—market opportunities were better there than in Japan. His sales to Free China during the war could be read as simply business opportunities. And what of his business in Shanghai? The authors do not explore potential use of his products by Japanese or puppet institutions. In sum, a simple narrative could be read in many different ways. There is no easy way to characterize Wang's wartime experience.

Yet the historical narrative also suggests the serendipitous nature of war. Wang's actual war situation might have been quite different had things varied only slightly. Wang initially tried to relocate to the interior. Had he had better luck in transporting his materials, he might well have established his factory in Sichuan and avoided contact with occupation authorities altogether, despite his mixed heritage. His status as a patriotic industrialist would have been maintained, although his ability to produce high-quality glass in the interior might not have. Moreover, had Wang originally located his plant in the foreign concessions, it might have escaped occupation for four years. Had it been in Zhabei, it might have been totally destroyed. Had Wang not chosen the name "Zhongyang," he might have had less difficulty in regaining control.

In sum, unless one begins with a preset approach such as the "patriotic nationalist narrative," characterizing the wartime experiences of China's capitalists defies easy generalizations. With few exceptions, the categories of "resistance" and "collaboration" do not easily fit the actual war situations, as an examination of several key industrialists will reveal.

CAPITALISTS AND NATIONALISM

The Chinese capitalists of the Shanghai area had an ambiguous relationship with Chinese "nationalism." As an idea, most voiced their support. The capitalists, after all, felt the pressure of foreign competition, especially Japanese. The capitalists, as the wealthy elite of Shanghai, had felt exclusion from the parks, clubs, and institutions of semi-colonial Shanghai more than the population in general. Yet the relationship of most Chinese businessmen, especially the industrialists, to Japan was complex. A large proportion of Chinese manufacturers either had connections to Japan or Japanese training or made use of Japanese equipment and technicians. Japan had industrialized before China and in most areas of production enjoyed a substantial technical lead. At the same time, in order to develop a market niche, most Chinese businessmen had supported anti-Japanese and anti-foreign boycotts. Often undercut by foreign producers in technical quality, Chinese industrialists relied upon the "made in China" label to increase sales. This ambiguity continued even in wartime. Ning Sihong, the manager of the Leming Pen Company located in the International Settlement of Shanghai, proudly manufactured fountain pens with a "national product" label during the war. As such they were used in both unoccupied China and even by the New Fourth Army. Yet after the war, Ning admitted that some of the materials used in production during the war period were actually Japanese. To prevent workers from finding this out, Japanese materials were actually repackaged before being sent to the factory.[2]

Many Chinese businessmen had used the foreign enclaves for protection from Chinese governments of the 1920s and 1930s, which they did not fully trust. This tendency was strongest in banking, with all of the modern Chinese banks and most native banks in Shanghai establishing their headquarters in the foreign settlements. Manufacturers generally located plants in the Chinese city before 1937, but this was largely due to the cost of land, which was considerably more expensive in the foreign sectors. In terms of personal residences, most of the big mansions of the Chinese business leaders were located in the foreign zones, particularly the prestigious French Concession. The record of most Chinese businessmen as "patriotic nationalists" before the war was certainly mixed, viewed from the perspective of the "patriotic nationalist narra-tive." Their actions during the war perhaps reflect this ambiguity. As Wang Ke-wen has argued, "To an extent, the behavior of the Shanghai capitalists during the war simply reaffirmed the symbiotic relationship between the Chinese business class and foreign interests in the treaty ports that had existed since the mid-nineteenth century."[3]

In sum, on entering the war, most capitalists would be defined as "na-tionalistic" but in an ambiguous way. Most professed to support na-tionalist ideals and did so with enthusiasm when it met their needs (as with Japanese boycotts). Few refused to take advantage of the foreign enclaves or of foreign equipment and technical ties, however. Ultimately the key goal of most of the businessmen was business itself, which could often override the emotional issue of nationalism.

DIFFERENCES BY SECTOR

The responses of Chinese capitalists to the war were also much influenced by the types of businesses they operated. Not only was there a great dif-ference among banking, commerce, and industry as to the impact of the war, but the Japanese treated each of these in a different manner as well. In commerce, businessmen had perhaps the least flexibility of any sec-tor. The large modern department stores located on Nanjing Road in Shanghai survived, and did well during the flourishing period of island Shanghai. For store owners in the Chinese sectors of Shanghai and else-where in the occupied lower Yangzi, there were only two options: leave and abandon their property or stay and attempt to operate under Japa-nese strictures.

Industrialists had leeway simply because many had the option of re-locating to island Shanghai. Cotton textile production was the largest industrial sector in China. Yet it faced peculiar circumstances. Both Chi-nese and Japanese mills in China had been fierce competitors on the eve of the war, not only for sales of manufactured products but for control of raw materials as well. The war gave the Japanese mills the upper hand. Japanese firms received control of many of the Chinese mills in the oc-cupied zone, and they gained priority in obtaining raw materials, although Japanese military needs came first. After the war erupted, Chinese cot-ton textile industrialists had only one real option if they wished to re-main in operation in the lower Yangzi. They had to relocate to island Shanghai, they had to rely on imported cotton, and they had to turn to sales in southeast Asia and along the China coast if they were to remain profitable. Silk producers were likewise constrained. Since the Japanese took control of the source of raw materials, silk cocoons, and regulated the supply to fit the needs of the Japanese producers at home, Chinese industrialists in Shanghai had to find ways of smuggling in supplies from the countryside.

The Japanese considered some industries, such as chemical manufacturing, to be more strategic and made efforts to control supplies and output. Key sectors such as iron production, coal mining, railway transportation, and shipping were quickly monopolized by the Japanese and eventually turned over to the Central China Development Company. There was no room for any activity by individual Chinese capitalists in these sectors. Thus the actions and decisions of individual capitalists regarding collaboration and resistance reflected not only personal choice but also the widely varying options depending on the circumstances.

Bankers, for instance, were among the most constrained. Because of the currency war between the Japanese and the Chongqing government, they could not easily remain neutral. When confronted in 1941, they had to either accept fabi or the currency of the Nanjing regime. Some, like banker Li Ming, simply gave up and left for America.

CHINESE BUSINESS CULTURE

The actions of Chinese capitalists during the war were also influenced by the business culture that had developed in China—both the style of business activity and the organizational structure of firms. Although there was certainly a great deal of variation, particularly among banking, commercial activity, and manufacturing, in general there were two key features of Chinese business culture of the day. The first was the dominance of the family firm as a form of organization, and the second was a strong reliance on personal connections rather than impersonal, contractual ties. These characteristics were both a product of Chinese culture and, perhaps more important, of the social, legal, and political environment of the early decades of the twentieth century when most enterprises had been formed.

The family firm was certainly dominant in every sector, save perhaps modern banking. Although Chinese companies could be organized as limited liability corporations, William Kirby's study "China Unincorporated" reveals that even in the 1930s, few chose to organize in this way. Instead, most were organized as unlimited liability companies headed by a single dominant entrepreneur. Investors were usually family or those with personal connections. The rights of those who had invested in the company were not spelled out as would normally be done in incorporated firms.[4] In the latter, according to Kai Yiu Chan, the company law of 1904 provided that "accounts were subject to inspection by an inspector elected from and by the shareholders." These inspectors, Chan notes, could "recruit professional accountants to audit the accounts. By the 1920s, professional accounting firms in Shanghai were offering Western accounting methods."[5]

By contrast, complete personal control by a senior leader was the norm for the family firm. This highly individualistic authority was suited to an environment in which the legal system was confused, the political structure weak, and the future uncertain. The single leader dominated and had enormous flexibility in handling funds. As Siu-lun Wong has written, "The father, as head of a family firm, has maximum flexibility in his action. . . . The father-entrepreneur is also able to transfer funds from one line of business to another for mutual sustenance. Capital is mobile within the family group of enterprises because it belongs to a common, unified *jia* budget."[6]

Even when the legal form of an enterprise was a limited liability corporation, quite often in practice it followed the traditional approaches of the family firm. The scholar-entrepreneur Zhang Jian, for instance, used the incorporated form for his Dasheng enterprises in Nantong. Yet in her study of Dasheng, Elisabeth Köll concludes that "although from the 1910s onward the Da Sheng business was a limited liability company, it was not managed in such a way as to allow the shareholders to curtail the power of the founder-manager. Da Sheng had obviously continued traditional business practices and institutions which were characteristic of Chinese family enterprises."[7] Similarly, in his study of Liu Hongsheng and the Shanghai Cement Company, Kai Yiu Chan notes the strong degree of control that Liu exercised over a limited liability company. Using such tools as creative bookkeeping that overestimated depreciation, Liu created pockets of reserves, manipulated profit rates, and limited the distribution of profits to shareholders. "To a great extent," notes Chan, "the corporation ceased to be an 'impersonalistic' institution and became 'personalized.'"[8]

Equally as important as the family firm in Chinese business culture was the strong preference for personal connections and ties in business operations as opposed to impersonal, contractual relations. Indeed, Siu-lun Wong has argued that the personalized nature of Chinese business arrangements was and is its most important characteristic. The crucial distinction in Chinese economic conduct, suggests Wong, is not between kin and non-kin so much as those between personal and impersonal. "In making business deals, [Chinese entrepreneurs] emphasise face-to-face contacts and verbal agreements which facilitate secrecy. They shun formal contracts and professional agents."[9]

Why was there such a strong emphasis on personal relationships? It might partly be attributed to traditional cultural influences. Chinese native banks (*qianzhuang*), for instance, traditionally loaned money based on personal introduction and guarantors rather than mortgages tied to collateral. Yet we now know that legal contracts were a critical feature of many aspects of life in late imperial China and that civil law, in fact, loomed large. In her study of merchant disputes in Zigong, Sichuan, Madeleine Zelin has clearly demonstrated that "Qing customary law left a deep imprint on legal practice during the early Republican period."[10]

The strong emphasis on personal relations in recent business practice is more attributable to a desire for protection from the state. Personal, secret relations can escape state supervision more effectively than open, contractual ones. "Why are the Chinese inclined to personalise their economic relations?" queries Siu-lun Wong. "Part of the reason may lie in their desire to erect a defence against the state."[11] Modern Chinese business had generally developed in an environment, particularly during the warlord years, in which Chinese government was viewed as predatory and/or ineffective. The rule of law, courts, and statues could not be relied upon. Even in the treaty ports and direct colonies such as Hong Kong and southeast Asian countries, Chinese businessmen generally viewed colonial governments as serving the interests of the ruling power rather than Chinese businessmen. As Tahirih V. Lee has written, "To achieve their hopes and dreams, Chinese in Shanghai tried to find ways to avoid the law. . . . Big business, simply by refusing to register with national authorities, avoided a succession of laws designed to regulate its organization, accounting practices, and profits."[12]

The desire for protection from the state was one of the driving forces that favored the family firm and inhibited the adoption of the limited liability corporation. In their article "On the Absence of Privately Owned, Public Traded Corporations in China: The Kirby Puzzle," Ray Bowen and David Rose argue in fact that fear of transparency inhibited organization of limited liability corporations. Because Chinese governments of the era relied so heavily on discretionary assessments and fees to raise revenue, businessmen felt that an open, registered corporation was simply too vulnerable to government extraction.[13] This may, as Bowen argues elsewhere, "explain the predominance of relationship-based business practices in China. . . . In China, the practice of *kejuan zashui* [discretionary fees] makes contractual-based business difficult and drives business into relationship networks. In such a hostile commercial environment, families act as economic lifeboats which provide support through family firms. The more hostile the environment, the more important is the family." If a firm chose a more open, contractual form of business, Bowen concludes, "it would be at a severe disadvantage in terms of official based extraction of revenue as compared to other, more secret network-based firms."[14] Thus, the history of Chinese business development reveals organization and structure designed to operate without reference to a reliable government. The limited liability corporation, that Western invention to control risk by capitalists, relied too heavily on statues and courts for most Chinese entrepreneurs.[15]

The development of Chinese business practices can be understood in terms of culture and in the uncertain political and social environment of Republican China. Yet there were clearly problems and limitations to this style of business organization and operation. The first was the difficulty of raising capital. Although not all scholars agree, it would seem that the family firm faced more obstacles in raising capital than would a limited liability company, provided that the latter could offer stock in an environment where property enjoyed legal and political protection. Indeed, the family firm had to turn to personal connections and ties to raise investments. A second, and potentially more fatal problem with the family firm, was its dependence on the individual leader. Because one man usually headed both the firm and the family, his presence was crucial to resolving disputes among managers of the firm, many of whom were often family members themselves. As David Faure has noted, "The continuation of a Chinese family business beyond the lifetime of the patriarch is fraught with difficulties." Almost inevitably, disputes over property developed upon (or even before) the death of the senior leader. "As a family business, the division between personal expenses and business expenses were never very clear-cut," notes Faure. "In many families, disputes over access to funds . . . led to family division (*fenjia*) shortly after the patriarch's death."[16] The business practices of China provided firms with strengths, such as defense against a sometimes predatory state, but had liabilities. Death of the patriarch and breakup of the firm was potentially a serious weakness.

BUSINESS CULTURE AND THE WAR

But whatever the business culture of China on the eve of the war, how did this impact the response of China's capitalists to the conflict? The nature of Chinese business, I would argue, strongly influenced the reaction of most Chinese businessmen to the war and contributed significantly to its survival under enemy occupation. The dominant characteristics that Chinese business had developed—family organization, secrecy, reliance on personal connections—served them well during the conflict. As Gordon Redding has argued, one of the primary characteristics of Chinese family firms was the high degree of strategic adaptability. The uncertainty of the wartime environment required the ability to operate rapidly and with discretion. Decisions on moving resources to the solitary island or on relocating to the interior had to be made quickly. Formal consultation with a board of directors might well have delayed action until the issues were moot. The father-entrepreneur was also able to use sons, sons-in-law, and nephews for secret negotiations and contacts. Often Chinese businessmen tried to maintain smooth relations with Chongqing while operating in Shanghai and Hong Kong or even the occupied zone. Use of family members provided a mechanism for such actions. A son could be dispatched to the interior, act on behalf of the family firm, and be trusted even in the absence of regular communication.

Larger firms that began the war with more than one facility often found themselves operating with only a fraction of prewar equipment. Because investors in individual factories often did not own stock in a common company, the family firm could sometimes simply write off the lost facilities and concentrate resources on the remaining with little regard for minority investors. And because the family firm made little distinction between the capital of the business and the family *jia* or unified budget, it could shift investments quickly to meet war conditions. When island Shanghai suddenly became profitable in 1938, family firms reacted quickly to the new environment.

The business environment of wartime China was certainly different and much worse than that of the prewar period. Yet the difference was one of degree more than kind. The Republican period had seen numerous civil wars that had disrupted the lower Yangzi. Within cities violence and strikes had been common occurrences. Even urban conflict in Shanghai had occurred in the January 1932 Incident, with devastating consequences for Zhabei. The Battle of Shanghai went far beyond these previous conflicts, and the occupation was a harsh regime. Yet insecurity

and a hostile political situation were not completely new for businessmen of the Republican era. They were conditioned to survive in such an
atmosphere. For much of the first half of the twentieth century Chinese
businesses had operated in an environment of political and monetary insecurity. The rule of law, the protection of property and contracts, and
the security of long-term investments had been uncertain. This environment favored businessmen who were successful in making quick, flexible adjustments to short-term situations. Fast profits, small capital investments, low-skilled workers, limited risks—these were factors favored
in an insecure environment. This is not to argue that no Chinese businessman made long-term investments or that at times, such as during the
Nanjing decade, things appeared more stable. But Chinese capitalism had
germinated in this atmosphere of insecurity and distrust of government.

Yet if a desire to avoid government had characterized Chinese business behavior in the prewar years, then these traits were even more enhanced during the war. Chinese businessmen perceived Japanese occupation authorities to be hostile. At worst the occupation brought the
possibility of being arrested, of having your property confiscated. At best
it meant second-class status, fear of violence and assassination, and the
chaotic conditions of wartime. That Chinese businessmen survived the
war at all owed much to their ability to operate in an insecure environment, an ability developed over several decades. Wartime China was violent and insecure, but Chinese capitalists did not enter this era from a
pristine, peaceful environment. The characteristics developed in the warlord and even Guomindang eras aided them in surviving the war.

These characteristics also created problems. Distrust of government,
which was pervasive among businessmen, meant that most had only limited ties with the Guomindang government in 1937. There were major
exceptions, including "bureaucratic capitalists" such as T. V. Soong and
H. H. Kung, but others like the Rong family had developed strained relations with the Chiang Kaishek government. When government assistance was clearly needed to evacuate equipment from Shanghai when the
war erupted, the lack of links slowed the process. By the time government support for businesses had been organized, it was largely too late.[17]

A second difficulty was the vulnerability of the family firm to the death
of the individual. The very strength that the single leader brought was
also a source of potential weakness. Even in peacetime, as noted above,
the death of the senior patriarch could be fatal. In wartime it brought
even greater stress. Although few capitalists died in the line of fire, some
perished on planes and ships in the battle zone. Others were vulnerable

to arrest and torture by either Dai Li or Number 76 Jessfield Road. Harsh war conditions probably hastened the death from health problems of leaders like textile magnate Rong Zongjing. The problems of family firms surviving the death of the founder thus increased in wartime.

Finally, the nature of the family firm may have influenced the decisions of Chinese businessmen. In any number of cases, Chinese capitalists put the survival of their businesses above the broader concerns of patriotism. They compromised with the occupying force even though they appeared unhappy in doing so. Their business enterprises were not impersonal corporations in which one simply held stock. In most family firms, as noted above, the private property of the family and the income of the firm were held in common. Family expenses were often taken from the general revenue. In fighting to preserve one's business one was fighting to preserve the family income. Family and survival often won out over the more abstract concept of nationalism.

In sum, it is very difficult in the abstract to characterize easily the actions of most Chinese businessmen during the war. Few fit neatly into the "heroic nationalist narrative" currently touted in Chinese historical writing. Yet few also would clearly be defined as collaborators for the entire course of the war. Most operated between the poles of collaboration and resistance. It is even more difficult to determine motives for the businessmen. Survival seems to have been the dominant goal. Nationalism played a role but one that was less clear. The business culture and organization certainly affected the way capitalists responded to the war, but again individual variation was quite large. An analysis of the individual wartime experiences of some of the major capitalists of the Shanghai area will illuminate these issues.

CHAPTER 6

The Rong Family Industrial Enterprises and the War

Of all of the industrial capitalists in China, the Rong family group had the size and diversity to survive the war. A study of the fate of this group reveals both the strengths and weaknesses of Chinese business culture and organization under war conditions. Founded by Rong Zongjing and his younger brother Rong Desheng, the Rong industrial empire included Shenxin textile mills (ten in all) as well as the Maoxin and Fuxin flour mills (sixteen in all). Rong operations extended from their native Wuxi to Shanghai, Hankou, and beyond. Although the mid-1930s brought some difficult times for the Rongs, they had developed close relationships with a number of Chinese and foreign banks and used extensive bank loans to acquire new technology and to expand their empire. By the mid-1930s, the Rongs held almost 20 percent of all spindles in Chinese-owned textile mills and produced one-sixth of the milled flour. The Rongs were frequently called the "cotton and flour" kings by the Chinese press.

Although Shenxin, Fuxin, and Maoxin would commonly be referred to as individual companies and each had a general headquarters, every mill in the group was actually organized as a separate unlimited liability firm. Rong Zongjing, the senior figure, was named director-general of every factory in the group. Despite its size and complexity, therefore, the Rong group was organized as a family business.[1]

The war seemed to deal a crippling blow to the Rong fortunes. More than 36 percent of their spindles, 60 percent of their looms, and 18 percent of their flour grinders were destroyed in the fighting, and the Japanese seized much of the remainder. Yet out of this rubble, the Rongs survived and even earned substantial profits. More crippling to the firm was the death of senior figure Rong Zongjing, whose health suffered under war conditions. After the war erupted, Zongjing departed Shanghai for Hong Kong, where he died on February 10, 1938, at the age of sixty-six. His brother, Desheng, was unable to maintain complete control over his nephews, and the Rongs began to disagree over the strategy to pursue in wartime. Some spoke of a split between the Ximo Road group (where Rong Zongjing's home was located) and the Zhi'en Road group (site of Rong Desheng's home).[2]

THE SHENXIN COTTON TEXTILE GROUP AND THE BATTLE OF SHANGHAI

In August 1937 seven of the ten Shenxin textiles mills were in the Shanghai area and thus in the face of battle; yet the fate of the individual mills varied greatly depending on location. By year's end the Rongs had lost control of five of their Shanghai mills. Two were virtually destroyed— the Shenxin #1, founded in 1915 and having 72,800 spindles at the time, and the Shenxin #8, founded in 1930, with 50,000 spindles. Both were located in the Western Roads section of Shanghai and were bombed by the Japanese on the morning of October 27, 1937, heavily damaging the mills, killing more than 70 workers and injuring more than 350. The Western Roads area had been the object of a long-standing dispute between Chinese and foreigners in Shanghai. Not part of the International Settlement, it nonetheless had many foreign residents. The foreign-dominated Shanghai Municipal Council therefore attempted to exercise jurisdiction over the area.[3]

When the fighting first began, the Rongs halted production (on August 16) and contemplated moving the two mills. The managers gambled that this location would be protected by foreign presence and hence resumed operation on September 17. This strategy exposed the workers to great danger when the Japanese attacked and precluded removing equipment to a safer location in the International Settlement proper. Only about ten truckloads of raw cotton and cloth were salvaged. Later the sites of these two mills were occupied by the Japanese military, who turned them over to the Toyoda Textile Company, which already owned an adjacent facility. Toyoda partially rebuilt the two; they had a combined 40,000 spindles and 1,300 looms.[4]

Three other Shenxin mills, #5, #6, and #7, escaped with only limited damage but were in areas occupied by the Japanese. The Shenxin #5 had been purchased by the Rongs in 1935 and had 49,000 spindles. Located in the Pudong section of Shanghai, it was abandoned almost immediately when an air battle occurred right over the plant, frightening the workers. Shortly thereafter, Chinese and then Japanese forces occupied the plant. Shenxin #6 and #7 were both located in the Yangshupu section of Shanghai and suffered only moderate damage in the fighting, but both quickly fell under Japanese control. Shenxin #6, which had more than 75,000 yarn spindles, nearly 6,000 thread spindles, and 864 looms with 1,825 workers in 1937, lost several thousand spindles and 200 to 300 looms in the fighting. Shenxin #7, which had been purchased from European owners in 1929 and had nearly 54,000 spindles and 455 looms, suffered a warehouse fire that destroyed a large quantity of raw material.[5]

Despite this damage, these mills could easily be brought back into production. But by whom? Japanese military authorities sealed off the properties, denying access to the Rongs. The family engaged a German firm to move the equipment from Shenxin #6 to the International Settlement, but the Japanese blocked this action in March 1938. For a time it appeared that the Japanese might allow the Rongs some stake in these mills in exchange for active collaboration with puppet regimes, but ultimately these operations fell victim to the Japanese policy of entrusting Chinese textile mills to Japanese concerns. This policy not only strengthened Japanese control over the economy of the occupied area, but (as noted in Chapter 2) was designed to compensate Japanese companies for losses of property elsewhere in China. Shenxin #5 went to the Yūhō bōseki, Shenxin #6 went to Shanhai bōseki, and #7 went to the Kanegafuchi Company.[6]

COLLABORATION?

In the immediate aftermath of the battle of Shanghai, Japanese authorities hinted that Chinese businessmen might be partially compensated for confiscated property if they supported the Japanese cause. There is some evidence that the Rongs flirted with this idea. When the Shanghai Citizens Association was being formed to support the Dadao regime in Shanghai in late 1937, Rong Zongjing's name was mentioned in the press as one of the organizers. As the biggest Chinese industrialist of the day,

Rong Zongjing attracted considerable attention by his involvement, including criticism from Guomindang authorities who denounced the association as a collaborationist organization. Hoping to defuse criticism, Rong told reporters that the association was not a government organization; members were merchants, not politicians. The group was a strictly humanitarian body, Rong argued, attempting to aid refugees living in the foreign concessions by restoring the economy of Zhabei, Nanshi, Pudong, and Wusong, which would allow the refugees to return home. Since five of Rong's Shenxin plants were in Japanese hands, the "restoration" of production in those facilities would obviously have meant working with the Japanese. Rong, in fact, admitted that the group had been negotiating with the Japanese military authorities, but denied that the body was part of the Dadao government. Rong compounded the outcry by remarking that "China is virtually a nation without a government; at times such as these it requires fearless action on the part of citizens to reduce want and suffering." These remarks attracted so much criticism that Rong issued a clarification that he referred only to Shanghai when discussing the absence of Chinese authority.[7] Despite Rong's denials, Guomindang authorities considered the group collaborationist and participants became targets of the "war of terror." First Lu Bohong was assassinated in late December 1937; then few days later someone tossed a hand grenade into the courtyard of Gu Xinyi, merchant guild leader and "rice king." Rong Zongjing's house came under surveillance. This intimidation had the desired effect, as most quit the association. A panicky Rong Zongjing departed Shanghai on January 4, 1938, for the seemingly safer environs of Hong Kong, only to die there shortly thereafter. Zongjing's experience had been a lesson for the Rongs. Although remaining aloof from the Japanese had its difficulties, collaboration was risky.[8]

Following his older brother's death in Hong Kong, Rong Desheng, now the senior leader, avoided collaboration as much as possible. He rejected early attempts by the Japanese to gain his participation in puppet organizations in exchange for possible restoration of Rong property. Yet, pressure continued; in 1940, his second son, Rong Er'ren, was held fifty-eight days by puppet police in Pudong. Even then Desheng refused to ask puppet authorities for assistance in exchange for political favors. Because of the Rongs' refusal to collaborate actively with Japanese and puppet authorities, whatever the motivation, they were not able to regain possession of their mills in the occupied areas of Shanghai during the 1937–1941 period.[9]

LIFE IN THE SOLITARY ISLAND PERIOD

After the fall of Shanghai, the Rongs thus retained control of only two of their Shenxin textile mills, #2 and #9. Both were in the International Settlement and not occupied until December 1941. The #2 mill had been founded in 1919 and by 1937 had more than 53,000 spindles. The Rongs had purchased Shenxin #9 in 1931, and by 1937 it had more than 129,000 spindles and 615 looms. Despite pressure from the Guomindang government to relocate in the interior, the Rongs decided to make the Shanghai concessions the base of their operations. Rong Desheng, the younger brother who had initially fled Wuxi for Hankou with his sons, returned to Shanghai to lead the family.[10]

The foreign concessions were islands of neutrality in a sea of Japanese control, yet Chinese firms were not fully secure. As an added measure of protection, the Rongs, like many industrialists who stayed, turned to the cover of foreign registration. The Rongs "leased" their two mills to foreign owners in paper transactions (described in Chapter 1) so as to provide the protection of a foreign flag. The Shenxin #2 was registered as American, Shenxin #9 as British.[11]

Since the Rongs retained control of only two of their seven mills in Shanghai, one might suppose that their economic fortunes declined substantially. Yet in many respects the Rongs actually did rather well in the war. Plagued by overcapacity on the eve of the conflict, the Rongs were able to make fuller use of their remaining mills—both increased in output. Although Shenxin #2's capacity remained essentially unchanged, its output of yarn increased after 1937. The Rongs expanded the capacity of Shenxin #9, increasing the number of looms by 1940 to 815 and spindles to 148,220, making it the largest mill in China. Shenxin #9's output of both yarn and cloth increased substantially (see table 3).[12] The number of workers increased from 4,938 in 1937 to 5,917 in 1939. The Rongs not only sold textiles in China, but greatly increased exports to southeast Asia. The large communities of overseas Chinese began to boycott Japanese products and turned to the Rong's "Golden twin horses" brand.

But production and profit are not the same thing. Increased output from existing equipment, and a tilt in the supply-demand ratio was a formula for higher earnings. In 1936, Shenxin's seven mills in Shanghai earned a total profit of almost 1.6 million yuan, with Shenxin #1 being the most profitable. Shenxin #2 had lost more than 150,000 yuan that year, while #9 earned only 417,000 yuan. In 1938, both earned substantial

TABLE 3. COTTON YARN AND CLOTH OUTPUT
AT SHENXIN MILLS #2 AND #9*

	Shenxin mill #2: yarn	Shenxin mill #9: yarn	Shenxin mill #9: cloth
1937	100	100	100
1938	126.5	127.2	151.9
1939	139.6	151.1	164.8
1940	143.4	152.0	137.2
1941	117.0	64.5	41.6

SOURCES: SASS, *Rongjia qiye shiliao*, vol. 2, pp. 68, 73–74, 191; SASS, Rong Collection, R08, pp. 48, 52–53, and R05, pp. 35–41.
*Base = 100

profits; #2 earned more than 2.7 million yuan and #9 more than 6.9 million. Thus from the standpoint of profits, the Rongs earned more with only two mills in island Shanghai in 1938 than they had from all seven Shanghai mills in the prewar period. War had reduced the supply of cotton yarn and cloth while demand remained firm. The good times did not last; the strains of war eventually drove profits down. In 1941, Shenxin #2 earned less than half the income of 1938 (adjusted for inflation) and Shenxin #9 just over one-third as much. Still the Rongs did reasonably well during the first years of the war.[13]

Even wartime inflation benefited the Rongs to a certain extent. The Rongs had endured some difficult years during the mid-1930s and had accumulated substantial debts. The effects of the world depression, the suspension of business in early 1932 when fighting had erupted in Shanghai, and the adverse impact of American silver purchase policy, had created rather unfavorable economic conditions for Shenxin in the mid-1930s. The company had, in fact, teetered on the verge of bankruptcy for a time before conditions improved in 1936 and 1937. Total debts of Shenxin and Fuxin mills were estimated to be 80 million yuan in 1936. With wartime inflation, the real costs of repaying old loans dropped, while earnings measured in inflated fabi increased quickly. Debts were thus rapidly repaid. Shenxin #2's actual earnings (not adjusted for inflation) increased from 543,300 yuan in 1937 to more than 3 million in 1939 and nearly 6.6 million in 1941. Shenxin #9's profits were 2.25 million in 1937, increasing to more than 10.7 million for 1939 and to nearly 12.3 million in 1941. By 1941 Shenxin #2 and #9 were debt free; debts of other units were reduced to 20 million yuan. When in May 1942 the Wang Jingwei government required the exchange of old fabi for its currency at a two-for-one ratio, this was reduced to only 10 million yuan. Adjusted for inflation, this was the equivalent of only 4.56 percent of this sum in 1936 yuan. The Rongs thus quickly repaid the remaining portion and by the end of June 1942 the company was debt free. The Shenxin mills even began paying dividends, although this good fortune ignited tensions among the shareholders over the spoils.[14]

ORGANIZATIONAL ISSUES

Wartime profits did not entirely smooth relations within the Rong family. Despite its size, the Rong group was organized along very traditional lines, which certainly helped the family survive the initial battle and the loss of five of its seven textile mills in Shanghai. Yet the death of Rong Zongjing, the senior patriarch, left the firm without its founding leader at the very moment when he was most needed. Serious disputes developed within the remaining Shenxin structure.

Because only two of the mills of the Rong group continued to operate under their control, and the investments in each of the mills varied, some members of the Rong clan profited more than others. This disparity resulted from the organizational structure of the Rong enterprises. The Rong brothers had established a general headquarters for Shenxin, but the company was not organized under the Western-style business law as an incorporated limited-liability concern under the control of a board of directors. The general office handled purchase of materials and sales of goods, but individual factories were organized separately. The Rongs had raised capital investment individually for each mill, but rights for shareholders had not been clearly established. The real authority in Shenxin was not in the institution of the general headquarters but in the person of Rong Zongjing and to a lesser extent his brother, Desheng.[15]

This looseness of organization was common among Chinese enterprises of prewar China (as noted in Chapter 5). The father-entrepreneur therefore retained enormous power and flexibility as leader of the family firm. In the Rong firm, it had been Rong Zongjing who had combined the position of head of the company and head of family. With his death, however, the reliance on personal rather than institutional arrangements became more of an issue, especially under wartime conditions. Desheng was neither forceful enough nor healthy enough to assume dominant leadership at the general headquarters. Although Rong Zongjing's son Hongyuan took over as general manager, he could not control his brothers and cousins. The surviving #2 and #9 mills became increasingly independent of the general headquarters, as did the Hankou Shenxin #4. The Maoxin and Fuxin flour companies also split off, with Rong Desheng dominating Maoxin and Wang Yuqing the Fuxin.[16]

As the #9 mill became more profitable, for instance, the manager, Wu Kunsheng, moved to make it more independent of the general headquarters, repaying to the center capital owed from the prewar period and accepting less interference in management decisions. Moreover, when the mill began to distribute wartime profits to the investors, the senior Rong branch of Rong Zongjing, now headed by Rong Hongyuan, held considerably more of the investment than Rong Desheng and his heirs and gained more of the profits.

In January 1939, the firm reallocated the stock to provide for both Rong branches and the managers of #9, but this did not resolve disagreement. The paperwork defining stockholder rights in the firm was held in a safe deposit box at a British bank, custody of which was jointly held by Rong Hongyuan and Rong Weiren (Desheng's eldest son). The latter's death led his widow to attempt to retrieve the documents, resulting in a quarrel between the two branches. Additional disputes arose because some of the stock from the 1939 distribution had been sold to outsiders who then raised questions about their rights.

On August 20, 1941, the capital of the mill was reset at 50 million yuan (in Nanjing banknotes), with a new distribution. The senior branch headed by Rong Hongyuan and his brothers Rong Hongsan and Rong Hongqing still controlled the majority—59.8 percent, with 25.6 percent held by Rong Desheng and his children. Smaller amounts were held by the managers, including 4.8 percent by Wu Kunsheng. The firm was defined as a partnership, which meant that the shares of ownership could not be transferred to a third party. In this way, the privacy of the family firm was to be maintained.[17]

In the meantime, Rong Er'ren, feeling that he was being shut out of real authority in Shenxin #9, began to press for changes in Shenxin #2. With the death of his brother Weiren, he was now the senior figure among Desheng's sons. In July 1938, Er'ren drafted an economic plan for Shenxin #2, key to which was the repayment of bank loans. Accumulated debts had left #2's management in the hands of bank authorities on the eve of the war. Er'ren's plan, however, was predicated on Shenxin #2 becoming independent of the general headquarters of Shenxin and coming under his domination. When Rong Hongyuan became aware of this plan, he devised a counterproposal. The debts of Shenxin #2 and #5 (then under Japanese control) would be retired together and the two reorganized as one group, but as a unit of the general headquarters of the Shenxin company.

The competing plans led to an intense dispute between the two factions, which was finally resolved, much as were disputes over #9. In a May 1942 agreement (when conditions were no longer so profitable), the two sides agreed that the debts of #2 and #5 would be retired together and that they would be reorganized as one unit. The stock was set at 30 million yuan (in Nanjing currency) in June 1942, with 56.7 percent going to Rong Hongyuan and his brothers and 43.3 percent to Rong Desheng and his sons. Rong Hongyuan took the title general manager, while Rong Er'ren was manager. Despite the title, it was agreed that day-to-day control would rest with Er'ren. In late 1942 a distribution of dividends occurred, with the senior Rongs getting 2,811,000 yuan and the junior branch 2,149,000. The following year, 1943, the distribution was 6,664,000 for the seniors and 5,499,000 for the juniors, with a modest 370,000 being returned to the general company headquarters and high level personnel.[18]

These disputes illustrate the difficulties faced by a Chinese family firm on the death of the patriarch. Only the strained conditions of 1941 and 1942, with the rapid growth of inflation, the decrease in real profits, and the Japanese seizure of Rong property in December 1941, led the family to compromise. These resolutions of conflict still left minority investors in Shenxin #1 and #8 out in the cold. They had received no income since the war began, while Shenxin #2 and #9 earned profits. Many of these investors protested that since Shenxin as a group was an unlimited liability firm, they should be entitled to compensation for their losses from the profits being earned by other branches. This dispute was not easily resolved, and the acrimony continued through the war era. In early 1943 (when all of Shanghai was under Japanese control) several of the investors launched a protest with the Ministry of Industry in Nanjing. The bickering also surfaced at an April 7, 1943, meeting of Shenxin #1 and #8 shareholders that was chaired by Rong Hongyuan. Several stockholders protested his leadership under the grounds that the position of chair of the board was not inherited. As a consequence Hongyuan withdrew and was replaced as chair by Zhang Zhipeng.[19]

Under Zhang's direction, a committee formed to examine the account books of the Shenxin system. When the group of seven arrived at the Shenxin headquarters, however, they were denied access to the accounting records on the grounds that these were the property of the Rong family. The minority shareholders then approached puppet official Chu Minyi through an intermediary with the hope of getting his support for their efforts. The Rongs, however, had already approached Chu, forcing the group to enter direct talks with Rong Hongyuan.

Always plotting to increase his authority, Rong Er'ren attempted to use the protests of the minority stockholders to his advantage. He suggested the creation of a new "Greater Shenxin" structure, with a revised and strengthened role for the central headquarters and for himself. He told the stockholder committee, "You are Shenxin's seven gentlemen (qi junzi). When the Greater Shenxin is set up, it will be because of your effort."[20] The minority stockholders, however, lacked the clout to force restructuring of Shenxin. Rong Desheng and the older leaders resisted the idea of changing the family firm into a limited liability company. On January 5, 1944, the minority shareholders agreed to recognize the existing organizational structure for Shenxin #2, #5, #6, #7, and #9, but would pursue the eventual reorganization of Shenxin #1 and #8 as a limited liability company. The latter form of organization would provide for specified legal rights for shareholders.[21]

It is not surprising that the senior Rongs resisted change. The loose structure of Shenxin had allowed them to garner profits from #2 and #9 while minority shareholders in the other mills gained nothing. Little of the income from the #2 and #9 mills had been returned to the general headquarters of Shenxin. The central office actually lost money in 1938 and 1939 (1,666,780 yuan and 1,593,870 yuan, respectively) before earning 775,710 in 1940. The central office lost funds because so many unemployed personnel from #1, #6, #7, and #8 depended on the general office for support, straining its resources. Under these circumstances, most of the Rongs preferred to separate #2 and #9 and their profits from the liabilities of the general headquarters.[22]

Rong Er'ren still maintained a goal for a centrally organized Rong group for postwar China. In March 1944, he issued two draft plans, one for Shenxin textiles and one for Maoxin and Fuxin flour production. The Shenxin plans called for postwar expansion to twenty mills with 2 million spindles and 20,000 looms. Flour production would expand within ten years to include sixteen mills and daily flour production of 220,000 bags. These plans would be implemented by newly organized central headquarters for the three firms, which would have a modern, scientific management and would actually control operations of the various mills of the Rong group.[23]

The continual disputes between the senior and junior branches of the Rong family actually led Rong Desheng to attempt to create a separate firm to be controlled by his side of the family. As early as 1941, De-sheng had been planning for an industrial company that would include textiles, flour, electrical production, and a foundry, to be entirely sepa-rate from the Zongjing branch. Desheng would be general manager and his seven sons would serve as assistant general managers. The firm was still in the planning stages, however, when the war ended.[24]

These disputes reflect both the strengths and weaknesses of the fam-ily firm as an organizational form. Wartime conditions coupled with deaths of key personnel put great strains on the family enterprise and led to the disputes. At the same time, the flexibility of the family firm may have been essential to its survival in the insecure and rapidly changing environment of war. Had the company had a more formal bureaucratic structure it might not have survived the early phase of the war.

FLOUR MILLS

The Rongs were also able to save some of their flour milling empire. In Shanghai the Rongs' eight Fuxin mills with a total annual capacity of 15.4 million bags of flour (see table 4) The Maoxin mills, discussed be-low, were located in Wuxi.

As with the Shenxin textiles, many of the Rongs' Fuxin and Maoxin mills were heavily damaged. Fuxin #1, #3, and #6, all located in Zhabei, sustained some of the heaviest destruction. Japanese troops also occu-pied all three, which were given in early 1938 to the Japanese Mikyō flour company. Three other mills, Fuxin #2, #7, and #8, were in the for-eign concessions and remained under Rong control. As a precaution, the family registered the mills as foreign enterprises.[25]

As with textiles, this remaining portion of the Fuxin system proved extraordinarily profitable during Shanghai's "flourishing" period of 1938 and 1939. The influx of refugees kept demand, and profits, high. Fuxin #2 and #8, which had produced 3.4 million bags of flour in 1937, produced 4.8 million in 1939. Fuxin #7 increased production from 2.5 million bags to 3.8 million during the same period. Profits rose even faster. Fuxin #2 and #8 had lost 323,720 yuan in 1937; Fuxin #7, 31,860 yuan. Both quickly turned profitable. Fuxin #2 and #8 earned 2.1 million yuan in 1939; Fuxin #7, 1.3 million.

The biggest difficulty for the mills was the source of wheat. Shipments from north China were disrupted by the war, so Fuxin turned to imported wheat. A negligible source before 1939, imported wheat accounted for almost 84 percent of the purchases of the three mills in that year. The

TABLE 4. CAPACITY OF THE FUXIN FLOUR
MILLS IN SHANGHAI IN 1936

Mill #	Number of grinders	Annual capacity (in million bags)
Fuxin #1	15	1.2
Fuxin #2	48	3.0
Fuxin #3 and #6 combined	24	1.6
Fuxin #4	32	2.0
Fuxin #7	49	4.0
Fuxin #8	56	3.6

SOURCES: Xu Weiyong and Huang Hanmin, *Rongjia qiye fazhan shi*, p. 132; Shanghai shi liangshi ju, *Zhongguo jindai mianfen gongye shi*, p. 155.

outbreak of the war in Europe, however, played havoc with supplies, and output began to drop. Fuxin #2 and #8, which had produced 4.8 million bags in 1939, could manage only 1.4 million in 1940. Fuxin #7 dropped from 3.8 million in 1939 to 1.1 in 1940. High prices kept profits up, even on the smaller volume, until Pearl Harbor.[26]

AN END TO THE SOLITARY ISLAND

The foreign concessions were not totally solitary islands. Especially after the outbreak of the European War, Japanese authorities intimidated the settlement authorities and exercised increasing dominance over Shanghai. Targets such as the lucrative Shenxin and Fuxin mills drew attention. The aloof attitude of Rong Desheng toward the occupation led to pressure from both the Japanese and Number 76 Jessfield Road. In the summer of 1941 Shenxin #9 manager Wu Kunsheng and his son were arrested by Japanese military police in the French Concession and held for more than a month until the Rongs paid a substantial sum for their release.[27]

When the Pacific war erupted, all vestiges of the sanctity of the International Settlement and French Concession evaporated. Shenxin #2 and #9 textile mills and Fuxin #2, #7, and #8 flour mills all came under Japanese control. The British and American registry, previously used to provide protection, now proved a detriment. Japanese military police arrived at the factories on December 13, seizing Shenxin #2 and #9, and five other textile mills in Shanghai, on the grounds that they were now enemy property. Rong Er'ren tried unsuccessfully to forestall the takeover on the grounds that the firms were really Chinese. Both textile mills suffered some losses while occupied. An estimated 300,000 to 500,000 yuan of material was taken from the plants during this period, including raw cotton, yarn, and cloth.[28]

In contrast to 1937 when the Japanese parceled out seized property to Japanese firms, military leaders were now more ready to restore mills to Chinese industrialists prepared to work with the occupation. The Rongs, who had been reluctant to deal with the occupiers as long as they could operate in the solitary island, now began a carefully orchestrated campaign of discrete overtures to the Japanese. They brought in new personnel with close ties to the Japanese. Shenxin hired as an assistant manager Tong Luqing, who had studied in Japan. Jiang Junhui, a Japanese language professor in Shanghai when war erupted, joined the board of directors of Shenxin #9. Jiang was a longtime associate of #9's manager Wu Kunsheng, both being natives of Changzhou. Not only did Tong and Jiang bring Japanese language skills to Shenxin, but Jiang eventually served as secretary of the Cotton Control Commission. Shenxin also invited Wen Lanting to join their board on February 1, 1942. Wen had accepted the Japanese offer to head the cotton board. Shenxin #9 even engaged a Japanese adviser, Ogawa Gorō, to smooth the way toward regaining its property.[29]

The Rongs and other groups that lost property in December 1941 opened direct negotiations with the Japanese military, which expressed a willingness to negotiate a return of industries to Chinese control by late 1942. Opposition surfaced, however, from the Japanese Mill Owners Association in China, which favored continued Japanese control over these properties. Jiang Shangda, a textile industrialist in Shanghai, began negotiations with the military on behalf of all seven mills that had been seized in December 1941, including Shenxin #2 and #9. (Others were the Yong'an mill, Anda, Baofeng, Defeng, and Hefeng.) Jiang attempted to drive a wedge between the Japanese mill owners and the Japanese military. The latter had a vested interest in reviving the prosperity of the occupied areas and restoring production, not only to win over the Chinese population, but to provide the cloth, uniforms, and blankets needed by the Japanese army. Chinese manufacturers, it was argued, could more easily operate in the China market and gain access to cotton produced in rural areas than could outside Japanese merchants. To press these arguments, Jiang Shangda dispatched Jiang Junhui to Tokyo.[30]

Jiang Shangda took advantage of one other tie, to Japanese right-wing leader Ōkawa Shūmei. Ōkawa was a mainstay of the radical right, an earlier associate of Kita Ikki, and had been imprisoned for his role in the

May 15 Incident in Tokyo. A strong advocate of Pan-Asianism and a Shōwa restoration, Ōkawa was highly regarded by many Japanese military commanders in China. (He was tried as a class A war criminal after the war.) Ōkawa came to Shanghai and negotiated between the Japanese Mill Owners Association and the military, pressing for the return of all seven plants to Chinese control. Such a policy was considered to be necessary for implementation of a true Pan-Asianist ideal.[31]

With this solid backing, the seven mills, including Shenxin #2 and #9, were returned to their Chinese owners. A formal ceremony of rendition occurred in May 1942. The group conspicuously left out of these negotiations had actually been the Nanjing puppet authorities, who nominally had real authority. Jiang Shangda and the Japanese did invite Mei Siping, Minister of Industry of the Nanjing government, to attend the rendition ceremony, but he had not been an active party in the negotiations.[32]

As the Japanese became even more interested in working with Chinese capitalists, the Rongs attempted to regain control over properties lost since 1937, including the old Shenxin #5, #6, and #7 as well as the rebuilt #1 and #8. On April 7, 1942, after the Wang government issued a proclamation that property would be returned, Rong Hongyuan submitted a petition thanking the Japanese for "protecting" the properties during the war and asking for the return of these old mills under the broad principles of Sino-Japanese cooperation through the Greater East Asia Co-Prosperity Sphere. Obstacles remained, and the process of rendition moved slowly. Japanese firms had operated some of these mills for nearly five years and invested in extensive repairs. The Japanese Yūhō Company objected to returning Shenxin #5 without compensation. Rong Er'ren opened negotiations with the firm, which culminated in an eventual agreement on July 24, 1943. Shenxin #6, which had been operated by Shanghai bōseki, was returned at the same time but was in poor shape. The Rongs called for workers to return on July 26, but, except for making repairs and producing some wool yarn, the plant remained out of production until the end of the war. The Japanese navy, it will be recalled, blocked return of Shenxin #7 until convinced that its plans to use the site were not viable. The Rongs regained title in July 1943 but agreed to lease the mill to a Japanese firm. Only in September 1945 would the Rongs resume management of the plant.[33]

Even more difficulties surrounded the return of Shenxin #1 and #8. Gutted in the early fighting, the two mills were rebuilt as one unit under the Toyoda company. The Japanese firm claimed that their repairs were equal to three-fourths of the value of the plant and demanded that the Rongs either sell the plant to them or compensate them for the repairs. Toyoda decided on a purchase price for the mill of 2.5 million yen. The Rong management contested Toyoda's figures, saying that the major buildings were old facilities and that most of the looms and spindles also were not new. Before the war the two mills contained 120,000 spindles, the management noted. In 1943 only 40,000 remained.

The dispute with Toyoda made the return of the mills problematic. This situation exacerbated the stockholder dispute initiated by the minority stockholders in #1 and #8 (discussed above). Many of the stockholders were suspicious of the Rongs' leadership, feeling that they were pursuing the interests of the other mills while writing off Shenxin #1 and #8. When the stockholders met on April 7, 1943, and again on July 10, 1943, they refused to sell their title to Toyoda or to agree to a joint management proposal, despite the urging of the Wang government. Stockholders wanted to regain the property and reorganize it as a limited liability company, so they instructed Rong Hongyuan to demand full return of the facility. Unable to reach an agreement, Shenxin did not regain control of the #1 and #8 plants until the war's end, when only 5,000 spindles were found immediately usable.[34]

The post–Pearl Harbor situation was thus fraught with difficulties for the Rongs. Although they desired to regain as much of their property as possible, and revealed a willingness to work with puppet authorities and the Japanese military in doing so, they still rejected the idea of a junior partnership with a Japanese firm, and attempted to keep collaboration as low-key as possible. The limits of this approach were revealed in the Rongs' attempt to regain control of Maoxin #4 in Ji'nan, one of the few Rong ventures in north China. This flour mill, which had twelve grinders and a capacity of only 600,000 bags annually, had come under Japanese military control when Ji'nan fell. Japanese control in north China was even tighter than in the south, with multiple agencies involved. The Rongs discovered these complexities when they began in the summer of 1941 to regain possession of this mill. Rong Baochun was dispatched north to negotiate the restoration.

The young Rong immediately discovered the difficulties. Plans for restoration had to be coordinated with the Xinmin Hui (People's Renovation Society), which was associated with the Beijing regime, as well as the special services of the Japanese military. As negotiations continued into the autumn of 1941, Maoxin representatives also had to deal with officials from the Beijing office of the Asian Development Board, the Ji'-

nan city government, and the Mitsubishi Corporation, which was to co-ordinate the operation of the mill with Maoxin. Ultimately, the negotiations failed. Rong Desheng abandoned the efforts to restore Maoxin #4, because he felt that satisfactory arrangements could not be made given the complexities of the Ji'nan situation. The Rongs thus experienced mixed results in getting restoration of their property that had been seized earlier in the war.[35]

WARTIME DECLINE IN PRODUCTION

Even with some of their mills restored, the Rongs found the glory days of "flourishing Shanghai" long over. The returned properties were not in good condition. Shenxin #5 had lost about one-half of its spindles, and its south building was totally destroyed. The #6 was partially gutted, and #7 had only 30,000 of the earlier 54,000 spindles remaining. A more serious problem was the general decline of the economy, including the development of hyperinflation, and the heavy demands of the Japanese procurement system. Island Shanghai had depended on imported cotton, and this supply was disrupted after Pearl Harbor.

The Japanese controlled the supply of raw cotton in China and, even after the Cotton Control Commission of the Wang government took nominal charge of supplies, made little of this available to Chinese mills. In 1942 Rong Hongyuan complained that 60 percent of China's raw cotton was appropriated by the Japanese military for shipment to Japan and three-fourths of the remaining portion given to Japanese mills in China. In the later war years, therefore, the Rong textile mills operated at only a fraction of capacity. Shenxin #2 and #9, for instance, resumed production in June 1942. Yet Shenxin #2 produced only 10 percent of the cotton yarn and thread in 1942 that it had in 1936, and Shenxin #9 only 7.5 percent. Shenxin #9 had used 321,812 piculs of cotton in 1940 but only 12,050 in 1942. Overall the Rongs' mills operated at only 20 percent of capacity in 1942, and #5 and #6 later ceased production entirely.[36]

As the Cotton Control Commission pressed Japanese procurement demands, while hyperinflation simultaneously gutted normal economy activity, the Rongs turned to speculation and black market activity to survive. Not only did the cotton commission keep procurement prices of raw cotton low, but it attempted to set the price for manufactured cotton products. In an era of hyperinflation, few manufacturers chose to produce at that price level. The commission set prices for the procurement of cotton yarn and cloth on August 9, 1943. For twenty-count cotton yarn the price was 10,000 yuan per *jian,* while the market price in September was more than 35,000. By June of 1944, the government was paying only 6 to 7 percent of market value in its procurement purchases. Under these conditions, Shenxin mills could not operate profitably, at least not without evading government rules.[37]

The Rongs farmed some of their equipment out to small-scale enterprises, which could more easily evade control and taxes. By operating workshops in rural areas in particular, they could purchase raw cotton from farmers, often circumventing puppet and occupation authorities. Small workshops could also use diesel generators, easing some of the energy problems that plagued the urban plants. Shenxin #2, able to operate only a fraction of its spindles by 1944, helped establish three small workshop groups in nearby areas such as Pudong. Eventually it leased out almost 3,000 spindles.[38]

The Rong "success" in regaining their properties from Japanese control was thus somewhat hollow. Their facilities were not in good condition and the lack of raw materials and the disruption of markets meant lean times during the late war period. Still, losses in production could be offset partially by hoarding of commodities and currency speculation. The Rongs seem to have had the resources and skills to survive in wartime.

FUXIN FLOUR MILLS

The Rongs also regained control of Fuxin flour mills #2, #7, and #8, which had been in the old foreign settlements and seized by the Japanese after Pearl Harbor. The three mills in Zhabei, formerly Fuxin #1, #3, and #6, remained under the management of the Mikyō company. The latter was reluctant to surrender these, so Nanjing puppet authorities pressed the Rongs to sign a three-year lease agreement with Mikyō in April 1942. Even with only half the number of mills they had prior to the war, the Rongs were able to maintain a strong presence in Shanghai. As late as 1944, each of their three mills produced 13,000 to 14,000 bags of flour per day. Two other flour mills in Shanghai were operating under Chinese ownership in 1944. The Fufeng produced 26,780 bags daily and the Huafeng, 8,000. Meanwhile, the seven mills managed by the Japanese could manage a total of only 33,800. The Rongs thus maintained their position of "flour kings" even under full Japanese occupation. When the war ended, the Rongs were thus positioned to continue that role. In 1948 the Fuxin mills in Shanghai produced a total of 4.5 million bags of flour.[39]

As with cotton textile production, flour milling increasingly shifted to very small producers in the countryside late in the war as the Chinese sought to evade Japanese control. When the Japanese military had difficulty in procuring sufficient foodstuffs, it had the Wheat Flour Control Commission tighten requirements for sales and transport of grain, especially in 1944. For more than 20 *jin* of grain or 10 *jin* of flour or bran, any agent was required to register with a branch of the commission and gain a permission ship for sales or transport. As a consequence, the number of small mills in the Shanghai hinterland grew rapidly. By early 1945 there were 107 small mills in the Jiangwan, Wusong, and Pudong areas, most with three to eight workers and some using stone grinders. Production capacity ranged from 20 to 500 bags per day. The strength of these mills was the ability of their managers to covertly obtain raw materials directly from farmers and to engage in the black market. Tight Japanese controls drove up prices and created a market niche.[40]

COLLABORATION AFTER PEARL HARBOR

In return for restoration of the textile and flour mills, the Japanese required a quid pro quo from the Rongs—public support for the Japanese and the Wang Jingwei regime. Rong Desheng attempted to minimize the family's involvement. Plant managers, most often not of the Rong surname, joined the control organizations of the puppet government. Many of these, such as Tong Luqing and Jiang Junhui, had been employed by Shenxin specifically because of their Japanese connections. Tong and Jiang, for instance, both served on Nanjing's Cotton Control Commission, Tong on the parent Commerce Control Commission. Fuxin's Shi Fuhou joined the Wheat Flour Control Commission.[41]

Despite this cooperation with the Japanese, Rong Desheng strove to keep good relations with Chongqing, particularly after an allied victory looked certain. He sent his son Rong Er'ren, along with a delegation of ten, to Baoji and Chongqing in September 1943 to make contact with Guomindang authorities. Er'ren registered all of the Rongs' property with the Nationalist government to avoid being labeled a traitor. Rong Er'ren had also brought a substantial sum for investment in the interior, setting up a new company (controlled entirely by the Desheng branch of the family) and opening a hemp production factory in Chongqing. Through this somewhat belated move to unoccupied China, the Rongs survived the postwar transition without loss of their property.[42]

WUXI AND WUHAN

Although the Rongs' empire was centered in Shanghai when the war erupted, their native place was Wuxi. Their Shenxin #3 textile mill was then the largest factory in that city, with 71,000 spindles, 1,478 looms, and three electric generators. When the war reached Wuxi, the mill was a total loss; only the steel-and-concrete structure was left standing. The managers spirited some raw materials and equipment out of the city before the Japanese arrived, but Japanese soldiers later found most of this. Although Japanese authorities restored title of Shenxin #3 to the Rongs on June 27, 1943, little remained. Rong Desheng sent his son Rong Yixin to handle the task, but the young Rong could only get 10,000 spindles operating at the site. The mill's electric generators had apparently been removed by Shanhai bōseki. The Rongs approached both the Nanjing government's Ministry of Industry and the Japanese consulate in Shanghai for assistance in regaining this missing equipment but apparently without success. Only in 1947, when the Rongs ordered 40,000 spindles from America and repaired 56,000 was the mill fully operating.[43]

A similar fate befell the two Maoxin flour mills in Wuxi, which before the war had fifty-four grinders and an annual production capacity of 2.8 million bags of flour. In the battle of Wuxi, Maoxin #1 was totally destroyed; Maoxin #2 was heavily damaged and then used as horse stables. Both ceased production after September 1937. The Japanese military authorities wanted to restart the #2 mill to produce flour for their armed forces. In 1939 they approached Rong Desheng about reopening under those terms, a request he rejected. The Japanese then entrusted the facility to a Japanese firm, the Kayū Flour Company (Kayū seifun).[44]

Completely shut out of Wuxi, some of the stockholders in Shenxin #3 and the Maoxin mills moved to Shanghai, where, under the leadership of Rong Hongyuan and Rong Yixin, they organized the very modest Hefeng Dyeing and Weaving Company with a capital investment of only 100,000 yuan. The firm, which opened in January 1939, expanded into new areas of business during Shanghai's "flourishing" period. It was registered as an American firm.[45]

When the Japanese and Wang Jingwei announced their goal of restoring Chinese firms, the Rongs hoped to regain the Maoxin mills. The Kayū firm offered a junior partnership to Rong Desheng in the old Maoxin #2, but he rejected the offer, not wishing to accept that status. When the Rongs' property rights were returned in June 1942, however, the board of directors decided to lease the mill to Kayū. Desheng dispatched his nephew Xiang Jiarui to work out terms. Kayū paid the Rongs rent from May 1942 until May 1944. Overall, the Rongs salvaged little from the enterprises in their native city. With so little at stake, Maoxin suffered few stockholder disputes. Its ownership was also simpler than that of the Shenxin company. In 1940 there were only eight stockholders. Rong Desheng held 45.7 percent of the stock; Zongjing's son Rong Hongyuan held 16.2 percent, sons Hongsan and Hongqing held 15.7 percent each, and the remainder was split among outsiders.[46]

In the first years of the war, Rong losses in Wuxi were partially offset by increased profits from plants in Wuhan. The Rongs had two mills in Wuhan, the Fuxin #5 flour mill and the Shenxin #4 textile mill. The flour mill had opened in 1919 and remained steadily profitable; the textile mill had been established in 1922, in large part to manufacture flour bags, and had experienced considerable financial difficulties. When war erupted, the immediate result was a sharp increase in profits for the textile firm. Shenxin #4, although posting only a modest increase in output, saw profits increase to 1.85 million yuan from less than 500,000 the previous year. The cutoff of competition from the mills of Shanghai, the large needs of the Chinese military, a consequent rapid rise in prices of finished products, and a good supply of raw cotton at modest prices fueled these high profits. Local farmers could not ship their raw cotton down the Yangzi to the traditional markets in Shanghai and Wuxi. The plant succeeded in retiring its debts.[47]

This favorable situation came to a rather sudden end in 1938 as Japanese forces began to close on Wuhan. At this time the textile plant had 50,000 spindles and 875 looms; the flour mill had the capacity to produce 13,500 bags a day. Li Guowei, son-in-law of Rong Desheng, planned to move the factories to the Chongqing area, but many of the Shanghai-based stockholders and Desheng himself objected. Since their continued operations in Shanghai were vulnerable to Japanese pressure, they feared actions which that anger the Japanese. At that point the evacuation of factory equipment to the interior would have required cooperating with the Guomindang's Industry and Mining Adjustment Office. The Shanghai group proposed instead operating the Wuhan plants under Japanese occupation using American registry.[48]

Li ultimately ignored these concerns of the Shanghai group and attempted to move the Wuhan plants to Chongqing. Li's decision may not have been entirely voluntary. When Guomindang authorities had difficulty persuading some of the industrialists to evacuate, they suggested that the army's scorched-earth policy would require destruction of remaining factories. Madame Chiang Kaishek met personally with Zhang Jianhui, a Shenxin manager and also a cousin of Li Guowei, to persuade them to move the plant.

In order to appease the Shanghai partners, Li did agree to use the name Qingxin, not Fuxin or Shenxin, for the Chongqing mills. They could at least maintain the fiction that this was a separate company. For Zhang Jianhui and others in the new factories, however, the Qingxin name was also an indication that the firm had achieved autonomy from the Rong headquarters. Because of the delay these disagreements caused, only a part of the equipment could be moved. Exclusive of factory buildings and raw materials, only 60 percent of the Shenxin #4 materials and 30 percent of Fuxin #5 was evacuated. In delaying, Li discovered that Guomindang military and political groups had monopolized much of the shipping, and Japanese bombing took a heavy toll. Only 200 workers from Wuhan completed the migration, so the lack of skilled workers plagued the reopened plants.[49]

Despite these problems, Li Guowei established two textile mills in the interior, one in Chongqing that eventually would have 10,000 spindles and 80 looms, and one in Baoji, Shaanxi, that would have 20,000 spindles and 400 looms. The flour mill in Chongqing produced 500 bags a day and the mill in Baoji, 3,000. Conditions in the interior were hardly ideal, with a lack of electricity and the threat of Japanese bombing. Indeed, when the Shenxin material first reached Sichuan, its boat was hit by Japanese bombers, scattering the equipment in several places along the riverfront. Later, after the textile mill in Baoji was hit several times, facilities were moved into caves. Li Guowei also erected plants further inland—in Chengdu and Tiansui—to escape Japanese bombs.

Still, because of high demand and the lack of competition in the interior, these industries were very profitable. The company also benefited from currency manipulation and commodity hoarding to maximize its advantage. As Sherman Cochran has noted, "Once Shenxin's equipment was reassembled in Chongqing and Baoji, its management continued through the war to bribe officials, falsify financial records, maintain bank accounts under various names, exaggerate war damages, and hide caches of hoarded goods and raw materials."[50]

This approach enabled the Rong enterprises to evade the taxes and controls of the Chongqing government. Li was able to open an additional cotton mill and a flour mill in Chengdu and a paper mill in Baoji, as well as organize an ironworks. When the war was over, Li bragged to Rong Er'ren that he had one million U.S. dollars in foreign exchange. Li's success did not escape the notice of the Rongs. As economic conditions in Shanghai deteriorated, the profits of the operations in the interior held more import.

One goal of Rong Desheng in dispatching Er'ren to Chongqing was to regain control of the enterprises managed by Li Guowei. Er'ren discussed with Li plans for a reunited Greater Shenxin company for the postwar period with a strong central headquarters, but Li was not supportive. When in March 1944 Rong Er'ren issued his draft plans for Shenxin and Fuxin/Maoxin for the postwar world, he called for massive expansion of both textile and flour mills. These expensive plans were funded in part through the foreign exchange reserves accumulated by Li Guowei. The latter, however, was reluctant to surrender control of facilities he had developed and capital he had accumulated. Li felt that he alone had been responsible for rescuing the assets from Wuhan, with no help from Shanghai. Further, the mills and factories that Li controlled were a much larger portion of total Rong holdings than in prewar days. As a consequence, Li Guowei felt his position within the group was much stronger, and he was less deferential to Rong Desheng and his sons and nephews.[51]

Even as allied victory moved closer, however, production difficulties in the interior mounted. The Japanese success in Operation Ichigō, particularly in the spring of 1944 in Henan, which was a cotton producing area, endangered the supply of cotton to the interior plants.[52]

A few other industrialists from the Rong group made it to Free China. Xue Mingjian, a native of Wuxi, had been an assistant manager for Shenxin and a close associate of Rong Zhongjing and Desheng. He and Rong Desheng had established the Yunli Industrial Company, which produced carbonic acid, bleaching powder, caustic soda, calcium carbide, and other products. By the war period, the firm had six plants and a capital investment of several million yuan. When Wuxi fell, the Japanese seized all of the Yunli property. Xue left for the interior, where he took advantage of connections with Guomindang leader Wu Zhihui. He rebuilt Yunli with his and Wu's capital and obtained support from Li Wujui, the former manager of Shenxin #4. With good connections to the Guomindang, Xue was able to move into textile and flour mills.[53]

The end of the war did not heal the breach between the Shanghai and

Chongqing branches of the Rong system, nor that between Zongjing's children and Desheng's. Rong Er'ren pushed for a Greater Shenxin that would reunite the group in the postwar era. As victory appeared inevitable on August 10, 1945, the Rongs did reorganize the general headquarters and registered it as a limited liability corporation under the Republic of China's company law. Called the Maoxin Fuxin Shenxin Flour and Textile Company, Ltd. (Maoxin, Fuxin, Shenxin Mianfen Fangzhi Gufen Youxian Gongsi), it could in theory bring the Rong empire back together. But this registration was undertaken primarily to protect Rong property from being confiscated as enemy property, not to restructure the firm.[54]

Immediately after the war, both Rong Er'ren and Rong Desheng presented the family with new plans for revision of the firm. Er'ren, as before, advocated a strong general headquarters, with firm control over all branches of Shenxin, Fuxin, and Maoxin. Hongyuan opposed this, suggesting a much more restricted general headquarters for Shenxin only. Even Er'ren's father, Rong Desheng, felt his son's plan was not workable, and both Li Guowei and Wang Yuqing rejected it as well. As a consequence, no real structural change won approval and the Rong empire remained divided into three segments. The central headquarters did not have controlling interest in the individual plants, and mill managers were unwilling to surrender the autonomy they had garnered during the war. The general headquarters was thus unable to assert its control and remained only the nominal leader of the group.[55]

Rong Hongyuan was apparently nervous about Rong Er'ren's status. Because Er'ren had been in Free China, at least in the latter part of the war, there was always the danger he could label the Shanghai group as collaborators and confiscate some of their holdings. To prevent such an occurrence, Rong Hongyuan began to cultivate T. V. Soong and his brother T. A. Soong. He visited Nanjing and met with the Soongs in order to block any action by Er'ren.[56]

The Rong empire thus survived the war but was divided into segments. Zhongjing's eldest son, Rong Hongyuan, was the general manager of the central office but directly managed only Shenxin #1, #6, #7, and #9. Wang Yuqing managed the Fuxin flour mills, except #5, which was affiliated with Hongyuan's group. Desheng's sons and sons-in-law, led by Rong Er'ren, managed Shenxin #2, #3, and #5, as well as the Maoxin flour mills and the Hefeng Company. The Fuxin #5 flour mill, together with the Shenxin #4 mill, remained in Li Guowei's group, which also included plants in Chongqing, Chengdu, and Baoji. The dream of re-creating Greater Shenxin when the war ended was not to be.[57]

Still, despite the lack of unity, the Rong family emerged from the conflict as a major force in China. Through their early use of foreign registry and later substantial cooperation with puppet authorities, the Rong enterprises survived the war and even profited, especially before December 1941. After the war, the Rongs largely avoided being labeled traitors and losing their property. True, there were many problems in the postwar period. Rong Desheng would be kidnapped on April 20, 1946, and held until May 28, when the family paid a ransom of US $500,000. Rong Hongyuan was arrested in 1948 in Shanghai for unauthorized purchase of Hong Kong currency. After two months in jail (and payment of yet another US $500,000), he received a suspended sentence and departed for the Crown Colony. The wealth of the Rongs made the family a target.[58]

Despite these setbacks, Shenxin, Fuxin, and Maoxin began to recover from the war. By 1947 Shenxin mills had 596,000 spindles (compared to about 620,000 before the war) as well as 4,100 looms (compared to 5,300 in 1936). These were not all in full operation. In 1947 Shenxin mills produced only 89,510 reels of cotton yarn compared to 316,695 in 1936. Still, the Rongs were well on the way to recovery, with most Shenxin units planning expansion until late in the civil war. The company petitioned Guomindang banks for recovery loans, and Shenxin #9 had purchased property in the Xujiahui section of Shanghai for a new factory. By 1949 the Shenxin group headed by Rong Hongyuan held almost 340,800 spindles; that by Rong Desheng, 216,900; and that by Li Guowei, 83,000.[59]

When the Communist Revolution occurred, the Rong family split into many directions, paralleling their movements during the war. This strategy divided the family but also gave it opportunities to survive in different environments. As a consequence the Rong family name remains prominent both within the People's Republic of China and without. Rong Zongjing's son Hongqing and son-in-law Wang Yuncheng became major textile industrialists in Hong Kong. Li Guowei established the Kowloon Mill using capital from Shenxin #4 but remained in China, serving in various official capacities in Hubei and Beijing. Rong Hongyuan opened a mill in Hong Kong and then relocated to Brazil, where he focused on the flour milling industry. Hongsan went to the United States. Rong Desheng's branch set up a factory in Thailand in March 1949 managed by Yanren, while Er'ren moved to America and Hongren to Australia. Not all of these efforts succeeded. The Thai mill failed in 1950, and an effort by Hongyuan to set up a mill in Taiwan was dashed because he could not secure electricity for the venture.[60] Rong Desheng himself retired in 1949 at age 74 and died three years later. In September 1985, the Wuxi City government held a special commemorative service in honor of the 110th anniversary of Desheng's birth.[61]

Perhaps the most famous of Desheng's sons was Rong Yiren, who remained in China. As his older brother Er'ren wrote in 1949 from Hong Kong, "One stays in China; one goes overseas. If there are no problems, then I can return."[62] But soon the wall between the capitalist world and People's China became a major barrier. Er'ren went on to the United States while Yiren found a prominent (if somewhat volatile) career in industry and politics. As Tahirih V. Lee has recently written, "The Rong family's acumen and its networks built in Shanghai during the Republican period survived fifty years of Communist rule to give rise to mainland China's most powerful promoter of capitalist-style economic development in the 1980s and 1990s—Vice Premier Rong Yiren."[63] The fourth son of Desheng, Yiren survived some difficult years during the Cultural Revolution to emerge in 1978 as a vice chairman of the Standing Committee of the National People's Congress.

Rong Yiren's political rise opened the door to a renewed Rong prominence in China. He headed the China International Trust and Investment Corporation (CITIC, Zhongguo guoji xintuo zi gongsi), which became a major player in China's economy. Family members thus had access to strong government connections. Yiren's son Rong Zhijian, for instance, moved to Hong Kong in 1978 following a few rough years during the Cultural Revolution. Tapping into Rong connections and capital, he organized a joint venture in 1982 with IBM, including a plant in San Jose, California. Eventually he came to head the CITIC branch in Hong Kong, CITIC Pacific.[64]

Many of Rong Desheng's grandsons are prominent. One of the most successful has been Rong Zhixin, son of Weiren, who moved to Hong Kong and studied electrical engineering in the United States. After a brief stint working in America, he returned to Hong Kong, where in 1960 he founded a company that distributed American cigarettes. Ten years later the American Lorillard Company bought Zhixin out, providing a capital base for new investments. In 1975 he and some associates began a computer firm (Rongwen keji youxian gongsi), which went public in 1982. When China began to open up under Deng Xiaoping's reforms, Zhixin began reinvesting in the mainland, establishing production plants in Shanghai and Guangzhou.[65]

Another grandson, Rong Zhiqin, had been part of the Brazil branch of the family. The opening of China fueled his interest, which led to eight visits to China during the early 1980s. Eventually he set up a joint venture in Wuxi to manufacture shoes, and pursued other interests in the lower Yangzi area. He moved his family to Hong Kong from Brazil to be closer to the Rong revival.[66] The Rong clan now extends to six generations, with more than 400 Rong relatives scattered over the world. On June 15, 1986, nearly 200 gathered in Beijing for a reunion that included a personal greeting by Deng Xiaoping. Although the gathering included sightseeing trips to Wuxi and Shanghai, the Rong clan is obviously not the tightly knit group of Zongjing and Desheng's day. The long years of separation created barriers between a figure like Rong Yiren, who had become for all intents and purposes an official of the People's Republic, and someone such as his brother Er'ren, who was a retired industrialist in Brazil. The family unit provided a basis for the earlier unity but could not bridge such large gaps. Indeed, the split within the family clearly dated from the wartime era and the death of Zongjing.[67]

The experience of the Rong family during the war does not really fit the "patriotic nationalist narrative." The Rongs made little effort to relocate in the interior, preferring the profits and security of island Shanghai. Although the Rongs resisted dealing with the Japanese as long as possible, they eventually cooperated when return of properties became a real possibility. Their earlier reticence, in fact, might be construed as fear of assassination by Guomindang agents and the poor terms initially offered by the Japanese, rather than nationalism. Their overtures to the Chiang government come late, when an Allied victory seemed likely.

Similarly, the war experience reveals both the strengths and weaknesses of the Chinese family firm. Without the flexibility of the family structure, the Rongs might have been less able to survive the war. With part of the industrial empire destroyed, part seized, part being relocated in caves in the interior, and part operating full throttle in island Shanghai, the loose organization of the business aided in the Rong's financial survival. Still, the death of Rong Zongjing opened the door to infighting among the Rongs themselves and between the Rongs and minority shareholders. The strains of war were exacerbated by the death of the patriarch. The pattern of division and splitting risks, practiced during the war era, was followed after 1949 as family members were spread from Shanghai, Hong Kong, America, Brazil, and elsewhere. Amazingly, the Rong name retains its luster half a century after the Communist Revolution.

CHAPTER 7

Textile and Consumer Industries in the War Era

Beyond the Rong Model

The experiences of the Rong family, although revealing much about war-time conditions, were not typical. The Rongs were simply too large for this to be the case. In the Rongs' situation, some plants were destroyed, some were occupied and given to Japanese firms, some relocated in the interior, and some flourished in island Shanghai. Most Chinese firms were much smaller and experienced only one piece of this scenario. Yet an analysis of experiences of other textile and consumer industry groups during the war era demonstrates some of the same patterns of the Rong experience. The nature of the Chinese business firm conditioned the response to war. Most industrialists placed survival of the firm and the family ahead of abstract concepts of nationalism.

THE GUO BROTHERS AND THE YONG'AN GROUP

Perhaps the closest parallel to the Rong group in pre-Communist China was the Guo family's Yong'an group. Like the Rongs, the Guos (usually referred to as Kwok in English) were headed by two brothers, Guo Le (Kwok Lock or James Gocklock) and Guo Quan (Kwok Chin or Philip Gockchin), although there were several younger brothers as well. As with the Rongs, the Guos became major textile magnates. On the eve of the war, the five Yong'an mills in Shanghai, together with a dyeing plant, made the Guos second only to the Rongs among Chinese textile indus-trialists. In sharp contrast to the Rongs, however, the Guos came from a base in marketing and department stores and moved into textiles only later in their career.

Although natives of Xiangshan (now Zhongshan) county in Guangdong, the Guos actually got their start in Sydney, Australia, where Guo Le had emigrated in 1892 to join an older brother. His younger brother, Guo Quan, emigrated first to Honolulu and then joined his brother in Sydney in 1899. Guo Le founded the Yong'an Fruit Company in 1897, which imported and wholesaled bananas and other produce in Australia. Eventually three other Guo brothers joined the firm, which even became involved in banana cultivation in Fiji. The Guos then expanded into general retail, importing Chinese products for sale to Chinese workers in Australia. The Guos gradually moved into financial activities, mostly by providing a reliable remittance service for Chinese who wished to send income back to China. Many of the Chinese immigrants in Australia had limited literacy, spoke little English, and suffered racial discrimination. They were reticent to use regular Australian banks for sending money to China. The Guos, natives of the Guangdong, as were most Chinese in Sydney, developed a reliable remittance service. In doing so, the Guos gained access to substantial capital flows, which they used to their advantage.[1]

The Guos nonetheless realized that business opportunities for Chinese in Australia at that time were limited and planned investment in China and Hong Kong. Perhaps influenced by the actions of Ma Yingbiao, a former employer, who returned to Hong Kong to set up the Sincere Department Store (Xianshi baihuo gongsi), the Guos decided to follow suit. The Guos raised about HK $160,000 in Sydney to fund the creation of the Yong'an (better known in English as Wing On) Department Store in Hong Kong in August 1918. Both Yong'an and the Sincere Company were large, well-designed department stores, modeled on stores in Sydney such as Anthony Hordern and Sons and completely unlike traditional Chinese shops. By offering elegant displays of goods in window cases, special sales and promotions, a courteous staff, and a one-price policy, Yong'an became a major retailer in Hong Kong. By 1933, its anchor store in Hong Kong Central had more than 40,000 square feet of floor space.[2]

The Yong'an Company began as a partnership, with the two Guo brothers as the dominant partners and other family members and associates as minor partners. Guo Le was chairman of the board and Guo Quan the general manager. In 1916 the company was reorganized as a limited liability corporation with a capital of HK $2 million. Control of the firm remained in the hands of senior partners, however. And as Yen

Ching-hwang has noted, "The employees of the Wing On Company after 1916 still viewed it as a Kwok family-controlled enterprise and Kwok Chin's General Managership still commanded the authority of ownership." Wellington Chan, in his study of the group, similarly concludes, "In spite of its 'public' nature, the Wing On Company's shareholding remained, at least through the 1940s, in the hands of the Guo brothers and their original partners."[3]

The great success of the department store led the Guo brothers to open new businesses in collateral areas. Yong'an opened a native bank (in Xiangshan county); hotels in Hong Kong, Guangzhou, and Wuzhou; a travel company; and (in 1933) a modern bank, the Wing On Commercial and Savings Bank, Ltd., of Hong Kong. Perhaps the most innovative enterprises were the Wing On Fire and Marine Insurance, founded in 1918, and Wing On Life Assurance Company, founded in 1925. Both types of insurance were relatively novel in China, but the Guos' overseas experience convinced them of a potential demand for these services in China. Yong'an also owned substantial commercial property in Hong Kong, and income from rents would be a major source of revenue for the parent firm.[4]

Although they had a solid base in Hong Kong, Sydney, and elsewhere, the Guos sought to establish themselves in Shanghai, which was considered China's economic center in the pre-1949 era. Shortly after Yong'an Hong Kong became a public corporation in 1916, the Guo brothers began to discuss raising capital for a Shanghai operation. Eventually, HK \$2.5 million was raised for the new company, with HK \$670,000 coming from the Guos and most of the remainder from overseas Chinese. In 1917 the Guos arranged for a property on Nanjing Road in Shanghai, then as now the premier shopping street in China. On September 5, 1918, the Shanghai store opened to great success. The company stressed high-quality merchandise, much of it foreign, as well as a strong emphasis on staff training and indoctrination, a somewhat novel concept in China. By the early 1920s, the Shanghai Yong'an Department Store was extraordinarily profitable.[5]

On paper, each of these companies was organized as a separate corporation with independent stockholders and a board of directors. In reality, Yong'an operated as one group. Usually, Guo Le was established as the chair of the board of directors and Guo Quan was listed as general manager. Often another figure, either a younger Guo brother or nephew, was the assistant manager. Funds were freely transferred from one unit to another as needed. As Yen Ching-hwang points out, an "obvious advantage of diversification was the accumulation and inter-firm dispersal of capital. The surplus capital in either the Wing On [Yong'an] parent body in Hong Kong or the Wing On Company in Shanghai could be absorbed into the subsidiary companies." The generous profits from the Yong'an Department stores thus provided low-cost capital for expansion into new areas. The result was a virtual interlocking of capital among the various portions of the Guo empire. During 1930 and 1931, for instance, the Yong'an Department Store in Shanghai invested 425,000 yuan in the fire and marine insurance company, 310,000 yuan in Yong'an [Wing On] Bank in Hong Kong, and 202,000 yuan in the parent company in Hong Kong.[6]

As Wellington Chan concludes, "The Guo brothers by the early 1920s had fashioned out a complex multi-unit organisation that bound its subsidiaries and affiliates together through the use of interlocking directorships and inter-company loans whenever they were needed. . . . In this sense, Guo Luo [Le] and Guo Chuan and their Wing On group of companies were probably as close as any other enterprise group in China at the time to forming a consolidation of capital and control."[7]

The makeup of investors in the Yong'an Company was key to Guo control. In analyzing the stockholders in the Shanghai department store, Wellington Chan points out that the Guo Brothers and the Hong Kong company held only about one-fourth of the stock. An additional one-twelfth was held by old Guo partners. The remaining two-thirds was held by approximately 1,400 stockholders, most of whom owned only a few shares. In raising capital for their Shanghai venture, the Guos had turned to the vast array of old customers among overseas Chinese, most of whom had deep trust of the Guos and the Yong'an name. These investors were ideal, for they provided a large amount of capital, which was critical to the start of the expensive Shanghai store. At the same time, none held large numbers of shares and most lived overseas or in Hong Kong. They did not pose a challenge to Guo control; yet they provided a ready source of capital. In contrast to entrepreneurs such as the Rongs, who had to turn to expensive bank loans to finance expansion, the Guos had a large pool of capital on which to draw at a relatively low cost.[8]

This access to low-cost capital permitted the Guos to venture into a relatively new area—textile manufacturing. Although they had purchased a small knitting factory in Hong Kong in 1919 that produced underwear, the Guos' experience had mostly been related to sales, marketing, and finance. Yet the rapid expansion of the textile industry in China during and immediately after World War I and the anti-Japanese boycotts of

1919 convinced the Guos that this would be a profitable area. In June 1921 they announced the formation of the Yong'an Textile Manufacturing Company of Shanghai [Yong'an shachang; later Yong'an fangzhi gongsi]. Shares were offered for sale at Yong'an Department stores in Shanghai, Canton, Hong Kong, and Sydney. They were snapped up by their usual supporters. When the firm began production in late 1922, the Shanghai concern was capitalized at 6 million yuan. The Guo family subscribed to less than 3 percent of the capital; slightly less than 20 percent came from other Yong'an companies. Yet the block of Guo/Yong'an shares and the large number of small, scattered shareholders meant that the Guos retained full control, as they had in other enterprises. Guo Le chaired the board of directors. A younger Guo brother, Guo Shun, served as the general manager.[9]

In the 1920s, Yong'an Textiles was very successful. By the early 1930s the company expanded to include five main textile mills, one dyeing mill, and an electric power generating plant. The firm employed 14,000 and had 240,000 spindles and 2,000 looms. The capital investment was doubled to 12 million yuan, making the Guos' operation second only to the Rongs among Chinese industrialists.[10] Yet the Guos' foray into textile manufacturing was not without its problems. The Guos lacked expertise in the technology of manufacturing yet were reluctant to bring in complete outsiders. Eventually a nephew, Guo Dihuo (son of the eldest Guo brother who had died earlier in Sydney), was dispatched to the United States to study. He returned to Shanghai and in 1929 at the young age of twenty-five sui was made assistant general manger of Yong'an Textiles. Dihuo worked to improve the technical quality of the company's production, purchasing American, British, and Germany equipment and employing returned students from the United States and Britain as engineers in his factories.[11]

Trouble would nonetheless plague Yong'an Textiles in the 1930s. When the January 28th Incident occurred in 1932, both the Yong'an #2 mill and #4 mill were heavily damaged by fighting and fires. Total losses of Yong'an Textiles were estimated at 1.8 million yuan. Then the combined effects of the world depression and American silver purchase policy dampened demand in the mid-1930s. Like the Rongs, the Guos found themselves with too much capacity and too little demand. Unlike the Rongs, the Guos had greater access to capital. Both the Shanghai and Hong Kong branches of the department store provided a capital infusion. Yet other sectors of the Guo empire suffered, particularly their bank

in Hong Kong. Late in the 1930s, Yong'an textiles had to seek loans outside of the Guo group.[12]

The Guos turned to the Bank of China and T. V. Soong for liquidity.
Soong headed the Bank of China and, as former minister of finance and
brother-in-law of Chiang Kaishek, had the clout to rescue Yong'an textiles. Soong also headed his own semi-private company, the China Development Finance Corporation (Zhongguo jianshe yin gongsi), which became very active in acquiring companies during the 1935–1937 period.
Soong apparently had been eyeing the Guo properties for some time. Eventually Yong'an Textiles borrowed 5 million yuan from the Bank of China,
mortgaging the mills, some commercial property, and even the private
homes of the Guo brothers in the upscale Jing'an section of Shanghai. The
company used the loan to issue industrial bonds in August 1936, which
reinfused Yong'an Textiles with cash. For his part in the deal, T. V. Soong
was apparently allowed to buy stock in the department store and textile
mills at a reduced price, and his China Development Finance Corporation purchased company bonds at a discount rate. Soong's China Development Finance Corporation dispatched two advisers to the Yong'an
group, one of whom was Soong himself.[13]

In 1936 as China's urban economy revived, Yong'an Textiles had both
the liquidity and the market to recover. The Guos' expansion into textiles, however, suggests some of the limitations of the family firm as a
form of business organization. The diversification policy of the Guo
brothers had worked well as long as they had expanded into collateral
areas. When they moved into a new field, manufacturing, they ran into
problems. The easy access to capital investment through the support of
overseas stockholders might even have been a detriment because it made
expansion possible at such a low cost. Indeed, this pattern has repeated
itself in Asia in more recent times. In the late 1990s, the sudden con-
traction in the economies of previously booming countries such as Thailand, Malaysia, Indonesia, and South Korea, as well as (to a much lesser
extent) Singapore, Hong Kong, and Taiwan, provided a jolt to the "Asian
economic miracle." In retrospect, many economists believe that businesses in the area expanded and diversified too rapidly, creating substantial overcapacity. An enormous infusion of global capital into the
area provided the source of the expansion without really requiring businessmen to assess the actual costs of the capital being used.[14] The Guos
seem to have fallen victim to that syndrome in their diversification before 1932.

When war erupted, the Guos had both strengths and weaknesses. On the plus side, they were a very diverse company with assets scattered in Hong Kong, Australia, London, and the Pacific as well as China. Although each portion of the empire was organized separately as a limited liability corporation, the company actually functioned as a family firm in most respects and could move capital from one unit to the next with limited worry about stockholder rights. On the negative side, the company had experienced financial difficulties with its large textile division and compromised Guo control to some extent. The company's assets, large department stores and textile mills, were also vulnerable to the destructions of war.

THE YONG'AN GROUP AT WAR

The initial days of the war were a disaster for Yong'an. In the accidental bombing on Nanjing Road on August 14, 1937, one of the explosives landed between the Yong'an and Sincere Department stores. Hundreds of shoppers, employees, and passersby were injured or killed. Yong'an lost fifteen staff members and scores of others were injured. All of the Yong'an store windows were blown out and merchandise was destroyed. Damage was estimated at 410,000 yuan.[15] Yet after a few days the Yong'an Department store reopened, and within a few months business began to boom. During the solitary island period, Yong'an did quite well, in fact. The shortage of commodities drove up prices, while the swollen refugee population kept demand high. Although some Chinese products from the interior were unavailable, foreign products could still be imported through international shipping. Since Yong'an had generally marketed many foreign products and specialized in more expensive items, it kept shelves full of desirable goods. In 1938 sales totaled 10.5 million yuan, and the profit margin was 13.33 percent. The following year sales rose to 18.2 million yuan and the profit margin to 17.26 percent before slipping to 13.19 percent in 1940 on sales of 34.6 million. In the last year of the solitary island, 1941, sales increased to 68.9 million and profits were more than 25 percent.[16]

There were difficulties, however. The outbreak of the war in Europe drove some products off the market. Foreign exchange shortages made purchase of imported goods more difficult as the war continued. The Shanghai department store had been registered as a British company, as had the Hong Kong firms, but a dispute led to termination of this connection. The Guos felt that the British consul in Shanghai had done nothing to protect their property. They approached the American consulate in Shanghai in an effort to register the firm, but the United States required that substantial numbers of the board of directors and management be American citizens for this process to be completed. After much effort in rounding up suitable persons to be added to the board, the Shanghai Yong'an Department Store was registered as an American company in July 1939. Guo Le, the patriarch, departed China for America, where he would remain until his death in 1956. The elder Guo established Yong'an offices in San Francisco and New York, in part to supply commodities to Shanghai.[17]

Yong'an Textiles in Shanghai did not fare as well as the department store. Of the five mills and dyeing plant in the greater Shanghai area, only one, Yong'an #3, which was located on Markham Road in the foreign zone, remained in Guo hands. Yong'an #1 in the Yangshupu sector was occupied by the Japanese and used as a field hospital. Its equipment (nearly 50,000 spindles and 1,200 looms) was damaged or removed during this period. Neither it nor the adjacent dyeing plant would resume significant operations until after the war. Yong'an #2 and #4 were both located at Wusong and had a combined total of about 120,000 spindles. Both mills were heavily damaged in the fighting and captured by the Japanese, who stripped supplies and equipment from the site. Yong'an #5, also in Yangshupu, was seized as well. Mills #2 and #4 were entrusted to the Yūhō bōseki kaisha; Toyoda textiles received permission to rehabilitate Yong'an #1.[18] The Guos retained control of only Yong'an #3, which was located in the International Settlement. As with the Rongs, the Guos did relatively well during the solitary island period, with demand and prices high. Yet the #3 mill was small, with only 50,000 spindles and 200 looms, which limited its success.[19]

After Pearl Harbor the Japanese seized both the Yong'an Department store and the #3 mill. The American registration now led Yong'an to be considered "enemy property." On March 25, 1942, the Japanese announced that three "foreign" department stores, Yong'an, the Sincere Company, and the Xinxin Company, would be placed under joint Japanese control. The Guos quickly struggled to regain their property. With Guo Le in America, Guo Linshuang (son of Guo Quan) managed the store. He petitioned the Wang Jingwei government to have the American registration replaced by a Chinese one. Finally in April 1943 Nanjing registered the company, which returned to Guo control in June 1943. (Guo Linshuang later claimed that the Japanese stripped company funds and placed them in the Bank of Taiwan).[20]

The glory days of Shanghai Yong'an were long gone, however. The supply of foreign goods had dried up with the outbreak of the Pacific War. Hyperinflation and the collapse of the economy left few goods on the shelf and few customers able to purchase them. The company had to provide commodities such as cloth and soap at low, fixed prices to the Japanese as part of the procurement system. Profits of the Yong'an store (adjusted for inflation to reflect 1936 valued yuan) plummeted. In 1936 the Shanghai store had garnered profits of nearly 1.3 million yuan (see table 5). During the solitary island era the company exceeded this figure in both 1939 and 1941. By the time the Guos regained control, profits were only a small fraction of this amount—for 1944 the equivalent of only 45,000 yuan measured in its 1936 value. Perhaps the surprise is that the Guos earned any profit whatsoever.

The pattern at Yong'an Textiles was similar. The initial concern of Guo Shun, as with the Rongs, was to regain possession of the property the family had held during the island period, in this case Yong'an #3. Only later would the Guos attempt to get the mills seized in 1937. Guo Shun, in fact, took a very public lead in negotiations with the Japanese and the Wang government. Guo's efforts led to the rendition of Yong'an #3 on May 22, 1942, in a ceremony that also saw the return of six other properties, including the Rongs' Shenxin #2 and #9. Guo Shun agreed to cooperate with the Wang regime and joined the Nanjing government's Cotton Control Commission as well as the board of supervisors of the parent Commerce Control Commission. When additional factories were returned to Chinese owners in July 1943, Guo Shun led the ceremony in thanking the Japanese.[21]

Behind the scenes negotiations were difficult. Yong'an mills #2 and #4 had been taken over by the Japanese Yūhō textiles, which had invested in repairing the facilities. Guo Shun finally agreed to a joint venture with the Japanese firm. Mills #2 and #4 were reorganized as the Yongfeng Company (Yongfeng qiye gongsi in Chinese; Eihō kigyō kōgyo in Japanese). Guo Shun served as chair of the board of directors; the vice chair, general manger and key personnel were all Japanese who essentially retained control. Guo Shun was more direct and flexible in his dealings with the Japanese than the Rongs. It is difficult to directly establish a motive, but one factor was probably key. The Guos were deeply concerned with regaining the Yong'an Department Store, which they finally did in June 1943. They showed greater flexibility in textiles perhaps in part because that portion of their enterprise group had not been highly profitable prior to the war. In any event, the Guos were no more successful than the Rongs in operating textile mills in Shanghai during the

TABLE 5. PROFITS OF THE SHANGHAI
YONG'AN (WING ON) DEPARTMENT STORE

Year	Profits in 1,000 yuan	Profits in yuan*
1936	1,299	1,299
1937	658	553
1938	1,398	978
1939	3,141	1,354
1940	4,570	903
1941	17,275	1,572
1942	17,657	511
1943	24,945	174
1944	45,126	45

SOURCE: Shanghai shehui kexue yuan, jingji yanjiu suo, ed., *Shanghai yongan gongsi de chansheng, fazhan he gaizao*, pp. 178–79.
*Discounted for inflation to 1936 value.

last months of the war. The strictures of the Japanese commodity control demands and the collapse of the economy left the mills mostly idle.[22]

The Guo family survived the war; Yong'an [Wing On] remains a dominant name in Hong Kong today in banking, real estate, and department stores. Although its Hong Kong properties were confiscated during the occupation, Yong'an quickly regained its position after the Japanese surrender. The firm did lose control of its Shanghai properties in the socialist era, yet today Yong'an has actually returned to the People's Republic as an investor. Yong'an's survival in the war was quite different from the Rong group. Because textiles were only a small part of the empire, their loss did not stymie the Guos. Because they had a strong base in Hong Kong, Australia, and overseas, they could shift resources out of China. Indeed, the patriarch himself left Asia entirely for America. The Guo family in no way conformed to the "patriotic nationalist narrative." Moving to the interior was never an option for a business that dealt in department stores and real estate. Although the Guos avoided working with Japanese before Pearl Harbor, once the Japanese occupied Shanghai and Hong Kong, the Guos were willing to collaborate. Guo Shun negotiated with both the Japanese authorities and the Nanjing government. His nephew Guo Dihuo was likewise cooperative. As with the Rongs, the cooperation brought little to the Guos except survival. They earned little profit from 1942 to 1945.

The Guos and the Rongs were similar in one other key aspect: both were at a similar stage in their evolution. Both had been founded by brothers, and both were at the point of turning over the enterprise to the second generation. Both had developed as pure entrepreneurs, not relying on government connections. Indeed, both attempted to evade political authorities as much as possible. By dint of shrewd maneuvering, hard work, and timing, both had parlayed their initial small businesses into vast business empires. Yet the differences are pronounced as well. The Guos had better luck perhaps. Both brothers survived into the 1950s to provide leadership for their group during and after the war. Even from America and Hong Kong, when they were out of touch with Shanghai during the Pacific War, the elder Guos' presence was felt. Guo Linshuang realized that ultimately the elders would retain control. The unfortunate death of Rong Zongjing, by contrast, created a leadership vacuum in the Rong group just at a time when the war imposed great stress. As with a monarchical system, the family enterprise group was subject to the whims of the fate of the individual.

HENGFENG TEXTILES

Enterprises like the Guos' and Rongs' were not the only modern businesses in China. There was another type of business that had been created with government involvement. These businesses dated from the *guandu shangban* (official supervision and merchant management) enterprises of the late Qing era. Many of these had initially flourished with government patronage but had suffered during the Republican era. Often in the case of manufacturing concerns, their equipment and method of production were dated. Nonetheless several key enterprises remained in 1937, although one of the most prominent, the China Merchants Steam Navigation Company, was essentially destroyed early in the conflict.[23]

One enterprise of this type was the Hengfeng textile mill located in the Yangshupu zone of Shanghai. This plant had its origins in the *guandu shangban* system. Originally named the Huaxin mill, it was reorganized in 1891 as a subsidiary of Sheng Xuanhuai's Huasheng company and is generally considered the first modern Chinese-owned textile mill. A principal backer of the Huaxin mill was Nie Qigui, the son-in-law of Zeng Guofan. Although the firm did have profitable periods, especially during World War I and in 1929–1930, it suffered substantial losses in the early 1930s, when it purchased large quantities of cotton in the United States just before prices collapsed. The firm received a loan of 3.5 million yuan from the Zhejiang Xingye Bank (called the National Commercial Bank in English), but to no avail. The mill closed in 1935, idling

3,000 workers. The older enterprises of this era had difficulty competing with Chinese entrepreneurs such as the Guos and Rongs, not to mention Japanese mills located in Shanghai.[24]

Eager to recover its investment, the National Commercial Bank
worked with the China Cotton Company (Zhongguo mianye gongsi), a
semi-official holding enterprise controlled by T. V. Soong, to reorganize
the firm in the spring of 1936. It reopened as the Hengfeng Mill, with
95 percent of any profits to be divided between the bank and the company, and 5 percent going to the Nie family for a three-year period. When
business conditions improved in 1936 and early 1937, the mill began to
turn a profit. Indeed, in the last half of 1936 the mill had netted a million yuan. After war erupted, the Japanese occupied the Yangshupu area.
Although the mill escaped serious damage, it was forced to close for several months because the Japanese military blockaded the area and workers could not reach the plant.

As with so many other plants, the management tried to protect the
firm by reorganizing it as a British concern. On paper the British-owned
Industrial Development Company leased everything from the National
Commercial Bank, which then held all of the stock as collateral. A British
"front man" was provided. Japanese authorities refused to accept this
arrangement, which they considered a ruse. In May 1938 the Japanese
military seized the firm and entrusted its management to the Daikō Textile Company (whose parent company was Dai Nippon). It began limited production under this new direction in October 1938, operating
about two-thirds of the approximately 55,000 spindles. The Daikō company sent nineteen people to the plant, including the factory head and
technical personnel.[25]

Yet Japanese authorities sought some formal, if perhaps nominal, Chinese participation in Hengfeng's management. The background of the Nie
family made them desirable as collaborators. As early as December 1937,
the leader of the Japanese Mill Owners Association, Funatsu Tatsuichirō,
pressed Nie Lusheng to cooperate publicly with the Japanese. He hinted
of possible loans as compensation for cooperation and of an intimidat-
ing blacklisting if he refused. Yet as was generally the case, few Chinese
capitalists (even those with political backgrounds) collaborated with the
Japanese before Pearl Harbor, both out of fear of assassination by Guomindang agents and because of the poor terms offered by the Japanese.

After the Japanese inaugurated the great departure and made more
attractive offers, many Chinese wavered. The Nies began negotiations
with the Japanese in autumn 1942. In February 1943, the Nie family and

Daikō agreed to reorganize the Hengfeng enterprise, with the Nies becoming minority owners. The reorganized firm would be registered as a Japanese company with the Japanese consulate, in exchange for which the Nie family would receive fair compensation, based on an estimate by a Japanese military specialist. Ultimately the Nie family received 830,000 yen as well as stock in the new firm, 135,000 yen of which they sold to the Daikō company.

With this cash settlement, the Nie family cleared the debts to the National Commercial Bank. The Nie family also received a share of profits, as well as returns on their stock, in the period from May 1938 up until August 1945. After the war, the Nies acknowledged making 1.45 million yen in profit. In the later months of the war, their earnings dropped, as did those of nearly all Chinese industrialists. The shortage of cotton and coal was compounded by American bombing, which increased the difficulty of workers who commuted to the plant.[26]

What did the Japanese receive from the settlement? Essentially they purchased the public support of the Nie family for the puppet government, no small matter given the prestige of the clan, as well as their business expertise and ties. Members of the Nie family, including Nie Lusheng and Nie Guangqi, served on the board of directors of the reorganized Hengfeng Company, under the chairmanship of Yamadera Gengo. In addition, the Nies joined the agencies of the Wang Jingwei government. Nie Lusheng, for instance, chaired for a time the Cotton Control Commission. After the war, the Guomindang labeled Nie Lusheng as a collaborator. He stepped down from his business posts, and his older brother Nie Yuntai was brought out of retirement to salvage the family name. From the family's point of view, they had essentially lost control of their firm to the National Commercial Bank and T. V. Soong's China Cotton Company. Collaboration with the Japanese was their only avenue to regain their status as industrialists and their lost profits.[27]

The experience and actions of the Nies therefore differ sharply from those of the Rongs and Guos. The Nies came more from a political than an entrepreneurial background. They were similar to those old bureaucrats and warlords bypassed by the Guomindang who came forward to work with the Japanese. They clearly fit the profile of collaborators.

NANTONG–DASHENG TEXTILE MILLS

The Dasheng (Dah Sun) textile mills near the city of Nantong were in similar circumstances to the Hengfeng mill. Dasheng was a legacy of the famous reformer Zhang Jian, who inaugurated the facility in 1899 with strong official backing. Located in a relatively backward area on the north bank of the Yangzi River, the mills did enjoy proximity to cotton supplies. Dasheng generally purchased cotton at 10 to 15 percent below the cost in Shanghai. The company developed close ties with local merchants and even peasant handicraft producers, who used yarn from the mills to produce cloth. Initially quite successful, Dasheng had three mills in 1925, with more than 175,000 spindles. By the early 1920s, however, the mills experienced serious financial losses, hard hit by financial mismanagement and the cotton crisis of 1922. Years of distributing profits rather than reinvesting had prevented the enterprise from continuing to progress. Many stockholders felt that Zhang Jian milked the firm to finance other of his operations in Nantong. Japanese textile mills in Shanghai, meanwhile, began to compete for purchase of local cotton. The accumulation of debts from the early 1920s reached a crisis with the death of Zhang Jian in 1926. A consortium of banks placed their own management team, headed by Li Shengbo, in charge of the company.[28]

In the initial weeks of the war, the Dasheng mills profited. The conflict sundered trade connections between the north shore of the Yangzi and Shanghai. Without a market in the city, the cost of raw cotton fell, while the price of Dasheng's manufactured products, lacking competition from Shanghai, increased. Still, the worsening situation in Shanghai and frequent overflights of Japanese airplanes made the management nervous. Dasheng decided to take the approach used by so many others— foreign registration. The company had purchased equipment from a German firm on which it still owed 172,000 pounds sterling. Taking advantage of this tie, the management arranged for the German firm to "foreclose" on Dasheng on January 10, 1938. A German manager was hired, the company registered with the German consulate (for a fee of more than 5,000 yuan), and the plant was draped with swastikas in hopes of warding off Japanese bombers. Signs on the plant read "The Dasheng Textile Manufacturing Company managed by the German Far Eastern Equipment Company" (Deshang yuandong jiqi gongsi jingli Dasheng fangzhi gongsi). The German firm also received 200 pounds monthly in management fees.[29]

The Japanese finally got around to invading Nantong on March 17, 1938, forcing the plants to close for a couple of months. In May, however, the Japanese permitted to them to resume operations, accepting the German connection. Dasheng operated, in fact, under its "German management" until March 1939, during which time it earned substantial profits. The favorable balance of low prices for raw materials and high value for output continued. From January through August 1938, for instance, the three Dasheng mills earned more than 2.35 million yuan. Moreover, as with other debt-ridden industries, the company benefited from wartime inflation by liquidating its debt with cheapened yuan.[30]

The good times did not last. Shortly after the Japanese occupation of Nantong, the Kanegafuchi Company (associated with the Mitsui group) established an office in the city. A longtime rival of Dasheng for cotton supplies, the Japanese firm sought control of the Chinese firm. In October 1938, the local head of Japanese special services ordered Dasheng to begin discussions with Kanegafuchi for the formation of a joint company. With little choice, Dasheng management dispatched Chen Baochu for the discussion. Although some, including Chen, felt that collaboration with the Japanese was inevitable, much of the Dasheng board wanted to resist as long as possible. Not only did they fear losing control of their company, but they worried that a victorious Guomindang would punish Dasheng if China won the war. The management thus dragged out the talks through the spring of 1939, offering to accept "technical cooperation" with Kanegafuchi, or management "leadership." They resisted an actual joint ownership.[31]

Suddenly in March 1939, Japanese military forces occupied all of the factories and placed them under military management. The mills ceased operations and the workers dispersed, many returning to their nearby villages. Special services then entrusted the factories to Kanegafuchi, which renamed the mills and restored production on May 23. The Japanese firm initially had difficulty getting sufficient workers but ultimately reached substantial levels of production. Under Japanese control, the output of the plant was geared toward production of cloth for use by the Japanese army. Some plant facilities were used for storage of weapons and ammunition and the billeting of troops.[32]

Dasheng management later accused Kanegafuchi of virtually destroying the mills, with losses up to 70 percent. The Japanese used poor quality raw materials, which damaged equipment, much of which was then given up for scrap metal drives. When the Japanese restored the mills to Chinese owners on July 28, 1943, as part of the great departure, the facilities were in poor shape. These problems, plus the energy shortages and lack of transportation, crippled production in the last two years of the war. Yet Dasheng survived by collaborating with the Japanese and the Nanjing government. Dasheng did not provide collaborators as prominent as the Nie family; Zhang Jian was long deceased, and his only son followed him in death in 1935. Still, the remaining management chose to work with the Japanese.[33]

Collaboration with puppet authorities kept Dasheng afloat. With currency inflation rendering market conditions unstable, and with extreme pressure on the commodity procurement system, the late war period brought disaster to most Chinese textile manufacturers. As noted earlier, the prices fixed for most commodities were only a fraction of the black market rate, encouraging the development of an underground economy. Chen Baochu, on behalf of Dasheng and himself, negotiated a special arrangement with Tang Shoumin of the Commerce Control Commission that allowed Dasheng to operate on a barter system. Dasheng would purchase raw cotton using cotton yarn at favorable exchange rates. For the control commission this helped secure a supply of cotton as Dasheng had sources to tap in the countryside. For Dasheng it meant that they could evade currency altogether. Under Chen's leadership, Dasheng survived the final months of the war through close cooperation with the Nanjing government and the Japanese and manipulation of the barter system.[34]

Hengfeng and Dasheng enterprises were both legacies of the first wave of industrialization in China. Both had been founded with official backing. Both had languished in the years preceding the war and fallen under the control of banks. Neither responded as well to the challenge of wartime as the Rongs and Guos did, yet the management of both firms had no real options given the location and scale of the facilities. In the case of Hengfeng, the prestigious Nie family collaborated with the Japanese to regain some profits. In neither case, however, did the factories really operate during the war as Chinese-controlled enterprises. Whatever the vulnerabilities of the family-style firm, both the Guos and Rongs were more successful in dealing with the war environment. The rather tired response of these old firms stands in even sharper contrast with the experiences of another textile company, Dacheng of Changzhou. With its leadership in the hands of a founder-owner, this company survived the conflict even under the most trying circumstances.

LIU GUOJUN AND THE
DACHENG COMPANY OF CHANGZHOU

The Dacheng Company was the creation of industrialist Liu Guojun, who began the enterprise in Changzhou, located between Nanjing and Shanghai in Jiangsu province. As with Nantong, the location away from Shanghai offered the same ease of access to local cotton and labor. Not only was cotton cheaper, but land costs and labor costs were significantly lower in outlying cities such as Changzhou, Wuxi, and Nantong. Liu began his career as a cloth merchant but then expanded into manufacturing, building three mills in Changzhou. In 1935 Liu purchased a failed mill in Wuhan, the Zhenhuan Mill, which had closed in 1933 with substantial debts. The old owners received 40 percent of the stock in Dacheng #4 in exchange for the plant and equipment, while Dacheng assumed the mortgage of the old firm.

By 1936 Liu's Dacheng Company was a small but successful cotton textile operation with a capital of 4 million yuan and 80,000 spindles. Liu had developed his operation carefully, investing in advanced equipment to produce such products as printed cotton cloth. His success was due in part to three trips he made to Japan to acquire new technology and to observe manufacturing techniques. At the same time, as was often the case with Chinese businessmen, he benefited handsomely from surges in sales accompanying anti-Japanese boycotts.[35]

With its location on the Shanghai-Nanjing Railway, Changzhou was hard hit when war erupted, and Liu Guojun's mills suffered heavily. Dacheng #2 was reduced to rubble, a total loss. The Dacheng #1 received the least damage but suffered some looting. Liu was unable to evacuate material from the #1 mill before the Japanese military arrived and placed the facility under military management. Dacheng #3 was also damaged, but Liu was able to remove most of its equipment for shipment to Wuhan or Shanghai before the Japanese arrived. The Japanese military turned the stripped mill into stables.[36] The looms from #3 (250 in all), arrived safely in Wuhan at Dacheng #4, but the shipment of spindles was damaged heavily en route by Japanese bombing. A portion that survived eventually made it to Shanghai. Liu himself escaped from Changzhou to Wuhan just two days before the Japanese captured the city in November 1937.[37]

Liu Guojun established a new mill in the concessions in Shanghai. Dacheng had nearly 14,800 spindles that had been ordered from Sweden before the war but had not been shipped to Changzhou and were in the International Settlement. Together with an additional purchase of 10,000 spindles and the remains salvaged from Dacheng #3, Liu was able to put together enough to open a new mill in Shanghai, the Anda Textile Mill (Anda shachang), in space rented from the China Book Company. He registered this as a British Company using two British subjects, one an Indian, as the nominal general manager and the chairman of the board of directors. Liu himself, of course, was the actual manager. Much of the staff of the mill, which opened in 1938, was recruited from Dacheng #1.[38]

In the meantime, the security of Dacheng #4 in Wuhan was threatened as the Japanese approached. Liu decided, as did Li Guowei of the Rong group, to relocate to Chongqing, working with other mill owners in Wuhan. He also had some earlier contacts in Sichuan with Lu Zuofu, general manager of the Minsheng Industrial Company (Minsheng shiye gongsi). Together with Lu and other Wuhan refugees, Liu organized the Daming Textile Spinning, Weaving, and Dyeing Company (Daming fangzhi ran gongsi). Lu served as the general manager.[39]

By 1939 both the Shanghai and Chongqing operations showed a profit. When the Japanese occupied the isolated island after Pearl Harbor, the Anda mill was seized on the grounds that it was enemy property—British. But Anda was one of the group of seven such mills, including Shenxin #2 and #9 and Yong'an #3, which were returned on May 22, 1942, so Liu was back in charge. Severe shortages of electricity in Shanghai permitted the firm to operate no more than 7,000 spindles in 1943 and 3,000 in 1944. In the meantime, two of Liu's lieutenants who had remained in Changzhou, Hua Du'an and Zhang Yifei, were able to get the Dacheng #1 back into limited production. Local Japanese military officials were willing to restore the mill. About 10,000 spindles and 150 looms were in the plant when it was returned.[40]

Liu earned substantial profits in the war not only from production but also from speculation. He established a firm in Hong Kong, the Dafu Development Company (Dafu jiangye gongsi), through which he could, prior to December 1941, purchase raw material and equipment overseas. He or his agents traveled between Chongqing, Hong Kong, Kunming, Rangoon, Hanoi, and elsewhere, buying and selling textiles and raw materials. Liu accumulated foreign currency reserves of an estimated US $1 million by 1944. Liu used some of these funds to purchase a huge villa (200 rooms) and gardens in Suzhou both for himself and as a recreation area for this employees. Throughout the war, even after Pearl Harbor, Liu traveled from Suzhou to Shanghai to Hong Kong to Sichuan. He had the ready cash such travel required and was not averse to taking risks.[41]

Yet travel between the occupied and unoccupied areas was not always easy. As the Rongs discovered, puppet forces would often "arrest" wealthy citizens for the equivalent of ransom. In 1942, Liu and his wife were in Suzhou when they received word from Hua Du'an and Zhang Yifei about the restored production of the #1 mill in Changzhou. Liu decided to make a quick trip to his old home, his first visit in nearly five years. Arriving with his wife by train, Liu toured the rubble of the #2 mill, then crossed the river to view the site of the #3 mill, then vacant but with clear evidence of its earlier use as a military stables. Finally arriving at the #1 mill, Liu and his entourage were greeted by several hundred workers. Overnight however, Liu and his wife were arrested by local authorities, who also pulled in Hua and Zhang. Held for two days, Liu was forced to pay a substantial ransom in cloth. After his release, Liu returned, rather shaken, to Shanghai. He quickly settled his affairs there and moved on to Chongqing via Luoyang and Xi'an.[42]

In July 1944, with the end of the war in sight, Liu sensed opportunity. He departed for the United States via India in order to purchase spindles for postwar operations. He left his oldest son Liu Hankun in charge of his operations in Sichuan and Hong Kong, his close relative Liu Jingji in Shanghai and Suzhou, and Hua Du'an in Changzhou. Liu had limited success. Because he had rejected cooperation with T. V. Soong, Liu was denied the right to transfer much of his funds from China. He was able to buy only 20,000 spindles in the United States. While overseas, he learned of the Japanese surrender, and his immediate reaction was to purchase U.S. cotton. Shortly after the war was over he was able to restore production of all three mills in Changzhou as well as the Anda mill in Shanghai. In 1949, after flirting with Hong Kong and Taiwan, Liu decided to remain in China, where he died in 1978 at the age of ninety-two sui.[43]

Liu Guojun is perhaps the classic entrepreneur, operating at the peak of his powers. He responded to the danger and destruction of war with incredible energy and daring, managing to survive and even earn profits in wartime. The contrast between the fate of the Dasheng mills in Nantong and the Dacheng mills in Changzhou is instructive. Although the Dasheng mills were larger than Dacheng, and suffered significantly less damage, the management in Nantong responded to the war with little vigor or imagination, with the possible exception of the German connection. Liu Guojun, by contrast, although losing two or three mills in Changzhou, rushed as much equipment out as possible and reestablished production in Shanghai and in Sichuan. He also responded to war conditions by engaging in speculation and profiteering activities. Aside from purchasing his villa in Suzhou, however, most of this income seems to have been retained for rehabilitating Dacheng in the postwar era.

Liu Guojun made free use of old associates and family members. He felt comfortable leaving China in 1944 with relatives and longtime associates in temporary charge. Liu not only demonstrated greater flexibility than the leadership of older enterprises such as Hengfeng and Dasheng, but even fared well compared to the older family firms such as the Guos and Rongs. In the latter case, the age of the founders and the death of Rong Zongjing, not to mention the greater size and complexity of these enterprise groups, constricted their responses in comparison to Liu's.

Liu's wartime experiences have been read by some Chinese scholars as part of the "patriotic nationalist narrative." Xu Dingxin, in his treatment of Liu during the war, notes his "deep feelings, strongly patriotic heart and enterprising spirit in an environment of extreme difficulty." Despite the "plundering and destruction of Dacheng by Japanese troops and heavy losses," Liu persevered. His visit back to Changzhou in autumn 1942 is interpreted as a brave attempt to check on his factory with no fear of injury to himself. Yet a more cynical reading of Liu's actions would suggest that he put survival of the firm first and patriotic concerns a distant second. True, Liu did evacuate much of his material to Wuhan, and then Chongqing, but much of this could be attributed to circumstances. He already had a plant in Wuhan, and he had pre-existing business ties in Sichuan, which facilitated the move there. In opening the Anda plant in Shanghai and using British registration, he followed the actions of many other Chinese capitalists. In negotiating with the Japanese to regain Anda in 1942 and his travels to occupied Suzhou and Changzhou, Liu certainly revealed a willingness to operate in the occupied area. Indeed, his decision to move to Chongqing in 1942 was probably a result of his arrest and ransom by local authorities rather than purely patriotic concerns. Survival of the firm seems to have been his primary goal. The persistence and endurance of businessmen such as Liu Guojun are remarkable features of the war era.[44]

WUXI — FLOUR AND TEXTILE MILLS

The wartime experiences of flour and textile industrialists in Wuxi provide yet another window to observe the wide range of responses to war conditions in China. After Shanghai, Wuxi was the most important industrial center of the lower Yangzi. Close to Shanghai by rail, it nonetheless enjoyed the advantages of Changzhou and Nantong of lower wages and easier access to raw materials than the big metropolis. The Rong family members were, of course, the most famous of Wuxi's industrialists. Rong Zhongjin and Desheng had their origins in the small city, and their Shenxin #3 textile mill, with its 71,000 spindles, was the largest such facility in Wuxi. The Rongs also had their two flour mills, Maoxin #1 and #2, as well. Yet by the mid-1930s, the Rongs had largely moved on. The bulk of their holdings were in Shanghai.

Five other families remained important industrialists in Wuxi—the Tangs, Xues, Yangs, Cais, and Chengs—dominating the important cotton, flour milling, and silk industries there. In 1934 the capital holdings of the Rong family enterprises in Wuxi were 5.64 million yuan, the Tang-Cai family group 3.21 million, the Xues 2.57 million, the Tang-Cheng group 2.04 million, and the Yangs 1.76 million. These six families controlled about 70 percent of all industrial and commercial capital in Wuxi.[45] Unfortunately, the battle of Wuxi was very intense and most Chinese factories sustained major damage during the fighting. Wuxi industrialists who survived pursued a variety of strategies in the new era. Responses of the Wuxi industrialists thus illustrate the full range from resistance to collaboration to something in between.

Both the background and actions of the Yang family in Wuxi parallel the Nies of the Hengfeng mill. The Yangs turned to collaboration to survive during the war. One of China's oldest industrial families, the Yangs traced their industrial beginnings back to two brothers, Yang Yifang and Yang Oufang, who had ties to Li Hongzhang's *mufu* and who created the Yeqin enterprise group. Although descendants of the founders were active in both industry and banking, by the 1930s the key industrial leader of the Yang clan was Yifang's son, Yang Hanxi. The Yeqin textile mill was profitable in the early 1920s, but then went into bankruptcy and reorganization on several occasions after 1927 when economic conditions were less favorable for Chinese industrialists. Yeqin's situation was similar to that of many of the early textile enterprises founded with political assistance. In 1936, however, Yeqin had resumed production.

Yang Hanxi had also established a second mill, the Guangqin plant, during the "golden age" of industrial expansion in the shadow of World War I. Guangqin was organized as a completely separate entity, in part so that Yang Hanxi would not have to share profits with this cousins, the sons of Yang Oufang. Hanxi obtained capital from both family sources and from industrial and banking associates and relatives. Guangqin began with 19,968 spindles in 1919, which gradually increased to 23,040 by 1930. Although its capacity grew little after this period, it remained profitable prior to the war, in contrast to the Yeqin mill. In 1937 Yang Hanxi also managed to expand into flour production. With the aid of family capital and the support of Hua Shuqin, manager of the Qingfeng cotton mill, and Ren Zhuoqun, manager of the Wuxi branch of the Jiangsu bank, Yang created the Guangfeng Flour Mill.[46]

When war erupted, the Yang clan was hard hit. Their two major textile mills, the Yeqing and Guangqin, were both completely destroyed, but the Guangfeng flour mill suffered only limited damage. Yang Hanxi was eager to reopen the flour mill after the Japanese gained control of Wuxi in order to preserve some income, even though this required direct dealings with the Japanese military and puppet authorities. Guangfeng mill began to supply the Japanese military with flour and consequently remained quite profitable, especially through 1941. The firm paid off prewar debts owed to the Bank of Communications. Later, Yang collaborated with the Wang Jingwei government, agreeing to have his son, Yang Jingrong, participate in the Wheat Flour Control Commission; Jingrong eventually headed its Wuxi office. Although Guangfeng's output and size expanded little during the war, the Yangs earned substantial profits from speculation. When the war ended, however, Yang Hanxi was arrested by Guomindang authorities as a traitor.[47]

So successful was Yang Hanxi that he organized a new textile enterprise in Shanghai, the Zhaoxin mill, funded by investments from the Yang group and associated capitalists. The new enterprise grew rapidly, incorporating 17,000 spindles and 126 weaving machines. Yang's willingness to cooperate with the Japanese brought his family fortunes back, despite the disastrous losses of the early war period. The price was cooperation with the Japanese occupier. After the war the Yang family business declined because of Hanxi's problems.[48]

The Xue family suffered similar losses during the battle of Wuxi. Another prominent family in that city, they traced their origins to Zeng Guofan's *mufu*. Xue Nanming, the family leader, established or purchased several silk filatures, such as the Yongtai Company, with a total of more than 1,700 silk reeling machines. He sent his youngest son, Xue Shouxuan, to the University of Illinois, and entrusted him with the leadership of the family's industrial base. The younger Xue solidified his ties to the industrial community by marrying the daughter of Rong Zongjing. Xue Shouxuan also established a reputation for using advanced technology and for the training of workers, a relatively novel concept in China. He added to the family's holdings, creating the Huaxin filature in 1931. By 1934 the Xue group included the Yongtai, Jinji, and Huaxin plants and had 2,400 silk reeling machines, 20 percent of the total in Wuxi.[49]

Although China produced much of its silk for export, traditionally foreign merchant houses in China handled the overseas marketing. Xue Shouxuan felt this practice limited Chinese profits because producers were unable to benefit easily from changing conditions in foreign markets. Determined to break this foreign monopoly, he dispatched Xue Zukang to America to set up a branch of the Yongtai Company in New York City in 1934. The Xues then marketed their silk output directly to the U.S. market. While many other silk producers suffered during the economically troubled 1930s, the Xue group kept profits high through direct marketing. So successful was Xue Shouxuan that in 1935 he organized a trust group, the Xingye Company, which included sixteen filatures, totaling 6,000 reeling machines from both the Xue group and allied firms. The final months before the war thus proved quite profitable for the family.[50]

The Xues' success was derailed by the war. Many of their factories were completely destroyed, including the Jinji and Longchang filatures, while others, Yongtai and Huaxin, were heavily damaged. After the war, only one of their mills, the Yongtai, could be immediately reopened, and that with only seventy reeling machines at first. In 1949, the Xues possessed only one-fifth of their industrial capacity of 1937. In the face of these overwhelming losses, the strategy of Xue Shouxuan was simply to flee. After the Marco Polo Bridge Incident, Xue used available cash in the firm to purchase American currency and assets. He shipped both the current stock of silk and his family to America, where he established a silk stocking factory in New York, leaving a relative to monitor the family's assets in Wuxi. Xue's strategy was available to him because of his American education and ties and because Yongtai already had an American office. Xue thus avoided collaboration, but he never returned to China and died in the United States in 1972.[51]

The Zhou family was a smaller group involved in silk production and allied with the Xues. The great patriarch of the clan, Zhou Shunqing, had founded the Yuchang Mill, which had 330 reeling machines in 1930. His son, Zhou Zhaofu, founded a second mill, the Dingchang, in 1929, with 256 machines. The total capital of the Zhou's enterprises was 434,0000 yuan in 1934, but by that date their property was heavily mortgaged and much of its control lost to bankers. In 1936 Zhaofu leased Dingchang to the Xingye Company. The woes of the Zhou clan were compounded by the war, which left the Yuchang mill in ruins.

The Zhous' junior partner in the Dingchang mill, Qian Fenggao, salvaged the plant by collaborating with the Japanese. He worked with the Central China Sericultural Company, the subsidiary of the Central China

Development Company. Qian's cooperation enabled him to gain Japanese capital to rehabilitate the Dingchang mill, which further benefited from the reduced competition in the area following the destruction of rival factories. At its peak the mill had 512 reeling machines. When the war ended, Qian was charged with being a traitor, so the mill was turned over to his younger brother. The much reduced Zhou family had only a token share in the firm. As with the Nies, who had lost control in the Hengfeng mill to bankers, collaboration with the Japanese was the path for a junior partner to gain the upper hand, at least until the end of the war.[52]

Two other prominent families in Wuxi, the Tangs and the Cais, had long formed joint industrial ventures. Tang Baoqian and Cai Jiansan had cofounded the Jiufeng flour mill in 1909. During the boom period in the wake of World War I, the two men decided to move into cotton textile production, establishing the Qingfeng mill in 1922 using capital mostly from their families. Tang served as general manager, Cai as assistant general manager. The mill began with 14,800 spindles and 250 looms. The company benefited heavily from the anti-foreign boycott movement that occurred during the May Thirtieth Movement of 1925. When Tang Baoqian's son, Tang Xinghai, returned from America in 1927 having obtained a master's degree in textile management, he took over day-to-day direction of the mill. Under his leadership, the Qingfeng company modernized and added a second plant. He purchased 50,000 spindles and 400 looms directly from England, bringing the total of spindles for Qingfeng to 64,768 and looms to 720 in 1937. From 1930 to 1936, the annual value of production of Qingfeng increased from 5,140,000 yuan to 11,430,000 yuan, profits from 310,000 yuan to 1,100,000 yuan.[53]

When war reached Wuxi, both the Qingfeng textile mill and the Jiufeng flour mill suffered heavy losses. Although Tang Xinghai, anticipating the fall of Wuxi, had moved 6,120 spindles to Shanghai before the Japanese arrival, the Tang and Cai properties were caught in Japanese bombardment. In all, Qingfeng lost 28,448 spindles, 277 looms, and its dyeing equipment. Together with electric generators and raw materials, the losses totaled more than 5,000,000 yuan. The Japanese military occupied the textile plant and then turned over management to the Japanese Daikō company, which rehabilitated the mill and reopened it in May 1939. The new plant had only 28,000 spindles and 300 looms, yet even these were not fully utilized because of shortages of raw materials and poor worker relations.[54]

The Tangs meanwhile had set up a new mill in Shanghai, the Baofeng (also called the Qingfeng #2), using equipment and funds salvaged from the Qingfeng mill, together with investments from the National Commercial Bank. Xinghai served as general manager and was assisted by his younger brother. In the "flourishing" conditions of wartime Shanghai, this enterprise did well, increasing to 27,140 spindles and 768 looms. After Pearl Harbor, when the Japanese began to stress salvaging the economy of occupied China, they began to press Tang Xinghai to collaborate, urging him to return to Wuxi (he was living in Shanghai) to resume a role in Qingfeng. The Daikō Company offered a joint management agreement with Tang and the original Qingfeng shareholders. Feeling that the Japanese "partners" would completely control the situation, Tang and the directors rejected the offer.[55]

Still, with Shanghai no longer a haven after December 1941, the Tangs ultimately engaged in some collaboration with the Wang Jingwei puppet government. Tang Xinghai served on Nanjing's Cotton Control Commission, and the family resumed a role in the management of Qingfeng. When Nanjing and the Japanese initiated their policy of returning factories to their Chinese owners, Tang petitioned to get Qingfeng back. The stumbling block was repaying Daikō for its investment in repairing the mill. Nanjing's Ministry of Industry arranged for Qingfeng stockholders to pay Daikō 6,200,000 yuan in Nanjing currency to regain their firm. Tang Xinghai spent more than a year trying to restart Qingfeng and resumed limited production in 1944. After the war, he was able to restore Qingfeng to a level of 62,728 spindles and 364 looms in 1947. Xinghai relocated to Hong Kong in 1949, establishing the Nanhai Textile Mill. The Tangs thus tried to avoid collaboration for as long as possible, preferring to operate in unoccupied Shanghai at first, and then refusing the initial terms of accepting a joint management agreement under Japanese control. Ultimately, as with the great majority of Shanghai area capitalists, Tang worked with the occupation authorities to regain control of his mill.[56]

Another branch of the Tang family, related but financially separate from the Qingfeng Tangs, had invested with the Chengs. In 1918 Tang Xiangting, a cousin of Tang Baoqian, and Cheng Jingtang established the Lihua Cloth Company, which by 1934 had three mills in Wuxi. In 1920 they invested in new technology, creating the Lixin Cloth Printing and Dyeing Company. After a shaky start, Lixin prospered when the May Thirtieth Movement led many Chinese consumers to boycott rival Japanese products. Perhaps the most daring investment by the Tang-Cheng pair occurred in 1934 when they established the first woolen mill in Wuxi. On the eve of the war the Tang-Cheng group was one of the most successful in Wuxi, with total capital of 4.8 million yuan, 40,000 spindles, and 1,200 looms.[57]

War devastated their enterprises. The Lihua #1 and #2 mills were completely destroyed. Lihua #3 and the Lixin printing and dyeing plant were heavily damaged. The buildings were occupied by the Japanese; the woolen mill was in ruins. The strategy of the Tangs and Chengs was to move to Shanghai. They took the remaining capital from Lixin and set up the Changxing textile mill and dyeing company, which had separate facilities for weaving, spinning, and dyeing. The textile mills began operations in June 1939 and the dyeing plant in December of that year. By the end of the war the plant had 14,760 spindles and 280 looms. They also opened a woolen mill in Shanghai to replace the one lost in Wuxi. Lixin did not resume operations in Wuxi until after the war, when it recovered to a level of 30,000 spindles and 700 looms by 1947. Despite moving the mill to Shanghai, some cooperation with the Japanese was required to continue operations after Pearl Harbor. Cheng Jingtang joined the puppet government's Cotton Control Commission.[58]

The industrialists of Wuxi thus exhibited a wide range of responses to the war. All suffered heavily because of the intensity of the fighting. Yang Hanxi chose to work with the Japanese to salvage his enterprises and was labeled a traitor after the war. Xue Shouxuan chose to leave for America and had the necessary connections to do so. The Zhou clan, financially weak on the eve of the war, was forced out by a partner who gained control by collaborating with the Japanese. The Tangs and Cais and the Tangs and Chengs all relocated in Shanghai to enjoy the "flourishing of the isolated island." After Pearl Harbor, they too faced the necessity of dealing with the occupiers.

These enterprises in Wuxi also represented a variety of different types of Chinese businesses—older, politically connected enterprises such as the Yangs and Xues, as well as partnerships such as the Tang-Cai and Tang-Cheng groups. Most were in the second generation of leadership. The founders had either had political ties or a mercantile background or both. The second generation was often educated to improve the technical know-how of the enterprise, such as Xue Shouxuan. Yet except for the Zhous, whose company was on the verge of failure in 1937, all were really under the control of a dominant and usually dynamic figure.

The actions of Yang Hanxi, although perhaps considered traitorous after the war, were a vigorous response to the conflict that enabled his family to prosper throughout much of the war. Xue Shouxuan's decision to move into marketing and emigrate was yet another response, as were the moves to Shanghai by the other groups. Yet all of these individual business leaders responded with speed and flexibility to the destruction of war.

CHAPTER 8

Chemical and Match Industrialists

On the eve of the war, China's chemical industry was quite small, though growing rapidly. As James Reardon-Anderson points out (citing statistics developed by D. K. Lieu), only 4.5 percent of factories in China in 1933 (148 total) were chemical factories; these had an average workforce of 186 and capital of 178,000 yuan. The vast majority (80 percent) manufactured consumer goods, such as matches, soap, candles, enamelware, cosmetics, and medicines. By comparison with the chemical industries in Europe, America, and Japan, China's remained relatively primitive. Still, Chinese manufacturers had achieved production breakthroughs in several areas, such as alkali soda ash, acids, and ammonium sulfate. Inadequate demand, rather than technical limitations, was the greatest barrier to expanding production. As Reardon-Anderson states, "China had few or none of those industries, such as iron and steel, coal tar, chemical fertilizer, and synthetic dyes, that consume large quantities of acid."[1]

The war dealt a sharp blow to the budding chemical industry, particularly "to those industries such as acids, sodas, and fertilizers, where most progress had been made before the war and where the prospects for continued development were the brightest." Annual production of acids and sodas in Guomindang China during the war was only one-eighth the prewar level, despite the efforts of the Chongqing government to restore this vital sector.[2]

What was the wartime experience of China's chemical industrialists, and how did it compare with those of the textile manufacturers, flour millers, and department store owners we have studied thus far? Because advanced chemical industries were few in number and of great strategic importance, these manufacturers tended to be more public figures than all but a handful of the textile manufacturers. Both Japan and China sought their collaboration because of the potential military uses for their products. Three key manufacturers, chemical producers Fan Xudong and Wu Yunchu and "match king" Liu Hongsheng, were the dominant individuals in this business sector. All had achieved public recognition prior to the war, all were pressed to collaborate, and all ultimately relocated to Free China. All seem to fit the "patriotic nationalist narrative," and indeed are often cited as prime examples. Yet a close reading of their wartime experiences reveals the same patterns of reaction we have seen in the textile and consumer industries.

TWO CHEMICAL MANUFACTURERS

On of the eve of the war, two Chinese manufacturers dominated the chemical industry. "In the north there is Fan Xudong, in the south Wu Yunchu," the saying went.[3] Perhaps of all manufacturers in China, these two came closest to fulfilling the "heroic capitalist" model. Both relocated to the interior after the war began, avoiding the stigma of collaboration. Fan in particular is often cited in the new literature from China as a capitalist who was motivated by patriotic goals, seeking to "save the nation through industrialization" (*gongye jiuguo*). One recent publication on Fan, Tim Wright notes, is titled "Fatherland, Industry, Science, Talent." When Fan died in Chongqing in October 1945, he was praised by Mao Zedong for his contributions to the nation, while Zhou Enlai personally visited Fan's family. Leftist figures Guo Moruo and Shen Junru attended a memorial service on November 13, and on the Guomindang side, Chiang Kaishek, H. H. Kung, and T. V. Soong sent condolences.[4]

Fan was a native of Hunan from an established literati family whose older brother had been a devoted follower of Liang Qichao. When the older Fan departed for Japan after the failure of 1898, he paved the way for Xudong, who studied there from 1900 until 1911, eventually graduating from Kyoto University. While in Japan during these formative years, Fan was exposed to the very public image of the "patriotic industrialist." As Peter Duus has noted, "Meiji business leaders did not consider themselves as heirs of the old merchant class." Instead they presented a very public image that they were, as Duus describes it, "working for 'national profit' not mere personal gain." The model for this new self-styled heroic capitalist was Shibusawa Eiichi, who coined the term "man of affairs" (*jitsugyōka*) to distinguish himself and the new industrialists from the old business class. Whatever the impact of these images on Fan, in his later career he projected himself very much as had the new Meiji industrial leaders.[5]

When Fan Xudong first returned from Japan he worked for the Tianjin Mint, but a tour of European salt and alkali soda plants as part of an official Chinese delegation pushed him into a new career. In 1914 he established the Jiuda Refined Salt Company (Jiuda jingyan gongsi, later called Jiuda yanye gongsi) in Tanggu. This plant used modern, Western-style equipment to manufacture pure, refined salt. By the end of the following year, Fan's Haiwang Xing brand of salt began to replace imported salt on the market. Production grew from a mere 30,000 piculs in 1916 to more than 1.25 million by 1919 and 4 million by 1924.[6]

From the beginning of his career, Fan depended on political ties. Connections to the Political Study Clique enabled him to gain support from the Chinese government crucial to the Jiuda Company. Salt remained a key item in the government's tax structure and thus a very politicized commodity. Further evidence of Fan's political strength came when the Beiyang government recovered the Qingdao Salt Fields from the Japanese following the Washington Conference. Unable to operate the facility themselves, Beijing authorities entrusted it to Fan, further enhancing Jiuda.[7]

Although political connections were important, perhaps the most critical element in Fan's career was his willingness to move up the technology ladder. Fan became known as a pioneer for new technology in China, employing numerous chemists and engineers who had been trained in the West or Japan, and using their skills to open up new manufacturing processes. In 1922 he even established the Huanghai Chemical Industrial Research Society (Huanghai huaxue gongye yanjiu she) in Tanggu to promote technical research. To head the institute, Fan brought in Harvard-trained chemist Sun Xuewu. But Sun was only one of the many gifted chemists and engineers employed by Fan. The most famous was Hou Debang, the outstanding Chinese chemical engineer of the Republican era. After receiving a B.S. at M.I.T. in 1917, Hou earned a Ph.D. at Columbia University in chemical engineering in 1921 before returning to China.[8]

Fan's approach led to eventual success in the manufacture of alkali soda ash (sodium carbonate), China's supply of which had been mostly imported. Widely used in the manufacture of glass, paper, textiles, and dyestuffs, soda was a fundamental product for the modern chemical industry. When World War I threatened the availability of this crucial commodity and sent prices skyrocketing, Fan sensed an opportunity. He established the Yongli Alkali Company (Yongli jian gongsi) to manufacture the product. Because of the earlier success of his Jiuda firm, Fan raised 400,000 yuan to invest in this difficult new challenge. Zhou Zuomin of the Jincheng Bank and Chen Guangfu of the Shanghai Commercial and Savings Bank were key sources of investment. Fan also needed his political connections. The key ingredient in soda is salt, which Beijing still taxed at many times its base value. Payment of the tax would have made salt prohibitively expensive as a raw material to produce soda ash, but Fan gained an exemption from the tax for salt used as an industrial commodity.[9]

Fan placed Hou Debang together with engineer Chen Tiaofu to work on the task. Although ground was broken for the soda plant in Tanggu in 1919, mastering production was difficult. Knowledge of the standard Solvay process was tightly controlled, so Hou had to devise the method himself. Even when the plant began operation in August 1924, the purity of the product was substandard. Only in June 29, 1926, did Hou achieve a complete success, producing a product of greater than 99 percent purity. The following year, Yongli manufactured 37 tons of soda daily, with production steadily increasing until 1936 when it reached 152 tons daily. Profits reached 2,000,000 yuan in 1933. Yongli also produced caustic soda (sodium hydroxide).[10]

Fan's industrial base had been almost entirely in north China, but the establishment of the Guomindang regime in Nanjing inevitably drew a politically connected industrialist such as Fan to the south. The vulnerability of Tanggu following the Tanggu truce put further pressure on Fan to move into the Yangzi basin. In 1936 Jiuda set up a salt-producing plant at Dapu in Jiangsu. Fan's major venture into the south, however, came with the establishment of an ammonium sulfate factory. The Nanjing government had sought the establishment of a plant to manufacture ammonia using atmospheric nitrogen and to produce sulfuric acid. The end product, ammonium sulfate, could be used for commercial fertilizer but also for military purposes. A China-based factory would also stem the foreign exchange loss from the growing quantity of imported chemical fertilizer.

In 1931 Nanjing authorities had discussed the issue with the British Imperial Chemical Industries and the German I. G. Farben, but Fan approached both T. V. Soong and H. H. Kung, Chiang Kaishek's brothers-in-law, with a proposal for Yongli to establish the plant. In 1933 the Nanjing government backed Yongli's effort with a substantial loan, based on the understanding that production must begin by the end of 1936 and that the plant be located in Nanjing. If Fan failed to achieve this, the government would turn anew to foreign firms. Nanjing granted Yongli certain tax breaks for the new venture, including a thirty-year exemption on export or transit taxes for products of the plant, assistance to Yongli in floating bonds, and some relief from import taxes on equipment for the plant.[11]

Despite this agreement, Fan's relations with Soong and Kung were not close. Kung preferred a joint government-private venture, but Fan was distrustful of government ownership. Soong apparently suggested that he would invest in the project providing he was named chairman of the board of directors. Unwilling to surrender control, Fan turned to a banking consortium of the Shanghai Commercial Bank, the Jincheng Bank, and the Zhongnan Bank to provide investment. Fan retained close ties to the old Political Study Clique, a connection that became more valuable when Wu Dingchang, a clique leader, became Minister of Industry in 1936. Fan was thus assured of political backing for the new facility.[12]

Fan pressed forward and dispatched Hou Debang to America to acquire equipment. By the end of the 1936, the Yongli facility in Nanjing succeeded in fixing nitrogen from the atmosphere. On February 5, 1937, the Nanjing Yongli Ammonium Sulfate Factory (Yongli liusuan yachang) began production of nitrogen and ammonia, nitric and sulfuric acid, and ammonium nitrate. Production of ammonium sulfate for fertilizer reached 150 tons daily by the early summer of 1937 and nitric acid 40 tons. Then war erupted. Because the Japanese realized that the plant could be used for war production, their bombers targeted the facility on August 21, 1937, barely a week after the fighting began in Shanghai. Fan tried to ship as much of the equipment as possible upriver to Hankou, but most was sunk en route. As late as December 5, just eight days before the Japanese occupied the site, a small batch made it onto the last ship out of Nanjing. The Japanese removed some of the remaining factory equipment and shipped it to Kyushu following their occupation of Nanjing. Later the plant resumed production of ammonium sulfate under the direction of the Mitsui and Tōyō companies.[13]

SURVIVING THE WAR

Most of Fan's facilities suffered a similar fate, as the company sites in Tanggu and Tianjin quickly came under Japanese control. Fan dispatched

Li Zhuchen to Tanggu to help escort personnel and equipment to Sichuan. Fan himself left from Hong Kong and then Hankou, following the Guomindang into retreat. Although the Japanese reportedly approached him in Hong Kong suggesting collaborative ventures with the Xingzhong Company, he rejected their offers. As a consequence, plants not destroyed in the fighting quickly came under Japanese control. Mitsubishi took over the Tanggu facilities in 1938. Fan did manage to evacuate some equipment from the Jiuda salt plant in Jiangsu that he had taken to Sichuan, along with material from other branches of his empire. To facilitate recovery, Fan united these remnants of Jiuda, Yongli, and the Huanghai research group to form a united Yongjiu group. By combining all of his meager resources, Fan hoped to establish the basis for wartime revival. Although Fan first planned to relocate in Xiangtan, Hunan, the Japanese conquest of Wuhan and Guangzhou in 1938 forced him to look westward. A new site in Sichuan was found and given the nickname the "new Tanggu." [14]

Still, only a minuscule amount of equipment made it to Sichuan. Fan struggled to recover. With help from the Guomindang government, he eventually set up a small salt manufacturing facility that produced approximately 200,000 tons of salt annually from brine wells at Wutongqiao, Sichuan. The firm encountered considerable hostility from the traditional salt producers in the area. The government also promised a substantial loan to assist in reestablishing soda and acid production in the interior. Because the salt brine in Sichuan was impure, the Solvay process that worked at Tanggu was too inefficient. Hou Debang strove to find alternative methods of production. The chemist departed for the United States, where he remained during much of the war, trying to acquire new equipment for the interior base. Yongjiu made extensive purchases in America, but most never arrived in Sichuan. One large order got as far as Haiphong only to be confiscated by the Japanese in August 1940 when they moved into northern Vietnam. The next ill-fated shipment made it to Burma, only to be captured there when the Pacific war erupted. Fan himself was in Hong Kong on December 8, 1941, and was unable to return to Chongqing until March 1943. [15]

Facing such daunting obstacles, Fan's plants managed only modest production in the interior, some salt and limited alkali soda ash output. The latter was achieved by returning to the old Leblanc method, which had been abandoned decades earlier in the West. Only five tons of soda could be produced each day, a small fraction of the output in Tanggu of nearly 60,000 tons annually. Indeed, total soda production in all Guomindang areas in 1944 was only 5,600 tons. To assist in maintaining the livelihood of workers, the united Yongjiu even attempted a bit of coal mining. Wartime inflation created an economy wherein commodities such as coal were far more valuable than wages paid in currency, for both workers and management.[16]

Even in wartime, Fan attempted to maintain the research arm of his enterprises. The Huanghai Chemical Industrial Research Society evacuated to Chongqing, although it suffered a loss of most of its equipment and much of the library. The old headquarters was taken over by the Japanese Imperial Navy. When the unit reopened in 1939, it could undertake only modest research during the war, yet it did keep the technical personnel occupied and raised morale. Its greatest achievement in the war was continuing to publish the journal *Haiwang*, which had begun in 1928 and publicized the latest scientific scholarship.[17]

Under wartime conditions, Fan's political connections were more crucial than ever, particularly his ties with the Jincheng Bank, which was affiliated with the Political Study Clique. Fan had also been a classmate in Japan with Zhou Zuomin, the key leader of the bank, and the two were longtime friends. Working with the Chongqing branch of the bank, Fan set up the China Chemical Manufacturing Company with the hopes of creating a new industrial base. Despite these valiant efforts, Fan's firms had very limited production in Sichuan because of the lack of equipment and raw materials. On a personal level, Fan continued to play a semigovernmental role, joining Zhang Jia'ao, Cheng Guangfu, and Li Ming in representing China at the international commercial conference held in the fall of 1944.[18]

Yet Fan's political involvement brought problems as well as opportunities. Although Fan was closely tied with the Political Study Clique, his relations with T. V. Soong and H. H. Kung remained strained. The retreat to Sichuan placed Fan further in their shadows. He desperately needed government assistance, yet was reluctant to invite either man to join his board of directors. Independence carried a price. While in America in 1944, Fan attempted to arrange a $16 million loan from the American Import Export Bank to be used to restart his enterprises after the war concluded. The bank wanted a guarantee from Chongqing, which failed to materialize, so Fan returned home empty handed in June 1945.[19]

Fan's international prominence and independence from Soong and Kung opened other political doors. When Mao visited Chongqing in August 1945, he personally met with Fan and offered him an opportunity to establish chemical factories in the liberated areas. Mao's gesture was clearly a recognition of the importance of Fan's industrial achievements. Fan's sudden death in October 1945 at sixty-three sui cemented his role as a "patriotic industrialist," since he was not tainted by actions in the Civil War period.[20]

So how does one evaluate Fan's wartime record? Can his actual experiences be distilled from the ideology of the historical literature about his career? If we examine his entire life, several features are prominent. First, Fan consciously promoted the idea of himself as a patriotic, industrial pioneer. This image was continuously publicized through the journal *Haiwang* and public discussion about his enterprises. Second, Fan recognized that acquiring higher technology was key to the success of his chemical industry. One could not simply use knock-off methods and cheap labor as other sectors of industry in China sometimes attempted to do. Third, Fan consistently utilized political connections. From early in his career, he realized that political ties were essential to his success and he played the game well. Nonetheless, Fan was determined to retain control over his enterprises.

Available historical resources make it difficult to reconstruct Fan's mental world, but his formative years were spent in Japan. The most likely model for his career was one of the great Japanese industrialists of the Meiji era so familiar to Fan during his youth in Japan. The Japanese industrialists had projected themselves as part of the Meiji project for developing Japan as a strong and independent nation. This approach not only reflected their personal patriotism, but deflected traditional prejudice against mercantile activity. These Japanese entrepreneurs also relied on close political ties but retained their independence from government control. Fan seems to have duplicated this strategy in his public persona.

Within that framework, Fan's wartime role makes sense. As a patriotic Chinese, he rejected any possibility of collaboration with the Japanese. He used political ties to maintain his enterprises but avoided entanglements that limited his control. He considered publication of the journal *Haiwang* to be a top priority. Yet Fan's wartime record, unblemished as it was, is subject to a slightly different reading. Did Fan really have an option of staying in the occupied area and collaborating with the Japanese? Despite reports that the Japanese sought his collaboration, it is unlikely that they would have extended any real chance of permitting autonomous enterprises in the occupied zone. Fan's industries had strong military implications and competed too closely with Japanese manufacturing to have created much room for autonomy. In other words,

Fan probably had no real option to operate his firms under Japanese control. It was really surrender or retreat. He chose the latter.

WU YUNCHU: THE "MSG KING"

China's second most famous chemical industrialist, Wu Yunchu, was based in Shanghai. As with Fan Xudong, Wu's wartime record seems to fit closely the patriotic capitalist narrative. He established manufacturing enterprises in Free China during the war. A native of Jiading, Jiangsu, Wu began his career in wake of World War I. Noticing that the war had created a shortage of raw materials for match manufacturing, Wu establish a small firm to fill this niche. His real breakthrough as an industrialist came in 1922 when he established the Tianchu Weijing (MSG) Company (Tianchu weijing chang). Developed and patented by Ikeda Kikunae, a professor of chemistry at Tokyo Imperial University, monosodium glutamate (MSG) had found a ready market in China. Armed with a mere 50,000 yuan in capital, Wu's facility used half-machine, half-handicraft methods of production. Not only did Wu ignore Japanese protests that he had violated their patent rights, but he also took advantage of anti-Japanese boycotts of the 1920s. Wu advertised that his product was "Chinese made" and successfully competed with the Japanese to become a dominant force in the market. Throughout his career Wu was known as the "MSG king." As his success grew, Wu continually upgraded the technical level of production.[21]

In July 1935, after some difficulties with his original partners, Wu reorganized Tianchu as a limited liability corporation. Now called the Shanghai Tianchu MSG Company, Ltd. (Shanghai tianchu weijing gufen youxian gongsi), it had a total capital of 2.2 million yuan. Wu served as general manager and dominant stockholder with more than 500,000 yuan of stock. In 1936 the company produced 220,000 kilograms of MSG.[22]

Unlike many early Chinese industrialists, but in common with Fan Xudong, Wu shared a commitment to research and investment in new technology. When he began manufacturing MSG, many of the raw materials had to be imported. Hydrochloric acid, a key element in the process, was supplied entirely by Japanese. Fearing that this supply might not be reliable, since his prime competitor was Japanese, Wu attempted to manufacture this ingredient himself. Fortunately, he discovered a failed French plant in Haiphong for the manufacture of the acid. Wu purchased the facility, together with electric generating equipment, and shipped it to Shanghai. Wu inaugurated the new plant in 1929, labeling it the Tianyuan Electric Powered Chemical Factory (Tianyuan dian hua chang). Wu could now manufacture the key ingredients that Tianchu needed to produce MSG.[23]

With the opening of the new facility, Wu joined Fan Xudong as a major leader of China's nascent chemical industry. Aside from hydrochloric acid, Tianyuan manufactured such complex products as liquefied caustic soda and bleaching powder. Tianyuan's daily production of the acid reached two tons; of bleach, three tons; and of caustic soda, four tons. The "national product" label helped Tianyuan's bleach to enter a market heretofore dominated by the Japanese.[24]

Wu's ambitions continued to grow. A 1932 trip to the United States convinced him that new areas of production were possible. The Tianyuan plant had a growing demand for acid-resistant ceramics. The factory relied on Japanese or French products. Convinced he could manufacture pottery of sufficient durability, Wu established the Tiansheng Ceramics Company (Tiansheng taoqi chang) in 1934, which used white clay from Yixing. It produced twenty to forty tons monthly of specialized pottery for chemical production.[25]

In the mid-1930s Wu developed the technology to produce nitrogen, nitric acid, and ammonia, partly using byproducts of the Tianyuan factory. The critical step was a visit to France in 1934, when Wu was able to purchase equipment to produce nitric acid. By 1936, his Tianli Nitrogen Plant (Tianli danqi chang) could produce four tons of ammonia daily.[26]

Wu's career paralleled Fan's in many ways, although he did not rely on political connections to the extent that his northern counterpart did. As had Fan, however, Wu stressed research, promoted himself as a pioneer of new technology, and established a research office. In 1928 he founded the China Chemistry Research Institute (Zhonghua gongye huaxue yanjiu suo). Meanwhile, the China Chemical Industrial Society (Zhonghua huaxue gongye hui), which had been founded in Beijing in 1922, decided to move to Shanghai and work with Wu's group. The society's major publication was *Huaxue shijie* (The world of chemistry), and the group assembled a small library.[27]

Although Wu's career was less involved with politics than Fan's, he did occasionally assume a semigovernmental role. In 1937 he traveled to Germany representing the Nanjing government's National Resources Commission. He had just negotiated an agreement with I. G. Farben to supply China with equipment for petroleum refining when war erupted and he rushed back to Shanghai.[28]

WU AT WAR

Wu attempted to move his plants out of harm's way but with limited success. The Tianli and Tianyuan factories, located in Western Shanghai, made chemical products of strategic value, and so were among early targets bombed by the Japanese. Wu sought to remove as much equipment as possible, first to the safety of the foreign concessions and then by ship to the interior. Finding transport was difficult; the plants were in the midst of fighting and troop movements. On several occasions Wu arranged shipping only to have it commandeered by Chinese forces. Finally on October 22, Wu's personnel began loading equipment onto eleven boats, only to fall victim to Japanese bombs four days later. Much of the equipment was sunk in the Suzhou Creek, from which it would be dredged up and confiscated by the Japanese. In the meantime, Wu received a subsidy from Nanjing to assist in the evacuation. About 600 tons of equipment were shipped to Hankou before Shanghai fell, although this included only 112 tons from the more strategic Tianli and Tianyuan plants. More than 360 tons from Tianchu (MSG) and 24 tons from Tiansheng (ceramics) were included. Nearly two months en route, the shipment suffered significant damage.[29]

Although Wu made some effort to reopen in the Wuhan area, he quickly concluded that real security would be found only in Sichuan. Indeed, no less than Chiang Kaishek himself recommended the move. In early 1938, Wu began shipping equipment upriver toward Chongqing. Losses continued as one shipment was bombed at Yichang in late February 1938. Of the four groups, that of the Tiansheng Ceramics Company fared best and began production in Sichuan. Ironically, nearly ten tons of new equipment for Tianyuan ordered from overseas arrived in Wuhan via Hong Kong on October 21, 1938, on the eve of the city's fall. It had to be abandoned.[30]

Wu utilized two routes in evacuating his enterprises from the Shanghai area—one to the interior, the other to Hong Kong. Wu himself departed for the Crown Colony in late 1937 (where he spent several weeks) and attempted to find factory space in Kowloon. Using some equipment shipped from Shanghai, and an additional 2 million yuan of investment, the Tianchu MSG facility in Hong Kong began production in 1939, averaging 100,000 kilograms annually until the eruption of the Pacific war. Wu's wife, Wu Yi, remained in Hong Kong to keep an eye on things. She was one of the few women to take so active a role. When the Japanese moved in after Pearl Harbor, she had as much equipment as possible smuggled out by foot and transported to Chongqing. Only a very small amount was rescued, so Wu's factory in the interior actually used handicraft techniques rather than the more modern processes the company had adopted in the late 1920s. The plant, managed by Wu's son Wu Zhichao, produced only 200 pounds of MSG per month, a far cry from the 1,600 pounds of daily production in Shanghai during the prewar period. Even this level was difficult to maintain. When a shortage of wheat gluten threatened production, Tianchu workers devised a method of using beans instead as a raw material.[31]

Wu also established a branch of Tianyuan in Hong Kong that produced bleaching powder. In the period from the fall of Wuhan until Pearl Harbor, Wu continued to ship some equipment to Sichuan using a very complex transport system of British-registered ships from Shanghai to Hong Kong then Haiphong. From there equipment shifted to railroad to Guiyang. Thereafter it went by truck and then train to Chongqing. In March 1939 Wu purchased thirty tons of machinery from abroad for Tianyuan, and managed to ship part of this to Chongqing. Despite this complex and dangerous route, Tianyuan received enough equipment in the interior to operate a plant in Sichuan. On June 22, 1940, Tianyuan resumed very modest operations, with about 100 workers producing bleaching powder. Life in the interior was still fraught with danger, however. In May 1944 the Tianyuan plant suffered severe damage when bombed by Japanese airplanes. Wu's group weathered the other hazard of Free China—hyperinflation—more successfully. Any commodity, even MSG or bleaching powder, could be traded on the black market or bartered.[32]

The equipment of the Tianli nitrogen plant had been totally destroyed in the fighting or sunk during the evacuation. The only hope was for new purchases, so in August 1941, Wu traveled to America to acquire the items needed for nitric acid production. Before delivery could be made, however, Pearl Harbor intervened. Wu's heroic efforts to reestablish his enterprises had met with obstacle after obstacle. Faced with severe shortages of capital, equipment, and raw materials, Wu finally turned to the Guomindang government for assistance. In 1943 he received a substantial infusion of capital from the National Resources Commission and Wu's plants became "state-owned enterprises." Technically Wu and the private shareholders controlled 51 percent of the stock and the National Resources Commission 49 percent, but clearly Wu's independence was curtailed. Although funding from government banks was essential, Wu remained uncomfortable in the role of bureaucratic capitalist; prior to the war he had largely steered clear of politics.[33]

Meanwhile in Shanghai, the Japanese had seized the site of the Tianyuan and Tianli plants and sealed them up. Wu kept an office in unoccupied Shanghai under the direction of Li Shi'an, who made several unsuccessful attempts to visit the factories. Li even tried a ruse by using a connection to a secretary to the British consul. Li told Japanese authorities that the firm had been sold to the British Brunner-Mond and Company (Buneimen) and that this British subject must check the facilities. The secretary was paid US $200 for participating in this scheme but failed to enter the plants. Finally in February 1938 Japanese troops lifted the blockade. Li and plant personnel were permitted to reenter the factory and frantically packed up equipment for shipment to the foreign concessions in Shanghai. Some portion of this was transported to Hong Kong and on to Hankou, arriving just before the city fell in October 1938.[34]

Dealing with the Japanese in Shanghai was not easy. One of Wu's employees, Gu Naizhi, was arrested by Japanese authorities in August 1938 in a dispute over salvage of the factory equipment found in the Suzhou Creek. A nearby Japanese company claimed that Tianyuan personnel had actually stolen the equipment during the heat of battle and tried to ship it out to Wuhan. Gu died after three months in prison. Wu arranged for compensation for his family. Eventually most of the equipment that Tianyuan left in the occupied areas was entrusted to the Japanese Ishin chemical company. Already operating factories in Tianjin and Qingdao, Ishin made acids, salts, and other chemical products. It established a branch in Shanghai using the Tianyuan and Tianli sites (which were adjacent). The Tianli plant was put in production first. Destruction at the Tianyuan facility had been so extensive that no immediate plans were made to reopen, and indeed much of the equipment had been taken as scrap metal. In the summer of 1941, with the support of the Kōain, the Ishin Company began to clean up the Tianyuan site. After Pearl Harbor, strategic considerations led the Japanese to invest heavily in the plant, which after months of delay began producing hydrochloric acid and alkali.[35]

Wu had also left some material in the foreign concessions in Shanghai, which had not been evacuated. On August 12, 1937, the day before fighting spread to Shanghai, Wu had hastily rented space in the French Concession and began moving equipment from two Tianchu plants in the abutting Nanshi section of Shanghai. Gao Baixun was left in charge of the equipment, although not everything was moved before Nanshi fell. Nonetheless, in April 1938 Gao opened a small Tianchu factory in island Shanghai to produce MSG. By 1939 the economy of unoccupied Shanghai revived and Shanghai Tianchu produced almost 30,000 pounds of MSG monthly, still well short of prewar levels. Trade with occupied China was difficult, but Tianchu Shanghai sent much of the production to the Hong Kong branch, which marketed it widely to overseas Chinese communities in Southeast Asia.[36]

Relations between the Sichuan branch and those who remained in Shanghai and Hong Kong were not always smooth. Patriotism was certainly one issue—some were working for Free China while others stayed in territory surrounded by the enemy. Questions of authority also surfaced. Wu's enterprises, like most such Chinese firms, had been under his personal control. With incomplete communication among Sichuan, Hong Kong, and Shanghai, differences naturally arose. Finally, there was the contradiction between the Tianchu stockholders, whose firms continued production, and those of the Tianyuan and Tianli concerns, who saw no income from their investments. Although Wu had been the key figure, he had raised capital for each of the enterprises separately. In Chongqing, equipment, supplies, personnel, and capital were being merged into one company. In Shanghai and Hong Kong they had been separate.

Tension flared between Wu and Gao, forcing the latter to resign in late June 1940. Although they had been very close, and Gao had been appointed to the standing committee of the board of directors, Wu and Gao did not meet face to face after Wu departed for Hong Kong and Sichuan. Contact by mail and telegram did not easily resolve differences of opinion that developed in the two very different environments in which the managers found themselves. After Gao's departure, Wu appointed Wang Huaigen director of Shanghai Tianchu operations. Meanwhile, Tianyuan stockholders in Shanghai pressed Wu to declare bankruptcy in the summer of 1938 and settle remaining capital on the investors. Wu became angry because he felt that he was sacrificing for China, whereas the Shanghai group was concerned only with their personal interests.[37]

Many of these concerns became moot after Pearl Harbor when Japan occupied all of Shanghai. Gao had registered Tianchu as a German firm, even hiring a German manager, Flug, as a cover. Gao hoped to counter

Tianchu's major Japanese competitor in the MSG market, the Suzuki Company. In a bold move, Suzuki registered the Tianchu trademark with the Wang Jingwei government in Nanjing and began to market their MSG under a Tianchu label. Gao felt that only the protection of a foreign flag, one friendly with Japan, could secure Tianchu's copyrights. The Shanghai group telegraphed Wu, who endorsed the plan to register with Germany. A dummy German company (Koch) was set up, which "foreclosed" on a mortgage of Tianchu and appeared to claim the brand name copyrights.[38]

After Pearl Harbor this approach was ineffective. Tianchu officials in Shanghai, now led by Wu Yunzhai, felt they had to have connections with the Nanjing puppet regime. Wu contacted two Nanjing officials, Lin Kanghou and Chen Riping, who agreed to organize a new firm, the Tiancheng Company, to serve as a front. It took over the Tianchu factories in Shanghai, although production dropped because of the lack of raw materials.[39]

When Japanese authorities began returning some Chinese factories in 1943, the Shanghai group hoped to regain the Tianyuan and Tianli plants, but they had little success. The Japanese Ishin Company had already invested 3 to 4 million yen in the Tianyuan chemical plant, since so much equipment had been damaged or removed. The adjacent Tianli nitrogen plant (which then produced nitric acid) had required a smaller yet still significant investment. Under these conditions, the Japanese firm was unwilling to surrender control, despite pleas from Nanjing. On July 1, 1943, Ishin and the Ministry of Industry in Nanjing signed an agreement whereby the Japanese firm kept control but paid a monthly rental fee and a percentage of any profits to the Chinese side. The actual amount paid was rendered rather trifling by hyperinflation. Moreover, Nanjing apparently retained these funds since Wu Yunchu was not within its jurisdiction. With conditions unfavorable for production, Ishin gave up in March 1945 and left management of the factory in the hands of the Tōa company.[40]

Wu Yunchu's wartime actions fit the narrative of "patriotic capitalist," although perhaps not so clearly as Fan Xudong's. Wu followed the Guomindang government to Sichuan, where he valiantly attempted to restore production. On the other hand, he kept personnel in Shanghai and tacitly approved their registration as a foreign firm. It is unclear whether he authorized the Tianchu group to work with puppet authorities after the Japanese takeover of the foreign concessions. Perhaps the key difference between Fan and Wu was circumstances, however. Fan's factories were immediately bombed or seized by the Japanese. Wu had the opportunity to move equipment into the foreign concessions in Shanghai. Wu's product line was also less strategically important than Fan's was. Although he produced a range of chemical products, the "MSG king" was geared more toward consumer products of less interest to the Japanese military. Finally, Wu's political links were less significant than Fan's. Throughout his entire career, Fan had utilized and developed political ties. These created both opportunities and difficulties for him in wartime Sichuan. Wu had some links, but his ties were less developed, and he received less assistance in reopening his plants. Both men did ultimately succeed in operating manufacturing plants in the interior; neither achieved production levels approaching their prewar outputs.

THE LIU HONGSHENG GROUP

Liu Hongsheng (O. S. Lieu) is considered one of the greatest of the "patriotic industrialists." Liu's reputation is built on many factors, including his leadership in organizing relief work during the battle of Shanghai as well as his prominent role as an industrialist in Free China during the war.[41] Liu Hongsheng began his career as a compradore for the British Kailuan Mines, earning a fortune as director of sales of its coal in the lower Yangzi area. Liu parlayed this success into a career in manufacturing, organizing such concerns as the Shanghai Cement Company (Shanghai shuini gongsi) at Longhua in the early 1920s, the Zhanghua Woolen Manufacturing Company (Zhanghua maorong fangzhi chang) located in Pudong across the river from Shanghai's Bund, and the Huafeng enamel plant (Huafeng tangci chang). His China Godown Company (Zhonghua matou gongsi) ran three wharves in Pudong, and Liu developed interests in banks and shipping. Liu is best remembered, however, as China's "match king" *(huochai dawang)* because of the central position of his Great China Match Company (Da Zhonghua huochai gufen youxian gongsi).[42]

Liu began his match company in Suzhou in 1920 as the Hongsheng Match Mills (Suzhou Hongsheng huochai chang), seeking to avoid the intense competition and higher labor costs in Shanghai. He quickly followed with the opening of a second factory, the Yusheng plant (Yusheng huochai chang), in Jiujiang, about 200 kilometers east of Wuhan on the Yangzi. Liu merged with two other companies in the summer of 1930, forming the Great China Match Company with Liu as the general manager, although Liu and his brother owned only about 30 percent of the stock. The anti-Japanese boycotts of 1931 and 1932 were a godsend; the new company supplied more than 46 percent of the matches sold in the lower Yangzi during the year from July 1931 to June 1932. By 1934, Great China had seven plants in the lower Yangzi, from Shanghai to Suzhou, Zhenjiang, Jiujiang, Hankou, and Hangzhou.[43]

Times were much less profitable in the mid-1930s when increased competition led to lower prices and reduced profits. In February 1936, T. V. Soong approached Liu and suggested collaboration in establishing a holding company over Liu's enterprises. The two men had personal ties through St. John's University in Shanghai; they referred to each other by the English initials "T.V." and "O.S." Like most entrepreneurs, however, Liu jealously guarded his authority. He assumed that cooperation with Soong would lead to the latter's dominance of Great China Match, so Liu resisted the partnership. To salvage his match operations, Liu instead negotiated a cartel arrangement with other producers, including the giant Swedish Match Company. In the last two years before the war, prices of matches rose nearly 50 percent under the arrangement, enabling Liu to fend off Soong.[44]

Liu's prominence as an entrepreneur was matched by his role in public affairs, particularly after the creation of the Guomindang government. Nanjing appointed Liu the general manager of the China Merchants Steam Navigation Company in 1933 and as a member of the National Economic Council. Moreover, in the early 1930s Liu served as a councillor on the Shanghai Municipal Council, which governed the International Settlement, and he was vice chair of the Shanghai branch of the Red Cross. When the war erupted, Liu continued his public leadership, directing the Commission to Aid Wounded Soldiers (Shanghai shi shangbing jiuhu weiyuan hui). This group organized the transportation of wounded Chinese soldiers from the front to hospitals in Shanghai, while the Red Cross helped with refugee relief. Working with other groups in Shanghai, Liu was able to provide more than 5,000 beds for wounded soldiers, far short of what was needed but significant nonetheless given the inadequacies of military medical services on the Chinese side.[45]

Liu was the quintessential Chinese entrepreneur, founding, financing, and personally directing a wide variety of enterprises. Although he entrusted management to others and turned to many investors, ultimately he insisted on personal control. As with many other businessmen, Liu used family members as part of his empire, combining the control of the *jia* with control of the business empire. His younger brother, Liu Jisheng, handled day-to-day concerns of much of his business, and Liu produced fourteen children (by four different women). Hedging his bets, Liu sent three sons and one daughter to study in England, three sons and one daughter to the United States, and two sons and one daughter to Japan. Liu thus had a rich family base on which to draw.[46]

LIU HONGSHENG AND THE OUTBREAK OF THE WAR

The war dealt a crushing blow to Liu's fortunes. Most of his major enterprises in the Shanghai area were located in areas such as Longhua and Pudong and fell under Japanese control. His cement factory halted production on August 16. Although some attempt was made to protect the company by registering it as German and hanging swastikas around the plant, workers and management abandoned the property when Japanese bombers attacked on October 27. Cement was a strategic commodity for the Japanese; they seized the facility. The military entrusted its management to the Onoda Cement Works (Onoda yōkai kabushiki kaisha) and Mitsui Bussan, which restored production on July 18, 1938. After a slow start of producing only 25,485 metric tons of cement in 1939, the company managed almost 67,000 in 1940. Even after Pearl Harbor the company turned out nearly 52,000 tons in 1943 and more than 48,000 tons in 1944.[47]

The Zhanghua woolen mill in Pudong fared somewhat better. In the five weeks between the Marco Polo Bridge Incident and the eruption of fighting in Shanghai, Liu and the management frantically tried to move equipment across the Huangpu River to the International Settlement. Ultimately a large number of spindles, looms, dyeing machines, and raw materials were salvaged. Using this and other equipment, Zhanghua management succeeded in opening a new mill in the solitary island on October 21, 1937. With equipment previously ordered from France, Zhanghua established a second plant on November 22, 1938. Meanwhile Liu worked with a German bank, which registered the Pudong factory as German and attempted to protect it from Japanese seizure. This ploy seemed to have been more successful in Zhanghua's case than in others, perhaps in part because a German national remained on the plant site, which flew the Nazi flag. Although they controlled Pudong by autumn 1937, Japanese troops did not enter the mill grounds until June 1939, at which time they finally rejected the German claims of ownership. In the meantime, Liu's son, Liu Nianzhi, turned to a Swede, E. Widler, with good connections to the Japanese. He arranged for five to six boatloads of equipment to be removed at a fee of 5,000 yuan per boat, part of which he paid to Japanese as bribes. The Japanese military entrusted the Pudong plant to Shanghai bōseki, which restored production on December 1, 1939. Meanwhile, the two plants operating across the river put the equipment to good use. They produced 168,300 meters of woolen products in 1939—a substantial output, although much less than Zhanghua's production of 502,920 meters in 1936.[48]

Liu's Great China Match Company suffered serious losses as well. Several of its seven plants were either damaged in the fighting or had material looted. Those that escaped destruction ceased production as they came under Japanese control. Suzhou closed on November 11, Hangzhou on November 17, and Zhenjiang on November 23. By the end of the year only the plant in Jiujiang, Jiangxi, remained in operation, and it closed in June 1938. Great China's total production for 1938 was only 22.6 percent of the level of 1936. Liu's losses from Great China Match were estimated at 30 million yuan. Perhaps because of long-standing competition between Chinese and Japanese firms, the strategic importance of the raw materials in match production, and the certain market for matches, the Japanese were eager to gain control over this business and the revenue it generated. The Japanese created the National Match Production and Marketing Joint Operations Company (Quanguo huochai chanxiao lianying she), which became a subsidiary of the Central China Development Company. This group controlled access to raw materials, set prices, and set production limits for match plants in the occupied areas.[49]

The Lius did not immediately give up on salvaging their match-making factories in the occupied area, since several had escaped destruction. Shortly after Chinese forces retreated westward, Great China Match began petitioning the Japanese for permission to reopen. The Yingchang plant in Zhenjiang (located on the Yangzi about 70 kilometers northeast of Nanjing), for instance, had closed in November 1937, but by July 1938, the headquarters of Great China Match contacted the Japanese consulate in Shanghai seeking to restore production. Locally, the company's representative, Zhou Yangqiao, who spoke Japanese, began cooperating with Japanese officials. Eventually the head of Special Services of the Japanese Military at Zhenjiang gave approval for Yingchang to resume production. The plant agreed to pay a tax of ten yuan per case of matches to the local puppet government, the Zhenjiang Self-Governing Commission (Zhenjiang zizhi weiyuan hui).[50]

Similarly, a representative of Great China, Qi Fuming, petitioned the Japanese consulate on July 26, 1938, for permission to reopen the Suzhou

Hongsheng plant. The Japanese had already set up a commission to regulate the sales of matches (later to be part of their development companies), which the Suzhou plant agreed to join. Great China Match did report to the Chinese authorities that they were attempting to reopen plants
in the occupied zone; they justified this effort as necessary for the wel-
fare of the workers, who otherwise would be left with no income. Perhaps the only cautionary move was that members of the Liu family were
not usually listed as the responsible parties. The petition of Liu's Suzhou
plant was made by Qi Fuming; the plant manager was listed as Wang
Shouyi. Use of the Liu name was avoided when possible. Yet all of these
early efforts at collaboration eventually failed. In September 1938, when
the Japanese became annoyed at Liu's unwillingness to collaborate personally (discussed below), they decreed Great China factories to be "enemy property," and seized them. Several of the plants continued to operate but under the direction of the Joint Operations Company, which
controlled prices, supplies, and payment of dividends to shareholders.
Still, in 1939, Great China produced more than 45 percent of the 1936
level of production.[51]

There were other losses. Pudong fell to the Japanese in November
1937, and with it went Liu's wharves. Liu Nianren and his father attempted to use an Italian connection to salvage the operation, but the
Japanese wanted the facilities for military use. Pleas through the Italian
consulate and petitions to the Japanese in 1938 and 1939 produced no
relief. The enamel factory was a loss as well. Only Liu's China Enterprise Bank (Zhongguo qiye yinghang), insurance firm (Dahua baoxian
gongsi), and real estate in the foreign settlement escaped Japanese occupation. The bank felt an immediate shock from the outbreak of conflict
but continued to function. Liu's most important property was his eight-
story building on Sichuan Road near the Bund.[52]

Early in the conflict, the Japanese had sought the cooperation of several prominent capitalists such as Yu Xiaqing, Rong Zongjing, and Liu
Hongsheng, individuals whom the Japanese felt would bring prestige to
their puppet regimes. According to Liu's sons, Liu Nianzhi and Liu Nianyi, their father was approached early in 1938 by representatives of Mitsui and Mitsubishi, with whom he had earlier had business dealings. They
urged him to renounce the Chiang Kaishek government and cooperate
with the Japanese. Perhaps the Japanese felt Liu was approachable because he had remained in Shanghai and had endorsed a plan to have
Shanghai declared an "open port," with access for all countries. Liu apparently stalled the negotiations for several months until he was visited

by a Japanese military official who had been handling the management of the Chinese match factories that had been confiscated in the Shanghai area. This representative, Ueda Jiichirō, was polite but firm, informing Liu that the safety of his family could not be guaranteed if he refused to cooperate. Conversely, the Japanese considered Liu a valuable potential ally and would reward his support, presumably by allowing him a partnership in his enterprises that were in Japanese hands. Ueda met with Liu and his sons. Liu Nianzhi recalls four to five such meetings, which included his brother, Liu Nianyi. An uncle, Liu Qinghong, who had studied extensively in Japan, translated. The Japanese suggested that Liu could head the chamber of commerce and implement a cooperative policy with Japan.[53]

Liu became subject to intense pressure from both sides. When the wave of assassinations by both pro-Chiang and pro-Japanese agents began in earnest in early 1938, Liu became extremely nervous about remaining in Shanghai, even in the foreign settlement. Eventually in June of that year Liu fled for the safer haven of Hong Kong, leaving other family members to manage the unoccupied holdings in island Shanghai. Ueda informed the family that the Liu enterprises seized by the Japanese would be held as hostage as long as the senior Liu refused to collaborate.[54]

Ever the entrepreneur, Liu attempted to initiate match production in Hong Kong. Working with T. L. Soong (Song Ziliang, T. V. Soong's younger brother), who would head the board of directors, and Weng Wenyi, the chief engineer, Liu drew on about forty investors from his Great China Match, funds from the Shanghai office, and the backing of the China National Products Bank (Zhongguo guohuo yinhang). Liu's Hong Kong plant began in April 1940 with a capital of HK $300,000. With sales to Hong Kong, the interior, and southeast Asia, the firm earned HK $500,000 to $600,000 in the months before the Japanese takeover in December 1941. Personnel were as important as equipment for Liu, so he instructed the technicians and accountants of Great China Match Company who were still in Shanghai to transit to Hong Kong.[55]

LIU HONGSHENG IN FREE CHINA

Even as he remained in the British colony, Liu attempted to establish production in unoccupied China. Some material from his plants was already there. Equipment from his Yusheng match factory in Jiujiang had been evacuated upriver before the Japanese arrival, and Liu tried to ship material from Shanghai. By the end of 1940 Liu would already be in production in Sichuan as well as Guizhou. Liu combined forces with Sun Shupei of the Huaye Match Company, and the two men organized the Huaye Heji Match Company (Huaye heji huochai gongsi), with Great China controlling 60 percent of the stock. Enjoying a virtual monopoly on the manufacture of safety matches in the unoccupied zone, the company was quite profitable, especially through 1943, and was able to open eight plants in Free China. Perhaps the most difficult feat was manufacturing the raw materials for matches, such as phosphorus, much of which had previously been supplied by Japanese sources. When the European war further reduced supplies, Liu has determined to manufacture the materials himself. In May 1940 Liu established the China Match Raw Materials Company (Zhongguo huochai yuanliao gongsi) in east Sichuan, the only such manufacturer in the unoccupied zone, which could supply his plants with the needed ingredients for producing matches.[56]

Liu's industrial empire in the interior was only a fraction of his prewar holdings. Nonetheless, he did attempt to restore his woolen concern. Machinery from the Zhanghua woolen mill, which had been moved from Pudong to island Shanghai, was then shipped to the interior via Haiphong or Rangoon. Zhanghua had established sales offices in Nanjing and Hankou before the war, and some material from these facilities was moved as well. Liu organized the China Woolen Company (Zhongguo mao fangzhi gongsi) in Sichuan. Liu also noted the large supply of raw wool in the northwest and the complete absence of factories. Manufactured textiles fetched high prices while raw wool was relatively cheap—a situation ripe for profits. Later in 1943 Liu established the Northwest Woolen Manufacturing Company, Ltd. (Xibei mao fangzhi chang gufen youxian gongsi), in Lanzhou in order to tap these woolen supplies. Liu ordered additional equipment overseas in order to expand, but unfortunately 300 tons of machinery for woolen production was captured by the Japanese in Burma in April 1942.[57]

As for Liu himself, he wavered throughout 1940 as to whether or not he should attempt to relocate to Sichuan from the supposed security of Hong Kong. In December Chiang Kaishek telegraphed, encouraging him to come west and promising support for his industries. H. H. Kung pledged to assist with his match production in the interior. In late December 1940, Liu boarded a plane for Chongqing. Several of his family members followed, although others stayed in Shanghai and Hong Kong during the entire war, keeping an eye on their remaining property. His son Liu Nianli stayed in Hong Kong to handle the Great China Match factory there, while Liu Nianren, Nianyi, and Nianzhong managed in

Shanghai. As with so many entrepreneurs, Liu relied on family connections to handle property, especially when communications were difficult.[58]

Shortly after his arrival in Chongqing, Liu was entertained by none other than Chiang Kaishek himself, an indication of Liu's status and the eagerness of Chiang to attract capitalists from the coast. Liu still had connections with the Soongs as well. Government investments and bank loans had been crucial for the China Match Raw Materials Company, which had five government appointees on the nine-man board of directors. T. L. Soong was chair of the board, while Liu served as general manager. Liu's China Woolen Company was also a joint government-private venture. Of 40,000 shares of stock, 10,000 were held by the Ministry of Finance, 5,000 by Liu, 5,000 by T. L. Soong, and 5,000 by Weng Wenhao. Yet Liu's relations with the Guomindang government were not totally smooth. Although Guomindang officials valued Liu's skills and leadership, they forced him to operate within private-government partnerships. Liu found his independence curtailed, not a circumstance he tolerated easily. In his partnership with H. H. Kung and the Soongs, Liu found himself second in command, a difficult role for someone use to being the dominant figure. Liu apparently expressed his dismay to family members, telling his son Liu Nianzhi that "my being general manager has become being their clerk."[59]

Still, Liu undoubtedly played a major role in developing industry in Free China. He even organized cement production, first in Ba county, Sichuan, and then in Lanzhou. Liu began the war with substantial earnings, so even with his losses in Shanghai, he had capital in reserve to invest. By war's end he had investments in eight match factories, three woolen mills, two cement plants and assorted other concerns in Free China. He served on several official and semi-official agencies in Chongqing, all designed to support the war economy. He would seem to deserve very strongly the designation "patriotic industrialist."[60]

LIU FAMILY PROPERTY IN THE OCCUPIED AREAS

Even Liu's record is subject to a variety of readings. Although Liu had moved to Chongqing, several sons and a younger brother stayed in Shanghai and continued to act on behalf of family businesses. The Liu bank, the China Enterprise Bank located in the International Settlement, continued operations even after December 1941. Liu Nianren wrote to his father in Chongqing to keep him informed of the bank's situation. In September 1942, for instance, he told Hongsheng that the bank had survived the exchange for old fabi for the currency of the Nanjing regime and continued to prosper. It would earn significant profits through 1944. After Pearl Harbor, when the Lius were unable to retail coal supplies in Shanghai, they sought new ventures. In February 1942, Nianren and Liu Nianzhong (the seventh son) established the Hongye Real Estate Company (Hongye dichan gongsi). They focused their real estate purchases in Nanshi and Zhabei, since these areas were much less developed than the old foreign settlements. Through speculation, the Hongye firm remained profitable into 1945. Taking advantage of wartime inflation, Liu Nianren paid off the debts of the Liu enterprises and increased the family's share of holdings. As the Japanese became more open to cooperation, Nianren apparently entered into joint agreements regarding several of the enterprises, given the Liu family some stake in the cement and match plants taken in 1937 and 1938 by the Japanese.[61]

The Shanghai Cement Factory, for instance, had been seized by the Japanese military and entrusted to the Japanese Onoda Company and Mitsui in 1938. As noted earlier, the firm had been very successful, maintaining a high level of production until 1945. Because of the strategic significance of cement, the Japanese military did not wish to return the factory to Chinese control. Instead, it pressed for a cooperative arrangement that would leave management in Japanese hands. In 1942 a representative of the Mitsui bank informed the Lius that the Japanese wished to replace the military control by a "rental" arrangement between the Chinese company and the Japanese companies who were operating the plant. The Lius were pressured to sign. Liu Jisheng, Hongsheng's younger brother, discussed the matter with Nianren and Nianzhong, among others, and concluded that since the agreement had been presented as a fait accompli they should acquiesce. Under the rental contract, which became official on January 14, 1943, Onoda and Mitsui would pay the stockholders of the Chinese firm a monthly rent (12,000 military yen) for a five-year period. The Lius thus regained some income from their facility, while the Japanese demonstrated their new policy of cooperation.[62]

A similar process developed for the Zhanghua woolen mills. The Shanhai bōseki company had operated the Pudong mill since 1939, and the Japanese had seized the plants in island Shanghai in December 1941. But when conditions appeared suitable, the Lius attempted to recover this property. On June 30, 1942, Zhanghua management petitioned the Ministry of Industry of the Wang Jingwei government to restore their mills. Yet Shanhai bōseki claimed to have invested heavily in the Pudong facility and did not wish to yield its rights. The Japanese consulate pressured the two sides to agree to a joint operation. After several weeks of discussion they formed a joint company, Shang Zhang Woolen Manufacturing Company (Shang Zhang maorong fangzhi gufen youxian gongsi, the Chinese name; Shan Shō Seijō kabushiki kaisha, the Japanese name). The new firm was capitalized at 2 million military yen, with half coming from each of the two parties. On December 17, 1942, representatives of Zhanghua, led by Liu Nianren, Shanhai bōseki, and Japanese military and civilian officials met at a hotel in Shanghai to celebrate the new joint company. Liu Nianren was the major shareholder on the Chinese side and Kuroda Keitarō the Japanese. Although the arrangement salvaged property rights for the Lius, and Liu Nianren served on the board of directors, the Japanese retained control of operations. The general manager of the firm was from Shanhai bōseki.[63]

The Lius were more successful in regaining control of the two plants they had established in the former island Shanghai. These had remained in production throughout the war and employed more than 300 workers, until seized in December 1941. When the plants were restored, the Lius struggled to find adequate sources of raw material. One of the plants dabbled in silk weaving to cope with the shortage of wool. In 1942 and 1943, the two plants produced 52,000 and 58,143 meters of woolen products, respectively (compared with 168,300 in 1939). The company maintained good relations with several banks in Shanghai, including the puppet Central Bank, which enabled them freely to borrow funds. Late in the war, the Lius found new supplies and produced a wartime record 202,000 meters in 1944. Profits for that year reached 27 million yuan on sales of 115 million.[64]

The Lius even salvaged a bit of their match empire. The factories of the Great China Match Company had been designated "enemy property" and placed under military direction after Liu Hongsheng had refused to collaborate in 1938. The Chinese management actually stayed on for the most part, but the Japanese controllers prevented them from removing profits or paying dividends to shareholders. Following his relocation in Hong Kong, Liu resigned as general manager of Great China Match, leaving his son, Liu Nianyi, to represent his interests in the company. The young Liu sent numerous letters to his father in Hong Kong and later Chongqing, reporting on conditions. In May of 1940 the board of directors of Great China Match realized that it might be possible to regain control of the plants by cooperating with the new Wang Jingwei government in Nanjing, though the process of rendition was slow. In March 1942, the Japanese organized the Central China Match Company (Hua-

zhong huochai gufen youxian gongsi) as a subsidiary of the Central China
Development Company. This new entity, called Kachō matchi kabushiki
kaisha in Japanese, was given control of sales and production of nearly
fifty-five factories previously controlled by Chinese.[65]

To take advantage of the new situation, the board of directors of Great
China Match appointed as its chair, in March 1942, Chen Bofan, an
official in Nanjing with good connections. Chen was to negotiate an end
to the designation of Great China Match as "enemy property." In December 1942, military management of the six surviving factories was ter-
minated and the "enemy property" label abolished. In exchange, the company agreed to accept terms of cooperation with the Central China
Development Company and its subsidiary the Central China Match Company. The terms included giving up two of the six plants to a joint venture, the Yingchang factories in Shanghai and Zhenjiang.[66]

On December 1, Chen Bofan formally signed an agreement with Japanese representatives of the CCDC and Taguchi Takeo of Central China
Match, creating a joint enterprise. On paper the Chinese side retained
majority control. Sixty percent of the capital came from Great China
Match, as did three of the five members of the board of directors. Control of raw materials and sales of matches, however, remained in the hands
of the CCDC for the entire match industry. Eventually, Chen Bofan was
appointed chair of the board of directors of the Central China Match
Company; a Japanese, Yasuno Takekazu, was vice director; Taguchi
Takeo and Liu Nianyi served on the board of directors. By giving up the
two plants to the joint venture, the owners of Great China Match, though
still under the general restrictions on supplies and price, were free to uti-
lize the profits from the other four operations.[67]

The one property that Great China could not regain was the Yusheng
plant in Jiujiang. The Great China board petitioned the Wang government on January 7, 1943. In a June 23 reply, Wang's Ministry of Industry informed the board that the Japanese military needed the site for military purposes and the plant could not be returned until later.[68]

Despite collaboration with the Wang government and the Japanese,
Great China Match could not keep up production during the later years
of the war. Shortage of materials and the collapse of the currency affected
the match industry, much as it had other sectors of business (see table 6).

The Liu family also had problems with the Hong Kong plant, which
Hongsheng had established there in 1940. When Hongsheng left for
Chongqing, his son Liu Nanli assumed control, although he reported to
his father throughout the war. The company, which had garnered

TABLE 6. MATCH PRODUCTION
BY THE GREAT CHINA MATCH COMPANY*

Year	Number of boxes produced
1936	100
1937	65.8
1938	22.6
1939	45.7
1940	37.4
1941	27.7
1942	11.4
1943	7.4
1944	9.4

SOURCE: SASS, *Liu Hongsheng qiye shiliao*, vol. 3, p. 96.
*Figures exclude the two Yingchang plants after December 1942.

HK $500,000 to $600,000 profit in 1940 and 1941, was placed under military control after the Japanese occupation of Hong Kong and remained closed until August 1943. Great China management finally received permission to reopen in that month, but production was limited by shortages of raw materials and fuel.[69]

When Guomindang forces liberated Shanghai after the war, they confiscated as enemy property many businesses that had collaborated with the Japanese. Yet Liu Hongsheng worked vigorously to regain his empire. On August 15, 1945, he wrote separate letters to his brother Liu Jisheng and sons Nianren and Nianyi regarding the state of the Liu enterprises. Hoping to use his official connections, he agreed to become the head of the Shanghai office of the government's Relief and Rehabilitation Administration (Shanhou jiuji zongshu). Returning to Shanghai on October 2, 1945, he worked to reacquire family property, arguing that the Sino-Japanese joint agreements had been coerced and did not represent "collaboration." He wrote to the Shanghai District Enemy and Puppet Property Office (Shanghai qu diwei chanye chu) on December 15, 1945, detailing the pressures that led to joint agreements involving Great China Match plants in the occupied zone. With his political connections, Liu was able to get his properties returned to family control. Although the Liu enterprises had been joint stock companies in which the family had sometimes been a minority stockholder in prewar China, the Lius actually emerged from the war with firmer control over the surviving enterprises.[70]

Liu's wartime record is thus subject to multiple readings. His personal actions in eventually moving to Chongqing and establishing numerous plants there certainly fit the "patriotic nationalist narrative." Yet he left other family members in Hong Kong and Shanghai, where they made substantial compromises with the Japanese in order to retain some control over their property. When the war ended, Liu used his status with the Guomindang to regain this property and to minimize charges of collaboration. In sum, Liu, like many others, attempted to survive the war by keeping one foot in each camp.

All three of the figures discussed in this chapter were among the most prominent industrialists in Republican China. All played both private and public roles. All manufactured products of interest to the Japanese. All eventually left for Free China and have been identified as "patriotic entrepreneurs" in the recent literature from China. Yet a close reading of their experiences suggests other possible interpretations. Both Liu and Wu had substantial property in the occupied area, and left family members to tend the store. Fan's record is the most unblemished, yet he had little property left to protect. If one were to draw a clear distinction between these three individuals and the textile industrialists, it might be their prominence and the important nature of the products they produced. The Japanese sought their political cooperation while demanding control of their industrial plants. The Chiang Kaishek government was eager for their public support and their expertise, even while members of the Chiang entourage sought to gain a share of their enterprises. However patriotic the investments in Free China may appear in retrospect, at the time it meant significant compromises with government authorities, in effect becoming "bureaucratic capitalists." For Fan there was little choice. For Wu and Liu, perhaps one reason why they wished to regain control of their properties in the occupied area is that in the postwar era this could be a basis for a rebirth of their industrial empire—a rebirth they would not have to share with the Soongs and Kungs.

CHAPTER 9

China's Rubber Industry

Production of rubber goods was one of the newest segments of Shanghai's industry, with most factories being established after 1925. Totally dependent on importation of raw materials and requiring a sophisticated technical base, rubber production got off to a slow start. From its inception, Chinese rubber manufacturing found itself intertwined with Japan. Virtually all Chinese producers used some Japanese equipment and even personnel to begin production. Yet the biggest obstacle they faced was competition from Japanese companies. Although few Japanese firms manufactured in China before 1937, they enjoyed better access to raw materials and superior technology, enabling them to underprice their Shanghai competitors. Anti-Japanese boycotts were critical for Chinese producers; the May 30th movement, in fact, was the real beginning of the Chinese industry. A second great expansion occurred with the boycotts of 1931 and 1932, although some producers suffered extensive damage in the January 28th incident.[1]

When the lift from these emotional events subsided and Japanese imports began to recover, Chinese producers sought a more permanent advantage. In October 1932 they organized the Shanghai Rubber Manufacturers Association (Shanghai xiangjiao gongye tongye gonghui), whose key activity was to petition for higher import tariffs on rubber goods. The Nanjing government responded the following year, raising the tariffs of imported rubber shoes/slippers (virtually all of which were Japanese) to 30 percent from 17.5 percent, permitting the takeoff of the

Chinese industry. By 1937 there were thirty-one plants in Shanghai making rubber products. The biggest producers were the Da Zhonghua, Yisheng, Zhengtai, Minsheng, Hongda, and Yonghe plants. Most firms acquired raw rubber materials from British Malaya using connections in Singapore.[2]

Initially, major items of production were cheap consumer goods such as rubber shoes, rain coats, and hot water bottles. By 1937 China produced 30 million pairs of rubber slippers, for instance. Gradually some firms added more sophisticated products such as tires for bicycles, rickshaws, and automobiles and insulated electric wiring. On the eve of war, Chinese companies manufactured 170,000 rickshaw tires annually. Because rubber production developed rather late compared to textiles, most plants were located in the outer areas of Shanghai; many were in the western Hongkou district, some in Zhabei, and a few south of the city or in Pudong.[3]

These conditions all played a key role in the fate of the rubber industry after August 13, 1937. First, because of their location, most rubber plants were either damaged or destroyed in the fighting and/or fell under Japanese control. Nearly all of the plants in Zhabei were destroyed, and those in Hongkou heavily damaged. Of the thirty-one Chinese owned plants, five were totally destroyed, ten heavily damaged, fifteen lightly damaged, and only four undamaged. Particularly hard hit were the Da Zhonghua, Zhengtai, Hongda, and Yonghe factories. The latter's Zhabei plant had the misfortune to be destroyed in both January 1932 and in 1937. Those Chinese owners who could do so scrambled to move equipment to the foreign concessions. Minsheng and a smaller company called Da Shanghai, both previously located in Nanshi (south city), raced equipment into the French Concession and were among the first to reopen.

More typical was the ill-fated Yonghe, a firm that had lost its major factory in Zhabei in January 1932, then painstakingly rebuilt it only to suffer a similar fate in 1937. A newly opened branch factory in Nanjing was a total loss, and a plant set up in Chongqing in 1936 was destroyed by Japanese bombers in April 1939. In Shanghai it took almost two years and two moves before the firm resumed production on Changshou Road in the settlement, producing water bottles, bike tires, and rubber slippers. As late as May 1938, only six Chinese-owned factories in Shanghai were in operation.[4]

And yet, with the "flourishing" of the solitary island, Chinese rubber production would resume. By the latter half of 1938, Da Zhonghua, Yisheng, Hongda, and others were back in action, some renting new property in the concessions. A host of smaller new companies opened, many with personnel and capital from earlier groups. Although trade with the immediate hinterland was difficult, the sea route to Southeast Asia and the South China coast kept important markets open. By 1940, twenty-nine Chinese-owned firms were in production in Shanghai, almost as many as in 1936. Output did not achieve prewar levels, however. In 1938, Chinese factories produced only 10 million pairs of rubber shoes and in 1939 only 12 million (compared to more than 30 million in the last year before the war). But profits were strong; wartime shortages drove prices upward and kept profit margins high.[5]

The war also afforded Japanese firms a chance to begin production in Shanghai, either by establishing a factory or forcing a Chinese firm to join a partnership. When war erupted only three Japanese rubber plants were operating in the city. By 1941 there would be nineteen Japanese factories and three joint ventures. Most of these Japanese plants remained quite small; the only large-scale rubber plants were in Manchukuo, Tianjin, and Qingdao. The Japanese plants in Shanghai, for instance, produced about 7,000 pairs of rubber slippers daily, compared to about 50,000 for Chinese plants in 1940.[6]

Even during the island Shanghai era, many Chinese manufacturers made compromises with the Japanese in order to maintain production. Not only did much equipment fall into Japanese hands, but reliance on imported raw materials left Chinese producers vulnerable to Japanese military pressure. After Pearl Harbor, of course, that control was total. Japan considered rubber supplies a war commodity to be strictly regulated; full cooperation with the Japanese and puppet authorities became necessary. The Greater East Asia Ministry confiscated existing supplies of raw rubber and released them, together with petroleum, only when its conditions were met. A control board, the Sino-Japanese Rubber Manufacturing Association (Rihua xiangjiao gongchang lianhe hui), implemented the controls. Chinese had to serve on this and other commodity control boards, register with puppet governments, and accept orders from the Japanese military.

Even so, the shortage of raw materials and the lack of electricity and petroleum became chronic. Many Chinese producers simply closed (the number of plants dropped to fourteen in 1942), and production dropped to less than a third of capacity. Some firms upgraded the product line to gain more profit from limited raw materials. Instead of manufacturing rubber slippers, producers such as Da Zhonghua and Zhengtai turned increasingly to tires, which earned a greater return.[7]

By the summer of 1944, the Japanese would release raw materials only for production contracted with the Japanese or Nanjing military. Most firms accepted these conditions. In June, for instance, Nanjing's Commerce Control Commission reached agreement with four firms, Yisheng, Zhengtai, Da Zhonghua, and Hongda, that they would receive electricity, raw rubber, and petroleum to produce 50,000 pairs of rubber shoes each for military use. The Yisheng company actually increased its order to 150,000 pairs. Faced with the choice of collaboration or ceasing production, the managers chose the former. Of course, production was not the only door to profit. Many manufacturers had secretly hoarded raw materials and, as prices rapidly inflated, did well through speculation and black market activity. Profit rates on capital investment in 1942 for Da Zhonghua, for instance, were nearly 48 percent; for Zhengtai, 47 percent; for Hongda, a hearty 273 percent; and for Mingsheng, 97 percent. Among major producers, only Yonghe, at 25 percent, and Yisheng at 11.5 percent, fared less well.[8]

As was the case with textiles and other industries, the wartime experience of individual companies varied widely. Often simply bad luck (a stray artillery shell) marked the difference between profits and losses. A grasp of the experience of the rubber manufacturers can perhaps best be gained by examining in greater detail the case of two of the major producers of the war era, Da Zhonghua and Zhengtai.

THE DA ZHONGHUA RUBBER COMPANY

Da Zhonghua (The Great China Rubber Company) was the largest such firm in Shanghai, with four major plants and capitalization of 3 million yuan on the eve of war. All of the key founders—Yu Zhiqing, Xue Fuji, and Wu Zhesheng—had lived and worked in Japan. Indeed, Yu had primarily been a merchant who sold imported Japanese goods in Shanghai, including the very popular rubber shoes. When the May 30th boycott devastated sales, Xue suggested that they manufacture the product themselves and use the "made in China" label as an asset. The entrepreneurs sent agents to Japan to negotiate a partnership with a Japanese firm, but this move appears to have been industrial espionage. Eventually they simply advertised in an Osaka newspaper for technicians skilled in rubber production. Through the use of these Japanese advisers, they mastered the necessary technique, and Da Zhonghua began operation in October 1928, producing rubber shoes and some hot water gloves. Later the company produced rickshaw, bicycle, and automobile tires.[9]

War produced a chaotic situation for Da Zhonghua. Their manager Xue Fuji was killed in the tragic bombing in front of the Great World Emporium on August 14, 1937, creating a leadership vacuum at the height of the crisis. The company's most important factory, the #4, which was located in the Nanshi section and produced tires, was hit by artillery fire and burned almost completely. Workers raced to remove surviving equipment and supplies from the war zone. The #3 plant in Hongkou was quickly occupied by Japanese forces and would be entrusted to a Japanese company.

Only two plants remained, one in the French Concession and one in the Western Roads area. Facing an uncertain future, Da Zhonghua leadership took two steps. The first was to remove the general headquarters of the company to Hong Kong for security. Because Yu Zhiqing had extensive experience living in Japan, Japanese sought him out to join the Shanghai municipal government, which they established. Unwilling to collaborate and fearing for his safety, Yu chose Hong Kong as an alternate base. (Personnel returned to Shanghai when both were occupied after Pearl Harbor.)

The second step was to register the company as a German firm with the German consulate. On paper Da Zhonghua was sold to a German company. The factories then flew the Nazi flag and employed two German managers, G. Scholz and K. Bartelt. The former had the added advantage of being a member of the Nazi Party, while Bartelt had connections to an American firm that would provide cover for a warehouse in the occupied zone.[10]

In the meantime, the National Resources Commission urged Da Zhonghua to relocate its tire-making facilities to Hunan province. Unfortunately, much of that equipment had been destroyed at the #4 plant, but what could be salvaged (approximately 120 tons) was loaded onto four boats and sent upriver. Da Zhonghua seemed destined for misfortune, however, and three of the ships went down after being struck by enemy fire. Only one surviving boat, with 31 tons of equipment, made it to Wuhan on January 18, 1938. The initial plan was for the NRC to create a tire factory in Xiangtan, Hunan, which had been the site where Chiang Kaishek had planned to set up a secure heavy industrial center. When this too was threatened, the government decided on Kunming as the final locale.

Alas, Da Zhonghua seemed to have an uncanny knack for having shipments arrive at the scene of nearly every major disaster of the China war. Through unfortunate timing, the firm lost material in the fall of Wuhan, the fall of Guangzhou, and the great fire in Changsha, as well as to aerial bombardment in Chongqing and Guiyang. The National Resources Commission still hoped to open a plant in Kunming and planned a joint government-private project, with firms such as Da Zhonghua contributing capital, personnel, and equipment. Wu Zhesheng, the Da Zhonghua leader, was sent to England to purchase additional tire-making equipment. With Da Zhonghua's knack for bad timing, the equipment arrived in Vietnam just in time to be seized by the Japanese. Further shipments were blocked when the British closed the Burma Road. The Kunming plant never became operational.[11]

Back in Shanghai, Da Zhonghua's fortunes revived during the "flourishing" period of the solitary island. Strong capital reserves allowed for repair and relocation of equipment, while contacts in Singapore kept supply lines open for raw materials. Overall, output was well below the prewar level. In 1940, for instance, the firm produced 5.6 million pairs of rubber slippers, less than 64 percent of the 1936 level; tire production dropped to 54 percent of the 1936 level. Only rickshaw tires increased overall from 340,000 in 1936 to 731,000 in 1940. Still profits remained high.[12]

As with most firms in island Shanghai, trade was easier with Southeast Asia than with the immediate hinterland. In addition, the company took advantage of the porous southeast coast of China, particularly the unoccupied port of Wenzhou, to trade with the Free China. Through that avenue or (before 1940) through Vietnam, Da Zhonghua sent more than 3.4 million pairs of rubber shoes, 70,000 rickshaw tires, 30,000 vehicle tires, and even 1,000 airplane tires to unoccupied China. Much of this had obvious military value and attracted the attention of the Japanese authorities. On May 8, 1941, Japanese military police arrested assistant manager Hong Nianzu, charging him with supplying material for military use to the Chongqing government. Hong was released after ten days, apparently after pledging greater cooperation with the Japanese.[13]

Following Pearl Harbor, the Japanese ignored the German registration and closed Da Zhonghua on January 25, 1942, releasing its 207 workers. Management began making strong efforts to regain the property, indicating a willingness to collaborate in order to do so. They registered the company with the Nanjing government and pledged to work with occupation agencies. In May 1942 the plant reopened, one of the first Chinese plants to do so. Managers of the plant would join the Commerce Control Commission and the Shanghai rubber producers group. Nor were they shy about joining in public ceremonies. In September 1943 the company's representatives joined in an assembly to celebrate the Greater East Asia Co-Prosperity Sphere, and on the seventh anniversary of the Marco Polo Bridge Incident in 1944, plant managers attended a program of the city government to promote industrialization.

This cooperation allowed the Da Zhonghua access to the materials needed to restore operations, although at a much reduced level. In 1943 it produced 830,000 pairs of shoes (only 9.5 percent of the prewar total) and 3,290 vehicles tires (12.5 percent of the prewar level). Much of this was to provide for the Japanese military. More than fifty-nine orders were placed for the Japanese and puppet military or security forces; these included shoes, tires, and gas masks. Da Zhonghua was one of the Chinese firms involved in the June 1944 agreement with Nanjing under which it was to provide 50,000 pairs of rubber shoes for military use, and an agreement on tires concluded as late as July 1945. After December 1944, however, very little raw rubber, petroleum, or electricity was available.[14]

In viewing Da Zhonghua's wartime activities in retrospect, it appears that the leadership's overwhelming desire was to remain autonomous and in operation. The firm showed no qualms about using the cover of imperialism—German registration, moving the headquarters to Hong Kong—but clearly shrank from cooperating with the Japanese for as long as possible. Indeed, Da Zhonghua's management consistently rejected offers from Japanese companies to form a partnership, even as late as 1943 when the Yūhō Textile Company pressed them to pool resources. Dealing directly with the Japanese military or Nanjing puppet authorities was preferable to giving up control of the firm. Certainly Da Zhonghua did attempt to move its tire production to the interior to help the war effort, and certainly it sold materials to Free China until 1941, but these efforts were part of a mixed record of survival and collaboration.[15]

THE ZHENGTAI RUBBER COMPANY

A rather different wartime narrative emerges when examining the Zhengtai Rubber factory of Shanghai. This company, which had been established in 1927 with Japanese technical assistance, principally manufactured rubber shoes. Despite its early Japanese connections, the firm directly benefited from the anti-Japanese boycotts that occurred after the Jinan and Manchurian Incidents. Its total workforce reached about 1,000 in the early 1930s. Although the firm suffered a setback in 1933 when an industrial accident claimed the lives of eighty workers, its sales soared in 1934 when the Chinese tariff on imported rubber shoes was raised to 30 percent.[16]

When the war erupted, the Zhengtai plant, located in the Hongkou section of Shanghai, was directly in the line of battle. On August 15 management fled to the French Concession; each worker was given five yuan and dispersed. In early September 1937, two leaders of the firm, Hong Fumei and Yang Shaozhen, made contact with a Japanese businessman, Fujimura Ichinori, of the Aikokuryū Company, who visited the plant site on their behalf. He found the buildings heavily damaged and the remaining materials plundered by Japanese soldiers. Fujimura had signs placed on the site proclaiming that it was a branch of his Japanese firm and arranged for two Japanese to stand watch over the facility. When Zhengtai managers received 370,000 yuan in insurance damages in 1938, they began to repair the plant, reopening in July. As an added protection, the Chinese registered the firm under the Japanese name at the German consulate. In exchange for providing this cover, Fujimura received fourteen fen for every dozen pair of rubber shoes Zhengtai produced, as well as monopoly rights for his firm to supply the Chinese partner with raw materials.[17]

Although the company lost more than 40,000 yuan in 1938, the following year Zhengtai became profitable again, garnering profits of 167,000 yuan. By 1940 it increased its capital from 550,000 to 800,000 yuan. Zhengtai management purchased an old textile mill on Wuding Road in the International Settlement and converted it into a second factory for producing rubber shoes. This activity, of course, required the acquiescence of the Japanese. Zhengtai lost its cover in 1939 when Fujimura's firm was reorganized and he was dismissed. His replacement demanded that Zhengtai make greater concessions and give his firm ownership of 51 percent of the stock in the enterprise. Yang Shaozhen refused, countering temporarily by using an American adviser as cover. This placed Zhengtai in a precarious position, but the managers were unwilling to become a junior partner with a Japanese firm.[18]

When the Pacific war erupted, supplies of raw materials fell completely under Japanese military control. Zhengtai had fortuitously stockpiled almost 100 tons of supplies in a Pudong warehouse, hiring a Japanese employee to escort ships across the river. This was only a temporary respite. As with other firms, Zhengtai had to pledge full cooperation in order to continue operations and to maintain its separate identity as a company. The company began dealing with the Japanese military, supplying thousands of pairs of shoes for Japanese soldiers in the Shanghai area. Later in the war, Zhengtai expanded to produce bicycle and car tires as well as electric wires. Profits continued up until the end of the war, despite the severe hyperinflation. As with many firms, hoarding and black market activity were as critical as manufacturing late in the war when supplies and energy sources all but disappeared.[19]

Zhengtai's management also had to work with puppet organizations established by the Japanese and the Wang Jingwei government. Yang Shaozhen joined the board of directors of the rubber production control association of the Shanghai puppet government. This organization controlled raw products for rubber production, which became increasingly scarce as the Pacific War continued. Zhengtai thus persisted as an independent entity but made considerable compromises with the Japanese, behavior that might be labeled collaborationist. Following Japanese surrender, Guomindang authorities confiscated Zhengtai facilities on the grounds that the firm had served the enemy.[20]

In sum, Chinese nascent rubber industry survived in the Shanghai area but ultimately had to collaborate with the Japanese after December 1941 in order to remain in production. Production levels remained remarkably high until after the start of the Pacific war, following which most firms had to rely on the black market or Japanese-controlled sources to survive. Access to the latter usually required contracts with the Japanese military. Overall, the industry and the Chiang Kaishek government were not able to remove a significant amount of equipment to the unoccupied interior, although several efforts were made. As a group, rubber manufacturers most closely fit the collaborationist narrative of any of the industrial groups we have studied. The strong connections most had to Japan in the early stages of nearly all of the firms, coupled with the Japanese control over supplies, made collaboration essential. Most rubber manufacturers demonstrated a willingness to work with the Japanese military but a strong reluctance to surrender control of their enterprises to a Japanese business partner.

Conclusion

In 1997 a Chinese American writer, Iris Chang, published *The Rape of Nanking: The Forgotten Holocaust of World War II*. The book quickly became a best-seller, and the author made the rounds of television talk shows. What was perhaps more surprising was the emotional reaction of many Chinese Americans and Chinese living in North America. Through internet connections, many began to urge their comrades to buy multiple copies of the work to keep it on best-seller charts, and to donate the extra copies to schools to promote awareness of the atrocities suffered by Chinese during the war. Meanwhile, a group of Chinese American scholars in North America began publishing a journal entitled *The Journal of Studies of Japanese Aggression Against China*. This outburst of interest and indignation regarding war atrocities, occurring more than half a century after the war ended, paralleled the "new remembering" of the war of resistance in China itself.[1]

At the turn of the century, remembrance of the war has become a touchstone of Chinese identity, a point of unity between Chinese in the People's Republic and those living outside. Yet while this new interest in the war has produced an outpouring of both scholarly and popular writing on the war, it may not necessarily advance our understanding of the actual war experience. All historical writing reflects the viewpoint of the writer, of course. Yet the degree to which the new writing both in China and without is shaped by contemporary issues of identity, grievance, and national pride is pronounced. The introduction of this work addressed this issue in conjunction with the wartime experience of China's emerging capitalist class. A convergence of the new evaluation of Republican era capitalists as patriotic Chinese entrepreneurs (*aiguo shiye jia*) and the "new remembering" of the War of Resistance has created the "patriotic nationalist narrative."

This romanticized view has the heroic industrialist evacuating Shanghai for the harsh reality of the interior, selflessly devoting himself to building the resistance economy. But the evidence presented in this study would suggest that this does not fit the actions of the vast majority of the key business leaders in the lower Yangzi area. Most chose to stay in unoccupied Shanghai or perhaps Hong Kong. A few, such as banker Li Ming or Wuxi textile magnate Xue Shouxuan, left for America, a route that required good connections. Even the heroism of the handful of capitalists often cited as fitting the model, such as Fan Xudong, Wu Yunchu, and Liu Hongsheng, fades somewhat under close examination. Fan had little left to stay for in the coastal areas; Wu had to be lured from Hong Kong. Both he and Liu left family members to mind the store under the Japanese.

This description is not meant to belittle the achievements that were made in Free China, an area with little modern industry in 1937, virtually cut off from the global market, and subject to intense enemy air attack. Chinese industrialists who were in the interior often reinvented modern processes in order to use human or animal power and relocated factories to caves to escape Japanese bombs. What was produced was vital to China's war effort yet was only a fraction of what was needed or what Shanghai had in 1937. Nor can it be assumed that the businessmen in coastal China did not want to aid China's cause. As the evidence of this study clearly indicates, many sought desperately to remove equipment to the interior, only to be stymied by lack or shipping or disaster. For many industrialists there was simply no easy opportunity to relocate in Free China. Yet the "patriotic nationalist narrative" simply does not apply to the war experiences of most of these industrialists.

But if the question posed is "collaboration or resistance," neither do most businessmen easily fit the profile of collaborator. The vast majority made every effort to escape Japanese control and domination, hence the move to the unoccupied areas. When attempting to preserve control over properties in the occupied areas, most attempted to use foreign registration as a cover, not necessarily patriotic by the standards of the "patriotic nationalist narrative," but certainly indicating a desire to prevent Japanese control. In the four and one-half years from the Marco Polo Bridge Incident until Pearl Harbor, there are very few examples of Chinese capitalists who were willing to accept junior partnership with Japanese companies, and these exceptions are instructive. The Nie family of Wuxi, for instance, agreed to such status. Yet the Nies, descendants of Zeng Guofan's son-in-law, had lost control of their enterprise to bankers long before the arrival of the Japanese. Their collaboration bought them some income from an enterprise already lost to them. For the Japanese it brought the political support of a prominent local family. Similarly the Yang family of Wuxi, descendants of the entourage of Li Hongzhang, sought profits by selling milled flour to the Japanese military.

Such behavior was clearly collaborationist; yet it was the exception. It was only after Pearl Harbor, when most Chinese industrialists found themselves living directly under Japanese rule, that many began to compromise. Most would seek to regain factories and businesses even it if meant registering such property with the Nanjing collaborationist regime and serving on the commerce control commissions. The list of capitalists who participated in Nanjing activities did eventually grow long, but one would hardly label them eager collaborators.

But collaboration required two partners—Japanese and Chinese. Perhaps the most fundamental reason Chinese capitalists were so slow to collaborate was that Japan offered so little in return. The Japanese were eager to get the *political* support of prominent capitalists in the early stages of the war, hence the attempt to lure Rong Zhongjing and others into signing on to the first puppet government in Shanghai. They cut deals with prominent families like the Nies and pressed Liu Hongsheng to join them. They made similar offers to old warlords, bureaucrats, and other "public figures" as they sought to create their client states in China. And they lured in some prominent names. They had already secured Henry Puyi as the "emperor" of Manchukuo. They obtained Wang Kemin in Beijing and Fu Xiao'an in Shanghai and their greatest triumph, Wang Jingwei. Yet few businessmen collaborated as businessmen during the early phases of the war for a very simply reason—the Japanese gave them little opportunity to do so.

The New Order in East Asia and the Greater East Asia Co-Prosperity Sphere both promised a "paradise" for the peoples liberated by the Japanese. Undoubtedly there were Japanese intellectuals and perhaps some Chinese who sincerely believed in Pan-Asian ideals in the war era. But from an economic standpoint, as it was actually implemented, the New Order was nothing more than a colonial regime over China. The Japanese imposed controls over the economy of the lower Yangzi, confiscated factories and gave them to Japanese companies, and severely restricted market activity. If Japan had won the war, China's economy would have been organized and developed as that of a colony, with control in the hands of Tokyo and Japanese corporations. Few Chinese businessmen saw a role for themselves in such a China. Most already faced strong Japanese competition; many had relied on anti-Japanese boycotts to generate profits. If China had become a Japanese colony, perhaps Chinese entrepreneurs would eventually have regained their strength. Even in colonial Korea, as Carter Eckert's study shows, Korean capitalists eventually emerged.[2]

But to most Chinese businessmen in the lower Yangzi, a Japanese-controlled China looked bleak indeed. Nothing the Japanese offered from 1937 until nearly 1943 gave much hope that there would be a meaningful role for Chinese capitalists in the new order.

Only late in the war, after defeats in the South Pacific, when a sense of desperation set in, did Japan initiate the great departure. At that point, bereft of capital and manpower, the Japanese finally made offers that China's capitalists would accept, hence the marked increase in collaboration from 1943 to 1945. The Japanese program for China, therefore, was not one that attracted support among the Chinese business community; it offered them little. Thus neither collaboration nor resistance really describes the actions of most Chinese entrepreneurs.

Perhaps one reason the collaboration/resistance dichotomy seems ill fitted for the Chinese case is that most of the Western-language, scholarly literature on collaboration during World War II relates to Europe in general and Vichy France in particularly. As a consequence, the term "collaboration" carries an embedded meaning in English—support for and participation in the Holocaust. There were local Nazi movements in almost all of the occupied areas of Europe; there were indigenous anti-Semitic feelings as well. In the postwar debate over collaboration in Europe, the most loaded charge is that collaborators aided and abetted, even encouraged, the extermination of Jewish populations. In his study *The Vichy Syndrome: History and Memory in France since 1944,* Henry Rousso analyzes the ongoing debate in France about the Vichy legacy. The most damning charge is that French anti-Semitism led some to contribute more vigorously to the extermination of the Jews than even the Germans required. The trial of Maurice Papon in the 1990s placed such issues in the pubic arena anew. "Vichy officials acted without German pressure to exclude Jews from the civil service and from cultural professions," notes one commentator on the trial, "to make lists of their names and addresses, and to reduce Jewish influence in the economy."[3]

Compared to such charges, the collaboration of Chinese capitalists would seem to carry little moral weight. The worst offenses, that Zhengtai sold rubber shoes and bicycle tires to the Japanese or that the Wuxi Yangs sold milled flour to the Japanese army, seem trivial compared to complicity in the Holocaust.

Rousso identifies a second issue that has made the memory of Vichy such a scar in France. French politics and identity, he notes, have been deeply divided since the French Revolution. Vichy represented the conservative side of French politics, and it conducted a civil war against the left. "The internal quarrels left deeper scars than either the defeat or the German occupation," he argues.[4] China too had its own left/right divide. But the puppet governments never captured the real leadership of the Guomindang; Chiang Kaishek remained an anti-Communist alternative who persisted until the end of the conflict.

The "collaboration/resistance" dichotomy, with its loaded imagery in English-language literature, seems a poor tool for explaining the wartime activities of the Chinese capitalists. Although the vigor of the "new remembering" of the war experience has framed the current debate against the "patriotic nationalist narrative," it too seems limited as an analytical tool. Did the Chinese capitalists fit the mold of patriotic entrepreneur or were they collaborators with the Japanese enemy? Perhaps this is the wrong question to ask.

SURVIVAL OF THE FAMILY FIRM

I would suggest an alternative approach to understanding the wartime activities of China's capitalists. Most Chinese firms discussed in this study were organized as family enterprises with a single dominant head of household. Even in cases in which the company was legally a limited liability corporation with an elected board of directors, nearly all such firms actually functioned as family controlled enterprises. Some of these, such as the Rong family group and the Kwok/Yong'an group, were mature family firms whose leadership was being shifted rather uneasily to a new generation. Others, such as the enterprises of Liu Hongsheng, Wu Yunchu, and Liu Guojun of Changzhou, were led by founder-entrepreneurs at the peak of their power when the war erupted. Only a very few, such as the Xue family silk group of Wuxi, were firms in which power had been transferred completely to a younger generation, in this instance Xue Shouxuan. In all of these cases and many others, however, the firm was under the control of the family head.

The family form of organization, I have argued, was key to the survival of most businesses in the wartime environment. With very unstable and rapidly changing conditions, the single family leader could make critical decisions quickly, could overlook distinctions among different companies in the enterprise group, and could ignore the concerns of minority investors. Most important, the family form of organization made it possible for enterprises to operate, or attempt to operate, in different spheres of the war. Hence, Liu Hongsheng could be in Hong Kong or Chongqing but trust that his brother and sons in Shanghai would protect the family property even if it meant collaborating with the Japanese. The implicit trust of the family relationship permitted employment of this type of strategy.

There were limitations to the family form of organization. The mature and large Rong family experienced major divisions after the death of the senior patriarch. Indeed the Achilles heel for the family firm was generational transfer. But most Chinese firms had their origins in the period during and immediately after World War I and were relatively young. There were a few older firms with origins in the late Qing that had come under the control of professional management. The Dasheng mills of Nantong were controlled by leaders installed by a banking consortium after the death of the founder Zhang Jian. The Hengfeng mills were in a similar situation. Interestingly, these types of firms were among the least successful in adapting to wartime conditions.

What motivated most of the businessmen during the war era? Nationalism was often a factor; most demonstrated support for China's cause. The key, however, was survival of the family firm. For most of the founder-entrepreneurs, their enterprises were their entire life. Their personal wealth and prestige and the family wealth and prestige were tied to survival of their individual firms. Thus every effort was made to save the firms—whether by evacuating to the interior or to unoccupied Shanghai. Few had any qualms about using the semicolonial foreign enclaves for protection. Few thought twice about availing themselves of foreign flag protection. Yet few wished to collaborate with the Japanese if other alternatives were available. Perhaps the most unappealing aspect of collaboration was not that it was unpatriotic but that, until late in the war, it meant surrendering the personal control of their enterprises to a Japanese senior partner. For most founder-entrepreneurs this was a route to be taken only under the most desperate circumstances. Only later when the Japanese offered to grant them control in exchange for support for the Nanjing regime did most of the Shanghai capitalists sign on with the occupation.

This obsession with personal control of the family firm perhaps explains why so few capitalists were eager to head to Sichuan as long as Shanghai and Hong Kong were viable alternatives. During the mid-1930s, the Nanjing government under Chiang Kaishek had become an active player in the economic sphere. Following the "banking coup" of 1935, Nanjing held control over nearly three-fourths of the assets of modern Chinese banks, and Chiang promoted a program to develop state-controlled heavy industry. At the same time, members of Chiang's entourage, including brothers-in-law T. V. Soong, T. L. Soong, and H. H. Kung, had become active players in the economic arena. These moves had resulted in some tension between business and the Nanjing authorities, but before the war, the private sector had remained quite strong.[5]

After the retreat to Sichuan, the role of government and government-connected personnel in the economy was much greater. The private sector in the interior was underdeveloped. Wartime controls placed much more authority in the hands of Chongqing. As the experience of many of the capitalists who relocated testifies, operating in the interior often meant working with the Kungs and Soongs. For most of the founder-entrepreneurs, losing control to these leaders was almost as distasteful as becoming junior partners with the Japanese. They simply did not want to surrender the unchecked authority they had enjoyed in their family-controlled firms. Free China was not so free as businessmen wished.

In sum, if we escape from the contemporary concerns that have privileged the patriotic nationalist narrative and examine the war experiences from the standpoint of the Chinese capitalists who actually lived through the war years, we can gain a clearer understanding of their motivations. Although patriotism often surfaced, the driving force behind the actions of the capitalists seems to be the overwhelming desire to preserve their enterprises and to keep them under tight personal control. Viewed from this perspective, the response of the capitalists was creative, perhaps even heroic. Many responded to the horrendous conditions of war and destruction with innovative, daring actions designed to save their companies. Many of these enterprises survived the war remarkably intact.

THE IMPACT OF THE WAR ON CHINESE CAPITALISM

But was survival enough? Although many businessmen won that battle, they lost the war. The triumph of the Communist Revolution in 1949 brought an end to private business during the Maoist years. Those who stayed in the People's Republic were forced out, their creations now socialized. Others continued as businessmen but in Hong Kong, Taiwan, or overseas. When the Chinese communists triumphed in 1949, they faced little opposition from Chinese capitalists. Indeed the victory of the Chinese Revolution was largely determined elsewhere. China's modern businessmen who seemed to be rising to prominence in the prewar era were a marginal factor in the civil war period.

Clearly the war had greatly weakened the capitalists. Despite some profits during the "flourishing" period of the isolated island, most businessmen emerged from the war in reduced circumstances. Factories and shops had been destroyed, workers scattered. The currency was all but worthless; commerce had been crippled during much of the war. When the conflict ended, peace proved elusive. Far from reviving, the economy of the civil war period duplicated some of the worst features of the just ended foreign war. Hyperinflation, government red tape, chronic shortages of transport and energy—all limited economic recovery.

Many capitalists emerged from the war touched by the taint of collaboration. When Guomindang forces returned to the coastal areas, many of the businessmen who are discussed in this study found their property confiscated, labeled as "enemy property." In the early days of the return, the process often resembled plunder, as those who returned from years of hardship in the interior took revenge on those who had remained with the enemy. As Suzanne Pepper has noted, "By the end of October [1945], the word 'Chungking-ite' had become a popular term of derision in Shanghai, where the newly arrived personnel were rushing to appropriate for their own use property taken from the Japanese and their collaborators." Commercial establishments were closed and fleeced of large sums to gain permission to reopen.[6]

These seizures provided the Guomindang with an opportunity to extend its control over the private sector to a much greater degree than in pre-1937 China. A government textile group founded to operate confiscated mills (the China Textile Reconstruction Company, Zhongguo fangzhi jianshe gongsi) controlled almost 40 percent of the cotton spindles in China. William Kirby has suggested, in fact, that in 1945 and 1946, the Nationalist Government controlled 70 percent of China's total industrial capital. Nanjing regulated the supply of industrial raw materials, set prices for major commodities, and prohibited private holdings in foreign exchange. Thus, even those capitalists such as the Rongs and Liu Hongsheng, who took action to protect their enterprises that had been located in the occupied areas, now found themselves under much greater government restraint than in prewar days. When Rong Hongyuan criticized Guomindang controls on foreign exchange in 1948, he found himself arrested and held for two months in jail for unauthorized currency transactions. A payment of half a million dollars was required for his release.[7] However distasteful they found it, China's capitalists had to ingratiate themselves with the Soongs and Kungs. Even those who kept title to their property found themselves tainted by their wartime actions. Critiques of capitalists by leftist intellectuals found a ready audience in the late 1940s.

But if the wartime years left China's capitalists weaker in the face of the Communist surge, war also forced them to create a strategy for the new era. Survival in wartime had forced businessmen to adopt a scrambling, risk-taking style of operation. The heavy reliance on family connections, the strategy of splitting risks, and operating enterprises in both unoccupied China and Shanghai were key. Many of the capitalists continued to follow this approach in later struggles. In 1949, for instance, the Rong family kept some money in China, moved some to Hong Kong, and sent some overseas. As Wong Siu-lun noted in his study of the migration of Shanghai capitalists to Hong Kong, nearly 80 percent of the cotton-spinning industry in the Crown Colony in 1978 was owned by entrepreneurs of Shanghai origin. Virtually all had moved there after the Communist Revolution. "In terms of their acquiring experience in relocating their enterprises, the war was a rehearsal for the exodus of the Shanghai capitalists to Hong Kong."[8] Thus the businessmen responded in 1949 as many had in 1937 and 1938: disperse the family and resources, divide the risk.

Even today, many Chinese capitalists who moved outside of People's China are pursuing a similar strategy, keeping some capital in Hong Kong, investing some in China, and moving some overseas. As Wong's study indicates, many of the cotton mill owners now based in Hong Kong anticipate a second-step migration. Virtually all he studied had made investments in Southeast Asia, Canada, Latin America, and elsewhere. Moreover, these leaders tended to diversify the place of residence of their adult children, much as had been done during the war. Wong found only one example in which a textile magnate with adult children did not have at least one resident in a foreign country.

As during the war, survival of the family and the family firm was key; strategies of dividing risk maximized that chance. That these industrialists "sought shelter in a British colony rather than in Communist-rule China," notes Wong, "indicated that they were pragmatic men. Their commitment of private enterprise evidently transcended nationalistic considerations."[9] Heng Pek Koon, in her study of ethnically Chinese businessmen in Southeast Asia, makes the same point. "The modus operandi of the Sino-capitalists is to accommodate local power holders," she notes. Yet, "they can also circumscribe state autonomy, for they are essentially 'stateless' in that they and their families are domiciled in different countries. . . . Their business empires are so diversified and they have spread their risks so widely in the region and globally that they are not vulnerable to the authority of individual states, even as imposing as China."[10]

Yet migration of capital and individuals has become a two-way street. As investment by overseas Chinese in the mainland had flourished in the post-Mao era, many have revived connections with family and associates in China. The career of Rong Yiren is obviously the most notable success. His role as a vice chairman of the National People's Congress and head of CITIC has provided entrée for the family, particularly the offspring of Rong Desheng. Yiren's own son led CITIC Pacific in Hong Kong.[11] Nor were the Rongs the only example of such ties. In her study of joint ventures in China, Margaret Pearson noted that wealthy overseas Chinese often used "their familial and personal ties from the past, to the advantage of the venture."[12] Yet one cannot say that forging of these links was always easy. The long Maoist interlude, particularly the trauma of the Cultural Revolution years, created a real divide for former capitalists who remained in China and those who moved overseas.

The eight years of the war, although only a fraction of the twentieth century, left a deep imprint on Chinese capitalism. Certain characteristics of Chinese business enterprise—family control, distrust and avoidance of government, personalistic ties—predated the war and were essential for enterprises to survive the war. Yet the eight years of war and the subsequent civil war also reinforced the strength of these characteristics. The wartime experience weakened China's new capitalist class, but it gave many businessmen the strategy and direction to survive the Maoist revolution outside of the People's Republic.

Notes

Abbreviations used in notes:

JIANGSU WZXJ	Jiangsu wenshi ziliao xuanji
SASS	Shanghai shehui kexue yuan (Shanghai Academy of Social Sciences)
SHANGHAI WZXJ	Shanghai wenshi ziliao xuanji
WUHAN WZXJ	Wuhan wenshi ziliao xuanji
WZXJ	Wenshi ziliao xuanji
ZHEJIANG WZXJ	Zhejiang wenshi ziliao xuanji

INTRODUCTION

1. Ch'i, Hsi-sheng, "The Military Dimension, 1942–1945," in James C. Hsiung and Steven I. Levine, eds., *China's Bitter Victory: The War with Japan, 1937–1945* (Armonk, N.Y.: M. E. Sharpe, 1992), pp. 157–84. The difficulty in determining property damage is compounded by the controversy over war reparations.

2. Stephen MacKinnon, "The Tragedy of Wuhan, 1938," *Modern Asian Studies* 30, no. 4 (1996), p. 931.

3. Arthur Waldron, "China's New Remembering of World War II: The Case of Zhang Zizhong," *Modern Asian Studies* 30, no. 4 (1996), p. 949.

4. Arthur Waldron, "China's New Remembering," p. 951.

5. Stephen MacKinnon, "The Tragedy of Wuhan, 1938," p. 931.

6. Du Xuncheng, *Riben zai jiu Zhongguo de touzi* (Japanese investment in old China; Shanghai: Shanghai shehui kexue yuan chuban she, 1986), p. 58.

7. Du Xuncheng, *Riben zai jiu Zhongguo de touzi*, p. 58.

8. Henry Rousso, *The Vichy Syndrome: History and Memory in France since*

1944, trans. by Arthur Goldhammer (Cambridge, Mass.: Harvard University Press, 1991), passim.

9. Tim Wright, "'The Spiritual Heritage of Chinese Capitalism': Recent Trends in the Historiography of Chinese Enterprise Management," in Jonathan Unger, ed., *Using the Past to Serve the Present: Historiography and Politics in Contemporary China* (Armonk, N.Y.: M. E. Sharpe, 1993), p. 234.

10. A few examples are Wang Renze, "Kui Yanfang: rexin jiuji shiye de aiguo shiye jia" (Kui Yangfang: A patriotic industrialist who ardently strove to develop industry), *Zhejiang WZXJ*, no. 39 (1989), pp. 249–55; Wang Renze, "KangRi xunsheng de aiguo shiye jia Xiang Songmao" (The martyr of the War of Resistance, the patriotic industrialist Xiang Songmao), *Zhejiang WZXJ*, no. 39 (1989), pp. 177–91; Li Daofa "Aiguo shiye jia Chen Wanyun" (Patriotic industrialist Chen Wanyun), *Shanghai WZXJ*, no. 66 (1991), pp. 109–17; Ma Gongjin et al., "Aiguo shiye jia Chen Jingyu" (Patriotic industrialist Chen Jingyu), *Wuhan WZXJ*, no. 33 (1988), pp. 24–45.

11. Tim Wright, "The Spiritual Heritage of Chinese Capitalism," p. 229.

12. *China at War* 2, no. 6 (June-July 1939), p. 55; 3, no. 4 (Nov. 1939), p. 54.

13. Shen Zuwei, Du Xuncheng, *Guonan zhong de Zhongguo qiye jia* (Shanghai: Shanghai shehui kexue yuan chuban she, 1996).

14. Sun Guoda, *Minzu gongye da qiantu—kangRi shiqi minying gongchang de neiqian* (Beijing: Zhongguo wenshi chuban she, 1991), p. 1.

CHAPTER ONE

1. For a discussion of this battle, see Dick Wilson, *When Tigers Fight: The Story of the Sino-Japanese War, 1937–1945* (New York: The Viking Press, 1982), pp. 30–45; Ch'i Hsi-sheng, *Nationalist China at War: Military Defeats and Political Collapse, 1937–45* (Ann Arbor: The University of Michigan Press, 1982), pp. 41–43; Edward L. Dreyer: *China at War, 1901–1949* (London: Longman, 1995), pp. 216–20.

2. Ch'i Hsi-sheng, *Nationalist China at War*, pp. 42–43; Edward L. Dreyer, *China at War*, pp. 216–20. For a vivid description of the Nanjing Road bombing, see Zhu Zuotong and Mei Yi, eds., *Shanghai yiri* (One day in Shanghai; Shanghai: Meishang Huamei chuban gongsi, 1939), section 1, pp. 166–68.

3. The *Yinhang zhoubao* (Bankers' weekly) ran weekly columns during the autumn of 1937 detailing the Chamber's list of damaged facilities during the previous week. See volume 21, August through December, passim.

4. These figures are from Han Qitong, *Zhongguo duiRi zhanshi juanshi zhi guji, 1937–1943* (An estimate of China's wartime losses, 1937–1943; Shanghai: Zhonghua shuju, 1946), p. 32, and Tang Zhenchang, ed. *Shanghai shi* (A history of Shanghai; Shanghai: Shanghai renmin chuban she, 1989), p. 798; see also Robert W. Barnett, *Economic Shanghai: Hostage to Politics, 1937–1941* (New York: Institute of Pacific Relations, 1941), pp. 80, 101; Usui Katsumi, "The Politics of War, 1937–1941," in James W. Morley, ed., *The China Quagmire: Japan's Expansion on the Asian Continent, 1933–1941* (New York: Columbia University Press, 1983), p. 314; *Yinhang zhoubao* 23, no. 43 (October 31, 1939), pp. 4–5; and *Tōa* (East Asia) 11, no. 11 (November 1938), pp. 80–99.

5. *Yinhang zhoubao* 22, no. 24 (June 21, 1938), pp. 3–4; Du Xuncheng, *Riben zai jiu Zhongguo*, p. 121; Zong Yu, "Manhua modai Zhaoshang ju" (Rambling talk of the last era of the China Merchants Steam Navigation Company), *WZXJ*, no. 64 (1986), pp. 235–51.

6. Usui Katsumi, "The Politics of War," p. 314; Tang Zhenchang, ed., *Shanghai shi*, pp. 798–99.

7. Lu Renxian, "Kangzhan shiqi Rijun dui Shanghai gangtie shangye de sanci da lueduo" (The three great plunderings of Shanghai's iron and steel commercial industry by the Japanese Army during the war of resistance), *Jingji xueshu ziliao*, no. 11 (1982), pp. 29–30; *Yinhang zhoubao* 22, no. 35 (September 6, 1938), p. 5; 23, no. 28 (July 18, 1939), pp. 4–5; 23, no. 39, (October 3, 1939), p. 3.

8. Shanghai Municipal Archives, Collection Q61, Shanghai City Bank (Shanghai shi yinhang), folder 305; *Yinhang zhoubao* 21, nos. 32–34 (August 31, 1937), pp. 6–7. This was a consolidated issue. The journal previously published on August 10 but was interrupted by the conflict.

9. *Yinhang zhoubao* 21, no. 40 (October 12, 1937), pp. 2–4.

10. Qi Zhilu, "Kangzhan shiqi gongkuang neiqian yu guanliao ziben de lueduo" (The move inland of factories and mines during the war of resistance period and its seizure by bureaucratic capitalism), *Gongshang jingji shiliao congkan* (A collection of economic historical materials on industry and commerce; 1983, no. 2), p. 64.

11. Sun Guoda, "Kangzhan qijian da houfang minzu gongye fazhan yuanyin chutan" (A preliminary investigation of the causes of the development of national industry in the rear areas during the war of resistance period), *Dang'an yu lishi* (Archives and history), no. 2 (1986), p. 60; William C. Kirby, "The Chinese War Economy," in James Hsiung and Steven Levine, eds. *China's Bitter Victory: The War with Japan, 1937–1945* (Armonk, N. Y.: M. E. Sharpe, 1992), p. 190.

12. Huang Liren and Zhang Yougao, "KangRi zhanzheng shiqi Zhongguo bingqi gongye neiqian chulun" (A first discussion of the movement to the interior of China's weapons' industry during the anti-Japanese war of resistance period), *Lishi dang'an* (Historical archives, 1991, no. 2), pp. 118–125. China's production of weapons was still far below its requirements. Prior to the war China imported the vast major of its weaponry. After Pearl Harbor and the fall of Burma, only a limited amount could reach Free China. By late 1943 China's 3 million soldiers had a mere 1 million rifles, 83,000 machine guns, and 1,300 pieces of artillery. See Ch'i Hsi-sheng, *Nationalist China at War*, p. 64.

13. William Kirby, "The Chinese War Economy," p. 190; Ch'i Hsi-sheng, *Nationalist China at War*, p. 221; Sun Guoda, "Kangzhan qijian da houfang," p. 60.

14. Sun Guoda, "Kangzhan qijian da houfang," p. 60; Rhodes Farmer, *Shanghai Harvest: A Diary of Three Years of the China War* (London: Museum Press, 1945), p. 177; Chen Zhen, ed. *Zhongguo jindai gongye shi ziliao* (Material on the history of modern Chinese industry), vol. 4 (Beijing: Sanlian chuban she, 1961), pp. 249–51.

15. Yu Zhongnan, "Wo chuangban Zhonghua niantong chang de jingguo" (The experiences of the Zhonghua copper rolling mill which I founded), *Shanghai WZXJ*, no. 18 (1964), pp. 159–60.

16. Lloyd E. Eastman, "Nationalist China during the Sino-Japanese War,

1937–1945," in *The Nationalist Era in China, 1927–1949*, ed. Lloyd E. Eastman et al. (Cambridge: Cambridge University Press, 1991), p. 131; see also Tang Zhenchang, *Shanghai shi*, pp. 787–88; Sun Guoda, *Minzu gongye da qiantu*, pp. 5–7.

17. Tang Zhenchang, *Shanghai shi*, pp. 788–89; William Kirby, "The Chinese War Economy," p. 190; Sun Guoda, *Minzu gongye da qiantu*, passim.

18. Tang Zhenchang, *Shanghai shi*, pp. 786–90; Huang Liren and Zhang Yougao, "KangRi zhanzheng shiqi," pp. 118–25.

19. "Nanyang xiongdi yancao gongsi shiliao buji" (An addendum to historical materials on the Nanyang Brothers Tobacco Company), *Dang'an yu lishi*, no. 2 (1986), p. 35–38; Sherman G. Cochran, *Big Business in China: Sino-Foreign Rivalry in the Cigarette Industry, 1890–1930* (Cambridge, Mass.: Harvard University Press, 1981), pp. 197–98. Relations between the Shanghai capitalists and the Guomindang government are discussed in Parks M. Coble, *The Shanghai Capitalists and the Nationalist Government of China, 1927–1937*, 2nd ed. (Cambridge, Mass.: Harvard East Asian Monographs, 1986), passim.

20. Ning Kunnan, "Kong Xiangxi yu Fuxing gongsi" (H. H. Kung and the Fuxing Company), *WZXJ*, no. 105, pp. 158–63; Hu Xiyuan, "Zhongguo Yapu'er chang shou diguo zhuyi he fandong pai cuican zhaiji" (An abbreviated account of the Chinese Yapu'er Factory being destroyed by imperialism and the reactionary faction), *WZXJ*, no. 44, pp. 115–23.

21. *Yinhang zhoubao* 22, no. 34 (August 30, 1938), pp. 4–5; 22, no. 38 (September 27, 1938), pp. 6–7. Xu was general manager of the Shanghai Zhejiang Xingye yinhang and Hu the Zhongnan yinhang.

22. Robert W. Barnett, *Economic Shanghai: Hostage to Politics*, pp. 76–86, 102, 164; Yuan Xieming, "Shanghai gudao yu da houfang de maoyi" (The trade between the rear areas and the isolated island Shanghai), *KangRi zhanzheng yanjiu*, no. 3 (1994), pp. 48–52; Lu Yangyuan and Fang Qingqiu, *Minguo shehui jingji shi* (A social and economic history of the Republican period; Beijing: Zhongguo jingji chuban she, 1989), pp. 695–96; Itō Takeo, *Problems in the Japanese Occupied Areas in China* (Tokyo: Japan Council, Institute of Pacific Relations, 1941), p. 25. Japanese permitted foreign-owned factories located in the settlement area north of the Suzhou Creek to reopen in early 1938. Most Chinese plants remained closed.

23. Tōa kenkyūjo, ed., *Shina senryō chi keizai no hatten* (The development of the economy of occupied China; Tokyo: Tōa kenkyūjo, 1944), p. 229; Chao Kang, *The Development of Cotton Textile Production in China* (Cambridge, Mass.: Harvard East Asian Monographs, 1977), p. 13; Robert W. Barnett, *Economic Shanghai*, p. 102; Wei Dazhi, "Shanghai 'gudao jingji fanrong' shimo" (Shanghai's economic flourishing during the isolated island period, from beginning to end), *Fudan xuebao*, no. 4 (August 12, 1985), pp. 109–10.

24. Shanghai shehui kexue yuan, Zhongguo qiye shi ziliao yanjiu zhongxin, Rong Collection [hereafter Rong Collection, SASS], R03–1, *Shenxin xitong qiye shiliao* (Historical material on the Shenxin system enterprises), mimeographed material originally compiled by the enterprise, vol. 1, no. 2, pp. 146–51; Chen Zhen, *Zhongguo jindai gongye shi ziliao*, vol. 4, pt. 1, p. 240.

25. *China Weekly Review*, December 24, 1938, p. 121; June 3, 1939, p. 17; *Yinhang zhoubao* 22, no. 39 (October 4, 1938), pp. 3–4.

26. The Bank of Canton's Shanghai branch, for instance, showed an increase in savings deposits in individual accounts from Y6 million in July 1937 to Y11.3 million in October 1937. See Shanghai Municipal Archives, Q65, Bank of Canton files, folder 58. A similar increase occurred in the Hong Kong branch with an increase from 1.9 million yuan to 4 million during the same period.

27. Chūgoku tsushinsha chōsabu, ed. *Sengo ni okeru Shanhai kin'yū jōtai no kaibō* (An analysis of the financial situation in Shanghai after the war began; Shanghai, 1938), pp. 9–14; *Yinhang zhoubao* 22, no. 13 (April 5, 1938), p. 5; 22, no. 29 (July 26, 1938), p. 6; 22, no. 32 (August 16, 1938), p. 4; 23, no. 15 (April 18, 1939), pp. 3–5; *Chūgoku nenkan, 1939* (China Yearbook), pp. 184–87; Ishihama Tomoyuki, *Shina senji keizai ron* (On China's wartime economy; Tokyo: Keiō shobō, 1940), pp. 216–19. One of the few financial firms to leave Shanghai was T. V. Soong's China Development Finance Corporation, which moved its headquarters to Hong Kong. See *Yinhang zhoubao* 22, no. 26 (July 5, 1938), p. 5.

28. *Yinhang zhoubao* 22, no. 37 (September 20, 1938), p. 3; 22, no. 48 (December 6, 1938), p. 7; 23, no. 3 (January 24, 1939), p. 6.

29. An index of industrial output in Shanghai in 1939 (with 1936 equal to 100) shows cotton textile production at 104.5, silk textiles at 116.8, flour milling at 112.1, wool cloth at 164.8, rubber decreasing to 42.1, machinery at 121.1, and paper at 242.5. See Jiang Duo, "Shanghai lunxian qianqi de 'gudao fanrong'" (The "flourishing solitary island" of the first period of occupied Shanghai), *Jingji xueshu ziliao* (Materials on economic studies), 1983, no. 10, p. 25. See also D. K. Lieu, *The Silk Industry of China* (Shanghai: Kelly and Walsh, 1940), pp. 259; *Yinhang zhoubao* 22, no. 23 (June 14, 1938), p. 4; 22, no. 39, (October 4, 1938), p. 3; Tang Zhenchang, *Shanghai shi,* pp. 800–803; Masuda Yoneji, *Shina sensō keizai no kenkyū* (Researches on China's wartime economy; Tokyo: Daiyamondo sha, 1944), p. 43.

30. Lu Yangyuan, and Fang Qingqiu, *Minguo shehui jingji shi,* pp. 693–98; Wei Dazhi, "Shanghai 'gudao' fanrong," p. 109.

31. Robert Barnett, *Economic Shanghai,* pp. 129–30; Yuda Hua fangzhi ziben jituan shiliao bianxie zu, ed., *Yuda Hua fangzhi ziben jituan shiliao* (Historical materials on the Yuda Hua textile capitalist group; Wuhan: Hubei renmin chuban she, 1984), pp. 337–43.

32. Poshek Fu, "Projecting Ambivalence: Chinese Cinema in Semi-occupied Shanghai, 1937–41," in Wen-hsin Yeh, ed., *Wartime Shanghai,* p. 97; *Zhiye shenghuo* (Professional life) 1, no. 1 (April 15, 1939), p. 2.

33. Sun Choucheng et al., "Yu Xiaqing shilue" (A biographical sketch of Yu Xiaqing), in *Zhejiang WZXJ,* no. 32 (1986), p. 127; Wang Renze, "Jindai hangyun ye jubo Yu Xiaqing" (Modern shipping leader Yu Xiaqing), in Xu Dixin, ed., *Zhongguo qiye jia liezhuan* (Biographies of Chinese entrepreneurs: Beijing: Jingji ribao chuban she, 1988), vol. 2, pp. 42–43; Rhodes Farmer, *Shanghai Harvest,* p. 254; Xu Nianhui, "Yu Xiaqing de yisheng" (Yu Xiaqing, a life), *WZXJ,* no. 15 (1986), pp. 193–94.

34. Shanghai shehui kexue yuan, jingji yanjiu suo, ed., *Rongjia qiye shiliao* (Historical material on the Rong enterprises; Shanghai: Shanghai renmin chuban she, 1962), vol. 2, pp. 43–46; Chen Zhen and Yao Luo, eds., *Zhongguo jindai gongye shi ziliao,* vol. 1, p. 394; Shanghai shi liangshi ju, Shanghai shi gongshang

xingzheng guanli ju, and Shanghai shehui kexue yuan, jingji yanjiu suo jingji shi yanjiu shi, eds., *Zhongguo jindai mianfen gongye shi* (A history of the flour milling industry in modern China; Beijing: Zhonghua shuju chuban, 1987), p. 155.

35. Poshek Fu, *Passivity, Resistance, and Collaboration: Intellectual Choices in Occupied Shanghai, 1937–1945* (Stanford, Calif.: Stanford University Press, 1993), p. 33.

36. Zhongguo kexue yuan, Shanghai jingji yanjiu suo; and Shanghai shehui kexue yuan, Jingji yanjiu suo, eds., *Hengfeng shachan de fasheng fazhan yu gaizao* (The creation, development, and reform of Hengfeng textiles; Shanghai: Shanghai renmin chuban she, 1958), pp. 68–72, 78; Chen Zhen and Yao Luo, eds., *Zhongguo jindai gongye shi ziliao,* vol. 3, pt. 2, p. 1045. Daikō had lost 138,000 spindles at Qingdao and was given Chinese mills in compensation.

37. Yan Xuexi, "Riben dui Nantong Dasheng qiye de lueduo" (Japan's plundering of the Dasheng enterprises of Nantong), in Jiangsu sheng lishi xuehui, ed., *Kangri zhanzheng shishi tansuo* (Explorations into the history of the anti-Japanese war of resistance; Shanghai: Shanghai shehui kexue yuan chuban she, 1988), pp. 206–12.

38. Huang Shirang, "Yu DaHua qiye sishi nian" (Forty years of the Yu DaHua enterprises), *WZXJ,* no. 44 (1986), pp. 29–30.

39. Yang Shaozhen and Hong Furong, "Zhengtai xiangjiao chang ershi er nian de jingli" (The experience of twenty-two years of the Zhengtai Rubber factory), *Shanghai WZXJ,* no. 32 (1980), pp. 153–58.

40. Yuan Xieming, "Shanghai gudao yu ta houfang," pp. 62–64; Wang Jishen et al., eds., *Zhanshi Shanghai jingji.* (Wartime Shanghai's economy; Shanghai: Zhongguo kexue gongsi, 1945), pp. 10–36; Frederic Wakeman, Jr., *The Shanghai Badlands: Wartime Terrorism and Urban Crime, 1937–1941* (Cambridge: Cambridge University Press, 1996), pp. 95–96.

41. Jiang Duo, "Shanghai lunxian qianqi," p. 28; Tang Zhenchang, *Shanghai shi,* pp. 803–4; Wei Dazhi, "Shanghai 'gudao jingji fanrong' shimo," p. 112.

42. Technically the French Concession remained under the control of a Vichy French administration that was an "ally" of Japan. In July 1943, the Vichy authorities formally surrendered the concession to the Wang Jingwei regime. Japanese agents operated in the concession during the Vichy period, eliminating the quasi-independent character of the regime. See Marie-Claire Bergère, "The Purge in Shanghai, 1945–46: The Sarly Affair and the End of the French Concession." in Wen-hsin Yeh, ed. *Wartime Shanghai,* pp. 157–78.

CHAPTER TWO

1. Joyce C. Lebra, ed., *Japan's Greater East Asia Co-Prosperity Sphere in World War II: Selected Readings and Documents* (Kuala Lumpur: Oxford University Press, 1975), pp. 68–69. On Hirota's three principles, see Parks M. Coble, *Facing Japan,* p. 250.

2. Speech of December 22, 1938, *Contemporary Japan* 8, no. 1 (March 1939), p. 171; Joyce C. Lebra, *Japan's Greater East Asia Co-Prosperity Sphere,* pp. 69–70.

3. Quoted in Ryusaku Tsunoda, William Theodore De Bary, and Donald

Keene, eds., *Sources of Japanese Tradition* (New York: Columbia University Press, 1958), vol. 2, p. 295. See also Joyce Lebra, *Japan's Greater East Asia Co-Prosperity Sphere*, pp. 71–73, 91.

4. Takahashi Kamekichi, "Economic Significance of the East Asiatic Co-Prosperity Sphere," *Contemporary Japan* 10, no. 1 (January 1941), p. 39. Additional material from Takahashi is published in Joyce Lebra, *Japan's Greater East Asia Co-Prosperity Sphere*, pp. 48–54. The Shōwa Research Association was associated with Prince Konoe.

5. John W. Dower, *War Without Mercy: Race and Power in the Pacific War* (New York: Pantheon Books, 1986), p. 289.

6. Peter Duus, "Introduction," in Peter Duus, Ramon H. Myers, and Mark R. Peattie, eds., *The Japanese Wartime Empire, 1931–1945* (Princeton: Princeton University Press, 1996), p. xxxii.

7. Quoted in Louise Young, "Imagined Empire: The Cultural Construction of Manchukuo," in Peter Duus, Ramon H. Myers, and Mark R. Peattie, eds., *The Japanese Wartime Empire, 1931–1945*, p. 81.

8. Katsuji, Nakagane, "Manchukuo and Economic Development," in Peter Duus, Ramon H. Myers, and Mark R. Peattie, eds., *The Japanese Informal Empire in China, 1895–1937* (Princeton: Princeton University Press, 1989), p. 141.

9. Louise Young, "Imagined Empire," pp. 81–82.

10. Quoted in Louise Young, *Japan's Total Empire: Manchuria and the Culture of Wartime Imperialism* (Berkeley: University of California Press, 1998), p. 204.

11. Quoted in Institute of Pacific Relations, Secretariat, *Industrial Japan: Aspects of Recent Economic Changes as Viewed by Japanese Writers* (New York: Institute of Pacific Relations, 1941), pp. 51–52.

12. Peter Duus, "Introduction," p. xxxii. The concept of the "Greater East Asia Co-Prosperity Sphere" became even more distorted by the sudden expansion into Southeast Asia after December 7, 1941. See E. Bruce Reynolds, "Anomaly or Model? Independent Thailand's Role in Japan's Asian Strategy, 1941–1943," pp. 243–73, and Mark R. Peattie, "*Nanshin:* The 'Southward Advance,' 1931–1941, as Prelude to the Japanese Occupation of Southeast Asia," pp. 189–242 in Peter Duus, Ramon H. Myers, and Mark R. Peattie, eds., *The Japanese Wartime Empire, 1931–1945.*

13. Michael A. Barnhart, *Japan Prepares for Total War: The Search for Economic Security, 1919–1941* (Ithaca, N.Y.: Cornell University Press, 1987), p. 91.

14. William W. Lockwood, *The Economic Development of Japan: Growth and Structural Change* (Princeton, N.J.: Princeton University Press, 1968), p. 67.

15. Hata Ikuhiko, "Continental Expansion, 1905–1941," in *The Cambridge History of Japan*, vol. 6, *The Twentieth Century* (Cambridge: Cambridge University Press, 1988), p. 302.

16. Michael A. Barnhart, *Japan Prepares for Total War*, p. 151; W. G. Beasley, *Japanese Imperialism, 1894–1945* (Oxford: Oxford University Press, 1987), pp. 216–17.

17. Hon'iden Yoshio (Akio Honyiden) in the *Economist* (Tokyo), June 11, 1939, quoted in Institute of Pacific Relations, Secretariat, *Industrial Japan: Aspects of Recent Economic Changes*, pp. 55–56.

18. This schema is adapted from Shan Guanchu, "Riben qinHua de 'yizhan yangzhan' zhengce," (Japan's policy of 'using the war to sustain the war' in its invasion of China), *Lishi yanjiu*, 1991, no. 4, pp. 86–88.

19. Norman D. Hanwell, "Economic Disruption in Occupied China," *Far Eastern Survey* 8, no. 6 (March 15, 1939), pp. 64; see also Haldore Hanson, "Japan's Balance Sheet in China," *Amerasia* 4, no. 3 (June 1939), p. 158.

20. Wang Ke-wen, "Collaborators and Capitalists: The Politics of 'Material Control' in Wartime Shanghai," *Chinese Studies in History* 26, no. 1 (fall 1992), pp. 42–43. See also Chen Zhengmo, *Zenyang fengsui Rikou de "yizhan yangzhan"* (How to smash the Japanese bandits "using the war to sustain the war"; Chongqing: Zhongshan wenhua jiaoyu guan, 1939), pp. 1–15.

21. Robert W. Barnett, *Economic Shanghai: Hostage to Politics*, p. 184; He Zupei, "Banian lunxian hua Hangxian" (Talking of Hangzhou county during eight years of occupation), *Zhejiang WZXJ*, no. 2 (1962), pp. 176–77; Lu Yangyuan and Fang Qingqiu, eds., *Minguo shehui jingji shi*, p. 691; "Testimony of Searle Bates," *Tokyo War Crimes Trials* (Garland, 1981), vol. 2, p. 2,647.

22. "Report by M. S. Bates on conditions in occupied Kiangsu and Anhwei," January 4, 1940, PRO FO 371/2468.9 F 182/182/10; He Zupei, "Banian lunxian hua Hangxian," pp. 176–77; Chen Dingwen, "Hangzhou lunxian shiqi choulu" (The shameful record of occupied Hangzhou), *Zhejiang WZXJ*, no. 21 (1982), pp. 200–203.

23. Robert Barnett, *Economic Shanghai: Hostage to Politics*, pp. 178–79.

24. *Far Eastern Survey*, July 19, 1939, p. 176; Du Xuncheng, *Riben zai jiu Zhongguo*, p. 59.

25. The letter is reprinted in *The Tokyo War Crimes Trial*, vol. 3, p. 5,219.

26. F. C. Jones, *Japan's New Order in East Asia: Its Rise and Fall, 1937–1945* (London: Oxford University Press, 1954), p. 73; see also *China Weekly Review*, December 23, 1939, p. 127; Haldore Hanson, *"Humane Endeavour": The Story of the China War* (New York: Farrar and Rinehart, 1939), p. 210.

27. Tōa kenkyūjo, ed., *Shina senryō chi keizai no hatten* (The development of the economy of occupied China; Tokyo: Tōa kenkyūjo, 1944), pp. 74–75. Procurement of cotton in north China was higher than in central China. In 1938, Japan procured 2,676,000 piculs, an estimated 98.4 percent of the harvest. In 1941, this was 2,209,000, an estimated 73.7 percent of the harvest. See also Haldore Hanson, *"Humane Endeavour,"* pp. 204–8.

28. Tōa kenkyūjo, *Shina senryō chi keizai no hatten*, p. 222. Japan's domination of textiles was even greater in north China, controlling 97.2 percent of spindles in 1941, up from 78 percent in 1936. See also Chen Zhen and Yao Luo, eds., *Zhongguo jindai gongye shi ziliao*, vol. 1, p. 82; Xu Xinwu, "Kangzhan shiqi Riben diguo zhuyi dui Hua jingji qinlue gaishu" (The economic invasion of China by Japanese imperialism during the war of resistance period), *Jingji xueshu ziliao* (Materials on economic studies), 1982, no. 10, p. 31.

29. Altogether an estimated 82 factories or mines were placed under direct military management. Of these 38 were in Shanxi, 12 in Hebei, 11 in Henan, 18 in Shandong, 2 in Anhui, 1 in Suiyuan. In terms of the type of plant, 30 of these were flour mills and 15 textile mills, with the rest scattered among other cate-

gories. See Chen Zhen and Yao Luo, eds., *Zhongguo jindai gongye shi ziliao,* vol. 1, pp. 80–82; Lu Yangyuan and Fang Qingqiu, *Minguo shehui jingji shi,* p. 684; Zheng Kelun, "Lunxian qu de gongkuang ye" (Mining and industry in the occupied areas), *Jingji jianshe jikan* (Economic reconstruction quarterly) 1, no. 4 (April 1943), p. 249.

30. Chen Zhen and Yao Luo, eds., *Zhongguo jindai gongye shih zuliao,* vol. 1, pp. 81–83; Zhang Xichang et al., *Zhanshi de Zhongguo jingji* (China's wartime economy; Guilin: Kexue shudian, 1943), pp. 172–73; Lu Yangyuan and Fang Qingqiu, *Minguo shehui jingji shi,* pp. 684–85, Du Xuncheng, *Riben zai jiu Zhongguo de touzi,* p. 57; Zhongguo di'er lishi dang'an guan, "1942 nianqian Riben zai Zhongguo lunxian qu lueduo gongsi gongkuang ye jingying ji shouyi diaocha" (Materials concerning the investigation of Chinese industrial and mining enterprises robbed by the Japanese aggressors before 1942), *Mingguo dang'an,* 1992, no. 1, p. 31.

31. Chen Zhen and Yao Luo, eds., *Zhongguo jindai gongye,* vol. 1, pp. 80–81; Chao Kang, *The Development of Cotton Textile Production,* p. 131.

32. Takamura Naosuke, "NitChū sensō to zaiKa bō (The Sino-Japanese war and textiles in China), in Inoue Kiyoshi and Etō Shikichi, eds., *NitChū sensō to NitChū kankei: Rokōkyō jiken 50 shūnan NitChū gakujutsu tōronkai kiroku* (The Sino-Japanese War and Sino-Japanese relations: A record of a scholarly conference on the 50th anniversary of the Marco Polo Bridge Incident; Tokyo: Hara shobō, 1988), p. 339; Du Xuncheng, *Riben zai jiu Zhongguo de touzi,* pp. 199–200; Shanghai shehui kexue yuan, Zhongguo qiye shi ziliao yanjiu zhongxin (Shanghai Academy of Social Sciences, Resource Center for Chinese Business History), Rong Collection [hereafter Rong Collection, SASS], R03–1, *Shenxin xitong qiye shiliao* (Historical material on the Shenxin system enterprises, mimeographed material originally published by the enterprise), vol. 1, no. 2, p. 118; Guo Tingyi and Zhang Pengyuan, eds., *Lin Jiyong xiansheng fanwen jilu* (The reminiscences of Mr. Lin Jiyong; Taibei: Zhongyang yanjiu yuan, jindai yanjiu suo, 1983), pp. 47–52.

33. Du Xuncheng, *Riben zai jiu Zhongguo de touzi,* pp. 200–201. Many Japanese manufacturers, including the Kanegafuchi Company, sought to expand in China because industrial wages remained lower than Japan. See Robert Norton, "Japan's Drive for Cotton," *Amerasia* 3, no. 6 (August 1939), pp. 263–69.

34. Yūhō bōseki is sometimes listed by the name of the parent company, Tōa bōseki kaisha; Kanegafuchi used the name Kōdai on its mills. Yan Zhongping et al., eds., *Zhongguo jindai jingji shi tongji ziliao xuanji* (Selected statistics on modern Chinese economic history; Beijing: Kexue chuban she, 1955), pp. 144–45; Du Xuncheng, *Riben zai jiu Zhongguo touzi,* pp. 204–13; SASS, Rong Collection, *Shenxin xitong,* R03–1, pp. 191–93; 232–34. Takeo Itō, *Problems in the Japanese Occupied Areas in China,* p. 21, states that 37 mills in central China were entrusted to Japanese firms. These mills had contained 611,512 spindles and 5,275 weaving machines. Yan Zhongping lists 33 mills as entrusted and 14 (mostly in the north) under military management.

35. Robert Barnett, *Economic Shanghai: Hostage to Politics,* p. 92; Tōa kenkyūjo, ed., *Shina senryō chi keizai no hatten,* pp. 226–28.

36. Chen Zhen, ed., *Zhongguo jindai gongye shi ziliao*, vol. 4, pt. 1, p. 830; Guo Shijie, *Rikou qinHua baoxing lu* (The savage record of Japan's invasion of China; Beijing: Lianhe shudian, 1951), p. 93; Chen Zhen and Yao Luo, *Zhongguo jindai gongye*, vol. 1, pp. 414–15; Takeo Itō, *Problems in the Japanese Occupied Areas in China*, p. 22.

37. *Yinhang zhoubao*, April 19, 1938, p. 3; Robert Barnett, *Economic Shanghai: Hostage to Politics*, p. 89; Jack Shepherd, "Salvaging the Textile Industry in China," *Far Eastern Survey* 8, no. 15 (July 19, 1939), pp. 174–75; Zhongguo di'er lishi dang'an guan, "1942 nian-qian Riben zai Zhongguo lunxian qu," p. 31.

38. Robert Barnett, *Economic Shanghai: Hostage to Politics*, pp. 89–90; He Zupei, "Banian lunxian hua Hangxian," pp. 177–78.

39. Chen Zhen and Yao Luo, eds., *Zhongguo jindai gongye*, vol. 1, pp. 457–58.

40. From *The Economist* (Tokyo), June 11, 1939, quoted in Institute of Pacific Relations, *Industrial Japan: Aspects of Recent Economic Changes*, p. 61.

41. Sassa Hirō and Shintarō Ryū, *Recent Political and Economic Developments in Japan* (Tokyo: Japanese Council: Institute of Pacific Relations, 1941), p. 66; one obstacle to Japanese plans to populate the mainland with immigrants from Japan was the lack of enthusiasm among the Japanese themselves, making it difficult for the government to reach its target. In 1938 in Manchukuo, a total of 417,759 Japanese lived among a population of approximately 37 million. See Elizabeth B. Schumpeter, ed., *The Industrialization of Japan and Manchukuo, 1930–1940: Population, Raw Materials, and Industry* (New York: Macmillan, 1940), p. 68; Louise Young, *Japan's Total Empire*, pp. 352–98.

42. Testimony of Searle Bates, Professor of History, University of Nanjing, cited in Douglas R. Reynolds, "Training Young China Hands: Tōa Dōbun Shoin and Its Precursors, 1886–1945," in Peter Duus, Ramon H. Myers, and Mark R. Peattie, eds., *The Japanese Informal Empire in China, 1895–1937*, p. 265; see also *Tokyo War Crimes Trials*, vol. 2, p. 2,637. The Special Services of the Army (Tokumu-bu) referred to special units attached to the headquarters of each army command that dealt with political matters. According to John Hunter Boyle, "They operated with a minimum of control from the commanding generals and gained a singularly unpopular reputation among Chinese because of their real and suspected interference in Chinese internal politics." See John Hunter Boyle, *China and Japan at War, 1937–1945: The Politics of Collaboration* (Stanford, Calif.: Stanford University Press, 1972), p. 85.

43. *Tokyo War Crimes Trials*, p. 2646.

44. Du Xuncheng, *Riben zai jiu Zhongguo de touzi*, pp. 58–59, 247.

45. Tōa kenkyūjo, *Shina senryō chi keizai no hatten*, p. 276. Ironically, the fourteen Chinese-owned mills in central China operated at nearly 63 percent of capacity, but many of these operated in unoccupied Shanghai and used wheat imported from overseas.

46. See, for example, the Shanghai Municipal Archives, Shanghai City Bank collection (Shanghai shi yinhang), Q61 folder 308, pp. 1–41, which lists the property removed for use by a Japanese bank, including furniture, typewriters, supplies, and several vehicles, including a Ford auto. See also He Zupei, "Banian lunxian hua Hangxian," pp. 177–78, and Gail Hershatter, *The Work-*

ers of Tianjin 1900–1949 (Stanford, Calif.: Stanford University Press, 1986), p. 37.

CHAPTER THREE

1. Shan Guanchu, "Riben qinHua de 'yizhan yangzhan' zhengce," pp. 86–88.

2. Kobayashi Hideo, *Daitōa kyōeiken no keisei to hōkai* (The formation and collapse of the Greater East Asian Co-Prosperity Sphere; Ochanomizu shobō, 1973), pp. 180–84; Usui Katsumi, "The Politics of War, 1937–1941," p. 325; Hara Akira, "'Daitōa kyōeiken' no keizaiteki jittai" (The economic realities of the Greater East Asia Co-prosperity Sphere), *Tochi seido shigaku* (Journal of Agrarian History; April 1976), no. 71, pp. 6–7; Zhang Zuguo, "Ershi shijie shangban ye Riben zai Zhongguo dalu de guoce huishe" (Japanese national policy companies on the Chinese mainland in the first half of the 20th century), *Lishi yanjiu*, no. 6 (1986), pp. 161–70; Parks M. Coble, *Facing Japan,* p. 262–63; Nakamura Takafusa, *Senji Nihon kahoku keizai shihai* (Japan's wartime economic control over north China; Tokyo: Yamakawa shuppansha, 1983), pp. 162–91.

3. Sherman Cochran, "Business, Governments, and War in China, 1931–1949," in Akira Iriye and Warren Cohen, eds., *American, Chinese, and Japanese Perspectives on Wartime Asia, 1931–1949* (Wilmington, Del.: Scholarly Resources, 1990), pp. 129–31; Hara Akira, "Daitōa kyōeiken," pp. 6–7; Nakamura Takafusa, "Japan's Economic Thrust into North China, 1933–1938: Formation of the North China Development Corporation" in Akira Iriye, ed., *The Chinese and the Japanese: Essays in Political and Cultural Interactions* (Princeton, N.J.: Princeton University Press, 1980), pp. 242–50; Nakamura Takafusa, *Senji Nihon kahoku,* pp. 58–68; W. G. Beasley, *Japanese Imperialism, 1894–1945,* p. 216.

4. Zhang Zuguo, "Ershi shiji shangban ye," p. 167; Jerome B. Cohen, *Japan's Economy in War and Reconstruction* (Minneapolis: University of Minnesota Press, 1949), pp. 42–43; *Tokyo War Crimes Trials,* vol. 2, p. 3,863.

5. Tan Xihong, ed., *Kangzhan shiqi zhi Zhongguo jingji* (China's economy in the war of resistance period; Hong Kong: Longmen shudian, 1968), vol. 2, pp. L-88–89; Chuan-hua Lowe, *Japan's Economic Offensive in China* (London: Allen and Unwin, 1939), pp. 56–59; Ju Zhifen and Bi Jie, "Riben 'Bei zhina kaifa zhushi huishe' de jingji huodong ji qi lueduo" (The economic activities and the plundering of Japan's North China Development Company), *Jindai shi yanjiu* (Research on modern history), no. 3 (1993), pp. 254–57; "The Economic Situation in North China," Mr. G. C. Pelpham, commercial secretary to the British embassy, memorandum of April 8, 1940, PRO FO 371/2468.9 3659/182/10.

6. Ju Zhifen, Bi Jie, "Riben 'Bei zhina kaifa zhushi huishe,'" pp. 252–53; W. G. Beasley, *Japanese Imperialism, 1894–1945,* p. 218; Nakamura Takafusa, "Kita Shina shinkō kabushiki kaisha no seiritsu" (The creation of the North China Development Corporation), in Inoue Kiyoshi and Etō Shikichi, eds., *NitChū sensō to NitChū kenkei,* pp. 349–65.

7. Yan Zhongping, *Zhongguo jindai jingji shi,* pp. 143–50; Jerome Cohen, *Japan's Economy in War and Reconstruction,* p. 45; Du Xuncheng, *Riben zai jiu Zhongguo,* pp. 156–61, 167.

8. Gail Hershetter, *The Workers of Tianjin*, p. 37.

9. Chen Zhengmo, *Zenyang fensui Rikou*, pp. 1–52, passim.

10. John Hunter Boyle, *China and Japan at War*, pp. 97–110; Parks M. Coble, *Facing Japan*, pp. 267–303, passim.

11. Hara Akira, "Daitōa kyōeiken," p. 2; Ramon H. Myers, "Creating a Modern Enclave Economy: The Economic Integration of Japan, Manchuria, and North China, 1932–1945," in Peter Duus, Ramon H. Myers, and Mark R. Peattie, eds., *The Japanese Wartime Empire, 1931–1945*, pp. 136–70; Tōa kenkyōjo, *Shina senryō chi keizai no hatten*, p. 77; Zhang Limin, "Riben Huabei kaifa huishe zijin touxi" (An analysis of the capital of Japan's North China Development Corporation), *KangRi zhangzheng yanjiu*, no. 1 (1994), p. 94; Furukyu Tadao, "'Kankan' no shosō" (Various aspects of traitors), in *Iwanami kōza: kindai Nihon to shokuminchi* (The Iwanami lectures, modern Japan and colonies, vol. 6; Tokyo: Iwanami shōten, 1993), p. 151.

12. Asada Kyōji, *Nihon teikokushugika no Chūgoku: Chūgoku senryōchi keizai no kenkyū* (China under Japanese imperialism: Research on the economy of occupied China; Tokyo: Rakuyū shobō, 1981), p. 106; Itō Takeo, *Problems in the Japanese Occupied Areas*, p. 58.

13. Itō Takeo, *Problems in the Japanese Occupied Areas*, p. 62.

14. Quoted in Institute of Pacific Relations, Secretariat, *Industrial Japan*, p. 44.

15. Yoda Yoshiie, ed., *NitChū sensō senryō chiku shihai shiryō* (Materials on control of the occupied areas during the Sino-Japanese War; Tokyo: Ryūkai shosha, 1987), pp. 626–29; Usui Katsumi, "Politics of War," pp. 326–27; Chuanhua Lowe, *Japan's Economic Offensive*, p. 63; Tan Xihong, *Kangzhan shiqi zhi Zhongguo*, vol. 2, p. L-89; Kobayashi Hideo, *Daitōa kyōeiken*, p. 190.

16. Takahashi Yasuryū, "Riben zhanling shiqi Huazhong diqu de suiyun ye," trans. Qian Xiaoming and Cheng Linsu (Water transport industry in the Japanese occupied area of central China), *Jingji xueshu ziliao*, no. 10 (1983), pp. 57–58; *Chūgoku nenkan* (China yearbook), 1939, p. 31; Yoda Yoshiie, ed., *NitChū sensō senryō chiku*, pp. 560–61, 637–38.

17. Takahashi Yasuryū, "Riben zhanling shiqi," p. 58; Yoda Yoshiie, ed., *NitChū sensō senryō chiku*, pp. 562–563; Douglas Reynolds, "Training Young China Hands," p. 264; Robert W. Barnett, *Economic Shanghai*, pp. 172–74.

18. Robert Barnett, *Economic Shanghai*, p. 176; Kobayashi Hideo, *Daitōa kyōeiken*, p. 222; *China Weekly Review*, May 4, 1940, p. 335; Usui Katsumi, "The Politics of War," p. 429; *Gendaishi shiryō* (Source materials on contemporary history), vol. 9, pp. 617–20. The authorized capital of the firm was 50 million yen, with one-half to be supplied by the CCDC. Actual capital investment, as of 1940, was 33,815,000 yen.

19. Takahashi Yasuryū, "Riben zhanling shiqi," p. 54; *Programs of Japan in China, Extracts from FCC intercepts of short-wave broadcasts from Radio Tokyo and affiliated stations from December 1941 to January 1, 1945, and from OSS sources* (Honolulu: Office of Strategic Services, 1945), vol. 1, p. 12.

20. *Chūgoku nenkan*, 1939, p. 33; Yoda Yoshiie, ed., *NitChū sensō senryō chiku*, pp. 568–70.

21. Yoda Yoshiie, ed., *NitChū sensō senryō chiku*, pp. 571–72.

22. Yoda Yoshiie, ed., *NitChū sensō senryō chiku*, pp. 573–75, 639–40; *Chūgoku nenkan*, 1939, p. 32; Du Xuncheng, *Riben zai jiu Zhongguo de touzi*, p. 143.

23. Yoda Yoshiie, ed., *NitChū sensō senryō chiku*, pp. 575–80, 635–37; *Chūgoku nenkan*, 1939, p. 31; testimony of Tung Shu-ming, *The Tokyo War Crimes Trial*, vol. 2, pp. 4,425–429, 4,435–441.

24. Tan Xihong, *Kangzhan shiqi*, vol. 2, p. L-90; Yoda Yoshiie, ed., *NitChū sensō senryō chiku*, pp. 580–82.

25. Chūgoku seiji keizai kenkyūjo, ed., *Naka Shina keizai nempō* (An economic yearbook of Central China; Shanghai, 1942), vol. 2, pp. 309–10.

26. Tan Xihong, *Kangzhan shiqi*, vol. 2, p. L-89; Yoda Yoshiie, ed., *NitChū sensō senryō chiku*, pp. 583–86; Miyazaki Masayoshi, *Tōa renmei ron* (A discussion of the East Asian League; Tokyo: Kaizōsha, 1938), pp. 189, 301; Du Xuncheng, *Riben zai jiu Zhongguo de touzi*, pp. 156–57; Hara Akira, "Daitōa kyōeiken," p. 8.

27. Yoda Yoshiie, ed., *NitChū sensō senryō chiku*, pp. 587–88.

28. Yoda Yoshiie, ed., *NitChū sensō senryō chiku*, pp. 589–95; Chuan-hua Lowe, *Japan's Economic Offensive*, pp. 62–63; *China Weekly Review*, December 23, 1937, p. 127; Higuchi Hiroshi, *Nippon no taiShi tōshi kenkyū* (Research on Japan's investment in China; Tokyo: Seikatsusha, 1939), pp. 682–84.

29. Hara Akira, "Daitōa kyōeiken," p. 8.

30. Shanghai shi dang'an guan, ed., *Riwei Shanghai shi zhengfu* (The Japanese puppet government of Shanghai; Beijing: Dang'an chuban she, 1986), pp. 446–61; Kobayashi Hideo, *Daitōa kyōeiken*, p. 188; Tan Xihong, *Kangzhan shiqi*, p. L-90; "Shanghai hengchan gufen youxian gongsi wenjian" (Documents on the Shanghai Real Estate Company, Ltd.), *Dang'an yu lishi* (Archives and history), no. 1 (1986), pp. 31–32; *Naka Shina keizai nempō*, vol. 2, p. 310–11; Yoda Yoshiie, ed., *NitChū sensō senryō chiku*, pp. 640–42.

31. "Shanghai hengchan gufen youxian gongsi wenjian," pp. 36–37; Shanghai shi dang'an guan, ed., *Riwei Shanghai shi zhengfu*, pp. 451–53; Fang Yi, "Ri shang hengchan zhushi huishe zhenggou tudi de pianju" (The fraud of the requisition of land by the Japanese merchant Hengchan company), *Shanghai WZXJ*, no. 64 (1990), pp. 200–202; John Hunter Boyle, *China and Japan at War*, pp. 116–18.

32. Yoda Yoshiie, ed., *NitChū sensō senryō chiku*, pp. 644–45; Qiu Liangru and Jiang Youlong, "Zhejiang sichou shi jiyao" (A record of the major facets of the history of Zhejiang silk production), *Zhejiang WZXJ*, no. 24 (1982), pp. 49–52; Chen Ciyu, *Jindai Zhongguo de jixie saosi gongye, 1860–1945* (Recent China's machine woven silk industry, 1860–1945; Taibei: Zhongyang yanjiu yuan, 1989), pp. 115–16; *Yinhang zhoubao* 22, no. 39 (October 4, 1938), p. 3; Tōa kenkyūjo, *Shina senryōchi keizai*, p.254.

33. Qiu Liangru and Jiang Youlong, "Zhejiang sichou shi jiyou," pp. 49–50; Robert Barnett, *Economic Shanghai*, pp. 97–98; *China Weekly Review*, August 20, 1938, p. 405, and January 6, 1940; Kobayashi Hideo, *Daitōa kyōeiken no keisei*, pp. 224–25.

34. Kobayashi Hideo, *Daitōa kyōeiken no keisei*, p. 225–27; Robert Barnett, *Economic Shanghai*, pp. 99–100; D. K. Lieu, *The Silk Industry of China*, p. 81; Chen Ciyu, *Jindai Zhongguo de jixie*, pp. 115–16, 130–31.

35. Tang Kentang, "Dali sichang jianshi" (An abbreviated history of the Dali silk factory), *Shanghai WZXJ*, no. 53 (1986), pp. 233–36; Chen Ciyu, *Jindai Zhongguo de jixie*, pp. 115–16.

36. Matsuzumi Kyūzaburō, *Naka Shina seishi gyō no gaikō narabi ni haikyū kikō no chōsa* (An investigation of the general situation and rationing organizations of central China's silk industry; Tokyo: n.p., 1939), pp. 57–66.

37. Yoda Yoshiie, ed., *NitChū sensō senryō*, pp. 590, 595.

38. Zhu Zijia [pseud. of Jin Xiongbai], *Wang zhengquan di kaichang yu shouchang* (The beginning and end of the Wang regime; Hong Kong: Chunqiu zazhi, 1960), vol. 3, pp. 5–10.

39. Nakamura Takafusa, "The Yen Bloc, 1931–1941," in Peter Duus, Ramon H. Myers, and Mark R. Peattie, eds., *The Japanese Wartime Empire, 1931–1945*, p. 179.

40. Nakamura Takafusa, "The Yen Bloc, 1931–1941," pp. 171–79; Lincoln Li, *The Japanese Army in North China*, pp. 138–45; *Tōa* 11, no. 3 (March 1938), pp. 64–66; for details on the East Hebei regime, see Parks M. Coble, *Facing Japan*, pp. 272–73.

41. John Hunter Boyle, *China and Japan at War*, p. 98; Frank Tamagna, *Banking and Finance in China* (New York: Institute of Pacific Relations, 1942), pp. 309–311; Kimura Masutarō, *Jihen ka no Shina kin'yu oyobi kin'yu kikan* (Finance and financial organizations in China since the incident; Tokyo, 1941), pp. 59–61.

42. Letter of December 5, 1938. PRO FO.371/23445 F 758/75/10.

43. F. C. Jones, *Japan's New Order in East Asia*, p. 164; Lincoln Li, *The Japanese Army in North China, 1937–1941: Problems of Political and Economic Control* (Tokyo: Oxford University Press, 1975), pp. 141–42; Arthur N. Young, *China and the Helping Hand, 1937–1945* (Cambridge, Mass.: Harvard University Press, 1963), pp. 155–59.

44. Frank Tamagna, *Banking and Finance in China*, pp. 271–75; Nakamura Takafusa, "The Yen Bloc," pp. 178–81; Robert W. Barnett, *Economic Shanghai*, p. 121; 142–43.

45. Lincoln Li, *The Japanese Army in North China*, pp. 141–42; Ma Yinchu, quoted in *Zhanshi jingji lunwen ji* (A collection of essays on the wartime economy; Chongqing: Zuojia shushi, 1945), p. 197; letter of November 3, 1938, from E. L. Hall-Patch in Tianjin to the British Ambassador at Shanghai, Sir Archibald Clark Kerr, re currency situation in north China, PRO.FO 371/23445 F/806/75/10; Arthur N. Young Collection, Hoover Institution, Box 68, Memorandum of March 31, 1941.

46. Arthur N. Young, *China and the Helping Hand*, p. 158; Takafusa Nakamura, "The Yen bloc," p. 181; Robert W. Barnett, *Economic Shanghai*, pp. 121–25, 133–35.

47. Frank Tamagna, *Banking and Finance in China*, pp. 245–46; Takafusa Nakamura, "The Yen Bloc," p. 190; Robert W. Barnett, *Economic Shanghai*, p. 140.

48. Frank Tamagna, *Banking and Finance in China*, pp. 317–19; D. K. Lieu, "The Sino-Japanese Currency War," *Pacific Affairs* 12, no. 4 (December 1939), pp. 419–20.

CHAPTER FOUR

1. For details of the formation of these governments, see Gerald E. Bunker, *The Peace Conspiracy: Wang Ching-wei and the China War, 1937–1941* (Cambridge, Mass.: Harvard University Press, 1972), pp. 62–63; F. C. Jones, *Japan's New Order in East Asia*, p. 72–74; John Hunter Boyle, *China and Japan at War*, pp. 83–133, passim. Chen Gongbo took over as mayor of Shanghai on November 20, 1940, following the assassination of Fu on October 12. Hu Baoqi, "Toudi funi de Fu Xiao'an" (Fu Xiao'en who went over to the enemy), *WZXJ*, no. 106 (1986), pp. 156–77.

2. John Hunter Boyle, *China and Japan at War*, p. 115.

3. W. G. Beasley, *Japanese Imperialism, 1894–1945*, p. 208.

4. Yoda Yoshiie, ed., *NitChū sensō senryō*, pp. 562, 568, 573.

5. John Hunter Boyle, *China and Japan at War*, p. 116.

6. Quoted in Usui Katsumi, "The Politics of War," p. 314.

7. John Hunter Boyle, *China and Japan at War*, pp. 116–17.

8. Parks M. Coble, *The Shanghai Capitalists*, pp. 32–33, 189.

9. SASS, *Rongjia qiye shiliao*, vol. 2, pp. 18–19; Itō Takeo, *Problems in the Japanese Occupied Areas*, p. 69. Others included several managers of companies whose properties were located in the occupied zones as well as managers of small banks.

10. SASS, *Rongjia qiye shi liao*, vol. 2, pp. 19–20.

11. For a discussion of the war of assassinations in Shanghai, see Frederic Wakeman Jr., *The Shanghai Badlands: Wartime Terrorism and Urban Crime, 1937–1941* (Cambridge: Cambridge University Press, 1996), passim, and Wen-hsin Yeh, "Urban Warfare and Underground Resistance" in Wen-hsin Yeh, ed., *Wartime Shanghai*, pp. 111–32.

12. Frederick Wakeman Jr., *The Shanghai Badlands*, pp. 17, 59–64, 97; Wang Fan-hsi, *Memoirs of a Chinese Revolutionary*, trans. Gregor Benton (New York: Columbia University Press, 1991), p. 223; SASS, *Rongjia qiye shiliao*, vol. 2, pp. 21–23.

13. Chen Dingwen, "Hangzhou lunxian shiqi choulu," pp. 199–218.

14. Frederic Wakeman, *The Shanghai Badlands*, passim; Wen-hsin Yeh, "Urban Warfare and Underground Resistance," p. 125.

15. Frederic Wakeman, *The Shanghai Badlands*, p. 58; Hu Shuchang, "Yanliao maiban Zhou Zongliang" (Dyestuffs comprador Zhou Zongliang), *Shanghai WZXJ*, no. 56 (1987), pp. 196–97; Lynn Pan, *Tracing It Home: A Chinese Family's Journey from Shanghai* (New York: Kodansha International, 1993), pp. 77–79.

16. Wang Renze, "Jindai hangyun zhubai ye," vol. 2, pp. 43–44; Xu Nianhui, "Yu Xiaqing de yisheng" (The life of Yu Xiaqing), *WZXJ*, no. 15 (1986), p. 196; Sun Choucheng et al., "Yu Xiaqing shilue," *Zhejiang WZXJ*, no. 32 (1986), pp. 127–28.

17. Song Ziyun, "Yu Zuoting—cong Ningbo shanghui huizhang dao Shanghai shi zong shanghui zhuwei" (Yu Zuoting—from head of the Ningbo Chamber of Commerce to a director of the Shanghai General Chamber of Commerce), *Zhejiang WZXJ*, no. 39 (1989), p. 244.

18. *China Weekly Review,* March 23, 1940, p. 118; Robert Barnett, *Economic Shanghai,* pp. 92–96.

19. Quoted in *Heping fangong jianguo wenxian* (Writings on peace, anticommunism, and building the nation; Nanjing: Xuanzhuan bu, 1941), pt. 2, p. 105. On wheat shortages created by the Japanese procurement policy see SASS, *Rong jia qiye shiliao,* vol. 2, p. 161.

20. Itō Takeo, *Problems in the Japanese Occupied Areas in China,* p. 65.

21. Akira Iriye, *Power and Culture: The Japanese-American War, 1941–1945* (Cambridge, Mass.: Harvard University Press, 1981), p. 71.

22. Akira Iriye, *Power and Culture,* p. 38.

23. Akira Iriye, *Power and Culture,* pp. 45–46, 98–99; Iriye suggests that Japan originally vetoed a declaration of war by Nanjing because it feared its status as a co-belligerent could lead to "assert greater authority in internal matters of occupied China." See also Shan Guanchu, "Riben qin Hua de 'yizhan yangzhan,'" pp. 83–86.

24. Poshek Fu, *Passivity, Resistance, and Collaboration,* pp. 118–19.

25. Akira Iriye, *Power and Culture,* pp. 98–99; John Hunter Boyle, *China and Japan at War,* pp. 309–10; Shi Yuanhua, "Lun Riben dui Hua xin zhengce xia de RiWang guanxi" (On Japanese–Wang Jingwei relations under Japan's new China policy), *Lishi yanjiu,* no. 2 (1996), pp. 103–4; *Gendaishi shiryō,* vol. 38, pp. 66–90.

26. Yuan Yuquan, "Rikou jiaqiang lueduo Huazhong zhanlue wuzi paozhi 'shangtong hui' jingguo (The Japanese enemy's increased plundering of Shanghai strategic material and concoction of the National Commerce Control Commission"), *Dang'an yu lishi,* pt. 1, no. 4 (1986), pp. 82–83; Wang Ke-wen, "Collaborators and Capitalists: The Politics of 'Material Control' in Wartime Shanghai," pp. 48–49; Jiang Duo. "Shanghai lunxian qianqi 'Gudao fanrong,'" p. 30; Chūgoku seiji keizai kenkyūko, ed. *Naka Shina keizai nempō* (Central China annual economic report), p. 486. Kishi was later Prime Minister of Japan from 1957 to 1960.

27. Yuan Yuquan, "Rikou jiaqiang lueduo," pt. 1, p. 82; Tang Zhenchang, ed., *Shanghai shi,* p. 833; Zhongguo di'er lishi dang'an guan, "Wang wei sibu lianxi huiyi guanyu tiaozheng ZhongRi heban jiaotong shiye jueyi an" (Draft resolution of the Wang puppet four ministries conference regarding adjust of Sino-Japanese joint management of transportation facilities), *Mingguo dang'an,* no. 2 (1991), pp. 57–65; *Programs of Japan in China,* vol. 1, p. 14.

28. Yuan Yuquan, "Rikou jiaqiang lueduo," pt. 1, pp. 82, 101; Wang Ke-wen, "Collaborators and Capitalists," p. 50.

29. *Programs of Japan in China,* vol. 1, p. 62. Broadcast of June 30, 1944, from Tokyo.

30. Yuan Yuquan, "Rikou jiaqiang lueduo," pt. 1, pp. 83–85; Wang Ke-wen, "Collaborators and Capitalists," pp. 48–49. Wang suggests that Japanese preferred to transfer power to nongovernmental organizations of Chinese and Japanese merchants rather than surrender it to the Nanjing government. See also Masuda Yoneji, *Shina sensō keizai no kenkyū,* pp. 30–31.

31. Tang Xinyi, "Shanghai zhi tongzhi jingji" (Shanghai's controlled economy), in Wang Jishen et al., eds., *Zhanshi Shanghai jingji,* pp. 109–10; Yuan

Yuquan, "Rikou jiaqiang lueduo," pt. 1, pp. 84–85; Jin Zhanlu, "Wang wei quan-guo shanghe tongzhi weiyuan hui" (The National Commerce Control Commis-sion of the Wang puppet government), *Zhejiang WZXJ*, no. 6 (1963), pp. 57–73.

32. Yuan Yuquan, "Rikou jiaqiang lueduo," pt. 1, pp. 85–86; Wang Ke-wen, "Collaborators and Capitalists," p. 50.

33. Yuan Yuquan, "Rikou jiaqing lueduo," pt. 1, p. 86.

34. Wang Ke-wen, "Collaborators and Capitalists," pp. 50–51; Yuan Yuquan, "Rikou jiaqiang lueduo," pt. 1, p. 84; SASS, Rong Collection, R03–1, *Shenxin xitong* 1, no. 2, pp. 196–97; Zhou Fohai, *Zhou Fohai riji* (The diary of Zhou Fohai; Shanghai: Shanghai renmin chuban she, 1984), pp. 243–44; Xing Jian-rong and Qian Yuli, "Sange zuole hanjian de haishang wen ren" (Three coastal notables who became traitors) *Dang'an yu lishi*, no. 3 (1989), pp. 67–72.

35. Yuan Yuquan, "Rikou jiaqiang lueduo," pt. 1, p. 84; Zhu Zijia, *Wang zhengquan de kaichang*, vol. 3, pp. 6–8; Xing Jianrong and Qian Yuli, "Sange zuole hanjian," pp. 67–72; Xu Guomao, "Zhou Zuomin he Jincheng yinhang" (Zhou Zuomin and the Jincheng Bank), *[Shanghai] WZXJ*, no. 23 (1973), p. 150.

36. Furukyū Tadao, "'Kankan no shosō," vol. 6, p. 160; SASS, *Rong Jia qiye shiliao*, vol. 2, pp. 112–13; SASS, Rong Collection, R03–1, *Shenxin xitong* 1, no. 2, p. 194.

37. SASS, *Rong Jia qiye shiliao*, vol. 2, pp. 43–46; #2 was American, #9 was British.

38. *Xin Shenbao* (The new Shenbao), July 25, 1943, p. 3; Yuan Yuquan, "Rikou jiaqiang lueduo," pt. 3, no. 2 (1987), p. 97; *Programs of Japan in China*, vol. 3, p. 52; Du Xuncheng, *Riben zai jiu Zhongguo*, p. 203; SASS, Rong Col-lection, R03–1, *Shenxin xitong* 1, no. 2, pp. 194–95.

39. Yuan Yuquan, "Rikou jiaqiang lueduo," pt. 3, p. 97; Chen Zhen and Yao Luo, *Zhongguo jindai gongye*, vol. 1, pp. 457–58; Du Xuncheng, *Riben zai jiu Zhongguo*, p. 203; *Naka Shina keizai nempō* 3, no. 1, p. 55.

40. Qian Zhonghan, "Wuxi wuge zhuyao chanye ziben xitong," *WZXJ*, no. 24 (1986), p. 118; SASS, Rong Collection, R03–1, *Shenxin xitong* 1, no. 2, p. 195.

41. SASS, *Rong Jia qiye shiliao*, vol. 2, p. 142; Yuan Yuquan, "Rikou jiaqiang lueduo," pt. 3, p. 97.

42. On Ichigō see Hsi-sheng Ch'i, *Nationalist China at War*, pp. 70–82; *Pro-grams of Japan in China*, vol. 1, pp. 11–12.

43. Wang Ke-wen, "Collaborators and Capitalists," p. 51; Yuan Yuquan, "Rekou jiaqiang lueduo," pt. 2, p. 101.

44. Wang Ke-wen, "Collaborators and Capitalists," pp. 52–53.

45. Poshek Fu, *Passivity, Resistance, and Collaboration*, p. 123.

46. After the U.S. landing in the Philippines, for instance, rice prices jumped to 20,000 yuan per catty. See *Programs of Japan in China*, vol. 1, p. 75.

47. SASS, *Rong Jia qiye shiliao*, vol. 2, pp. 157–58; Yuan Yuquan, "Rikou jiaqiang lueduo," pt. 3, pp. 98–99.

48. Yuan Yuquan, "Rikou jiaqiang lueduo," pt. 3, p. 99; Shanghai shi liang-shi ju, Shanghai shi gongshang xingzheng guanli ju, and Shanghai shehui kexue yuan, jingji yanjiu suo jingji shi yanjiu shi, eds., *Zhongguo jindai mianfen gongye shi* (A history of the flour milling industry in modern China; Beijing: Zhonghua shuju chuban, 1987), pp. 152–53, 157–67.

49. SASS, Rong Collection, R03–1, *Shenxin xitong* 1, no. 2, pp. 198–99; Wang Ke-wen, "Collaborators and Capitalists," p. 51; Yuan Yuquan, "Rikou jiaqiang lueduo," pt. 2, p. 99. The commission actually took over the work of a commission of Chinese and Japanese textile firms, headed by the leader of the Japanese textile group in Shanghai, which had been established in September 1942. See *Naka Shina keizai nempō*, vol. 2, 1944, pp. 422–23.

50. Wang Ke-wen, "Collaborators and Capitalists," p. 52; Yuan Yuquan, "Rikou jiaqiang lueduo," pt. 2, pp. 99–100; Shanghai shi gongshang xingzheng guanli ju and Shanghai shi fangzhi pin gongsi, mianbu shangye shiliao zu, eds., *Shanghai shi mianbu shangye* (The cotton cloth business of Shanghai; Beijing: Zhonghua shuju, 1979), pp. 293–99.

51. Yuan Yuquan, "Rikou jiaqiang lueduo, pt. 3, p. 98; Xu Weiyong and Huang Hanmin, *Rongjia qiye fazhan shi* (A history of the development of the Rong family enterprises; Beijing: Renmin chuban she, 1985), pp. 165–67.

52. SASS, Rong Collection, R03–1, *Shenxin xitong* 1, no. 2, p. 187; Yuan Yuquan, "Rikou jiaqiang lueduo," pt. 3, p. 98; Shanghai shi gongshang xingzheng guanli ju, ed., *Shanghai shi mianbu shangye*, pp. 308–9; Chen Zhen, *Zhongguo jindai gongye shi ziliao*, vol. 4, pt. 1, pp. 252–54; Shanghai shi liangshi ju, *Zhongguo jindai mianfen gongye shi*, pp. 70–72, 161–62.

53. *Handbook of Japanese Industry in Japan and Occupied Areas* (Honolulu: Research and Analysis Branch, Office of Strategic Services, 1944), vol. 1, p. 103; *Programs of Japan in China*, vol. 1, p. 76.

54. Yuan Yuquan, "Rikou jiaqiang lueduo," pt. 3, pp. 100–101; Wang Ke-wen, "Collaborators and Capitalists," pp. 53–55.

55. Lin Wenyi, "KangRi zhanzheng shiqi lunxian qu de peiji zhi qingkuang" (The situation of the ration control system in the occupied areas during the anti-Japanese war of resistance), *Shangye ziliao*, no. 2 (1983), pp. 73–77.

56. William Kirby, "The Chinese War Economy," p. 204; Poshek Fu, *Passivity, Resistance, and Collaboration*, pp. 124–25; *Programs of Japan in China*, vol. 1, pp. 11–13.

57. Chao Kang, *The Development of Cotton Textile Production in China*, p. 133; *Programs of Japan in China*, vol. 1, p. 98; Gail Hershatter, *The Workers of Tianjin, 1900–1949*, p. 37. The Lihua coal mine was part of the Yuda Hua group. See Huang Shirang, "Yuda Hua qiye sishi nian," p. 56.

58. Robert Barnett, *Economic Shanghai*, pp. 133–35; Arthur N. Young, *China and the Helping Hand*, p. 159.

59. Frank Tamagna, *Banking and Finance in China*, p. 324; Shou Jinwen, *Zhanshi Zhongguo de yinhang ye* (The banking industry of wartime China; Chongqing: n. p., 1944), pp. 75–77; Robert Barnett, *Economic Shanghai*, p. 25; Yao Shengxiang and Shen Jiazhen, "Wangwei Zhongyang chubei yinhang shimo" (The puppet Wang government's Central Reserve Bank from beginning to end), *Jiangsu WZXJ*, no. 29 (1989), p. 240; Hu Xuantong, "Wosuo zhidao de Wangwei Zhongyang chubei yinhang" (The Wang Jingwei puppet Central Reserve Bank that I knew), *Shanghai WZXJ*, no. 33 (1980), p. 155. The new bank drew in and replaced the old Huaxin banknotes.

60. Ren Jiayao, "Xianshen jinrong gaige de Zhu Boquan" (Devoted finan-

cial reformer Zhu Boquan) in Xu Dixin, ed., *Zhongguo qiye jia liezhuan,* vol. 3, pp. 186–88.

61. Frederic Wakeman Jr., *The Shanghai Badlands,* pp. 119–23; Yao Shengxiang and Shen Jiazhen, "Wangwei Zhongyang chubei yinhang," pp. 242–44; Wang Zhixian, "Shanghai gudao de huobi zhan" (The currency war in solitary island Shanghai), *Shanghai difang shi ziliao* 1 (1982), pp. 167–69.

62. Wang Jishen, "Ji jinrong jia Li Fusun" (Remembering the financier Li Fusun), *Zhejiang WZXJ,* no. 32 (1986), pp. 171–72.

63. Shou Jinhua, *Zhanshi Zhongguo de yinhang ye,* pp. 78–79; Arthur N. Young, *China's Wartime Finance and Inflation* (Cambridge, Mass.: Harvard University Press, 1965), p. 180.

64. Wang Ke-wen, "Collaborators and Capitalists," p. 47; Eleanor Hinder, *Life and Labour in Shanghai* (New York: International Secretariat, Institute of Pacific Relations, 1944), p. 46.

65. *Programs of Japan in China,* vol. 1, pp. 124–26.

66. Robert Barnett, *Economic Shanghai,* p. 138; Frank Tamagna, *Banking and Finance in China,* pp. 324–26; *Programs of Japan in China,* vol. 1, p. 124; Arthur N. Young, *China's Wartime Finance and Inflation,* pp. 183–86, 366; Yao Shengxiang and Shen Jiazhen, "Wangwei Zhongyang chubei yinhang," pp. 245–46, 253. Central Reserve Bank notes increased much faster than this during the same period.

67. Shou Jinhua, *Zhanshi Zhongguo de yinhang ye,* p. 78.

68. See Table 1. For the communist base areas see Yu Songjing and Xue Wei, "KangRi genju di de wujie guanli" (Price control in the anti-Japanese base areas), *Lishi dang'an,* no. 1 (1999), pp. 125–30.

69. Zhu Zijia, *Wang zhengquan de kaichang,* vol. 3, p. 8.

CHAPTER FIVE

1. Zhang Jinsheng and Hu Xinsheng, "Zhongguo huaxue boli gongye xianqu—Wang Xinsheng" (China's vanguard in the chemical glass industry—Wang Xingsheng), *Renwu* (Personalities), no. 3 (1989), pp. 119–26.

2. Ning Sihong, "Guan leming jinbi chang shiliao" (Historical materials on the Leming golden pen factory), *Shanghai WZXJ,* no. 6 (1980), pp. 169–73.

3. Wang Ke-wen, "Collaborators and Capitalists," p. 58.

4. William C. Kirby, "China Unincorporated: Company Law and Business Enterprise in Twentieth-Century China," *The Journal of Asian Studies* 54, no. 1 (February 1995), pp. 43–63.

5. Kai Yiu Chan, "Capital Formation and Accumulation of Chinese Industrial Enterprises in the Republican Period: The Case of Liu Hongsheng's Shanghai Portland Cement Works Company, Ltd., 1920–1937," in R. A. Brown, ed., *Chinese Business Enterprise,* vol. 2, p. 153.

6. Siu-lun Wong, "The Chinese Family Firm: A Model," *The British Journal of Sociology* 36, no. 1 (1985), pp. 63–64.

7. Elisabeth Köll, "Controlling Modern Business in China: The Da Sheng Enterprise, 1895–1926," *Journal of Asian Business* 14, no. 1 (1998), p. 50.

8. Kai Yiu Chan, "Capital Formation and Accumulation," vol. 2, pp. 160–62. Chan does note that when some shareholders disputed the management plans for distribution of dividends, as occurred in 1929, the formalities of the corporation were useful. "When any conflict emerged," he notes, "'institutional' means of conflict resolution were used . . . The other shareholders used the shareholders' meeting to effect a decision against the board of directors" (p. 162).

9. Siu-lun Wong, "Business Networks, Cultural Values, and the State in Hong Kong and Singapore," in Rajeswary A. Brown, ed., *Chinese Business Enterprise in Asia* (London: Routledge, 1995), p. 143.

10. Madeleine Zelin, "Merchant Dispute Mediation in Twentieth-Century Zigong, Sichuan," in Kathryn Bernhardt and Philip C. C. Huang, eds., *Civil Law in Qing and Republican China* (Stanford, Calif.: Stanford University Press, 1994), p. 284.

11. Siu-lun Wong, "Business Networks, Cultural Values," p. 142.

12. Tahirih V. Lee, "Coping with Shanghai: Means to Survival and Success in the Early Twentieth Century—A Symposium," *Journal of Asian Studies* 54, no. 1 (February 1995), p. 10.

13. J. Ray Bowen II and David C. Rose, "On the Absence of Privately Owned, Publicly Traded Corporations in China: The Kirby Puzzle," *The Journal of Asian Studies* 57, no. 2 (May 1998), pp. 442–52.

14. J. Ray Bowen II, "Families, Firms, and Ancestors: The Effect of Government Behavior and Property rights on China's Businesses and Economic Development," *Chinese Business History* 6, no. 2 (fall 1996), pp. 1, 5–7.

15. Tahirih V. Lee, "Coping with Shanghai," *Journal of Asian Studies* 54, no. 1 (February 1995), p. 10.

16. David Faure, "The Control of Equity in Chinese Family Firms within the Modern Sector from the Late Qing to the Early Republic," in Rajeswary A. Brown, ed., *Chinese Business Enterprise in Asia,* p. 66.

17. S. Gordon Redding, *The Spirit of Chinese Capitalism* (Berlin: Walter de Gruyter, 1990), pp. 205–6. On the difficulties between many of the Shanghai capitalists and the Chiang government, see Parks M. Coble, *The Shanghai Capitalists,* pp. 208–60.

CHAPTER SIX

1. Shang Fangmin, "Jindai shiye jia Rongshi xiongdi jingying zhi daoxi" (Modern industrialists, the Rong brothers, and their way of management), *Minguo dang'an,* no. 2 (1992), pp. 86–91; Huang Hanmin, "Rongjia qiye dizao zhe—Rong Zongjing, Rong Desheng" (The founders of the Rong industries—Rong Zhongjing, Rong Desheng), in Xu Dixin, ed., *Zhongguo qiye jia liezhuan,* vol. 1, pp. 97–109; Wan Lin, "Wuxi Rongshi jiazu baofa shi" (The history of the sudden rise of the Rong family of Wuxi), *Jingji daobao* (Economic report), December 14, 1947, no. 50, p. 1; William Kirby, "China Unincorporated," p. 51; Sherman G. Cochran, *Encountering Chinese Networks: Western, Japanese, and Chinese Corporations in China, 1880–1937* (Berkeley: University of California Press, 2000), pp. 117–46. For a chart of the Rong family see Marie-Claire Bergère, *The Golden*

Age of the Chinese Bourgeoisie, 1911–1937, trans. Janet Lloyd (Cambridge: Cambridge University Press, 1989), pp. 154–55.

2. Qian Zhonghan, "Minzu ziben jia—Rong Zongjing, Rong Desheng" (National capitalists—Rong Zongjing, Rong Desheng), *Jiangsu WZXJ,* no. 2 (1963), pp. 131–39; Qian Zhonghan, "Wuxi wuge zhuyao chanye," p. 109; Huang Hanmin, "Rongjia qiye dizao," vol. 1, p. 109; Rong Shuren, "Wojia jingying mianfen gongye de huiyi" (Memoirs of management of the flour milling industry by my family), *Gongshang shiliao* (Historical materials on industry and commerce; Beijing: Wenshi ziliao chuban she, 1981), vol. 2, pp. 52–53; Gong Tingtai, "Rongshi jiazu de shiye juzi—ji Rong Zongjing, Rong Desheng xiongdi" (The Rong family industrial leaders—remembering Rong Zongjing and Rong Desheng), *Jiangsu wenshi ziliao,* no. 34 (1989), pp. 111–38; SASS, *Rongjia qiye shiliao,* vol. 2, p. 187. On the eve of the war the Rong mills held 570,000 spindles. An estimated 207,484, or 36.4 percent, were lost during the war. The number of looms was 5,304, of which 3,226, or 60.8 percent, were lost. The number of flour grinders was 347, of which 18.4 percent were lost.

3. For additional information on disputes between Chinese and the Shanghai Municipal Council, see Nicholas Clifford, *Spoilt Children of Empire: Westerners in Shanghai and the Chinese Revolution of the 1920s* (Hanover and London: University Press of New England, 1991). For information on the Western Roads issue, see Frederic Wakeman Jr., *Policing Shanghai, 1927–1937,* passim.

4. SASS, Rong Collection, R01–2, p. 59, and R03–2, *Shenxin xitong qiye shiliao 3,* no. 1, pp. 26–32; SASS, *Rongjia qiye shiliao 2,* pp. 3–4, 120; M. C. Bergère, "Zhongguo de minzu qiye yu ZhongRi zhanzheng: Rongjia Shenxin fangzhi chang" (China's national industry and the Sino-Japanese War, the Rong family's Shenxin textile company), in Zhang Xianwen et al., eds., *Minguo dang'an yu minguo shixue shu taolun lunwen ji* (A collection of essays on the study of Republican history and the Republican archives; Beijing: Dang'an chuban she, 1988), pp. 533–34; Chen Zhen and Yao Luo, eds., *Zhongguo jindai gongye shi ziliao,* vol. 1, p. 384; Xu Weiyong and Huang Hanmin, *Rongjia qiye fazhan shi,* pp. 132–34.

5. SASS, Rong Collection, R05, *Shenxin 2, 5 chang juan,* pp. 32–34.

6. SASS, *Rongjia qiye shiliao,* vol. 2, pp. 5–7, 36–37; Chen Zhen and Yao Luo, *Zhongguo jindai gongye shi ziliao,* vol. 1, pp. 391, 394; M. C. Bergère, "Zhongguo de minzu qiye yu ZhongRi zhanzheng," pp. 533–36; Xu Weiyong and Huang Hanmin, *Rongjia qiye fazhan shi,* p. 137; Rong Collection, SASS, R03–2, *Shenxin xitong 3,* no. 1, pp. 13–17, 65–66.

7. Xu Weiyong and Huang Hanmin, *Rongjia qiye fazhan shi,* pp. 139–40.

8. Frederick Wakeman Jr., *The Shanghai Badlands,* p. 25; Shanghai shehui kexue yuan, jingji yanjiu suo, ed., *Rongjia qiye shiliao,* vol. 2, pp.18–23; Xu Weiyong and Huang Hanmin, *Rongjia qiye fazhan shi,* p. 140; Gong Tingtai, "Rongshi jiazu de shiye juzi," pp. 130–32.

9. Gong Tingtai, "Rongshi jiazu de shiye juzi," p. 133. Rong Er'ren was released when Fuxin manager Rong Bing'gen paid the puppet police the equivalent of US$30,000. See SASS, *Rongjia qiye shiliao,* vol. 2, p. 88.

10. SASS, Rong Collection, R05, p. 42; RO8, p. 44.

11. SASS, *Rongjia qiye shiliao,* vol. 2, pp. 43–46; Chen Zhen and Yao Luo, *Zhongguo jindai gongye shi ziliao,* p. 394.

12. The number of spindles in Shenxin #2 did increase slightly from 53,123 in 1937 to 55,707 in 1940.

13. SASS, *Rongjia qiye shiliao,* vol. 2, pp. 68, 73–74, 191; SASS, Rong Collection, Ro8, pp. 48, 52–53, Ro5, pp. 35–41.

14. Gong Tingtai, "Rongshi jiazu de shiye juzi," pp. 125–32; SASS, *Rongjia qiye shiliao,* vol. 2, pp. 74, 166–73; Xu Weiyong and Huang Hanmin, *Rongjia qiye fazhan shi,* pp. 132, 153–54.

15. Because they were capitalized separately, profits and losses of individual mills had also varied greatly before the war. In 1936, for instance, the Shenxin general office had suffered a net loss of 1.6 million yuan, Shenxin #1 a profit of 1.1 million yuan, Shenxin #2 a loss of 154,000 yuan, Shenxin #3 a profit of 1.0 million yuan, Shenxin #4 a profit of 498,000 yuan, Shenxin #5 a loss of 184,000 yuan, Shenxin #6 a profit of 371,000 yuan, Shenxin #7 a loss of 4,100 yuan, and Shenxin #9 a profit of 417,000 yuan. See SASS, Rong Collection, Ro3–4, *Shenxin xitong* 7, no. 2, p. 131. On Zongjing's dominance, see Sherman G. Cochran, *Encountering Chinese Networks,* p. 124.

16. SASS, Rong collection, Ro3–3, *Shenxin xitong* 4, no. 2, pp. 107–9.

17. SASS, *Rongjia qiye shiliao,* vol. 2, pp. 166–69; SASS, Rong Collection, Ro8, pp. 28–30.

18. SASS, *Rongjia qiye shiliao,* vol. 2, pp. 169–71, 192; SASS, Rong Collection SASS, Ro5, p. 77. The 1942 figure includes 826,700 each for Rong Hongyuan, Rong Hongsan, and Rong Hongqing, and 992,040 for Rong Desheng. The increase in dividends from 1942 to 1943 was a result of inflation. The actual value of the total dividends distributed in gold *liang* was 1,576.6 in 1942 and 1,291.7 in 1943.

19. SASS, Rong Collection, Ro3–2, *Shenxin xitong,* p. 78.

20. SASS, *Rongjia qiye shiliao,* vol. 2, p. 176. The phrase *qi junzi* was widely used in conjunction with the seven leaders of the National Salvation Movement who had been arrested before the war. See Parks M. Coble, *Facing Japan,* pp. 334–42.

21. SASS, *Rongjia qiye shiliao,* vol. 2, pp. 171–77, 194.

22. SASS, Rong Collection, Ro3–3, *Shenxin xitong* 4, no. 2, p. 109.

23. Xu Weiyong and Huang Hanmin, *Rongjia qiye fazhan shi,* pp. 199–200; SASS, *Rongjia qiye shiliao,* vol. 2, pp. 284–89.

24. Xu Weiyong and Huang Hanmin, *Rongjia qiye fazhan shi,* pp. 145–46; SASS, Rong Collection, Ro1–3, pp. 141–42; Ro3–3, *Shenxin xitong* 4, no. 2, p. 109.

25. Xu Weiyong and Huang Hanmin, *Rongjia qiye fazhan shi,* p. 132; Shanghai shi liangshi ju, *Zhongguo jindai mianfen gongye shi,* p. 155.

26. Fuxin #2 and #8 earned almost as much in 1940 as in 1939 (1.9 million yuan versus 2.1 million), while Fuxin #7 even earned a bit more (1.6 million for 1940 compared with 1.3 million in 1939). These figures, however, partially reflect inflation. Expressed in ounces of gold, the figures for profits for Fuxin #2 and #8 were: 1937—loss of 2,822; 1938—profit of 2,525; 1939—profit of 7,052; 1940—profit of 3,558; 1941—loss of 46; 1942—loss of 288; 1943—profit of 205; 1944—profit of 90; 1945—profit of 4.4; for Fuxin #7: 1937—loss of 278; 1938—profit of 3,835; 1939—profit of 4,501; 1940—profit of 2,996; 1941—

profit of 119; 1942—loss of 48; 1943—profit of 153; 1944—profit of 93; 1945—profit of 4.3. See SASS, *Rongjia qiye shiliao,* vol. 2, pp. 10, 37, 46, 75-76, 79, 164, 193; Chen Zhen, *Zhongguo jindai gongye shiliao,* vol. 4, pt. 1, pp. 423-24.

27. Xu Weiyong and Huang Hanmin, *Rongjia qiye fazhan shi,* p. 156.

28. SASS, *Rongjia qiye shiliao,* vol. 2, pp. 104-5; SASS, Rong Collection, R08, p. 27.

29. SASS, *Rongjia qiye shiliao,* vol. 2, pp. 106-7; Qian Zhonghan, "Wuxi wuge zhuyao chanye," p. 118; Huang Hanmin, "Rongjia qiye dizao zhe," vol. 1, p. 109.

30. SASS, *Rongjia qiye shiliao,* vol. 2, pp. 107-8; SASS, Rong Collection, R01-3, pp. 73-74.

31. SASS, *Rongjia qiye shiliao,* vol. 2, pp. 107-8.

32. SASS, *Rongjia qiye shiliao,* vol. 2, pp. 107-8; SASS, Rong Collection, R01-2, pp. 186-17; R01-3, pp. 76-77; R03-2, *Shenxin xitong* 3, no. 1, p. 67.

33. SASS, *Rongjia qiye shiliao,* vol. 2, pp. 115-23; SASS, Rong Collection, R01-3, p. 81; R03-3, *Shenxin xitong* 4, no. 1, p. 41-45; Qian Zhonghan, "Wuxi wuge zhuyao chanye," p. 118; Sherman Cochran, "Business, Governments, and War in China," p. 124; Chen Zhen and Yao Luo, *Zhongguo jindai gongye shi ziliao,* vol. 1, pp. 391-95.

34. SASS, *Rongjia qiye shiliao,* vol. 2, pp. 124-31, 172, 188; SASS, Rong Collection, R03-2, *Shenxin xitong* 3, no. 1, pp. 75-79.

35. Rong Desheng's plan had been to sell the mill to a Sino-Japanese venture, the Hengfeng Company, if rendition could be negotiated. SASS, *Rongjia qiye shiliao,* vol. 2, pp. 99-104 and SASS, Rong Collection, R03-3, *Shenxin xitong* 4, no. 1. For a discussion of the Xinmin Hui, see Akira Iriye, "Toward a New Cultural Order: The Hsin-min Hui," in Akira Iriye, ed., *The Chinese and the Japanese,* pp. 254-74.

36. SASS, Rong Collection, R03-3, *Shenxin xitong* 4, no. 1, pp. 22-23; R05, p. 70; R08, pp. 52-54; M. C. Bergère, "Zhongguo de minzu qiye yu ZhongRi zhanzheng," p. 539; SASS, *Rongjia qiye shiliao,* vol. 2, pp. 121-23, 139-41, 188-89. In September 1943, for instance, Shenxin #2 had 56,584 spindles but only 3,993 in operation. The number of workers employed was only 152.

37. Xu Weiyong and Huang Hanmin, *Rongjia qiye fazhan shi,* pp. 165-67.

38. SASS, Rong Collection, R03-2, *Shenxin xitong* 3, no. 1, p. 87; R05, p. 45; Xu Weiyong and Huang Hanmin, *Rongjia qiye fazhan shi,* p. 167.

39. SASS, Rong Collection, R03-4, *Shenxin xitong* 7, no. 1, p. 56; Chen Zhen, *Zhongguo jindai gongye shiliao,* vol. 4, pt. 1, pp. 423-24; SASS, *Rongjia qiye shiliao,* vol. 2, pp. 133-34, 164, 186.

40. Shanghai shi liangshi ju et al. *Zhongguo jindai mianfen gongye shi,* pp. 162-67. The commission promulgated new regulations in December 1944 that required the permits for all sales and transport of grain, wheat, and bran.

41. Qian Zhonghan, "Wuxi wuge zhuyao chanye," p. 118; Tang Zhenchang, *Shanghai shi,* p. 803; SASS, *Rongjia qiye shiliao,* vol. 2, pp. 106-8.

42. The Chongqing factory was moved to Shanghai in 1946. SASS, Rong Collection, R01-3, pp. 141-42; R03-2, *Shenxin xitong* 3, no. 1, pp. 91-92; Qian Zhonghan, "Wuxi wuge zhuyao chanye ziben," p. 118; Sherman Cochran, "Business, Governments, and War in China," p. 125; SASS, *Rongjia qiye shi-*

liao, vol. 2, pp. 179–80; Xu Weiyong and Huang Manmin, *Rongjia qiye fazhan shi,* pp. 195–96.

43. SASS, Rong Collection, SASS, R01–3, p. 141; R03–3, *Shenxin xitong* 4, no. 1, p. 32; SASS, *Rongjia qiye shiliao,* vol. 2, pp. 115, 120–22; Chen Zhen and Yao Luo, *Zhongguo jindai gongye shi ziliao,* vol. 1, p. 392.

44. SASS, Rong Collection, SASS, R03–4, *Shenxin xitong* 7, no. 1, pp. 8, 51; SASS, *Rongjia qiye shiliao,* vol. 2, pp. 10–11.

45. SASS, *Rongjia qiye shiliao,* vol. 2, p. 47.

46. SASS, Rong Collection, R03–3, *Shenxin xitong* 4, no. 1, p. 3; Qian Zhonghan, "Wuxi wuge zhuyao chanye," pp. 117–18; Chen Zhen and Yao Luo, *Zhongguo jindai gongye shi ziliao,* vol. 1, p. 392; SASS, *Rongjia qiye shiliao,* vol. 2, pp. 11–12, 47, 135; Wang Gengtang, Feng Ju, and Gu Yiqun, "Wuxi jiefang qian zhuming de liujia minzu gongshang ye ziben" (The six famous national industrial and commercial capitalist families in Wuxi before liberation), *Jiangsu WZXJ,* no. 31 (1989), pp. 9–13.

47. Zhou Zhengang, "Wuhan de Rongjia qiye" (The Rong family enterprises in Wuhan), *Dang'an yu lishi,* 1986, no. 3, pp. 75–80; Li Guowei, "Rongjia jingying fangzhi he zhifen qiye liushi nian" (Sixty years of managing the Rong family textile and flour enterprises), *Gongshang shiliao* (1980), vol. 1, pp. 14; Tang Yongzhang and Gong Peiqing, "Hankou Fuxin diwu mianfen chang he Shenxin disi fangzhi chang" (Hankou's Fuxin #5 flour mill and Shenxin #4 textile mill), *Wuhan wenshi ziliao,* no. 33 (1988), pp. 5, 14–15; SASS, *Rongjia qiye shiliao,* vol. 2, pp. 48–52.

48. Zhang Jianhui, "Xueni zaji—wo de chuangye shengya" (A record of past events—my life as founder of industry), *WZXJ,* no. 122, p. 99; Qian Zhonghan, "Wuxi wuge zhuyao chanye," pp. 118–19; Zhou Zhengang, "Wuhan de Rongjia qiye," pp. 75–80.

49. SASS, Rong Collection, R03–2, *Shenxin xitong* 3, no. 1, p. 55; Rhodes Farmer, *Shanghai Harvest,* p. 177; Sherman Cochran, "Business, Governments, and War in China," p. 124; SASS, *Rongjia qiye shiliao,* vol. 2, pp. 61, 199; Zhou Zhengang, "Wuhan de Rongjia qiye," pp. 75–80; Zhang Jianhui, "Xueni zaji," pp. 95–99. After Pearl Harbor the Qingxin mills resumed use of the Shenxin and Fuxin names.

50. Sherman Cochran, "Business, Governments, and War in China," p. 124; see also Tang Yongzhang and Gong Peiqing, "Hankou Fuxin diwu mianfen chang," p. 5; Zhou Zhengang, "Wuhan de Rongjia qiye," p. 78, and SASS, *Rongjia qiye shiliao,* vol. 2, pp. 66–67, 200, 211, 304; Xu Weiyong and Huang Hanmin, *Rongjia qiye fazhan shi,* pp. 192–94; Sun Guoda, *Minzu gongye da qian tu,* p. 125.

51. SASS, Rong Collection, R03–3, *Shenxin xitong* 4, no. 1, pp. 39–40; 4, no. 2, pp. 111–12; R06–1, *Shenxin sanchang,* pp. 126–27; Zhou Zhengang, "Wuhan de Rongjia qiye," pp. 75–80; Qian Zhonghan, "Wuxi wuge zhuyao chanye ziben," pp. 118–19; SASS, *Rongjia qiye shiliao,* vol. 2, pp. 179–80, 289–91, 304; Xu Weiyong and Huang Hanmin, *Rongjia qiye fazhan shi,* pp. 199–201. According to Xu and Huang, Li Guowei argued that 28.2 percent of the spindles and 44.9 percent of the looms in the Shenxin group in 1944 were in his mills, compared to prewar figures of 8.4 percent and 13.2 percent.

52. Xu Weyong and Huang Hanmin, *Rongjia qiye fazhan shi*, p. 202.

53. Chen Zhen and Yao Luo, *Zhongguo jindai gongye shi ziliao*, vol. 1, pp. 450–51.

54. SASS, Rong Collection, R03–3, *Shenxin xitong* 3, no. 1, p. 98; 4, no. 2, pp. 111–13.

55. Xu Weiyong and Huang Hanmin, *Rongjia qiye fazhan shi,* pp. 213–14; SASS, *Rongjia qiye shiliao*, vol. 2, pp. 393–95.

56. SASS, *Rongjia qiye shiliao*, vol. 2, p. 388.

57. SASS, Rong Collection, R03–3, *Shenxin xitong* 4, no. 1, pp. 110–11; 4, no. 2, pp. 112–13, 127–30; SASS, *Rongjia qiye shiliao*, vol. 2, pp. 396–99.

58. SASS, Rong Collection, SASS, R16, pp. 8–15, 64; Wong Siu-lun, *Emigrant Entrepreneurs: Shanghai Industrialists in Hong Kong* (Hong Kong: Oxford University Press, 1988), p. 19; SASS, *Rongjia qiye shiliao*, vol. 2, pp. 470–74, 608–15.

59. SASS, Rong Collection, R01–3, pp. 117–18; R03–3, *Shenxin xitong* 4, no. 1, p. 46; R03–4, vol. 7, no. 1, pp. 5–12; SASS, *Rongjia qiye shiliao*, vol. 2, p. 672.

60. Wong Siu-lun, *Emigrant Entrepreneurs*, pp. 21–22; 29–31; Ma Kefeng, *Rongshi jiazu* (The Rong family; Guangzhou: Guangzhou chuban she, 1997), pp. 248–49. Li Guowei died on October 1, 1978, in Beijing at 85 sui.

61. Ma Kefeng, *Rongshi jiazu*, p. 245.

62. Ma Kefeng, *Rongshi jiazu*, p. 249.

63. Tahirih V. Lee, "Coping with Shanghai," p. 13; SASS, Rong Collection, R15, p. 81; Wan Lin, "Wuxi Rongshi jiazu baofa shi," pp. 1–5; Zhou Zhengang, "Wuhan de Rongjia qiye," pp. 75–80; Qian Zhonghan, "Wuxi wuge zhuyao chanye," pp. 118–19; Wong Siu-lun, *Emigrant Entrepreneurs,* pp. 28, 30–31; SASS, *Rongjia qiye shiliao*, vol. 2, pp. 178–79, 645–64.

64. Rong Zhijian goes by Larry Yung in English. *Far Eastern Economic Review,* Feb. 6, 1997, p. 43; Wong Siu-lun, *Emigrant Entrepreneurs*, p. 31.

65. Ma Kefeng, *Rongshi jiazu*, p. 254–56.

66. Ma Kefeng, *Rongshi jiazu*, p. 256.

67. Ma Kefeng, *Rongshi jiazu*, pp. 256–57.

CHAPTER SEVEN

1. Jiang Wei, "Xiongju 'baihuo dawang' baozuo sanshi nian" (Occupying the "department store king" throne for thirty years), *Jiangsu WZXJ,* no. 34 (1989), pp. 93–95; Wellington K. K. Chan, "The Origins and Early Years of the Wing On Company Group in Australia, Fiji, Hong Kong, and Shanghai: Organisation and Strategy of a New Enterprise," in Rajeswary A. Brown, ed., *Chinese Business Enterprise in Asia,* pp. 80–84; Wellington K. K. Chan, "Selling Goods and Promoting a New Commercial Culture: The Four Premier Department Stores on Nanjing Road, 1917–1937," in Sherman G. Cochran, ed., *Inventing Nanjing Road,* pp. 19–36; Yen Ching-hwang, "The Wing On Company in Hong Kong and Shanghai: A Case Study of Modern Overseas Chinese Enterprise, 1907–1949," in Rajeswary A. Brown, ed., *Chinese Business Enterprise,* vol. 1, pp. 368–72; Shanghai shehui kexue yuan, jingji yanjiu suo, ed., *Shanghai yongan gongsi*

de chansheng fazhan he gaizao (The creation, development, and reform of the Shanghai Yong'an [Wing On] Company; Shanghai: Shanghai renmin chuban she, 1981), pp. 17–19; Marie-Claire Bergère, *The Golden Age of the Chinese Bourgeoisie*, p. 156.

2. Jiang Wei, "Xiongju 'baihuo dawang' baozuo," pp. 96–97; Yen Ching-hwang, "The Wing On Company," vol. 1, pp. 372–74; Wellington Chan, "The Origins and Early Years," pp. 86–89; Wellington Chan, "Personal Styles, Cultural Values, and Management: The Sincere and Wing On Companies in Shanghai and Hong Kong, 1900–1941," *Business History Review* 70 (summer 1996), p. 145.

3. Yen Ching-hwang, "The Wing On Company in Hong Kong and Shanghai," vol. 1, p. 377; Wellington Chan, "The Origins and Early Years," p. 90.

4. Wellington Chan, "The Origins and Early Years," pp. 88–89; Xianggang Yong'an youxian gongsi, *Xianggang yong'an youxian gongsi nianwu zhounian jinian lu* (A record of 25 years of the Hong Kong Yong'an [Wing On] Company; Hong Kong: Yong'an Company, 1932), passim.

5. Yen Ching-hwang, "The Wing On Company," pp. 381–84; Jiang Wei, "Xiongju 'baihuo dawang,'" pp. 97–106.

6. Yen Ching-hwang, "The Wing On Company," p. 390; Jiang Wei, "Xiongju 'baihuo dawang,'" p. 108.

7. Wellington Chan, "The Origins and Early Years," pp. 89–90.

8. Wellington Chan, "The Origins and Early Years," p. 91; Yen Ching-hwang, "The Wing On Company," pp. 384–85.

9. Jiang Wei, "Xiongju 'baihuo dawang,'" pp. 107–8.

10. Jiang Wei, "Xiongju 'baihuo dawang,'" pp. 107–8; Yen Ching-hwang, "The Wing On Company," pp. 388–89; Chen Zhen and Yao Luo, *Zhongguo jindai gongye shi ziliao*, vol. 1, pp. 424–27.

11. Tan Renjie, "Guo Dihuo he Yong'an fangzhi gongsi" (Guo Dihuo and the Yong'an Textile Company), *Guangdong WZXJ*, no. 56 (1988), pp. 161–67; Marie-Claire Bergère, *The Golden Age of the Chinese Bourgeoisie*, p. 158.

12. Jiang Wei, "Xiongju 'baihuo dawang,'" p. 109.

13. Zheng Zeqing, "Song Ziwen he Shanghai yong'an gongsi de jiaowang" (T. V. Soong and his dealings with the Shanghai Yong'an Company), *Shanghai dang'an* (Shanghai archives), 1990, no. 2 (#32), pp. 43–46; Parks M. Coble, *The Shanghai Capitalists*, pp. 216–24; Tan Renjie, "Guo Dihuo he Yong'an," pp. 179–71.

14. Michael Lewis, "The World's Biggest Going-Out-of-Business Sale," *The New York Times Magazine*, May 31, 1998, pp. 34–41.

15. Pan Junxiang, "1937–1945 nian qijian Shanghai shangye qiyu de tucun huodong," (The survival activities of Shanghai commercial enterprises from 1937 to 1945), in Ding Richu, ed., *Jindai Zhongguo* (Modern China), vol. 5 (Shanghai: Shanghai shehui kexue yuan chuban she, 1995), pp. 332–44; Shanghai shehui kexue yuan, *Yong'an gongsi*, p. 148.

16. Shanghai shehui kexue yuan, *Yong'an gongsi*, pp. 148–50.

17. Chen Zhen and Yao Luo, *Zhongguo jindai gongye*, vol. 1, p. 423; Shanghai shehui kexue yuan, *Shanghai yong'an gongsi*, p. 148–50; Lu Xinglong, "Guo Linshuang: lunxian qu baihuo daiwang de xinsuan" (Guo Linshuang: The trou-

bles of the department store king in the occupied area), in Shen Zuwei and Du Xuncheng, *Guonan zhong de Zhongguo qiye jia,* pp. 219–31.

18. Chen Zhen and Yao Luo, *Zhongguo jindai gongye,* vol. 1, pp. 425–27.

19. Chen Zhen and Yao Luo, *Zhongguo jindai gongye,* vol. 1, pp. 426–27.

20. Xu Dingxin, "Yong'an qiye jituan de Guo Linshuang" (Guo Linshuang of the Yong'an enterprise group) in Xu Dixin, ed., *Zhongguo qiye jia liezhuan,* vol. 2, pp. 223–24; Pan Junxiang, "1937–1945 nian qijian," p. 336; Chen Zhen and Yao Luo, *Zhongguo jindai gongye,* vol. 1, p. 429.

21. See Chapter 4; see also *Xin shenbao,* July 25, 1943, p. 3; Shanghai shehui kexue yuan, *Shanghai yong'an gongsi,* p. 167.

22. Shanghai shehui kexue yuan, *Shanghai yong'an gongsi,* pp. 166–68.

23. The classic studies of this type of enterprise remain Albert Feuerwerker, *China's Early Industrialization: Sheng Hsuan-huai (1844–1916) and Mandarin Enterprise* (Cambridge, Mass.: Harvard University Press, 1958) and Wellington K. K. Chan, *Merchants, Mandarins, and Modern Enterprise in Late Ch'ing China* (Cambridge, Mass.: Harvard East Asian Monograph Series, 1977).

24. Albert Feuerwerker, *China's Early Industrialization,* p. 221; Zhongguo kexue yuan, Shanghai jingji yanjiu suo, and Shanghai shehui kexue yuan, jingji yanjiu suo, eds., *Hengfeng shachang de fasheng fazhan yu gaizao* (The development and reform of the Hengfeng textiles; Shanghai: Shanghai shehui kexue yuan, 1958), pp. 1–58; David Faure, "The Control of Equity in Chinese Family Firms within the Modern Sector from the Late Qing to the Early Republic," in Rajeswary A. Brown, *Chinese Business Enterprise in Asia,* pp. 64–67.

25. Parks M. Coble, *The Shanghai Capitalists,* p. 228; Zhongguo kexue yuan et al., *Hengfeng shachang de fasheng,* pp. 68–72, 78; Chen Zhen and Yao Luo, eds., *Zhongguo jindai gongye,* vol. 3, pt. 2, p. 1,045. Before the war, Dai Nippon had approximately 300,000 spindles and 4,368 looms. Nearly all of its 138,000 spindles and 3,000 looms in Qingdao were destroyed in the fighting. The Japanese military gave the company control of several Chinese mills to compensate these losses. See Chapter 2.

26. Zhongguo shehui kexue yuan et al., eds., *Hengfeng shachang,* pp. 71–73, 82–83.

27. Zhongguo shehui kexue yuan et al., eds., *Hengfeng shachang,* pp. 71–77; Marie-Claire Bergère, *The Golden Age of the Chinese Bourgeoisie,* pp. 161–63.

28. This account is based on Dasheng xitong qiye shi bianxie zu, ed., *Dasheng xitong qiye shi* (A history of the enterprises of the Dasheng system; Nanjing: Jiangsu guji chuban she, 1990) [the author thanks Elisabeth Köll for making available this source], and Yan Xuexi, "Riben dui Nantong Dasheng qiye de lueduo," pp. 206–12. For background on Zhang Jian and Dasheng, see Elisabeth Köll, "Controlling Modern Business in China," pp. 41–56; Samuel C. Chu, *Reformer in Modern China, Chang Chien, 1853–1926* (New York: Columbia University Press, 1965), pp. 21–31; Lu Yangyuan, "Jindai Zhongguo di yige da shiye jia: ji Zhang Jian de nanku chuangye" (Modern China's first big industrialist: Remembering Zhang Jian's hard work to begin an undertaking), *Jiangsu WZXJ,* no. 34 (1989), pp. 2–17; and Zhu Ronghua, "Zhang Jian yu Nantong Dasheng shachang" (Zhang Jian and the Nantong Dasheng textile mill), *Jiangsu wenshi ziliao,* no. 31 (1989), pp. 60–75. See also Kathy Le Mons Walker, *Chi-*

nese Modernity and the Peasant Path: Semicolonialism in the Northern Yangzi Delta (Stanford, Calif.: Stanford University Press, 1999), pp. 101–55.

29. Dasheng xitong, *Dasheng xitong qiye shi*, pp. 261–62.

30. Dasheng xitong, *Dasheng xitong qiye shi*, pp. 262–63.

31. Dasheng xitong, *Dasheng xitong qiye shi*, pp. 263–64.

32. Dasheng xitong, *Dasheng xitong qiye shi*, pp. 264–66.

33. Dasheng xitong, *Dasheng xitong qiye shi*, pp. 266–68.

34. Dasheng xitong, *Dasheng xitong qiye shi*, pp. 267–70.

35. Zhang Shijie, "Liu Guojun zhuanlue" (A brief biography of Liu Guojun), *Minguo dang'an*, no. 2 (1990), pp. 129–31; Chao Fuxie, "Shiye jia Liu Guojun" (Industrialist Liu Guojun), *WZXJ*, no. 100, pp. 266–74; Su Zhongbo, "Fangzhi qiye jia Liu Guojun" (Textile industrialist Liu Guojun), *Jiangsu wenshi ziliao*, no. 34 (1989), pp. 74–91; Liu Shousheng and Liu Meisheng, "Zhenhuan shachang zaoshou diguo zhuyi lueduo ji" (A record of the Zhenhuan textile mills suffering the plundering of imperialists), *WZXJ*, no. 44 (1986), pp. 80–81. Thomas Rawski argues that wages in the Shanghai textile industry averaged 23 to 32 percent above the national average in *Economic Growth in Prewar China* (Berkeley: University of California Press, 1989), p. 81.

36. Zhang Shijie, "Liu Guojun," pp. 130–31; Chao Fuxie, "Shiye jia Liu Guojun," pp. 277–79; Zhu Xiwu, "Dacheng fangzhi ran gongsi yu Liu Guojun" (The Dacheng textile mill and dyeing company and Liu Guojun), *Gongshang shiliao*, vol. 1, p. 49.

37. Chao Fuxie, "Shiye jia Liu Guojun," pp. 275–78.

38. Zhang Shijie, "Liu Guojun," p. 131; Chao Fuxie, "Shiye jia Liu Guojun," p. 278; Zhu Xiwu, "Dacheng fangzhi ran gongsi," p. 49.

39. Zhang Shijie, "Liu Guojun," p. 131; Chao Fuxie, "Shiye jia Liu Guojun," pp. 275–80. The Daming Company included several factories that had been evacuated from the Wuhan area. Lu Zuofu's Minsheng Shipping company usually provided transport in exchange for investment credit in the reorganized enterprise. See Wang Shijun, "Kong Song guanliao ziben shi zenyang yinmou bingtun Minsheng gongsi de" (How did the bureaucratic capitalists H. H. Kung and T. V. Soong plot to take over the Minsheng Company), *WZXJ*, no. 49 (1986), pp. 183–84.

40. Zhu Xiwu, "Dacheng fangzhi ran gongsi," p. 49; SASS, Rong Collection, R03–1, *Shenxin xitong* 1, no. 2, p. 147.

41. Chao Fuxie, "Shiye jia Liu Guojun," pp. 280–81.

42. Chao Fuxie, "Shiye jia Liu Guojun," pp. 281–82.

43. Chao Fuxie, "Shiye jia Liu Guojun," pp. 282–83; Su Zhongbu, "Fangzhi qiye jia Liu Guojun," p. 90.

44. Xu Dingxin, "Liu Guojun: 'Shijie mian wangguo' de kuxin zhuiqiu zhe" (Liu Gun, the painstaking quest of the 'Shijie mian wangguo'), in Sheng Zuwei, Du Xuncheng, *Guonan zhong de Zhongguo qiye jia*, p. 93.

45. Qian Zhonghan, "Wuxi wuge zhuyao chanye," p. 140; Wang Gengtang et al., "Wuxi jiefang qian zhuming," p.1.

46. Qian Zhonghan, "Wuxi wuge zhuyao chanye," pp. 101–7; Yang Tongyi, "Wuxi Yangshi yu Zhongguo mianfang ye de guanxi" (The relationship of

Wuxi's Yang family and China's cotton textile industry), *Gongshang shiliao,* vol. 2, pp. 54–56.

47. Qian Zhonghan, "Wuxi wuge zhuyao chanye ziben," pp. 104–7; Yang Tongyi, "Wuxi Yangshi yu Zhongguo mianfang," vol. 2, p. 62; Wang Gengting et al., "Wuxi jiefang qian zhuming," pp. 4–6.

48. Qian Zhonghan, "Wuxi wuge zhuyao," pp. 104–7; Yang Tongyi, "Wuxi Yangshi yu Zhongguo mianfang," p. 68; SASS, Rong Collection, R03–1, *Shenxin xitong* 1, no. 2, pp. 149–50.

49. Lynda S. Bell, *One Industry, Two Chinas: Silk Filatures and Peasant-Family Production in Wuxi County, 1865–1937* (Stanford, Calif.: Stanford University Press, 1999), pp. 171–76; Wang He, "Wei fazhan Zhongguo siye er xiangji fendou" (The development of the Chinese silk industry and its struggles), *Jiangsu wenshi ziliao,* no. 34 (1989), pp. 184–87.

50. Qian Zhonghan, "Wuxi wuge zhuyao chanye," pp. 123–28; Wang He, "Wei fazhan Zhongguo siye," pp. 190–92; Wang Gengting et al., "Wuxi jiefang qian zhuming," pp. 19–23; Lynda S. Bell, "From Comprador to Country Magnate: Bourgeois Practice in the Wuxi Country Silk Industry," in Joseph Esherick and Mary Backus Rankin, eds., *Chinese Local Elites and Patterns of Dominance* (Berkeley: University of California Press, 1990), pp. 134–35.

51. Qian Zhonghan, "Wuxi wuge zhuyao chanye," pp. 123–29; Wang Gengting et al., "Wuxi jiefang qian zhuming," p. 23. Xue Zukang managed the family's property in China after the war. Xue Shouxuan apparently lost most of his income in the United States. See Lynda S. Bell, *One Industry, Two Chinas,* p. 176.

52. Qian Zhonghan, "Wuxi wuge zhuyao chanye," pp. 125–26, 140; Wang Gengtang et al., "Wuxi jiefang qian zhuming," pp. 14–17; Lynda S. Bell, "From Comprador to Country Magnate," p. 126.

53. Xue Wenshi, "Ji jiefang qian Wuxi Qingfeng mian fangzhi chang" (On the Qingfeng cotton textile plant in Wuxi before liberation), *Jiangsu wenshi ziliao,* no. 31 (1989), pp. 76–88; Qian Zhonghan, "Wuxi wuge zhuyao chanye," pp. 130–32.

54. Qian Zhonghan, "Wuxi wuge zhuyao chanye," pp. 132–33; Xue Wenshi, "Ji jiefang qian Wuxi Qingfeng mian," pp. 86–88; Wang Gengting et al., "Wuxi jiefang qian zhuming," pp. 23–26.

55. Qian Zhonghan, "Wuxi wuge zhuyao chanye," pp. 132–33; Xue Wenshi, "Ji jiefang qian Wuxi Qingfeng," pp. 86–88; SASS, Rong Collection, R03–1, *Shenxin xitong* 1, no. 2, p. 148.

56. Qian Zhonghan, "Wuxi wuge zhuyao chanye," pp. 132–33; Xue Wenshi, "Ji jiefang qian Wuxi Qingfeng," pp. 86–88; Wang Gengting et al., "Wuxi jiefang qian zhuming," pp. 26–27.

57. Wang Gengting et al., "Wuxi jiefang qian zhuming," pp. 27–29; Zhang Jinhua, "Aiguo shiye jia Tang Junyuan" (Patriotic industrialist Tang Junyuan), *Shanghai WZXJ,* no. 80 (1996), pp. 19–21.

58. Qian Zhonghan, "Wuxi wuge zhuyao chanye," pp. 133–37; Wang Gengting et al., "Wuxi jiefang qian zhuming," pp. 29–30; SASS, Rong Collection, R03–1, *Shenxin xitong* 1, no. 2, p. 149; Zhang Jinhua, "Aiguo shiye jia," pp. 21–22.

CHAPTER EIGHT

1. James Reardon-Anderson, *The Study of Change: Chemistry in China,
1840–1949* (Cambridge: Cambridge University Press, 1991), pp. 281, 273–74.
2. James Reardon-Anderson, *The Study of Change*, pp. 300–301.
3. Chen Zhen, Yao Luo, *Zhongguo jindai gongye*, vol. 1, p. 513.
4. Tim Wright, "The Spiritual Heritage of Chinese Capitalism," p. 229. Examples of accounts of Fan's life that clearly fit the "patriotic nationalist narrative" include Xu Dingxin, "Fan Xudong: Quan quan aiguo xin, yi yi '*Haiwang*' hun" (Fan Xudong, the fists of a patriot, the brilliant and luminous spirit
of [the journal] *Haiwang*), in Shen Zuwei and Du Xuncheng, *Guonan zhong
de Zhongguo qiye jia*, pp. 135–49; Shi Junshan and Zhang Hongmin, "Zhongguo huagong xiandao Fan Xudong" (China's chemical industrial first leader,
Fan Xudong), in Zhao Yunsheng, *Zhongguo da ziben jia zhuan*, vol. 3, pp.
3–9; and Wang Zhong and Han Zhengbin, "Gongye xiandao, gong zai
Zhonghua: Ji huagong shiye jia Fan Xudong" (Remembering chemical industrialist Fan Xudong, a leader in China's industry), *Jiangsu WZXJ*, no. 34 (1989),
pp. 42–43.
5. Peter Duus, *Modern Japan*, 2d ed. (Boston: Houghton Mifflin, 1998),
pp. 159–60; Kishi Toshihiko, "Eiri kagaku kōgyō konsu to Han Kyokutō" (The
Yongli Chemical Industrial Company and Fan Xudong), in Soda Saburō, ed.,
Chūgoku kindaika, p. 254; James Reardon-Anderson, *The Study of Change*, pp.
160–62. The term "man of affairs" (*jitsugyōka/shiyejia*) became widely used in
both China and Japan to mean "industrialist."
6. Wang Zhong and Han Zhengbin, "Gongye xiandao, gong zai Zhonghua,"
pp. 47–50; Chen Zhen and Yao Luo, *Zhongguo jindai gongye*, vol. 1, pp. 513–14;
James Reardon-Anderson, *The Study of Change*, p. 162.
7. Shi Junshan, Zhang Hongmin, "Zhongguo huagong xiandao," vol. 3, p. 20;
Wang Zhong and Han Zhengbin, "Gongye xiandao, gong zai Zhonghua," pp. 48–
49; Zhang Gaofeng, "Kuhai yanbian chuangye jishi" (A true record of the endless difficulty in setting up the salt business), in *Huagong xiandao—Fan Xudong*
(The first leader of the chemical industry, Fan Xudong; Beijing: Zhongguo wenshi chuban she, 1987), p. 18.
8. James Reardon-Anderson, *The Study of Change*, pp. 165–66; Howard
Boorman, *Biographical Dictionary of Republican China*, vol. 2, p. 85; Chen Zhen
and Yao Luo, *Zhongguo jindai gongye*, vol. 1, p. 514.
9. James Reardon-Anderson, *The Story of Change*, pp. 163–64; Hou Te-pang
[Hou Debang], *Manufacture of Soda: With Special Reference to the Ammonia
Process* (New York: Reinhold, 1942), p. ix.
10. The Solvay process had been invented by Ernest Solvay in 1861. James
Reardon-Anderson, *The Study of Change*, pp. 163–67, 275; Chen Tiaofu, "Yongli
jianchang fendou huiyi lu" (A record of memories of the struggles of the Yongli
alkali soda plant), *Gongshang shiliao*, vol. 2, pp. 80–91; Wang Zhong and Han
Zhengbin, "Gongye xiandao, gongzai Zhonghua," pp. 49–53; Zhang Gaofeng,
"Kuhai yanbian chuangye jishi," p. 24; Zhang Zhizhong, "Aiguo shiye jia Fan
Xudong" (Patriotic industrialist, Fan Xudong), in *Huagong xiandao*, p. 38; Kishi
Toshihiko, "Eiri kagaku kōgyō konsu," pp. 262–63. Hou Debang became well

known in the west with the publication of *Manufacture of Soda,* under the auspices of the American Chemical Society.

11. Yongli's name was changed to the Yongli Chemical Industrial Company (Yongli huaxue gongye gongsi) in 1934 to reflect the broadening of its production. Zhang Gaofeng, "Kuhai yanbian chuangye jishi," pp. 24–26; Zou Bingwen, "Yongli liusuan ya chang jianchang jingguo" (The establishment of the Yongli ammonium sulfate factory) *WZXJ,* no. 19 (1986), pp. 95–111; Kishi Toshihiko, "Eiri kagaku kōgyō konsu," pp. 264; James Reardon-Anderson, *The Study of Change,* pp. 264–67.

12. Chen Zhen and Yao Luo, *Zhongguo jindai gongye,* vol. 1, pp. 513–14; Wang Zhong and Han Zhengbin, "Gongye xiandao, gong zai Zhonghua," pp. 58–60; Zhang Zhizhong, "Aiguo shiye jia," p. 38. For Wu's connections to the Political Study Clique and a discussion of why he was brought into the Nanjing government, see Parks Coble, *The Shanghai Capitalists,* pp. 242–43.

13. Chen Zhen and Yao Luo, *Zhongguo jindai gongye,* vol. 1, p. 519; James Reardon-Anderson, *The Study of Change,* pp. 267–68; Wang Zhong, Han Zhengbin, "Gongye xiandao, gongzai Zhonghua," pp. 58–60, 68; Kishi Toshihiko, "Eiri kagaku kōgyō konsu," pp. 260–62; Hou Te-pang, *The Manufacture of Soda,* p. ix; Du Xuncheng, *Riben zai jiu Zhongguo,* p. 297; Sun Guoda, *Minzu gongye da qiantu,* pp. 148–49; Yosa Yoshiie, ed., *Nitchū sensō senryō chiku,* p. 646.

14. He Xizeng, "'Yongjiu tuanti' za yi" (Various memories of the Yongli and Jiuda enterprise groups), *WZXJ,* no. 80 (1986), pp. 74–82; Zhang Gaofeng, "Kuhai yanbian chuangye jishi," p. 29; Kishi Toshihiko, "Eiri kagaku kōgyō konsu," pp. 267, 270; Sun Guoda, *Minzu gongye da qiantu,* pp. 148–49.

15. James Reardon-Anderson, *The Study of Change,* pp. 294–95; Chen Zhen and Yao Luo, *Zhongguo jindai gongye,* vol. 1, pp. 513–14; Wang Zhong and Han Zhengbin, "Gongye xiandao, gongzai Zhonghua," pp. 68–69; Guo Bingyu, "Yongli jianchang wushi nian jianwen" (A look at fifty years of the Yongli soda plant), in *Huagong xiandao,* p. 92; Zhang Tongyi, *Fan Xudong zhuan* (A biography of Fan Xudong; Changsha: Hunan renmin chuban she, 1987), p. 163.

16. Kishi Toshihiko, "Eiri kagaku kōgyō konsu," p. 276; Xu Tengba, "Fan Xudong yu Yongli Tanggu jianchang" (Fan Xudong and the Yongli Soda Plant at Tanggu), *Jiangsu wenshi ziliao,* no. 25, (1988), p. 43; Zhang Nengyuan, "Fan Xudong he Zhongguo jindai huaxue gongye" (Fan Xudong and China's modern chemical industry), in *Jiansgu wenshi ziliao,* no. 25 (1988), p. 89–90; James Reardon-Anderson, *The Story of Change,* p. 295; Sun Guoda, *Minzu gongye da qiantu,* pp. 148–49. American production of soda ash on the eve of the war was approximately 3 million metric tons, by contrast. See Hou Te-pang, *Manufacture of Soda,* p. 41.

17. Chen Zhen and Yao Luo, *Zhongguo jindai gongye,* vol. 1, pp. 515–16; Chen Tiaofu, "Fan Xudong yu Huanghai huaxue gongye yanjiu she" (Fan Xudong and the Huanghai Chemical Industrial Research Society), *WZXJ,* no. 80 (1986), pp. 60–67.

18. He Xizeng, "Yongjiu tuanti," pp. 74–82.

19. Wang Zhong and Han Zhengbin, "Gongye xiandao, gongzai Zhonghua,"

pp. 70–71; Chen Tiaofu, "Yongli jianchang fendou huiyi lu," vol. 2, p. 101; Xu Tengba, "Fan Xudong yu Yongli Tanggu," p. 44.

20. Wang Zhong and Han Zhengbin, "Gongye xiandao, gongzai Zhonghua," pp. 71–72.

21. Wu Zhichao, "Wu Yunchu ji qi huagong shiye" (Wu Yunchu and his chemical industrial enterprises), in *Shanghai WZXJ*, no. 22 (1978), pp. 86–92, 99–100; James Reardon-Anderson, *The Study of Change*, pp. 168–69; James R. Bartholomew, *The Formation of Science In Japan: Building a Research Tradition* (New Haven, Conn.: Yale University Press, 1989), pp. 180–81.

22. Chen Zhen and Yao Luo, *Zhongguo jindai gongye*, vol. 1, pp. 521–23; Xu Ying, "Wu Yunchu ji qi huagong shiye" (Wu Yunchu and his chemical industrial enterprises), in Xu Dixin, *Zhongguo qiye jia*, vol. 1, pp. 216–28.

23. Chen Zhen and Yao Luo, *Zhongguo jindai gongye*, vol. 1, pp. 521–23; Wu Zhichao, "Wu Yunchu ji qi huagong shiye," pp. 92–93; James Reardon-Anderson, *The Study of Change*, p. 259.

24. Chen Zhen and Yao Luo, *Zhongguo jindai gongye*, vol. 1, pp. 521–23; Wu Zhichao, "Wu Yunchu ji qi huagong shiye," pp. 92–94; Xu Ying, "Wu Yunchu ji qi huagong," p. 218.

25. Chen Zhen and Yao Luo, *Zhongguo jindai gongye*, vol. 1, pp. 521–23; Wu Zhichao, "Wu Yunchu ji qi huagong," pp. 94–99; Xu Ying, "Wu Yunchu ji qi huagong," p. 220.

26. Chen Zhen and Yao Luo, *Zhongguo jindai gongye*, vol. 1, pp. 521–23; Wu Zhichao, "Wu Yunchu ji qi huagong," pp. 94–100; Xu Ying, "Wu Yunchu ji qi huagong," pp. 219–20.

27. Chen Zhen and Yao Luo, *Zhongguo jindai gongye*, vol. 1, p. 522; Wu Zhichao, "Wu Yunchu ji qi huagong," pp. 94–100.

28. Wu Zhichao, "Wu Yunchu ji qi huagong," p. 100; Lu Xinglong, "Wu Yunchu: Guonan shiqi de 'Tianzi hao'" (Wu Yunchu: The Tian name brand during the period of national difficulty), in Shen Zuwei and Du Xuncheng, *Guonan zhong de Zhongguo qiye jia*, pp. 45–46.

29. Wang Daliang, *Weijing dawang, Wu Yunchu* (The MSG king, Wu Yunchu; Beijing: Jiefang jun chuban she, 1995), p. 112; Wu Zhichao, "Wu Yunchu ji qi huagong," p. 101; Xu Ying, "Wu Yunchu ji qi huagong," pp. 220–21; Lu Xinglong, "Wu Yunchu," pp. 46–48. Wu petitioned the Chinese government for assistance in evacuating his plants and received some aid. The Tianli Nitrogen Plant, whose production was closest to war needs, was awarded 334,000 yuan in subsidies and 510,000 yuan in loans. The Tianyuan facilities received 280,000 and 800,000, and the Tiansheng Pottery Company received 420,000 and 80,000. Tianchu, whose MSG production was not viewed as critical to the war effort, did receive 300,000 in loans. The Industry and Mining Adjustment Commission later reduced the subsidy to the collective Tian enterprises by 400,000 yuan. Sun Guoda, *Minzu gongye da qiantu*, p. 63–66.

30. Sun Guoda, *Minzu gongye da qiantu*, pp. 66–67.

31. Chen Zhen and Yao Luo, *Zhongguo jindai gongye*, vol. 1, pp. 521–23; Wu Zhichao, "Wu Yunchu ji qi huagong," pp. 101–6; Wang Daliang, *Weijing dawang*, p. 101; Xu Ying, "Wu Yunchu ji qi huagong," p. 223; Sun Guoda, *Minzu gongye da qian tu*, p. 66; Lin Xinglong, "Wu Yunchu," p. 51.

32. Chen Zhen and Yao Luo, *Zhongguo jindai gongye,* vol. 1, pp. 522–24; Wang Daliang, *Weijing dawang,* pp. 120–29; Xu Ying, "Wu Yunchu ji qi huagong," p. 223; Sun Guoda, *Minzu gongye da qiantu,* p. 66–67; Lin Xinglong, "Wu Yunchu," p. 52.

33. Chen Zhen and Yao Luo, *Zhongguo jindai gongye,* vol. 1, pp. 522–24; Wang Daliang, *Weijing dawang,* pp. 120–23; Wu Zhichao, "Wu Yunchu ji qi huagong," p. 110; Xu Ying, Wu Yunchu ji qi huagong," pp. 223–24; Sun Guoda, *Mingzu gongye da qiantu,* pp. 66–67.

34. Wang Daliang, *Weijing dawang,* pp. 118–20; Sun Guoda, *Minzu gongye da qiantu,* p. 65; James Reardon-Anderson, *The Study of Change,* p. 163.

35. Wang Daliang, *Weijing dawang,* pp. 183–84; Du Xuncheng, *Riben zai jiu Zhongguo,* pp. 296–97.

36. Wang Daliang, *Weijing dawang,* pp. 172–74; Wu Zhichao, "Wu Yunchu ji qi huagong," pp. 108–10; Lu Xinglong, "Wu Yunchu," pp. 51–52.

37. Wang Daliang, *Weijing dawang,* pp. 129–33, 174–78.

38. Wang Daliang, *Weijing dawang,* pp. 177–79; Wu Zhichao, "Wu Yunchu ji qi huagong," pp. 108–10.

39. Wu Zhichao, "Wu Yunchu ji qi huagong," pp. 108–10; Wang Daliang, *Weijing dawang,* pp. 178–79.

40. Wang Daliang, *Weijing dawang,* pp. 184–86; Zhongguo di'er lishi dang'an guan, "Wang wei zhengquan 'jieshou' Riben junguan gongchang de yizu shiliao" (Historical materials on the Wang puppet regime's "retaking" factories managed by the Japanese military), *Minguo dang'an,* no. 2 (1990), pp. 53–54.

41. The patriotic industrialist theme is stressed in such recent treatments as Zhang Qifu, "Kangzhan shiqi de Liu Hongsheng" (Liu Hongsheng during the war of resistance era), *Minguo dang'an,* no. 2 (1995), pp. 100–104; and Cheng Nianqi, "Liu Hongsheng: Zai gouan yu minzu dayi zhijian jueze" (Liu Hongsheng: Choosing between a false peace and national righteousness), in Shen Zuwei and Du Xuncheng, *Guonan zhong de Zhongguo qiye jia,* pp. 29–44.

42. This discussion is based on Shanghai shehui kexue yuan, jingji yanjiu suo, ed. [hereafter SASS], *Liu Hongsheng qiye shiliao* (Historical materials on the Liu Hongsheng enterprises, 3 vols.; Shanghai: Shanghai renmin chuban she, 1981); Kai Yiu Chan, "Capital Formation and Accumulation of Chinese Industrial Enterprises in the Republican Period: The Case of Liu Hongsheng's Shanghai Portland Cement Works Company, Ltd., 1920–1937," vol. 2, pp. 149–53; Howard Boorman, *Biographical Dictionary of Republican China,* vol. 2, pp. 398–400; Liu Nianzhi, "Kangzhan shiqi jian Liushi qiye qianchuan jingguo" (The experiences of the Liu family enterprises in relocating to Sichuan during the war of resistance period), *WZXJ,* no. 68 (1986), p. 170; Sherman Cochran, "Three Roads into Shanghai's Market: Japanese, Western, and Chinese Companies in the Match Trade, 1895–1937," in Frederick Wakeman Jr. and Wen-hsin Yeh, eds. *Shanghai Sojourners* (Berkeley: Institute of East Asian Studies, China Research Monograph, 1992), pp. 57–63; Sherman Cochran, *Encountering Chinese Networks,* pp. 147–76; Albert Feuerwerker, "Industrial Enterprise in Twentieth-Century China: The Chee Hsin Cement Co.," in Albert Feuerwerker, Rhoads Murphey, and Mary C. Wright, *Approaches to Modern Chinese History* (Berkeley: University of California Press, 1967), pp. 307–8.

43. Sherman Cochran, Three Roads into Shanghai's Market," pp. 57–63; Liu Nianzhi, "Kangzhan shiqi jian," p. 170. Liu merged with the Yingchang and Zhonghua Match Companies of Shanghai.

44. Sherman Cochran, "Three Roads into Shanghai's Market," pp. 68–70; Ma Bohuang, "Liu Hongsheng's Enterprise Investment and Management," in Tim Wright, ed., *The Chinese Economy in the Early Twentieth Century: Recent Chinese Studies* (New York: St. Martin's Press, 1992), p. 95.

45. Hu Shikui, "Wo suo zhidao de Liu Hongsheng xiansheng" (The Liu Hongsheng I knew), in *Shanghai wenshi ziliao xuanji, Tongzhan gongzuo shiliao zhuanji*, no. 8 (1989), pp. 167–72; Zhang Qifu, "Kangzhan shiqi jian," pp. 100–101; Liu Nianzhi, *Shiye jia Liu Hongsheng zhuanlue: Huiyi wode fuqin* (A biography of industrialist Liu Hongsheng: Remembering my father; Beijing: Wenshi ziliao chuban she, 1982), pp. 81–82.

46. Shi Qun, "Guangfan jingying gezhong qiye de Liu Hongsheng" (Liu Hongsheng who had extensive knowledge of managing various kinds of enterprises), in Xu Dixin, *Zhongguo qiye jia liezhuan*, vol. 2, pp. 116–17.

47. SASS, *Liu Hongsheng qiye*, vol. 3, pp. 11–12, 16, 25; Liu Nianzhi, "Kangzhan shiqi jian," p. 170; Zhang Qifu, "Kangzhan shiqi," p. 102.

48. SASS, *Liu Hongsheng qiye*, vol. 3, pp. 26–28, 32, 55–56; Liu Nianzhi, "Kangzhan shiqi jian," pp. 170–71; Liu Nianzhi, *Shiye jia*, pp. 88–89.

49. SASS, *Liu Hongsheng qiye*, vol. 3, pp. 62, 87, 96; Du Xuncheng, *Riben zai jiu Zhongguo*, pp. 293–94; Cheng Nianqi, "Liu Hongsheng," p. 30.

50. SASS, *Liu Hongsheng qiye*, vol. 3, pp. 67–69.

51. SASS, *Liu Hongsheng qiye*, vol. 3, pp. 70–72.

52. Liu Nianzhi, *Shiye jia*, p. 83; SASS, *Liu Hongsheng qiye*, vol. 3, pp. 108–15, 119–22.

53. SASS, *Liu Hongsheng qiye*, vol. 3, pp. 9–10; Liu Nianzhi, "Kangzhan shiqi jian," pp. 171–72; Liu Nianzhi, *Shiye jia*, pp. 83–85.

54. Frederick Wakeman Jr., *The Shanghai Badlands*, pp. 59–64; Liu Nianzhi, "Kangzhan shiqi jian," pp. 172–73; Zhang Qifu, "Kangzhan shiqi," p. 102.

55. Liu Nianzhi, *Shiye jia*, pp. 87–88; Cheng Nianqi, "Liu Hongsheng," p. 33; SASS, *Liu Hongsheng qiye*, vol. 3, pp. 140–50.

56. Zhang Qifu, "Kangzhan shiqi," p. 103; Liu Nianzhi, "Kangzhan shiqi jian," pp. 173–75; Cheng Nianqi, "Liu Hongsheng," p. 37; SASS, *Liu Hongsheng qiye*, vol. 3, pp. 150–57; 163–65.

57. SASS, *Liu Hongsheng qiye*, vol. 3, pp. 31–32; Hu Shikui, "Wo suo zhidao de Liu Hongsheng," pp. 174–75; Zhang Qifu, "Kangzhan shiqi," pp. 103–4.

58. Liu Nianzhi, "Kangzhan shiqi jian," pp. 175–82; Howard Boorman, *Biographical Dictionary of Republican China*, vol. 2, pp. 398–400; SASS, *Liu Hongsheng qiye*, vol. 3, p. 19; 137–40.

59. Liu Nianzhi, *Shiye jia*, p. 95; Chen Zhen and Yao Luo, *Zhongguo jindai gongye*, vol. 1, pp. 404–5; Cheng Nianqi, "Liu Hongsheng," pp. 38–41; SASS, *Liu Hongsheng qiye*, vol. 3, pp. 183–92.

60. Zhang Qifu, "Kangzhan shiqi," p. 104.

61. Cheng Nianqi, "Liu Hongsheng," pp. 43–44; SASS, *Liu Hongsheng qiye*, vol. 3, pp. 119–33.

62. SASS, *Liu Hongsheng qiye*, vol. 3, pp. 20–26.

63. SASS, *Liu Hongsheng qiye*, vol. 3, pp. 42–54.

64. SASS, *Liu Hongsheng qiye*, vol. 3, pp. 54–61.

65. Yoda Yoshiie, ed., *NitChū sensō senryō chiku*, pp. 589–95; SASS, *Liu Hongsheng qiye*, vol. 3, pp. 77, 84–87.

66. SASS, *Liu Hongsheng qiye*, vol. 3, pp. 74–80.

67. SASS, *Liu Hongsheng qiye*, vol. 3, pp. 80–87.

68. SASS, *Liu Hongsheng qiye*, vol. 3, pp. 86–87.

69. SASS, *Liu Hongsheng qiye*, vol. 3, pp. 148–50.

70. Cheng Nianqi, "Liu Hongsheng," pp. 43–44; Howard Boorman, *Biographical Dictionary of Republican China*, vol. 2, pp. 399–400; SASS, *Liu Hongsheng qiye*, vol. 3, pp. 239–41.

CHAPTER NINE

1. Meng Caiyi, "Kangzhan qianhou de Shanghai xiangjiao shiye" (The Shanghai rubber industry before and during the war of resistance), *Shangye zazhi* (Commercial magazine) 1, no. 4 (December 1940), pp. 39–40; Shanghai shi gongshang xingzheng guanli ju, Shanghai shi xiangjiao gongye gongsi, and Shiliao gongye zuozu, eds., *Shanghai minzu xiangjiao gongye* (Shanghai's national rubber industry; Beijing: Zhonghua shuju, 1979), pp. 15–19, 26–27; Du Xuncheng, *Riben zai jiu Zhongguo*, pp. 298–99.

2. SASS, Resource Center for Chinese Business History, Shanghai Rubber Manufacturers Association collection (unpublished material), vol. 1, pp. 17–18; vol. 2, pp. 60–64.

3. Meng Caiyi, "Kangzhan qianhou," p. 39.

4. SASS, Yonghe collection, item 2, item 13; Meng Caiyi, "Kangzhan qianhou," p. 40; Shanghai shi gongshang xingzheng guanli ju et al., *Shanghai minzu xiangjiao gongye*, p. 41.

5. Shanghai shi gongshang xingzheng guanli ju et al., *Shanghai minzu xiangjiao gongye*, pp. 42–43; SASS, Yonghe collection, item 2.

6. Du Xuncheng, *Riben zai jiu Zhongguo*, p. 299; Shanghai shi gongshang xingzheng guanli ju et al., *Shanghai minzu xiangjiao gongye*, pp. 43–49.

7. SASS, Da Zhonghua collection, no. 11, pp. 59–60; Shanghai shi gongshang xingzheng guanli ju et al., *Shanghai minzu xiangjiao gongye*, pp. 43–45, 52–53, 97–98.

8. SASS, Da Zhonghua collection, no. 11, pp. 59–61; Shanghai shi gongshang xingzheng guanli ju et al., *Shanghai minzu liangjiao gongye*, pp. 51–53, 97–98.

9. Wang Renze, "Da Zhonghua xiangjiao chang chuangban ren Yu Zhiqing" (The founder of the Da Zhonghua Rubber Factory, Yu Zhiqing), *Zhejiang WZXJ*, no. 39 (1989), pp. 195–98; SASS, Da Zhonghua collection, no. 1, p. 9; Sun Guoda, *Minzu gongye da qian tu*, p. 77.

10. SASS, Da Zhonghua collection, no. 11, pp. 54–57; Shanghai shi gongshang xingzheng guanli ju et al., *Shanghai minzu xiangjiao gongye*, pp. 49–50; Wang Renze, "Da Zhonghua xiangjiao chang," p. 199.

11. SASS, Da Zhonghua collection, no. 11, pp. 54–55, 58; Sun Guoda, *Minzu gongye da qiantu*, pp. 77–81.

12. SASS, Da Zhonghua collection, no. 11, pp. 56–57; Shanghai shi gongshang xingzheng guanli ju et al., *Shanghai minzu xiangjiao gongye,* pp. 49–50.

13. SASS, Da Zhonghua collection, no. 11, pp. 56–58.

14. Shanghai shi gongshang xingzheng guanli ju et al., *Shanghai minzu xiangjiao gongye,* pp. 50–51; SASS, Da Zhonghua collection, no. 11, pp. 56–58, 63–64.

15. SASS, Da Zhonghua collection, no. 11, pp. 62–63.

16. Yang Shaozhen and Hong Furong, "Zhengtai xiangjiao chang," pp. 148–67; Shanghai shi gongshang xingzheng guanli ju et al., *Shanghai minzu xiangjiao gongye,* pp. 17–19, 51–53; Meng Caiyi, "Kangzhan qianhou," pp. 39–40.

17. SASS, Zhengtai collection (original documents from the Shanghai Municipal Archives), pp. 21–22; Yang Shaozhen and Hong Furong, "Zhengtai xiangjiao chang," pp. 153–54; Shanghai shi gongshang xingzheng guanli ju et al., *Shanghai minzu xiangjiao gongye,* pp. 51–53. Some sources give the amount of the insurance settlement from the Tianyi Insurance Company as only 270,000 yuan.

18. SASS, "Zhengtai collection," pp. 20–25; Yang Shaozhen and Hong Furong, "Zhengtai xiangjiao chang," pp. 154–55. The profit of 167,000 yuan was earned from February 1939 to February 1940.

19. SASS, "Zhengtai collection," pp. 20–34; Yang Shaozhen and Hong Furong, "Zhengtai xiangjiao chang," pp. 154–58.

20. Yang Shaozhen and Hong Furong, "Zhengtai xiangjiao chang, pp. 155–58; Shanghai shi gongshang xingzheng guanli ju et al., *Shanghai minzu xiangjiao,* p. 522.

CONCLUSION

1. Iris Chang, *The Rape of Nanking: The Forgotten Holocaust of World War II* (New York: Basic Books, 1997). For a discussion of this issue, see Daqing Yang, "Review Essay: Convergence or Divergence? Recent Historical Writings on the Rape of Nanjing," *American Historical Review,* June 1999, pp. 842–65.

2. Carter J. Eckert, *Offspring of Empire: The Ko'chang Kims and the Colonial Origins of Korean Capitalism, 1876–1945.* Seattle: University of Washington Press, 1991.

3. Henry Rousso, *The Vichy Syndrome: History and Memory in France since 1944,* trans. Arthur Goldhammer (Cambridge, Mass.: Harvard University Press, 1991), passim.

4. Henry Russo, *The Vichy Syndrome,* p. 297.

5. Parks M. Coble, *The Shanghai Capitalists,* pp. 172–260, passim.

6. Suzanne Pepper, *The Civil War in China: The Political Struggle, 1945–1949* (Berkeley: University of California Press, 1978), pp. 21–24.

7. William C. Kirby, "The Chinese War Economy," p. 185; Wong Siu-lun, *Emigrant Entrepreneurs,* p. 19; SASS, *Rongjia qiye shiliao,* vol. 2, pp. 388, 608–15; *Jingji tongxun* (Economic newsletter), no. 9, March 23, 1946, pp. 12–13; SASS, *Rongjia qiye shiliao,* vol. 2, pp. 404–6.

8. Wong Siu-lun, *Emigrant Entrepreneurs,* pp. 14, 18; SASS, *Rongjia qiye shiliao,* vol. 2, pp. 45–649, 662–64.

9. Wong Siu-lun, *Emigrant Entrepreneurs,* pp. 39–41.

10. Heng Pek Koon, "Robert Kuok and the Chinese Business Network in Eastern Asia: A Study in Sino-Capitalism," in Timothy Brook and Hy V. Luong, eds., *Culture and Economy* (Ann Arbor: University of Michigan Press, 1997), p. 175.

11. *Far Eastern Economic Review,* Feb. 6, 1997, p. 43; Ma Kefeng, *Rongshi jiazu,* pp. 244–64.

12. Margaret M. Pearson, *Joint Ventures in the People's Republic of China: The Control of Foreign Direct Investment under Socialism* (Princeton, N.J.: Princeton University Press, 1991), p. 196.

Bibliography

Amerasia. New York, 1937–1940.

Asada Kyōji 浅田喬二. *Nihon teikokushugika no Chūgoku: Chūgoku senryōchi keizai no kenkyū* 日本帝国主義下の中国中国戦領地経済の研究(China under Japanese imperialism: Research on the economy of occupied China). Tokyo: Rakuyū shobō, 1981.

Barnett, Robert W. *Economic Shanghai: Hostage to Politics, 1937–1941*. New York: Institute of Pacific Relations, 1941.

Barnhart, Michael A. *Japan Prepares for Total War: The Search for Economic Security, 1919–1941*. Ithaca, N.Y.: Cornell University Press, 1987.

Bartholomew, James R. *The Formation of Science in Japan: Building a Research Tradition*. New Haven, Conn.: Yale University Press, 1989.

Beasley, W. G. *Japanese Imperialism, 1894–1945*. Oxford: Oxford University Press, 1987.

Bell, Lynda S. "From Comprador to County Magnate: Bourgeois Practice in the Wuxi Country Silk Industry." In *Chinese Local Elites and Patterns of Dominance*, edited by Joseph Esherick and Mary Backus Rankin, 113–39. Berkeley: University of California Press, 1990.

———. *One Industry, Two Chinas: Silk Filatures and Peasant-Family Production in Wuxi County, 1865–1937*. Stanford: Stanford University Press, 1999.

Bergère, Marie-Claire. *The Golden Age of the Chinese Bourgeoisie, 1911–1937*. Translated by Janet Lloyd. Cambridge: Cambridge University Press, 1989.

———. "The Purge in Shanghai, 1945–46: The Sarly Affair and the End of the French Concession." In *Wartime Shanghai*, edited by Wen-hsin Yeh, 157–78.

———. "Zhongguo de minzu qiye yu ZhongRi zhanzheng: Rongjia Shenxin fangzhi chang" 中国的民族企业与中日战争荣家申新纺织厂 (China's national industry and the Sino-Japanese War: The Rong family's Shenxin textile company). In *Minguo dang'an yu minguo shixue shu taolun lunwen ji,* edited by Zhang Xianwen et al., 533–44.

Boorman, Howard L., ed. *Biographical Dictionary of Republican China.* 4 vols. New York: Columbia University Press, 1967–1971.

Bowen, J. Ray, II. "Families, Firms, and Ancestors: The Effect of Government Behavior and Property Rights on China's Businesses and Economic Development." *Chinese Business History* 6, no. 2 (fall 1996): 1, 5–7.

Bowen, J. Ray, II, and David C. Rose. "On the Absence of Privately Owned, Publicly Traded Corporations in China: The Kirby Puzzle." *The Journal of Asian Studies* 57, no. 2 (May 1998): 442–52.

Boyle, John Hunter. *China and Japan at War, 1937–1945: The Politics of Collaboration.* Stanford: Stanford University Press, 1972.

Brook, Timothy, and Hy V. Luong, eds. *Culture and Economy: The Shaping of Capitalism in Eastern Asia.* Ann Arbor: University of Michigan Press, 1997.

Brown, Rajeswary Ampalavanar, ed. *Chinese Business Enterprise.* Vols. 1–4. London: Routledge, 1996.

———. *Chinese Business Enterprise in Asia.* London: Routledge, 1995.

Bruce, George C. *Shanghai's Undeclared War.* Shanghai: Mercury Press, 1937.

Bunker, Gerald E. *The Peace Conspiracy: Wang Ching-wei and the China War, 1937–1941.* Cambridge, Mass.: Harvard University Press, 1972.

Candlin, Enid Saunders. *The Breach in the Wall: A Memoir of the Old China.* New York: Macmillan, 1973.

Carey, Arch. *The War Years at Shanghai, 1941–45–48.* New York: Vantage, 1967.

Chan, Kai Yiu. "Capital Formation and Accumulation of Chinese Industrial Enterprises in the Republican Period: The Case of Liu Hongsheng's Shanghai Portland Cement Works Company, Ltd., 1920–1937." In *Chinese Business Enterprise,* edited by R. A. Brown, 149–70. Vol. 2.

Chan, Wellington K. K. *Merchants, Mandarins, and Modern Enterprise in Late Ch'ing China.* Cambridge: Harvard East Asian Monographs, 1977.

———. "The Origins and Early Years of the Wing On Company Group in Australia, Fiji, Hong Kong, and Shanghai: Organisation and Strategy of a New Enterprise." In *Chinese Business Enterprise in Asia,* edited by R. A. Brown, 80–95.

———. "Personal Styles, Cultural Values, and Management: The Sincere and Wing On Companies in Shanghai and Hong Kong, 1900–1941." *Business History Review* 70 (summer 1996): 141–66.

———. "Selling Goods and Promoting a New Commercial Culture: The Four Premier Department Stores on Nanjing Road, 1917–1937." In *Inventing Nanjing Road,* edited by Sherman G. Cochran, 19–36.

Chang, Iris. *The Rape of Nanking: The Forgotten Holocaust of World War II.* New York: Basic Books, 1997.

Chao Fuxie 巢福偕. "Shiye jia Liu Guojun" 实业家刘国钧 (Industrialist Liu Guojun). *WZXJ,* no. 100: 266–93.

Chao Kang. *The Development of Cotton Textile Production in China.* Cambridge: Harvard East Asian Monographs, 1977.

Chen Ciyu 陳慈玉. *Jindai Zhongguo de jixie saosi gongye, 1860–1945* 近代中國的機械繅絲工業 (Recent China's machine woven silk industry, 1860–1945). Taibei: Zhongyang yanjiu yuan, 1989.

Chen Dingwen 陳鼎文. "Hangzhou lunxian shiqi choulu" 杭州沦陷时期丑录 (The shameful record of occupied Hangzhou). *Zhejiang WZXJ*, no. 21 (1982): 199–218.

Chen Tiaofu 陈调甫. "Fan Xudong yu Huanghai huaxue gongye yanjiu she" 范旭东与黄海化学工业研究社 (Fan Xudong and the Huanghai Chemical Industrial Research Society). *WZXJ*, no. 80 (1988): 60–73.

———. "Yongli jianchang fendou huiyi lu" (A record of memories of the struggles of the Yongli alkali soda plant) 永利碱厂奋斗回忆录. *Gongshang shiliao*, vol. 2, 80–104.

Chen Zhen 陈真 and Yao Luo 姚洛, eds. *Zhongguo jindai gongye shi ziliao* 中国近代工业史资料 (Material on the history of modern Chinese industry). Vol. 1. Beijing: Sanlian chuban she, 1957; vol. 4, edited by Chen Zhen, 1961.

Chen Zhengmo 陈正谟. *Zenyang fensui Rikou de "yizhan yangzhan"* 怎樣粉碎日寇的以战養战 (How to smash the Japanese bandits "using the war to sustain the war"). Chongqing: Zhongshan wenhua jiaoyu guan, 1939.

Cheng Nianqi 程念祺. "Liu Hongsheng: Zai gouan yu minzu dayi zhijian jueze" 刘鸿生在苟安与民族大义之間抉择 (Liu Hongsheng: Choosing between a false peace and national righteousness). In *Guonan zhong de Zhongguo qiye jia*, edited by Shen Zuwei and Du Xuncheng, 29–44.

Ch'i, Hsi-sheng. "The Military Dimension, 1942–1945." In *China's Bitter Victory*, edited by James C. Hsiung and Steven I. Levine, 157–84.

———. *Nationalist China at War: Military Defeats and Political Collapse, 1937–45*. Ann Arbor: The University of Michigan Press, 1982.

China at War. Chongqing, 1939–1941.

China Weekly Review. Shanghai, 1937–1941.

Chu, Samuel C. *Reformer in Modern China, Chang Chien, 1853–1926*. New York: Columbia University Press, 1965.

Chūgoku nenkan 中國年鑑 (China yearbook). Shanghai, 1939.

Chūgoku seiji keizai kenkyūjo 中国政治经济研究所, ed. *Naka Shina keizai nempō* 中支那經済年報 (An economic yearbook of Central China). Shanghai, 1942, 1943, 1944.

Chūgoku tsushinsha chōsabu 中國通信社調查部, ed. *Sengo ni okeru Shanhai kin'yū jōtai no kaibō* 戰後に於ける上海金融状態の解剖 (An analysis of the financial situation in Shanghai after the war began). Shanghai: Chūgoku tsushinsha chōsabu, 1938.

Clifford, Nicholas R. *Spoilt Children of Empire: Westerners in Shanghai and the Chinese Revolution of the 1920s*. Hanover, N. H.: University Press of New England, 1991.

Coble, Parks M. "Chinese Capitalists and the Japanese: Collaboration and Resistance in the Shanghai Area, 1937–45." In *Wartime Shanghai*, edited by Wen-hsin Yeh, 62–85.

———. *Facing Japan: Chinese Politics and Japanese Imperialism, 1931–1937*. Cambridge: Harvard East Asian Monographs, 1991.

———. *The Shanghai Capitalists and the Nationalist Government of China, 1927–1937*. 2d ed. Cambridge: Harvard East Asian Monographs, 1986.

Cochran, Sherman G. *Big Business in China: Sino-Foreign Rivalry in the Cigarette Industry, 1890–1930*. Cambridge: Harvard University Press, 1981.

———. "Business, Governments, and War in China, 1931–1949." In *American, Chinese, and Japanese Perspectives on Wartime Asia, 1931–1949*, edited by Akira Iriye and Warren Cohen, 117–45. Wilmington, Del.: Scholarly Resources, 1990.

———. *Encountering Chinese Networks: Western, Japanese, and Chinese Corporations in China, 1880–1937*. Berkeley: University of California Press, 2000.

———. "Three Roads into Shanghai's Market: Japanese, Western, and Chinese Companies in the Match Trade, 1895–1937." In *Shanghai Sojourners*, edited by Frederic Wakeman Jr. and Wen-hsin Yeh, 35–75. Berkeley: Institute of East Asian Studies, China Research Monograph, 1992.

Cochran, Sherman G., ed. *Inventing Nanjing Road: Commercial Culture in Shanghai, 1900–1945*. Ithaca, N. Y.: Cornell University, East Asia Program, 1999.

Cohen, Jerome B. *Japan's Economy in War and Reconstruction*. Minneapolis: University of Minnesota Press, 1949.

Contemporary Japan: A Review of Far Eastern Affairs. Tokyo, 1940–1943.

Dang'an yu lishi 档案与历史 (Archives and history). Shanghai, 1986–1988.

Dasheng xitong qiye shi bianxie zu 大生系统企业史编写组, ed. *Dasheng xitong qiye shi* 大生系统企业史 (A history of the enterprises of the Dasheng system). Nanjing: Jiangsu guji chuban she, 1990.

Ding Richu 丁日初, ed. *Jindai Zhongguo* 近代中国 (*Modern China*), no. 5. Shanghai: Shanghai shehui kexue yuan chuban she, 1995.

Dower, John W. *War Without Mercy: Race and Power in the Pacific War*. New York: Pantheon Books, 1986.

Dreyer, Edward L. *China at War, 1901–1949*. London: Longman, 1995.

Du Xuncheng 杜恂诚. *Riben zai jiu Zhongguo de touzi* 日本在旧中国的投资 (Japanese investment in old China). Shanghai: Shanghai shehui kexue yuan chuban she, 1986.

Duus, Peter. *Modern Japan*. 2d ed. Boston: Houghton Mifflin, 1998.

———. "Zaikabō: Japanese Cotton Mills in China, 1895–1937." In *The Japanese Informal Empire in China, 1895–1937*, edited by Peter Duus, Ramon H. Myers, and Mark R. Peattie, 65–100.

Duus, Peter, Ramon H. Myers, and Mark R. Peattie, eds. *The Japanese Informal Empire in China, 1895–1937*. Princeton, N.J.: Princeton University Press, 1989.

———. *The Japanese Wartime Empire, 1931–1945*. Princeton, N.J.: Princeton University Press, 1996.

Eastman, Lloyd E. *The Abortive Revolution: China Under Nationalist Rule, 1927–1937*. Cambridge, Mass: Harvard University Press, 1974.

———. "Nationalist China during the Sino-Japanese War, 1937–1945." In *The Nationalist Era in China, 1927–1949*, edited by Lloyd E. Eastman et al., 115–76. Cambridge: Cambridge University Press, 1991.

———. *Seeds of Destruction: Nationalist China in War and Revolution, 1937–1949*. Stanford, Calif.: Stanford University Press, 1984.

Eckert, Carter J. *Offspring of Empire: The Koch'ang Kims and the Colonial Origins of Korean Capitalism, 1876–1945*. Seattle: University of Washington Press, 1991.

Fang Yi 方异. "Ri shang hengchan zhushi huishe zhenggou tudi de pianju" 日商
恒产株式会社征购土地的骗局 (The fraud of the requisition of land by the Japanese merchant Hengchan company [Kōsan kabushiki kaisha]). *Shanghai
WZXJ*, no. 64 (1990): 200–202.

Far Eastern Survey. New York, 1937–1945.

Farmer, Rhodes. *Shanghai Harvest: A Diary of Three Years in the China War.*
London: Museum Press, 1945.

Faure, David. "The Control of Equity in Chinese Family Firms within the Modern Sector from the Late Qing to the Early Republic." In *Chinese Business
Enterprise in Asia,* edited by R. A. Brown, 60–79.

Feuerwerker, Albert. *China's Early Industrialization: Sheng Hsuan-huai (1844–
1916) and Mandarin Enterprise.* Cambridge: Harvard University Press,
1958.

———. "Industrial Enterprise in Twentieth-Century China: The Chee Hsin Cement Co." In *Approaches to Modern Chinese History*, edited by Albert Feuerwerker, Rhoads Murphey, Mary C. Wright, 304–41. Berkeley: University of
California Press, 1967.

Fogel, Joshua A. "The Other Japanese Community: Leftwing Japanese Activities in Wartime Shanghai." In *Wartime Shanghai,* edited by Wen-hsin Yeh,
42–61.

Fu, Poshek. *Passivity, Resistance, and Collaboration: Intellectual Choices in Occupied Shanghai, 1937–1945.* Stanford, Calif.: Stanford University Press,
1993.

———. "Projecting Ambivalence: Chinese Cinema in Semi-occupied Shanghai,
1937–41." In *Wartime Shanghai,* edited by Wen-hsin Yeh, 86–109.

Furukyū Tadao 古廐忠夫. "'Kankan' no shosō" 漢奸の諸相 (Various aspects of
traitors). In *Iwanami kōza: kindai Nihon to shokuminchi* 岩波講座：近代日
本と殖民地 (The Iwanami lectures, modern Japan and colonies). Vol. 6,
149–71. Tokyo: Iwanami shōten, 1993.

Gendaishi shiryō 現代史資料 (Source materials on contemporary history). Tokyo:
Misuzu shobō, 1962–1967.

Gong Tingtai 龚廷泰. "Rongshi jiazu de shiye juzi: ji Rong Zongjing, Rong Desheng xiongdi" 荣式家族的实业巨子记荣宗敬荣德生兄弟 (The Rong family industrial leaders: Remembering the brothers Rong Zongjing and Rong Desheng).
Jiangsu WZXJ, no. 34 (1989): 111–39.

Great Britain. Public Records Office. (PRO) Selected files.

Guangdong wenshi ziliao xuanji 广东文史资料选辑 (Selections of literary and historical materials, Guangdong province). Guanzhou.

Guo Bingyu 郭炳瑜. "Yongli jianchang wushi nian jianwen" 永利碱厂五十年见文
(A look at fifty years of the Yongli soda plant). In *Huagong xiandao—Fan
Xudong,* 86–103.

Guo Shijie 郭士杰. *Rikou qinHua baoxing lu* 日寇侵华暴行録 (The savage record
of Japan's invasion of China). Beijing: Lianhe shudian, 1951.

Guo Tingyi 郭廷以, Zhang Pengyuan 張朋园, eds. *Lin Jiyong xiansheng fanwen
jilu* 林继庸先生訪問紀録 (The reminiscences of Mr. Lin Jiyong). Taibei: Zhongyang yanjiu yuan, jindai yanjiu suo, 1983.

Hamilton, Gary G., ed. *Business Networks and Economic Development in East and Southeast Asia.* Hong Kong: University of Hong Kong, Centre of Asian Studies, 1991.

———. *Cosmopolitan Capitalists: Hong Kong and the Chinese Diaspora at the End of the 20th Century.* Seattle: University of Washington Press, 1999.

Hamilton, Gary G., and Kao Cheng-shu. "The Institutional Foundations of Chinese Business: The Family Firm in Taiwan." *Comparative Social Research: A Research Annual* 12 (1990): 135–51.

Han Qitong 韩启桐. *Zhongguo duiRi zhanshi juanshi zhi guji, 1937–1943* 中国對日戰事捐失之估計 (An estimate of China's wartime losses, 1937–1943). Shanghai: Zhonghua shuju, 1946.

Handbook of Japanese Industry in Japan and Occupied Areas. 3 vols. Extracts from shortwave radio Tokyo and affiliated stations from December 1941 to March 1, 1944. Honolulu: Research and Analysis Branch, Office of Strategic Services, 1945.

Hanson, Haldore. *"Humane Endeavour": The Story of the China War.* New York: Farrar and Rinehart, 1939.

———. "Japan's Balance Sheet in China." *Amerasia.* 4, no. 3 (June 1939): 158–64.

Hanwell, Norman D. "Economic Disruption in Occupied China." *Far Eastern Survey* 8, no. 6 (March 15, 1939): 61–66.

Hara Akira 原朗. "'Daitōa kyōeiken' no keizaiteki jittai" 大東亞共榮圈の経済的実態 (The economic realities of the Greater East Asia Co-Prosperity Sphere). *Tochi seido shigaku* 土地制度史学 (Journal of Agrarian History), no. 71 (April 1976): 1–28.

Hata Ikuhiko. "Continental Expansion, 1905–1941." In *The Cambridge History of Japan,* 271–314. Vol. 6, *The Twentieth Century.* Cambridge: Cambridge University Press, 1988.

He Kuang 何况. *Huochai dawang—Liu Hongsheng* 火柴大王刘鸿生. Beijing: Jiefang jun chuban she, 1995.

He Xizeng 何熙曾. "'Yongjiu tuanti' za yi" 永久团体杂忆 (Various memories of the Yongli and Jiuda enterprise groups). *WZXJ,* no. 80 (1986): 74–82.

He Zupei 何祖培. "Banian lunxian hua Hangxian" 八年论陷話杭縣 (Talking of Hangzhou county during eight years of occupation). *Zhejiang WZXJ,* no. 2 (1962): 172–85.

Heng Pek Koon. "Robert Kuok and the Chinese Business Network in Eastern Asia: A Study in Sino-Capitalism." In *Culture and Economy: The Shaping of Capitalism in Eastern Asia,* edited by Timothy Brook and Hy V. Luong, 155–81.

Heping fangong jianguo wenxian 和平反共建国文献 (Writings on peace, anti-communism and building the nation). Nanjing: Xuanzhuan bu, 1941.

Hershatter, Gail. *The Workers of Tianjin, 1900–1949.* Stanford, Calif.: Stanford University Press, 1986.

Higuchi Hiroshi 樋口弘. *Nippon no taiShi tōshi kenkyū* 日本の対支投資研究 (Research on Japan's investment in China). Tokyo: Seikatsusha, 1939.

Hinder, Eleanor. *Life and Labour in Shanghai.* New York: International Secretariat, Institute of Pacific Relations, 1944.

Hou Te-pang [Hou Debang]. *Manufacture of Soda: With Special Reference to the Ammonia Process*. New York: Reinhold, 1942.

Hsiung, James C., and Steven I. Levine, eds. *China's Bitter Victory: The War with Japan, 1937–1945*. Armonk, New York: M. E. Sharpe, 1992.

Hu Baoqi 胡鲍淇. "Toudi funi de Fu Xiao'an" 投敌附逆的傅筱庵 (Fu Xiao'an who went over to the enemy). *WZXJ*, no. 106 (1986): 156–77.

Hu Linge 胡林阁, Zhu Bangxing 朱邦兴, and Xu Sheng 徐馨 eds. *Shanghai chanye yu Shanghai zhigong* 上海產業与上海職工 (Shanghai production and Shanghai employment). Hong Kong: Yuandong chuban she, 1939.

Hu Shikui 胡世奎. "Wosuo zhidao de Liu Hongsheng xiansheng" 我所知道的刘鸿生先生 (The Liu Hongsheng I knew). *Shanghai wenshi ziliao xuanji. Tongzhan gongzuo shiliao zhuanji*, no. 8 (1989): 167–81.

Hu Shuchang 户书锠. "Yanliao maiban Zhou Zongliang" 颜料买办周宗良 (Dyestuffs comprador Zhou Zongliang). *Shanghai WZXJ*, no. 56 (1987), pp. 191–201.

Hu Xiyuan 胡西园. "Zhongguo Yapu'er chang shou diguo zhuyi he fandong pai cuican zhaiji" 中国亚浦耳厂受帝国主义和反动派摧残摘记 (An abbreviated account of the Chinese Yapu'er Factory being destroyed by imperialism and the reactionary faction). *WZXJ*, no. 44 (1986): 115–23.

Hu Xuantong 胡宣同. "Wosuo zhidao de Wangwei Zhongyang chubei yinhang" 我所知道的汪伪中央储备银行 (The Wang Jingwei puppet Central Reserve Bank that I knew). *Shanghai WZXJ*, no. 33 (1980): 153–65.

Huagong xiandao—Fan Xudong 化工先导范旭东 (The first leader of the chemical industrial industry, Fan Xudong). Compiled by Quanguo zhengxie wenshi ziliao yanjiu weiyuan hui 全国政协文史资料研究委员会. Beijing: Zhongguo wenshi chuban she chuban, 1987.

Huang Hanmin 黄汉民. "Rong Desheng: Juebu yu diren 'hezuo'" 荣德生决不与砥人合作 (Rong Desheng who absolutely would not cooperate with the enemy). In *Guonan zhong de Zhongguo qiye jia*, edited by Shen Zuwei and Du Xuncheng, pp. 106–18.

———. "Rongjia qiye dizao zhe—Rong Zongjing, Rong Desheng" 荣家企业缔造者荣宗敬荣德生 (The founders of the Rong industries—Rong Zhongjing, Rong Desheng). In *Zhongguo qiye jia liezhuan*, vol., 1, edited by Xu Dixin, 96–116.

Huang Hanrui 黄汉瑞. "Huiyi Fan Xudong xiansheng" 回忆范旭东先生 (Remembering Mr. Fan Xudong). *WZXJ*, no. 80: 38–43.

Huang Liren 黄立人 and Zhang Yougao 张有高. "KangRi zhanzheng shiqi Zhongguo bingqi gongye neiqian chulun" 抗日战争时期中国兵器工业内迁初论 (A first discussion of the movement to the interior of China's weapons industry during the anti-Japanese war of resistance period). *Lishi dang'an*, no. 2 (1991): 118–25.

Huang Shirang 黄师让. "Yu Dahua qiye sishi nian" 裕大华企业四十年 (Forty years of the Yu Dahua Enterprises). *WZXJ*, no. 44 (1986): 1–75.

Inoue Kiyoshi 井上清 and Etō Shinkichi 衛藤瀋吉, eds. *NitChū sensō to NitChū kankei: Rokōkyō jiken 50 shūnan Nitchū gakujutsu tōronkai kiroku* 日中戰爭と日中關係盧溝橋事件50周年日中学術討論會記録 (The Sino-Japanese War and Sino-Japanese relations: A record of a scholarly conference on the 50th anniversary of the Marco Polo Bridge Incident). Tokyo: Hara shobō, 1988.

Institute of Pacific Relations, Secretariat. *Industrial Japan: Aspects of Recent Economic Changes as Viewed by Japanese Writers.* New York: Institute of Pacific Relations, 1941.

Iriye, Akira. *Power and Culture: The Japanese-American War, 1941–1945.* Cambridge, Mass.: Harvard University Press, 1981.

———. "Toward a New Cultural Order: The Hsin-min Hui." In. *The Chinese and the Japanese: Essays in Political and Cultural Interactions*, edited by Akira Iriye, 254–74. Princeton, N.J.: Princeton University Press, 1980.

Ishihama Tomoyuki 石濱知行. *Shina senji keizai ron* 支那戰時經濟論 (On China's wartime economy). Tokyo: Keiō shobō, 1940.

Itō Takeo. *Problems in the Japanese Occupied Areas in China.* Tokyo: Japan Council, Institute of Pacific Relations, 1941.

Japan Year Book, 1943–44. Tokyo: The Foreign Affairs Association of Japan, 1943.

Jiang Duo 姜铎. "Shanghai lunxian qianqi de 'gudao fanrong'" 上海沦陷前期的孤岛繁荣 (The "flourishing solitary island" of the first period of occupied Shanghai). *Jingji xueshu ziliao* 经济学术资料 (*Materials on economic studies*), no. 10 (1983): 25–31.

Jiang Wei 姜伟. "Xiongju 'baihuo dawang' baozuo sanshi nian" 雄踞'百货大王'宝座三十年 (Occupying the "department store king" throne for thirty years). *Jiangsu WZXJ*, no. 34 (1989): 92–110.

Jiangsu sheng lishi xuehui, 江苏省历史学会 ed. *Kangri zhanzhen shishi tansuo* 抗日战争史事探索 (Explorations into the history of the anti-Japanese war of resistance). Shanghai: Shanghai shehui kexue yuan chuban she, 1988.

Jiangsu wenshi ziliao xuanji 江苏文史资料选辑 (Selections from literary and historical materials, Jiangsu province). Nanjing.

Jin Zhanlu 金湛卢. "Wang wei quanguo shanghe tongzhi weiyuan hui" 汪伪全国商业统制委员会 (The National Commerce Control Commission of the Wang puppet government). *Zhejiang WZXJ*, no. 6 (1963): 57–73.

Jingji tongxun 经济通讯 (Economic newsletter). Hong Kong, 1946–1948.

Jinrong jie wei lu 金融界伪錄 (A record of puppets in financial circles). Shanghai: Huazhi shushe, n.d.

Jones, F. C. *Japan's New Order in East Asia: Its Rise and Fall, 1937–45.* London: Oxford University Press, 1954.

The Journal of Studies of Japanese Aggression Against China. Carbondale, Illinois.

Ju Zhifen 居之芬 and Bi Jie 毕杰. "Riben 'Bei zhina kaifa zhushi huishe' de jingji huodong ji qi lueduo" 日本北支那开发株式会社的经济活动及其掠夺 (The economic activities and the plundering of Japan's North China Development Company). *Jindai shi yanjiu* 近代史研究 (Research on modern history), no. 3 (1993): 245–67.

KangRi zhanzheng yanjiu 抗日战争研究 (Research on the anti-Japanese war of resistance). Beijing.

Katsuji, Nakagane. "Manchukuo and Economic Development." In *The Japanese Informal Empire in China, 1895–1937,* edited by Peter Duus, Ramon H. Myers, and Mark R. Peattie, 133–57.

Kimura Masutarō 木村増太郎. *Jihen ka no Shina kin'yu oyobi kin'yu kikan* 事變下の支那金融及び金融機關 (Finance and financial organizations in China since the incident). Tokyo: Kin'yu kenkyūkai, 1941.

Kirby, William C. "China Unincorporated: Company Law and Business Enterprise in Twentieth-Century China." *The Journal of Asian Studies* 54, no. 1 (February 1995): 43–63.

———. "The Chinese War Economy." In *China's Bitter Victory: The War with Japan, 1937–1945,* edited by James C. Hsiung and Steven I. Levine, 185–212.

Kishi Toshihiko 貴志俊彦. "Eiri kagaku kōgyō konsu to Han Kyokutō" 永利化学工業公司と範旭東 (The Yongli Chemical Industrial Company and Fan Xudong). In *Chūgoku kindaika katei no shidōsha tachi,* edited by Soda Saburō, 253–85.

Kobayashi Hideo 小林英夫. *Daitōa kyōeiken no keisei to hōkai* 大東亞共栄圈の形成と崩壊 (The formation and collapse of the Greater East Asian Co-Prosperity Sphere). Tokyo: Ochanomizu shobō, 1973.

Köll, Elisabeth. "Controlling Modern Business in China: The Da Sheng Enterprise, 1895–1926." *Journal of Asian Business* 14, no. 1 (1998): 41–56.

Lebra, Joyce C., ed. *Japan's Greater East Asia Co-Prosperity Sphere in World War II: Selected Readings and Documents.* Kuala Lumpur: Oxford University Press, 1975.

Lee, Tahirih V. "Coping with Shanghai: Means to Survival and Success in the Early Twentieth Century—A Symposium." *Journal of Asian Studies* 54, no. 1 (February 1995): 3–18.

Lewis, Michael. "The World's Biggest Going-Out-of-Business Sale." *The New York Times Magazine,* May 31, 1998, 34–41.

Li Daofa 李道发. "Aiguo shiye jia Chen Wanyun" 爱国实业家陈万运 (Patriotic industrialist Chen Wanyun). *Shanghai WZXJ,* no. 66 (1991): 109–17.

Li Guowei 李国伟. "Rongjia jingying fangzhi he zhifen qiye liushi nian" 荣家经营纺织和制粉企业之六十年 (Sixty years of managing the Rong family textile and flour enterprises). *Gongshang shiliao,* vol. 1, 1–15.

Li, Lincoln. *The Japanese Army in North China, 1937–1941: Problems of Political and Economic Control.* Tokyo: Oxford University Press, 1975.

Lieu, D. K. *The Silk Industry of China.* Shanghai: Kelly and Walsh, 1940.

———. "The Sino-Japanese Currency War." *Pacific Affairs* 12, no. 4 (December 1939): 413–26.

Lin Wenyi 林文益. "KangRi zhanzheng shiqi lunxian qu de peiji zhi qingkuang" 抗日战争时期沦陷区的配给制情况 (The situation of the ration control system in the occupied areas during the anti-Japanese war of resistance). *Shangye ziliao,* no. 2 (1983): 73–77.

Lishi dang'an 历史档案 (Historical archives). Beijing.

Lishi yanjiu 历史研究 (Historical research). Beijing.

Liu Nianzhi 刘念智. "Kangzhan shiqi jian Liushi qiye qianchuan jingguo" 抗战时期间刘氏企业迁川经过 (The experiences of the Liu family enterprises in relocating to Sichuan during the war of resistance period). *WZXJ,* no. 68 (1986): 170–81.

———. *Shiye jia Liu Hongsheng zhuanlue: Huiyi wode fuqin* 实业家刘鸿生传略回忆我的父亲 (A biography of industrialist Liu Hongsheng: Remembering my father). Beijing: Wenshi ziliao chuban she, 1982.

Liu Shousheng 刘寿生 and Liu Meisheng 刘梅生. "Zhenhuan shachang zaoshou diguo zhuyi lueduo ji" 震寰纱厂遭受帝国主义掠夺记 (A record of the Zhenhuan textile mills suffering the plundering of imperialists). *WZXJ*, no. 44 (1986): 76–84.

Lockwood, William W. *The Economic Development of Japan: Growth and Structural Change.* Princeton, N.J.: Princeton University Press, 1968.

Lowe, Chuan-hua. *Japan's Economic Offensive in China.* London: Allen and Unwin, 1939.

Lu Renxian 陸仁贤. "Kangzhan shiqi Rijun dui Shanghai gangtie ye de sanci da lueduo" 抗战时期日军对上海钢铁业的三次大掠夺 (The three great plunderings of Shanghai's iron and steel commercial industry by the Japanese Army during the war of resistance). *Jingji xueshu ziliao* 经济学术资料, no. 11 (1982): 29–30.

Lu Xinglong 陆兴龙. "Guo Linshuang: lunxian qu baihuo dawang de xinsuan" 郭琳爽沦陷区百货大王的辛酸 (Guo Linshuang: The troubles of the department store king in the occupied area). In *Guonan zhong de Zhongguo qiye jia*, edited by Shen Zuwei and Du Xuncheng, 219–31.

———. "Wu Yunchu: Guonan shiqi de 'Tianzi hao'" 吴蕴初国难时期的天字号 (Wu Yunchu: The Tian name brand during the period of national difficulty). In *Guonan zhong de Zhongguo qiye jia*, edited by Shen Zuwei and Du Xuncheng, 45–60.

Lu Yangyuan 陆仲渊. "Jindai Zhongguo di yige da shiye jia: ji Zhang Jian de nanku chuangye" 近代中国第一个大实业家记张謇的难苦创业 (Modern China's first big industrialist: Remembering Zhang Jian's hard work to begin an undertaking). *Jiangsu wenshi ziliao*, no. 34 (1989): 2–17.

Lu Yangyuan 陆仲渊 and Fang Qingqiu 方庆秋, eds. *Mingguo shehui jingji shi* 民国社会经济史 (A social and economic history of the Republican period). Beijing: Zhongguo jingji chuban she, 1991.

Ma Bohuang. "Liu Hongsheng's Enterprise Investment and Management." In *The Chinese Economy in the Early Twentieth Century: Recent Chinese Studies,* edited by Tim Wright, 85–97.

Ma Gongjin 马公瑾 et al. "Aiguo shiye jia Chen Jingyu" 爱国实业家陈经畬 (Patriotic industrialist Chen Jingyu). *Wuhan WZXJ*, no. 33 (1988): 24–45.

Ma Kefeng 马克锋. *Rongshi jiazu* 荣氏家族 (The Rong family). Guangzhou: Guangzhou chuban she, 1997.

Ma Yinchu 马寅初. *Zhanshi jingji lunwen ji* 战时经济论文集 (A collection of essays on the wartime economy). Chongqing: Zuojia shushi, 1945.

MacKinnon, Stephen. "The Tragedy of Wuhan, 1938," *Modern Asian Studies* 30, no. 4 (1996): 931–43.

Masuda Yoneji 増田米治. *Shina sensō keizai no kenkyū* 支那戰争經濟の研究 (Researches on China's wartime economy). Tokyo: Daiyamondo sha, 1944.

Matsuzumi Kyūzaburō 松角久三郎. *Naka Shina seishi gyō no gaikyō narabi ni haikyū kikō no chōsa* 中支那蠶絲業の概況並配合機構の調査 (An investigation of the general situation and rationing organizations of central China's silk industry). Tokyo: n.p., 1939.

Meng Caiyi 萌才譯. "Kangzhan qianhou de Shanghai xiangjiao shiye" 抗战前后的上海橡胶事业 (The Shanghai rubber industry before and during the war of resistance). *Shangye zazhi* 商业杂誌 (Commercial magazine) 1, no. 4 (December 1940): 39–40.

Minguo dang'an 民国档案 (Republican archives). Nanjing.

Miyazaki Masayoshi 宮崎正義. *Tōa renmei ron* 東亞聯盟論 (A discussion of the East Asian League). Tokyo: Kaizōsha, 1938.

Morley, James W., ed. *The China Quagmire: Japan's Expansion on the Asian Continent, 1933–1941.* New York: Columbia University Press, 1983.

Myers, Ramon H. "Creating a Modern Enclave Economy: The Economic Integration of Japan, Manchuria, and North China, 1932–1945." In *The Japanese Wartime Empire, 1931–1945,* edited by Peter Duus, Ramon H. Myers, and Mark R. Peattie, 136–70.

Nakamura Takafusa 中村隆英. "Depression, Recovery, and War, 1920–1945." In *The Cambridge History of Japan.* Vol. 6, *The Twentieth Century,* 451–93. Cambridge: Cambridge University Press, 1988.

———. "Japan's Economic Thrust into North China, 1933–1938: Formation of the North China Development Corporation." In Akira Iriye, ed., *The Chinese and the Japanese: Essays in Political and Cultural Interactions,* edited by Akira Iriye, 220–53.

———. "Kita Shina shinkō kabushiki kaisha no seiritsu" 北支那開發株式会社の成立 (The creation of the North China Development Corporation). In *NitChū sensō to NitChū kenkei,* edited by Inoue Kiyoshi and Etō Shikichi, 349–65.

———. *Senji Nihon kahoku keizai shihai* 戰時日本の華北經濟支配 (Japan's wartime economic control over north China). Tokyo: Yamakawa shuppansha, 1983.

———. "The Yen Bloc, 1931–1941." In *The Japanese Wartime Empire, 1931–1945,* edited by Peter Duus, Ramon H. Myers, and Mark R. Peattie, 171–86.

"Nanyang xiongdi yancao gongsi shiliao buji" 南洋兄弟烟草公司史料补辑 (An addendum to historical materials on the Nanyang Brothers Tobacco Company). *Dang'an yu lishi,* no. 2 (1986): 35–41.

Ning Kunnan 宁鲲南. "Kong Xiangxi yu Fuxing gongsi" 孔祥熙与复兴公司 (H. H. Kung and the Fuxing Company). *WZXJ,* no. 105 (1987): 158–63.

Ning Sihong 宁思宏. "Guan leming jinbi chang shiliao" 关勒铭金笔厂史料 (Historical materials on the Leming golden pen factory). *Shanghai WZXJ,* no. 6 (1980): 169–178.

Orru, Marco, Nicole W. Biggart, Gary G. Hamilton. *The Economic Organization of East Asian Capitalism.* Thousand Oaks, Calif.: Sage Publications, 1997.

Pan Junxiang 潘君祥. "1937–1945 nian qijian Shanghai shangye qiye de tucun huodong" 1937–1945 年期间上海企业的图存活动 (The survival activities of Shanghai commercial enterprises from 1937 to 1945). In *Jindai Zhongguo,* vol. 5, edited by Ding Richu, 332–44.

Pan, Lynn. *Tracing It Home: A Chinese Family's Journey from Shanghai.* New York: Kodansha International, 1993.

Pearson, Margaret M. *China's New Business Elite: The Political Consequences of Economic Reform.* Berkeley: University of California Press, 1997.

———. *Joint Ventures in the People's Republic of China: The Control of Foreign Direct Investment under Socialism.* Princeton, N.J.: Princeton University Press, 1991.

Peattie, Mark R. "*Nanshin:* The 'Southward Advance,' 1931–1941, as a Prelude to the Japanese Occupation of Southeast Asia." In *The Japanese Wartime Empire, 1931–1945,* edited by Peter Duus, Ramon H. Myers, and Mark R. Peattie, 189–242.

Pepper, Suzanne. *Civil War in China: The Political Struggle, 1945–1949.* Berkeley: University of California Press, 1978.

Programs of Japan in China. Extracts from FCC intercepts of short wave broadcasts from Radio Tokyo and affiliated stations from December 1941 to January 1, 1945, and from OSS sources. Compiled by Research and Analysis Branch, Office of Strategic Services. 3 vols. Honolulu, 1945.

Qi Zhilu 齐植鏴. "Kangzhan shiqi gongkuang neiqian yu guanliao ziben de lueduo" 抗战时期工矿内迁与官僚资本的掠夺 (The move inland of factories and mines during the war of resistance period and its seizure by bureaucratic capitalism). *Gongshang jingji shiliao congkan* 工商经济史料丛刊 (A collection of economic historical materials on industry and commerce), no. 2 (1983): 64.

Qian Zhonghan 钱钟汉. "Minzu ziben jia—Rong Zongjing, Rong Desheng" 民族资本家荣宗敬荣德生 (National capitalists—Rong Zongjing, Rong Desheng). *Jiangsu WZXJ,* no. 2 (1963): 131–41.

———. "Wuxi wuge zhuyao chanye ziben xitong de xingcheng yu fazhan" 无锡五个主要产业资本系统的形成与发展 (The formation and development of Wuxi's five most important industrial capitalists systems). *WZXJ,* no. 24 (1986): 98–153.

Qing Qingrui 清庆瑞. *Kangzhan shiqi de jingji* 抗战时期的经济 (The economy of the war of resistance period). Beijing: Beijing chuban she, 1995.

Qiu Liangru 求良儒 and Jiang Youlong 蒋猷龙. "Zhejiang sichou shi jiyao" 浙江丝绸史纪要 (A record of the major facets of the history of Zhejiang silk production). *Zhejiang WZXJ,* no. 24 (1982): 1–52.

Rawski, Thomas G. *Economic Growth in Prewar China.* Berkeley: University of California Press, 1989.

Reardon-Anderson, James. *The Study of Change: Chemistry in China, 1840–1949.* Cambridge: Cambridge University Press, 1991.

Redding, S. Gordon. *The Spirit of Chinese Capitalism.* Berlin: Walter de Gruyter, 1990.

Ren Jiayao 任嘉尧. "Xianshen jinrong gaige de Zhu Boquan" 献身金融改革的朱博泉 (Devoted financial reformer Zhu Boquan). In *Zhongguo qiye jia liezhuan,* vol. 3, edited by Xu Dixin, 178–91.

Reynolds, Douglas R. "Training Young China Hands: Tōa Dōbun Shoin and Its Precursors, 1886–1945." In *The Japanese Informal Empire in China, 1895–1937,* edited by Peter Duus, Ramon H. Myers, and Mark R. Peattie, 210–71.

Reynolds, E. Bruce. "Anomaly or Model? Independent Thailand's Role in Japan's Asian Strategy, 1941–1943." In *The Japanese Wartime Empire, 1931–1945,* edited by Peter Duus, Ramon H. Myers, and Mark R. Peattie, 243–73.

Rong Shuren 荣漱仁. "Wojia jingying mianfen gongye de huiyi" 我家经营面粉工业的回忆 (Memoirs of management of the flour milling industry by my family). *Gongshang shiliao* 2: 40–53.

Rousso, Henry. *The Vichy Syndrome: History and Memory in France since 1944.*

Translated by Arthur Goldhammer. Cambridge: Harvard University Press, 1991.

Sassa, Hirō, and Shintarō Ryū. *Recent Political and Economic Developments in Japan.* Tokyo: Japanese Council, Institute of Pacific Relations, 1941.

Schumpeter, Elizabeth B., ed. *The Industrialization of Japan and Manchukuo, 1930–1940: Population, Raw Materials, and Industry.* New York: Macmillan, 1940.

Shan Guanchu 单冠初. "Riben qinHua de 'yizhan yangzhan' zhengce" 日本侵华的以战养战政策 (Japan's policy of "using the war to sustain the war" in its invasion of China). *Lishi yanjiu,* no. 4 (1991): 77–91.

Shang Fangmin 尚方民. "Jindai shiye jia Rongshi xiongdi jingying zhi daoxi" 近代实业家荣氏兄弟经营之道析 (Modern industrialists, the Rong brothers, and their way of management). *Minguo dang'an,* no. 2 (1992): 85–93.

Shanghai baihuo gongsi 上海百货公司, Shanghai shehui kexue yuan, jingji yanjiu suo 上海社会科学院经济研究所, and Shanghai shi gongshang xingzheng guanli ju 上海市工商行政管理局, eds. *Shanghai jindai baihuo shanghe shi* 上海近代百货商业史 (A history of modern department stores in Shanghai). Shanghai: Shanghai shehui kexue yuan chuban she, 1988.

"Shanghai hengchan gufen youxian gongsi wenjian" 上海恒产股份有限公司文件 (Documents on the Shanghai Real Estate Company, Ltd.). *Dang'an yu lishi,* no. 1 (1986): 31–37.

Shanghai Municipal Archives, Q61, Shanghai City Bank (Shanghai shi yinhang 上海市银行), Q65, Bank of Canton files (Guangzhou yinhang 广州银行).

Shanghai shehui kexue yuan, jingji yanjiu suo 上海社会科学院经济研究所, ed. *Liu Hongsheng qiye shiliao* 刘鸿生企业史料 (Historical materials on the Liu Hongsheng enterprises). 3 vols. Shanghai: Shanghai renmin chuban she, 1981.

———. *Rongjia qiye shiliao* 荣家企业史料 (Historical material on the Rong enterprises). 2 vols. Shanghai: Shanghai renmin chuban she, 1962.

———. *Shanghai yongan gongsi de chansheng fazhan he gaizao* 上海永安公司的产生发展和改造 (The creation, development, and reform of the Shanghai Yong'an [Wing On] Company). Shanghai: Shanghai renmin chuban she, 1981.

Shanghai shehui kexue yuan, Zhongguo qiye shi ziliao yanjiu zhongxin (Shanghai Academy of Social Sciences [SASS], Resource Center for Chinese Business History) 上海社会科学院，中国企业史资料研究中心. Archives. The Rong collections, sections R01–08, and R 15; Da Zhonghua xiangjiao chang (Great China rubber factory) collection, 2 vols. (unpublished material); Shanghai xiangjiao gongye tongye gonghui (The Shanghai Rubber Manufacturers Association), 2 vols.; Yonghe shiye gongsi (Yonghe Industrial Company), 1 vol.; and Zhengtai xiangjiao chang (Zhengtai Rubber factory), 2 vols.

Shanghai shi dang'an guan 上海市档案馆, ed. *Riwei Shanghai shi zhengfu* 日伪上海市政府 (The Japanese puppet government of Shanghai city). Beijing: Dang'an chuban she, 1986.

Shanghai shi gongshang xingzheng guanli ju 上海市工商行政管理局, Shanghai shi diyi jidian gongye ju 上海市第一机电工业局 and Jiqi gongye shi zubian 机器工业史组编, eds. *Shanghai minzu jiqi gongye* 上海民族机器工业 (The Shanghai national machine tool industry). 2 vols. Beijing: Zhonghua shuju, 1966, 1979.

Shanghai shi gongshang xingzheng guanli ju 上海市工商行政管理局, Shanghai shi

fangzhi pin gongsi 上海市纺织品公司 and Mianbu shangye shiliao zu 棉布商业
史料组, eds. *Shanghai shi mianbu shangye* 上海市棉布商业 (The cotton cloth
business of Shanghai). Beijing: Zhonghua shuju, 1979.

Shanghai shi gongshang xingzheng guanli ju 上海市工商行政管理局, Shanghai shi
xiangjiao gongye gongsi 上海市橡胶工业公司, and Shiliao gongye zuozu 史料
工业作组, eds. *Shanghai minzu xiangjiao gongye* 上海民族橡胶工业 (Shanghai's
national rubber industry). Beijing: Zhonghua shuju, 1979.

Shanghai shi liangshi ju 上海市粮食局, Shanghai shi gongshang xingzheng guanli
ju 上海市工商行政管理局, and Shanghai shehui kexue yuan, jingji yanjiu suo
jingji shi yanjiu shi 上海社会科学院经济研究所经济史研究室, eds. *Zhongguo
jindai mianfen gongye shi.* 中国近代面粉工业史 (A history of the flour milling
industry in modern China). Beijing: Zhonghua shuju chuban, 1987.

Shanghai shi wenshi guan 上海史文史馆, Shanghai shi renmin zhengfu canshi shi
上海市人民政府参事室 and Wenshi ziliao gongzuo weiyuan hui, 文史资料工作委
员会 eds. *Shanghai difang shi ziliao* 上海地方史资料(Materials on the local history of Shanghai). 5 vols. Shanghai: Shanghai shehui kexue yuan chuban she,
1982–86.

Shanghai wenshi ziliao xuanji 上海文史资料选辑 (Selections from literary and historical materials, Shanghai). Shanghai.

Shanghai wenshi ziliao xuanji: tongzhan gongzuo shiliao zhuanji 上海文史资料选
辑：统战工作史料选辑 (Selections of literary and historical materials, Shanghai: special collections on United Front work). Shanghai.

Shangye ziliao 商业资料 (Materials on commerce and industry). Beijing.

Shen Zuwei 沈祖炜. "Xiang Songmao: Diyi ge kangRi xunnan de qiye jia" 项松
茂第一个抗日殉难的企业家 (Xiang Songmao: The first entrepreneur martyred
in the anti-Japanese war of resistance). In *Guonan zhong de Zhongquo qiye
jia*, edited by Shen Zuwei and Du Xuncheng, 1–13.

Shen Zuwei, Du Xuncheng 杜恂诚. *Guonan zhong de Zhongguo qiye jia* 国难中
的中国企业家 (Chinese entrepreneurs during the national difficulty). Shanghai:
Shanghai shehui kexue yuan chuban she, 1996.

Shi Junshan 师俊山, Zhang Hongmin 张鸿敏. "Zhongguo huagong xiandao Fan
Xudong" 中国化工先导范旭东 (China's chemical industrial first leader, Fan
Xudong). In *Zhongguo da ziben jia zhuan*, vol. 3, edited by Zhao Yunsheng,
1–183.

Shi Qun 史群. "Guangfan jingying gezhong qiye de Liu Hongsheng" 广泛经营各
种企业的刘鸿生 (Liu Hongsheng who had extensive knowledge of managing
various kinds of enterprises). In *Zhongguo qiye jia liezhuan,* vol. 2, edited by
Xu Dixin, 103–22.

Shi Yuanhua 石源华. "Lun Riben dui Hua xin zhengce xia de RiWang guanxi"
论日本对华新政策下的日汪关系 (On Japanese–Wang Jingwei relations under
Japan's new China policy). *Lishi yanjiu,* no. 2 (1996): 103–17.

Shou Jinwen 寿进文. *Zhanshi Zhongguo de yinhang ye* 戰時中国的銀行业 (The
banking industry of wartime China). Chongqing: n. p., 1944.

Soda Saburō, ed. 曽田三郎. *Chūgoku kindaika katei no shidōsha tachi* 中國近代
化過程の指導者たち (Leaders in the process of China's modernization). Tokyo:
Tōhō shoten, 1997.

Song Ziyun 宋紫云. "Yu Zuoting—cong Ningbo shanghui huizhang dao Shanghai shi zong shanghui zhuwei" 俞佐庭从宁波商会会长到上海市总商会主委 (Yu Zuoting—from head of the Ningbo Chamber of Commerce to a director of the Shanghai General Chamber of Commerce). *Zhejiang WZXJ*, no. 39 (1989): 239–45.

Su Zhongbo 苏仲波. "Fangzhi qiye jia Liu Guojun" 纺织企业家刘国钧 (Textile industrialist Liu Guojun). *Jiangsu wenshi ziliao*, no. 34 (1989): 74–91.

Sun Choucheng 孙筹成 et al. "Yu Xiaqing shilue" 虞洽卿事略 (A biographical sketch of Yu Xiaqing). *Zhejiang WZXJ*, no. 32 (1986): 104–28.

Sun Guoda 孙果大. "Kangzhan qijian da houfang minzu gongye fazhan yuanyin chutan" 抗战期间大后方民族工业发展原因初探 (A preliminary investigation of the causes of the development of national industry in the rear areas during the war of resistance period). *Dang'an yu lishi*, no. 2 (1986): 60–65.

———. *Minzu gongye da qiantu—kangRi shiqi minying gongchang de neiqian* 民族工业大迁徒抗日时期民营工厂的内迁 (The great movement of national industry—the move to the interior by private industry during the anti-Japanese war of resistance period). Beijing: Zhongguo wenshi chuban she, 1991.

Takahashi Kamekichi. "Economic Significance of the East Asiatic Co-Prosperity Sphere." *Contemporary Japan* 10, no. 1 (January 1941): 39.

Takahashi Yasuryū 高橋泰隆. "Riben zhanling shiqi Huazhong diqu de suiyun ye" 日本占领时期华中地区的水运业 (Water transport industry in the Japanese occupied area of central China). Translated by Qian Xiaoming 錢小明 and Cheng Linsun 程麟苏. *Jingji xueshu ziliao*, no. 10 (1983): 56–59.

Takamura Naosuke 高村直助. "NitChū sensō to zaiKa bō 日中戰争と在華紡 (The Sino-Japanese war and textiles in China). In *NitChū sensō to NitChū kenkei*, edited by Inoue Kiyoshi and Etō Shikichi, 329–47.

Tamagna, Frank M., *Banking and Finance in China*. New York: Institute of Pacific Relations, 1942.

Tan Renjie 谭仁杰. "Guo Dihuo he Yong'an fangzhi gongsi" 郭棣活和永安纺织公司 (Guo Dihuo and the Yong'an Textile Company). *Guangdong WZXJ*, no. 56 (1988): 161–80.

Tan Xihong 谭熙鸿, ed. *Kangzhan shiqi zhi Zhongguo jingji* 抗戰時期之中國經濟 (China's economy in the war of resistance period). 3 vols. 1948. Reprint, Hong Kong: Longmen shudian, 1968.

Tang Kentang 汤肯堂. "Dali sichang jianshi" 大利絲厂簡史 (An abbreviated history of the Dali silk factory). *Shanghai WZXJ*, no. 53 (1986): 233–36.

Tang Xinyi 湯心仪. "Shanghai zhi tongzhi jingji" 上海之统制经济 (Shanghai's controlled economy). In *Zhangshi Shanghai jingji*, edited by Wang Jishen et al., 108–49.

Tang Yongzhang 唐庸章 and Gong Peiqing 龚培卿. "Hankou Fuxin diwu mianfen chang he Shenxin disi fangzhi chang" 汉口福新第五面粉厂和申新第四纺织厂 (Hankou's Fuxin #5 flour mill and Shenxin #4 textile mill). *Wuhan wenshi ziliao*, no. 33 (1988): 1–23.

Tang Zhenchang 唐振常, ed. *Shanghai shi* 上海史 (A history of Shanghai). Shanghai: Shanghai renmin chuban she, 1989.

The Orient Year Book, 1942. Tokyo: The Asia Statistics Co., 1942.

Tōa 東亞 (East Asia). Tokyo.

Tōa kenkyūjo 東亞研究所, ed. *Shina senryō chi keizai no hatten* 支那占領地經濟

の發展 (The development of the economy of occupied China). Tokyo: Tōa ken-kyūjo, 1944.

The Tokyo War Crimes Trial: The Complete Transcripts of the Proceedings of the International Military Tribunal for the Far East in Twenty-Two Volumes. Edited by R. John Pritchard, Sonia Magbanua Zaide. New York: Garland, 1981.

Tsunoda, Ryusaku, William Theodore De Bary, and Donald Keene, eds. *Sources of Japanese Tradition.* Vol. 2. New York: Columbia University Press, 1958.

Usui Katsumi. "The Politics of War, 1937–1941." In *The China Quagmire,* edited by James W. Morley, 309–435.

Wakeman, Frederic, Jr. *Policing Shanghai 1927–1937.* Berkeley: University of California Press, 1995.

———. *The Shanghai Badlands: Wartime Terrorism and Urban Crime, 1937–1941.* Cambridge: Cambridge University Press, 1996.

———. "Urban controls in Wartime Shanghai." In *Wartime Shanghai,* edited by Wen-hsin, 133–56.

Waldron, Arthur. "China's New Remembering of World War II: The Case of Zhang Zizhong," *Modern Asian Studies* 30, no. 4 (1996): 945–78.

Walker, Kathy Le Mons. *Chinese Modernity and the Peasant Path: Semicolonialism in the Northern Yangzi Delta.* Stanford, Calif.: Stanford University Press, 1999.

Wan Lin 萬林. "Wuxi Rongshi jiazu baofa shi" 無錫榮氏家族暴發史 (The history of the sudden rise of the Rong family of Wuxi). *Jingji daobao* (Economic report), December 14, 1947, no. 50, 1–7.

Wang Daliang 王大亮. *Weijing dawang, Wu Yunchu* 味精大王吳蘊初 (The MSG king, Wu Yunchu). Beijing: Jiefang jun chuban she, 1995.

Wang Fan-hsi. *Memoirs of a Chinese Revolutionary.* Translated by Gregor Benton. New York: Columbia University Press, 1991.

Wang Gengtang 王賡唐, Feng Ju 冯炬, and Gu Yiqun 顾一群. "Wuxi jiefang qian zhuming de liujia minzu gongshang ye ziben" 无锡解放前著名的六家民族工商业资本 (The six well-known commercial and industrial capitalist families in Wuxi before liberation). *Jiangsu wenshi ziliao,* no. 31 (1989): 1–30.

Wang He 王河. "Wei fazhan Zhongguo siye er xiangji fendou" 为发展中国丝业而相继奋斗 (The development of the Chinese silk industry and its struggles). *Jiangsu wenshi ziliao,* no. 34 (1989): 180–194.

Wang Jishen 王季深. "Ji jinrong jia Li Fusun" 记金融家李馥荪 (Remembering the financier Li Fusun). *Zhejiang wenshi ziliao,* no. 32 (1986): 163–72.

Wang Jishen et al., eds. *Zhanshi Shanghai jingji* 戰時上海經濟 (Wartime Shanghai's economy). Shanghai: Zhongguo kexue gongsi, 1945.

Wang Ke-wen. "Collaborators and Capitalists: The Politics of 'Material Control' in Wartime Shanghai." *Chinese Studies in History* 26, no. 1 (fall 1992): 42–62.

Wang Renze 汪仁泽. "Da Zhonghua xiangjiao chang chuangban ren Yu Zhiqing" 大中华橡胶厂创办人余芝卿 (The founder of the Da Zhonghua Rubber Factory, Yu Zhiqing). *Zhejiang WZXJ,* no. 39 (1989): 195–200.

———. "Jindai hangyun ye jubo Yu Xiaqing" 近代航运业巨擘虞洽卿 (Modern shipping leader Yu Xiaqing). In *Zhongguo qiye jia liezhuan* (Biographies of Chinese entrepreneurs), vol. 2, edited by Xu Dixin, 32–44.

———. "KangRi xunsheng de aiguo qiye jia Xiang Songmao" 抗日殉身的爱国企业家项松茂 (The martyr of the war of resistance, the patriotic industrialist Xiang Songmao). *Zhejiang WZXJ*, no. 39 (1989): 177–91.

———. "Kui Yanfang: rexin jiuji shiye de aiguo shiye jia" 黄延芳热心救济事业的爱国实业家 (Kui Yanfang: A patriotic industrialist who ardently strove to develop industry). *Zhejiang WZXJ*, no. 39 (1989): 249–55.

Wang Shijun 王世均. "Kong Song guanliao ziben shi zenyang yinmou bingtun Minsheng gongsi de" 孔宋官僚资本是怎样阴谋并吞民生公司 (How did the bureaucratic capitalists H. H. Kung and T. V. Soong plot to take over the Minsheng Company). *WSZJ*, no. 49 (1986): 183–94.

Wang Zhixian 王志贤. "Shanghai gudao de huobi zhan" 上海孤岛的货币战 (The currency war in solitary island Shanghai). *Shanghai difang shi ziliao 1*, (1982): 167–69.

Wang Zhong 王忠 and Han Zhengbin 韩正彬. "Gongye xiandao, gong zai Zhonghua: Ji huagong shiye jia Fan Xudong" 工业先导功在中华记化学工实业家范旭东 (Remembering chemical industrialist Fan Xudong, a leader in China's industry). *Jiangsu WZXJ*, no. 34 (1989): 42–73.

Wasserstein, Bernard. "Ambiguities of Occupation: Foreign Resisters and Collaborators in Wartime Shanghai." In *Wartime Shanghai*, edited by Wen-hsin Yeh, 24–41.

Wei Dazhi 魏达志. "Shanghai 'gudao jingji fanrong' shimo" 上海孤岛经济繁荣始末 (Shanghai's economic flourishing during the isolated island period, from beginning to end). *Fudan xuebao*, no. 4 (August 12, 1985): 109–13.

Wenshi ziliao xuanji 文史资料选辑 (Selections from literary and historical materials). Beijing: Zhongguo wenshi chuban she. Vols. 1–100. Reprint 1986, and continuing.

Wilson, Dick. *When Tigers Fight: The Story of the Sino-Japanese War, 1937–1945*. New York: The Viking Press, 1982.

Wong, Siu-lun. "Business Networks, Cultural Values, and the State in Hong Kong and Singapore." In *Chinese Business Enterprise in Asia*, edited by R. A. Brown, 136–53.

———. "The Chinese Family Firm: A Model." *The British Journal of Sociology* 36, no. 1 (1985): 58–72.

———. *Emigrant Entrepreneurs: Shanghai Industrialists in Hong Kong*. Hong Kong: Oxford University Press, 1988.

Wright, Tim. *The Chinese Economy in the Early Twentieth Century: Recent Chinese Studies*. New York: St. Martin's Press, 1992.

———. "'The Spiritual Heritage of Chinese Capitalism': Recent Trends in the Historiography of Chinese Enterprise Management." In *Using the Past to Serve the Present: Historiography and Politics in Contemporary China*, edited by Jonathan Unger, 205–238. Armonk, N.Y.: M. E. Sharpe, 1993.

Wu Zhichao 吴志超. "Wu Yunchu ji qi huagong shiye" 吴蕴初及其化工事业 (Wu Yunchu and his chemical industrial enterprises). *Shanghai WZXJ*, no. 22 (1978): 83–118.

Wuhan wenshi ziliao 武汉文史资料 (Literary and historical materials, Wuhan). Wuhan.

Xianggang Yong'an youxian gongsi 香港永安有限公司. *Xianggang yong'an you-*

xian gongsi nianwu zhounian jinian lu 香港永安有限公司廿五週年纪念錄 (A record of 25 years of the Hong Kong Yong'an [Wing On] Company). Hong Kong: Yong'an Company, 1932.

Xin shenbao 新申报 (The new Shenbao). Shanghai, 1937–1945.

Xing Jianrong 邢建榕 and Qian Yuli 钱玉莉. "Sange zuole hanjian de haishang wenren" 三个做了汉奸的海上闻人 (Three coastal notables who became traitors). *Dang'an yu lishi,* no. 3 (1989): 67–72.

Xu Dingxin 徐鼎新. "Fan Xudong: Quan quan aiguo xin, yi yi '*Haiwang*' hun" 范旭东拳拳爱国心熠熠海王魂 (Fan Xudong: The fists of a patriot, the brilliant and luminous spirit of [the journal] *Haiwang*). In *Guonan zhong de Zhongguo qiye jia,* edited by Shen Zuwei and Du Xuncheng, 135–49.

———. "Liu Guojun: 'Shijie mian wangguo' de kuxin zhuiqiu zhe" 刘国钱世界棉王国的苦心追求者 (Liu Guojun: The painstaking quest of the 'Shijie mian wangguo') In *Guonan zhong de Zhongguo qiye jia,* edited by Shen Zuwei and Du Xuncheng, 93–105.

———. "Yong'an qiye jituan de Guo Linshuang" 永安企业集团的郭琳爽 (Guo Linshuang of the Yong'an enterprise group). In *Zhongguo qiye jia liezhuan,* vol. 2, edited by Xu Dixin, 216–228.

Xu Dixin 許滌新, ed. *Zhongguo qiye jia liezhuan* 中国企业家列传 (Biographies of Chinese entrepreneurs). 3 vols. Beijing: Jingji ribao chuban she, 1988–1989.

Xu Guomao 徐国懋. "Zhou Zuomin he Jincheng yinhang" 周作民和金城银行 (Zhou Zuomin and the Jincheng Bank). [*Shanghai*] *WZXJ,* no. 23 (1979): 137–71.

Xu Nianhui 許念晖. *Yu Xiaqing de yisheng* 虞洽卿的一生 (The life of Yu Xiaqing). *WZXJ,* no. 15 (1986): 170–200.

Xu Tengba 許滕八. "Fan Xudong yu Yongli Tanggu jianchang" 范旭东与永利塘沽碱厂 (Fan Xudong and the Yongli Soda Plant at Tanggu). *Jiangsu WZXJ,* no. 25 (1988): 38–46.

Xu Weiyong 許维雍 and Huang Hanmin 黄汉民. *Rongjia qiye fazhan shi* 荣家企业发展史 (A history of the development of the Rong family enterprises). Beijing: Renmin chuban she, 1985.

Xu Xinwu 徐新吾. "Kangzhan shiqi Riben diguo zhuyi dui Hua jingji qinlue gaishu" 抗战时期日本帝国主义对华经济侵略概述 (The economic invasion of China by Japanese imperialism during the war of resistance period). *Jingji xueshu ziliao* 经济学术资料 (Materials on economic studies), no. 10 (1982): 30–34.

Xu Ying 徐盈. "Wu Yunchu ji qi huagong shiye" 吴蕴初及其化工事业 (Wu Yunchu and his chemical industrial enterprises). In *Zhongguo qiye jia liezhuan,* vol. 1, edited by Xu Dixin, 216–28.

Xue Wenshi 薛聞史. "Ji jiefang qian Wuxi Qingfeng mian fangzhi chang" 记解放前无锡庆丰棉纺织厂 (On the Qingfeng cotton textile plant in Wuxi before liberation). *Jiangsu wenshi ziliao,* no. 31 (1989): 76–88.

Yan Xuexi 严学熙. "Riben dui Nantong Dasheng qiye de lueduo" 日本对南通大生企业的掠夺 (Japan's plundering of the Dasheng enterprises of Nantong). In *Kangri zhanzhen shishi tansuo,* edited by Jiangsu sheng lishi xuehui, 206–12.

Yan Zhongping 严中平 et al., eds. *Zhongguo jingdai jingji shi tongji ziliao xuanji* 中国近代经济史统计资料选辑 (Selected statistics on modern Chinese economic history). Beijing: Kexue chuban she, 1955.

Yang, Daqing. "Review Essay: Convergence or Divergence? Recent Historical Writings on the Rape of Nanjing." *American Historical Review* 104, no. 3 (June 1999): 842–65.

Yang Shaozhen 楊少振 and Hong Furong 洪福荣. "Zhengtai xiangjiao chang ershi er nian de jingli" 正泰橡胶厂二十二年的经历 (The experience of twenty-two years of the Zhengtai Rubber factory). *Shanghai WZXJ*, no. 32 (1980): 148–67.

Yang Tongyi 杨通谊. "Wuxi Yangshi yu Zhongguo mianfang ye de guanxi" 无锡杨氏与中国绵纺业的关系 (The relationship of Wuxi's Yang family and China's cotton textile industry). *Gongshang shiliao*, vol. 2, 54–70.

Yao Shengxiang 姚盛祥 and Shen Jiazhen 沈家振. "Wangwei Zhongyang chubei yinhang shimo" 汪伪中央储备银行始末 (The puppet Wang government's Central Reserve Bank from beginning to end). *Jiangsu WZXJ*, no. 29 (1989): 236–63.

Yeh, Wen-hsin. *Provincial Passages: Culture, Space, and the Origins of Chinese Communism*. Berkeley: University of California Press, 1996.

———. "The Republican Origins of the *Danwei*: The Case of Shanghai's Bank of China." In *Danwei: The Changing Chinese Workplace in Historical and Comparative Perspective*, edited by Xiaobo Lu and Elizabeth J. Perry, 60–88. Armonk, N.Y.: M. E. Sharpe, 1997.

———. "Urban Warfare and Underground Resistance: Heroism in the Chinese Secret Service during the War of Resistance." In *Wartime Shanghai,* edited by Wen-hsin Yeh, 111–32.

Yeh, Wen-hsin, ed. *Wartime Shanghai*. London: Routledge, 1998.

Yen Ching-hwang. "The Wing On Company in Hong Kong and Shanghai: A Case Study of Modern Overseas Chinese Enterprise, 1907–1949." In *Chinese Business Enterprise*, vol. 1, edited by R. A. Brown, 365–97.

Yinhang zhoubao 银行週报 (Bankers' weekly). Shanghai, 1937–1940.

Yoda Yoshiie 依田喜家, ed. *NitChū sensō senryō chiku shihai shiryō* 日中戰争占領地区支配資料 (Materials on control of the occupied areas during the Sino-Japanese War). Tokyo: Ryūkai shosha, 1987.

Young, Arthur N. *China and the Helping Hand, 1937–1945*. Cambridge, Mass.: Harvard University Press, 1963.

———. *China's Wartime Finance and Inflation, 1937–1945*. Cambridge, Mass.: Harvard University Press, 1965.

———. "Papers." Stanford, Calif.: Hoover Institution Archives, Boxes 68, 69.

Young, Louise. "Imagined Empire: The Cultural Construction of Manchukuo." In *The Japanese Wartime Empire, 1931–1945,* edited by Peter Duus, Ramon H. Myers, and Mark R. Peattie, 71–96.

———. *Japan's Total Empire: Manchuria and the Culture of Wartime Imperialism*. Berkeley: University of California Press, 1998.

Yu Songjing 于松晶. Xue Wei 薛微 "KangRi genju di de wujie guanli" 抗日根据地的物价管理 (Price control in the anti-Japanese base areas). *Lishi dang'an*, no. 1 (1999): 125–30.

Yu Xiaoqiu 余啸秋. "Yongli jianchang he yingshang buneimen yangjian gongsi douzheng qianhou jilue" 永利碱厂和英商卜内门洋碱公司斗争前后记略 (A complete record of the struggle between the Yongli Alkali Soda Company and the British Brunner, Mond and Co. Alkali Soda Company). *WZXJ*, no. 80 (1986): 44–59.

Yu Zhongnan 余中南. "Wo chuangban Zhonghua niantong chang de jingguo" 我
创办中华辗铜厂的经过 (The experiences of the Zhonghua copper rolling mill
which I founded). *Shanghai WZXJ*, no. 18 (1964): 152–63.

Yuan Xieming 袁燮铭. "Shanghai gudao yu da houfang de maoyi" 上海孤岛与大
后方的贸易 (The trade between the rear areas and the solitary island Shanghai). *KangRi zhanzheng yanjiu*, no. 3 (1994): 48–67.

Yuan Yuquan 袁愈佺. "Kangzhan shiqi Rijun shiyong jia chaopiao de zhenxiang"
抗战时期日军使用假钞票的真相 (The actual situation of the Japanese military
using bogus banknotes during the war of resistance period). *Shanghai WZXJ*,
no. 58 (1988): 103–12.

———. "Rikou jiaqiang lueduo Huazhong zhanlue wuzi paozhi 'shangtong hui'
jingguo" 日寇加强掠夺华中战略物资炮制商统会经过 (The Japanese enemy's increased plundering of Shanghai strategic material and concoction of the National Commerce Control Commission). *Dang'an yu lishi,* pt. 1, no. 4 (1986):
82–87; pt. 2, no. 1 (1987): 99–102; pt. 3, no. 2 (1987): 97–101.

Yuda Hua fangzhi ziben jituan shiliao bianxie zu, ed. 裕大华纺织资本集团史料编
写组. *Yuda Hua fangzhi ziben jituan shiliao* 裕大华纺织资本集团史料 (Historical materials on the Yuda Hua textile capitalist group). Wuhan: Hubei renmin chuban she, 1984.

Zelin, Madeleine. "Merchant Dispute Mediation in Twentieth-Century Zigong,
Sichuan." In *Civil Law in Qing and Republican China*, edited by Kathryn
Bernhardt and Philip C. C. Huang, 249–86. Stanford, Calif.: Stanford Uni-
versity Press, 1994.

Zhang Gaofeng 张高峰. "Kuhai yanbian chuangye jishi" 苦海盐边创业纪实 (A true
record of the endless difficulty in setting up the salt business). In *Huagong
xiandao—Fan Xudong,* 15–31.

Zhang Jianhui 章剑慧. "Xueni zaji—wo de chuangye shengya" 雪泥杂记我的创业
生涯 (A record of past events—my life as founder of industry). *WZXJ*, no.
122 (1991): 91–106.

Zhang Jinhua 张今华. "Aiguo shiye jia Tang Junyuan" 爱国实业家唐君远 (Patriotic industrialist Tang Junyuan). *Shanghai WZXJ*, no. 80 (1996): 16–23.

Zhang Jinsheng 张金盛 and Hu Xinsheng 胡新生. "Zhongguo huaxue boli gongye
xianchu—Wang Xinsheng" 中国化学玻璃工业先驱王辛生 (China's vanguard in
the chemical glass industry—Wang Xinsheng). *Renwu*, no. 3 (1989): 119–26.

Zhang Limin 张利民. "Riben Huabei kaifa huishe zijin touxi" 日本华北开发社
资金透析 (An analysis of the capital of Japan's North China Development Corporation). *KangRi zhanzheng yanjiu*, no. 1 (1994): 84–98.

Zhang Nengyuan 张能远. "Fan Xudong he Zhongguo jindai huaxue gongye" 范
旭东和中国近代化学工业 (Fan Xudong and China's modern chemical industry).
Jiangsu wenshi ziliao, no. 25 (1988): 47–96.

Zhang Qifu 张圻福. "Kangzhan shiqi de Liu Hongsheng" 抗战时期的刘鸿生 (Liu
Hongsheng during the war of resistance era). *Minguo dang'an*, no. 2 (1995):
100–104.

Zhang Shijie 张士杰. "Liu Guojun zhuanlue" 刘国钧传略 (A brief biography of
Liu Guojun). *Minguo dang'an,* no. 2 (1990): 129–31.

Zhang Tongyi 张同义. *Fan Xudong zhuan* 范旭东传. Changsha: Hunan renmin
chuban she, 1987.

Zhang Xianwen 张宪文 et al., eds. *Minguo dang'an yu minguo shi xueshu taolun wenji* 民国档案与民国史学术讨论文集 (A collection of essays on the study of Republican history and the Republican archives). Beijing: Dang'an chuban she, 1988.

Zhang Xichang 张锡昌 et al. *Zhanshi de Zhongguo jingji* 戰時的中國經濟 (Wartime economy of China). Guilin: Kexue shudian, 1943.

Zhang Zhizhong 章執中. "Aiguo shiye jia Fan Xudong" 爱国实业家范旭东 (Patriotic industrialist, Fan Xudong). In *Huagong xiandao—Fan Xudong*, 32–48.

Zhang Zuguo 張祖国. "Ershi shijie shangban ye Riben zai Zhongguo dalu de guoce huishe" 二十世纪上半叶日本在中国大陆的国策会社 (Japanese national policy companies on the Chinese mainland in the first half of the 20th century). *Lishi yanjiu*, no. 6 (1986): 161–73.

Zhao Yunsheng 赵云声, ed. *Zhongguo da ziben jia zhuan* 中国大资本家传 (Biographies of the big Chinese capitalists). 10 vols. Changchun: Shidai wenyi chuban she, 1994.

Zhejiang wenshi ziliao xuanji 浙江文史资料选辑 (Selections from literary and historical materials, Zhejiang province). Hangzhou.

Zheng Kelun 鄭克論. "Lunxian qu de gongkuang ye" 淪陷區的工鑛業 (Mining and industry in the occupied areas). *Jingji jianshe jikan* 經濟建設季刊 (Economic reconstruction quarterly) 1, no. 4 (April 1943): 247–58.

Zheng Zeqing 鄭泽青. "Song Ziwen he Shanghai Yong'an gongsi de jiaowang" 宋子文和上海永安公司的交往 (T. V. Soong and his dealings with the Shanghai Yong'an Company). *Shanghai dang'an* 上海档案 (Shanghai archives), no. 2 (1990): 43–46.

Zhiye shenghuo 職業生活 (Professional life). Shanghai, 1939.

Zhongguo di'er lishi dang'an guan 中国第二历史档案馆. "1942 nianqian Riben zai Zhongguo lunxian qu lueduo gongsi gongkuang ye jingying ji shouyi diaocha" 1942年前日本在中国沦陷区掠夺公私工矿业经营及收益调查 (Materials concerning the investigation of Chinese industrial and mining enterprises robbed by the Japanese aggressors before 1942). *Minguo dang'an*, no. 1 (1992): 31–39.

————. "Wang wei sibu lianxi huiyi guanyu tiaozheng ZhongRi heban jiaotong shiye jueyi an" 汪伪四部联席会议关于调整中日合办交通事业决议案 (Draft resolution of the Wang puppet four ministries conference regarding adjustment of Sino-Japanese joint management of transportation facilities). *Minguo dang'an*, no. 2 (1991): 57–65.

————. "Wang wei zhengquan 'jieshou' Riben junguan gongchang de yizu shiliao" 汪伪政权"接收"日本军管工厂的一组史料 (Historical materials on the Wang puppet regime's "retaking" factories managed by the Japanese military). *Minguo dang'an*, no. 2 (1990): 52–63.

Zhongguo kexue yuan, Shanghai jingji yanjiu suo 中国科学院上海经济研究所, and Shanghai shehui kexue yuan, Jingji yanjiu suo 上海社会科学院经济研究所, eds. *Hengfeng shachan de fasheng fazhan yu gaizao* 恒丰纱厂的发生发展与改造 (The creation, development, and reform of Hengfeng textiles). Shanghai: Shanghai renmin chuban she, 1958.

Zhongguo renmin zhengzhi xieshang huiyi quanguo weiyuan hui 中国人民政治协商会议全国委员会 and Wenshi ziliao yanjiu weiyuan hui 文史资料研究委员会,

eds. *Gongshang shiliao* 工商史料 (Historical materials on industry and commerce). 2 vols. Beijing: Wenshi ziliao chuban she, 1980, 1981.

Zhou Fohai 周佛海. *Zhou Fohai riji* 周佛海日记 (The diary of Zhou Fohai). Shanghai: Shanghai renmin chuban she, 1984.

Zhou Zhengang 周振刚. "Wuhan de Rongjia qiye" 武汉的荣家企业 (The Rong family enterprises in Wuhan). *Dang'an yu lishi*, no. 3 (1986): 75–80.

Zhu Ronghua 朱荣华. "Zhang Jian yu Nantong Dasheng shachang" 张謇与南通大生纱厂 (Zhang Jian and the Nantong Dasheng textile mill). *Jiangsu wenshi ziliao*, no. 31 (1989): 60–75.

Zhu Ting 朱婷. "Fang Yexian: daozai diwei qiangtan xia" 方液仙倒在敌伪枪弹下 (Fang Yexian: Under enemy gunfire). In *Guonan zhong de Zhongguo qiye jia*, edited by Shen Zuwei and Du Xuncheng, 14–28.

Zhu Xiwu 朱希武. "Dacheng fangzhi ran gongsi yu Liu Guojun" 大成纺织染公司与刘国钧 (The Dacheng textile mill and dyeing company and Liu Guojun). *Gongshang shiliao* 1, 44–54.

Zhu Zijia 朱子家 [pseud. of Jin Xiongbai]. *Wang zhengquan de kaichang yu shouchang* 汪政权的开场与收场 (The beginning and end of the Wang regime). 5 vols. Hong Kong: Chunqiu zazhi, 1959–1964.

Zhu Zuotong 朱作同 and Mei Yi 梅益, eds. *Shanghai yiri* 上海一日 (One day in Shanghai). Shanghai: Meishang Huamei chuban gongsi, 1939.

Zong Yu 宗于. "Manhua modai Zhaoshang ju" 漫话末代招商局 (Rambling talk of the last era of the China Merchants Steam Navigation Company). *WZXJ*, no. 64 (1986): 235–51.

Zou Bingwen 邹秉文 "Yongli liusuan ya chang jianchang jingguo" 永利硫酸铔厂建厂经过 (The establishment of the Yongli ammonium sulfate factory). *WZXJ*, no. 19 (1986): 95–111.

Glossary

Names of well-known places and people, as well as commonly used terms, have been omitted.

aiguo shiye jia 爱国实业家
Aikokuryū Yōkō 愛克隆洋行
Anda shachang 安达纱厂
Aoki shoten 青木書店
Ayukawa Yoshisuke 鮎川義介
Baofeng 保丰
Buneimen (Brunner, Mond, and Company) 卜内門
Cai Jiansan 蔡缄三
Cai Zengji 蔡增基
Changxing fangzhi yinran 昌兴纺织印染
Chen Baochu 陳葆初
Chen Bofan 陳伯蕃
Chen Deming 陳德铭
Chen Guangfu 陳光甫
Chen Lu 陳籙
Chen Riping 陈日平
Chen Tiaofu 陳调甫
Cheng Jingtang 程敬堂
Chōsen bōseki kōgyō kumiai 朝鮮紡績工業組會
Chu Minyi 褚民誼
Da Shanghai wasi gufen youxian gongsi 大上海瓦斯股份有限公司
Da Zhonghua huochai gufen youxian gongsi 大中华火柴股份有限公司
Da Zhonghua xiangjiao chang 大中华橡胶厂
Dafeng 大丰

Dafu jianye gongsi 大孚建业公司
Dahua 大华
Dahua baoxian gongsi 大华保险公司
Dai Nippon bōseki kaisha 大日本紡績會社
Dai Tōa kyōeiken 大東亞共栄圏
Dai Zimu 戴自牧
Daikō 大康
Dali sichang 大利丝厂
Daming fangzhi ran gongsi 大明纺纸染公司
Deshang yuandong jiqi gongsi jingli Dasheng fangzhi gongsi 德商远东机器公司
    经理大生纺织公司
Dingchang 鼎昌
Dōkō bōseki kabushiki kaisha 同興紡績株式會社
Fan Xudong 范旭东
Fenmai tongzhi weiyuan hui 粉麦统制委员会
Fu Xiao'an 傅筱庵
Fufeng 阜丰
Fujimura Ichinori 藤村一則
Funatsu Tatsuichirō 船津辰一郎
Fuxin 福新
Fuxing gongsi 复兴公司
Gao Baixun 高伯浚
Gongkuang diaozheng chu 工矿调整处
gongye jiuguo 工业救国
gongye Riben, nongye Zhongguo 工业日本农业中国
Gu Gengyu 古耕虞
Gu Naizhi 顾迺智
Gu Xinyi 顾馨一
Guangfeng mianfen chang 广丰面粉厂
Guangqin shachang 广勤纱厂
gudao 孤岛
Guo Dihuo 郭棣活
Guo Le 郭乐
Guo Linshuang 郭琳爽
Guo Quan 郭泉
Guo Shun 郭顺
Haiwang 海王
Haiwang xing 海王星
Hangzhou shi zhi'an weichi hui 杭州市治安维持会
Hangzhou shi zizhi weiyuan hui 杭州市自治委员会
hanjian 汉奸
Harada Kamakichi 原田熊吉
Hefeng gongsi 合丰公司
Hengfeng shachang 恒丰纱厂
Hidaka Shin'rokurō 日高信六郎
Hong Fumei 洪福楣
Hong'an 虹安

Hongda 宏大
Hongkou 虹口
Hong Nianzu 洪念祖
Hongqiao 虹桥
Hongye dichan gongsi 宏业地产公司
Hon'iden Yoshio 本位田祥男
Honjō Shigeru 本庄繁
Hou Debang 候德榜
Hu Bijiang 胡笔江
Hua Du'an 华笃安
Hua Shuqin 华叔琴
Huafeng 华丰
Huafeng tangci chang 华丰搪瓷厂
Huainan meikuang gufen youxian gongsi 淮南煤矿股份有限公司
Huang Chujiu 黄楚九
Huang Huannan 黄焕南
Huanghai huaxue gongye yanjiu she 黄海化学工业研究社
Huaxin 华新
Huaxing shangye yinhang 华兴商业银行
Huaxue shijie 化学世界
Huaye heji huochai gongsi 华业和记火柴公司
Huaye huochai gonsi 华业火柴公司
Huazhong cansi gufen youxian gongsi 华中蚕丝股份有限公司
Huazhong dianqi tongxin gufen youxian gongsi 华中电气通信股份有限公司
Huazhong dushi zidong che gufen youxian gongsi 华中都市自动车股份有限公司
Huazhong huochai gufen youxian gongsi 华中火柴股份有限公司
Huazhong kuangye gufen youxian gongsi 华中矿业股份有限公司
Huazhong shuichan gufen youxian gongsi 华中水产股份有限公司
Huazhong shuidian gufen youxian gongsi 华中水电股份有限公司
Huazhong tiedao gufen youxian gongsi 华中铁道股份有限公司
Huazhong yanye youxian gongsi 华中盐业有限公司
Huazhong yunshu gufen youxian gongsi 华中运输股份有限公司
huochai dawang 火柴大王
Ikeda Kikunae 池田菊苗
Inoue Yasutada 井上泰忠
Ishin 維新
issen yōsen 以戰養戰
Iwanami shoten 岩波書店
Jiafeng 嘉丰
Jiang Junhui 蒋君辉
Jiang Shangda 江上达
Jiang Yiping 江一平
Jin Jiang fandian 锦江饭店
Jin Xiongbai 金雄白
Jinji 锦记
Jin Zuhui 金祖惠
jitsugyōka 实业家

Jiuda jingyan gongsi 久大精益公司
Jiuda yanye gongsi 久大盐业公司
Jiufeng mianfeng 九丰面粉
Jiuji zongshu 救济总署
jun guanli 军管理
Kachū matchi kabushiki kaisha 華中燐寸株式會社
Kanegafuchi bōseki kabushiki kaisha 鐘淵紡績 株式會社
Kang Xinru 康心如
Katakura seishi 片倉製絲
Kayū seifun konsu 華友制粉公司
kejuan zashui 苛捐杂税
Kimura Masutarō 木村増太郎
Kinoshita Yae 木下八重
Kishi Nobusuke 岸信介
Kita Seiichi 喜多誠一
Kita Shina kaihatsu kabushiki kaisha 北支那開發株式會社
Kōain 興亞院
Kōdai 公大
Kodama Kenji 兒玉謙次
Kuroda Keitarō 黒田慶太郎
Li Enhao 李恩浩
Li Guojie 李国杰
Li Guowei 李国伟
Li Pingshu 李平书
Li Shengbo 李昇伯
Li Shi'an 李石安
Li Wujiu 厉无咎
Li Zhuchen 李烛尘
Liang Hongzhi 梁鸿志
Lihua 丽华
Lihua meikuang 利华煤矿
Lin Kanghou 林康候
Liu Guojun 刘国鈞
Liu Hangchen 刘航琛
Liu Hankun 刘汉坤
Liu Hongsheng 刘鸿生
Liu Jingji 刘靖基
Liu Jisheng 刘吉生
Liu Nianli 刘念礼
Liu Nianyi 刘念义
Liu Nianzhi 刘念智
Liu Nianzhong 刘念忠
Liu Qinghong 刘清洪
Lixin 丽新
Longchang chang 隆昌厂
Lu Bohong 陆伯鸿
Lu Zuofu 卢作孚

Ma Yingbiao 马应彪
Maoxin 茂新
Matsui Iwane 松井石根
Meiguang huochai 美光火柴
Mengjiang lianhe weiyuan hui 蒙疆联合委员会
Mengjiang yinhang 蒙疆银行
Mianhua tongzhi weiyuan hui 棉花统制委员会
Mianye tongzhi weiyuan hui 棉业统制委员会
Mianzhipin lianhe hui 棉制品联合会
Mikyō 三興
Miliang tongzhi weiyuan hui 米粮统制委员会
Minfeng 民丰
Minsheng shiye gongsi 民生实业公司
Mu Ouchu 穆藕初
Naigai wata kaisha 内外棉会社
Naka Shina shinkō kabushiki kaisha 中支那振興株式會社
Nie Guangqi 聂光琪
Nie Lusheng 聂潞生
Nie Qigui 聂缉椝
Nie Yuntai 聂云台
Nikka bōseki kaisha 日華紡績會社
Ning Sihong 宁思宏
Nippon menka kabushiki kaisha 日本棉花株式會社
Nishi Yoshiaki 西義顯
Nishio Toshizō 西尾寿造
Nisshin kisen kaisha 日清汽船会社
Nomura Michikuni 野村通邦
Ogawa Gorō 小河五郎
Ōkawa Shūmei 大川周明
Ōnishi Shōten kabushiki kaisha 大西商店株式會社
Onoda yōkai kabushiki kaisha 小野田洋灰株式會社
Ōtani Son'yū 大谷尊由
Pan Hannian 潘汉年
Qi Fuming 戚福铭
Qian Fenggao 钱風高
Qin Defang 秦德芳
Qingfeng 庆丰
Qingxin gongsi 庆新公司
Qiye yinhang 企业银行
Quanguo huochai chanxiao lianying she 全国火柴产銷联营社
Quanguo shangye tongzhi weiyuan hui 全国商业统制委员会
Ren Bao'an 任保安
Ren Zhuoqun 任桌群
Rihua xiangjiao gongchang lianhe hui 日华橡胶工厂联合会
Rong Baochun 荣宝椿
Rong Binggen 荣炳根
Rong Desheng 荣德生

Rong Er'ren 荣尔仁
Rong Hongqing 荣鸿庆
Rong Hongsan 荣鸿三
Rong Hongyuan 荣鸿元
Rong Shuren 荣漱仁
Rong wen keji youxian gongsi 荣文科技有限公司
Rong Weiren 榮伟仁
Rong Yiren (third son) 荣伊仁
Rong Yiren (fourth son) 荣毅仁
Rong Yixin 荣一心
Rong Zhijian 荣智健
Rong Zhiqin 荣智勤
Rong Zhixin 荣智鑫
Rong Zongjing 荣宗敬
Sanbei lunchuan gongsi 三北论船公司
Sansei sangyō kabushiki kaisha 山西産 業株式會社
Shan Shō seijū kabushiki kaisha 上章制絨株式會社
Shang Zhang maorong fangzhi gufen youxian gongsi 上章毛绒纺织股份有限公司
Shanghai dushi jiaotong gufen youxian gongsi 上海都市交通股份有限公司
Shanghai gongchang qianyi lindu weiyuan hui 上海工厂迁移临督委员会
Shanghai hengchan gufen youxian gongsi 上海恒产股份有限公司
Shanghai neihe lunchuan gufen youxian gongsi 上海内河轮船股份有限公司
Shanghai qu diwei chanye chu 上海区敌伪产业处
Shanghai shi guomin duiRi jingji juejiao weiyuan hui 上海市国民对日经济绝交委
    员会
Shanghai shi minxie hui 上海市民协会
Shanghai shi shangbing jiuhu weiyuan hui 上海市伤兵救护委员会
Shanghai shuini gongsi 上海水泥公司
Shanghai tianchu weijing gufen youxian gongsi 上海天厨味精股份有限公司
Shanghai xiangjiao gongye tongye gonghui 上海橡胶工业同业工会
Shanghai Zhejiang xingye yinhang 上海浙江兴业银行
Shanghai zilai huo gongsi 上海自来火公司
Shangtong hui 商统会
Shanhai bōseki kabushiki kaisha 上海紡 績株式會社
Shanhou jiuji zhongshu 善后救济总署
Shenchang 慎昌
Shenxin 申新
Shi Fuhou 施复侯
Shijie 世界
Song Feiqing 宋棐卿
Song Zejiu 宋则久
Su Taiyu 苏汰余
Sun Shupei 孙树培
Sun Xuewu 孙学悟
Sun Zhongli 孙仲立
suzhan sujue 速战速决
Suzhou Hongsheng huochai chang 苏州鸿生火柴厂

Suzuki Kakusaburō 鈴木格三郎
Taguchi Chōjiro 田口長治郎
Taguchi Takeo 田口武夫
Takahashi Yasutaka 高橋泰隆
Tang Baoqian 唐保谦
Tang Shoumin 唐寿民
Tang Xiangting 唐骧庭
Tang Xinghai 唐星海
Tang Yeru 唐哗如
Taochong 桃冲
Tiancheng 天承
Tianchu weijing chang 天厨味精厂
Tianli danqi chang 天利氮气厂
Tiansheng taoqi chang 天盛陶器厂
Tianyuan dianhua chang 天原电化厂
Tōa bōseki kabushiki kaisha 東亞紡績株式會社
Tōa kaiun kabushiki kaisha 東亞海運株式會社
Tōa shinchitsujo 東亞新秩序
Tong Luqing 童侣青
Toyoda bōseki kaisha 豐田紡績會社
Ueda Jiichirō 植田次一郎
Ueno Ryōsaku 上野良作
Wang Huaigen 王槐根
Wang Shijing 汪时璟
Wang Shouyi 王守义
Wang Xiaolai 王孝賚
Wang Xinsheng 王辛生
Wang Yiling 王毅灵
Wang Yintai 王蔭泰
Wang Yuncheng 王云程
Wang Yuqing 王禹卿
weiren jingying 委任经营
Wen Lanting 闻兰亭
Weng Wenyi 翁文猗
Wu Boseng 吴伯僧
Wu Dahuai 吴大槐
Wu Kunsheng 吴昆生
Wu Shihuai 吴士槐
Wu Tongqiao 五通桥
Wu Yi 吴仪
Wu Yunchu 吴蕴初
Wu Yunzhai 吴蕴斋
Wu Zhesheng 吴哲生
Wu Zhichao 吴志超
Wujin yinhang 武進银行
Wuzi tongzhi shenyi weiyuan hui 物资统制审议委员会
Xiang Jiarui 项家瑞

Xianshi gongsi 先施公司
Xibei mao fangzhi chang gufen youxian gongsi 西北毛纺织厂股份有限公司
Xie Hucheng 谢虎丞
Ximo lu 西摩路
Xingzhong gongsi 兴中公司
Xinhe shachang 信和纱厂
Xinmin hui 新民会
Xu Caicheng 徐采丞
Xu Jiqing 徐寄顇
Xu Xinliu 徐新六
Xue Fucheng 薛福成
Xue Fuji 薛福基
Xue Mingjian 薛明剑
Xue Nanming 薛南溟
Xue Shouxuan 薛寿萱
Xue Zukang 薛祖康
Yamadera Gengo 山寺源吾
Yan Yutang 严裕棠
Yang Cansan 楊粲三
Yang Hanxi 楊翰西
Yang Jicheng 楊济成
Yang Jingrong 楊景荣
Yang Oufang 楊藕芳
Yang Shaozhen 样少振
Yang Tongyi 楊通誼
Yang Yifang 楊艺芳
Yangshupu 楊树浦
Yao Mulian 姚慕莲
Yapu'er chang 压浦耳厂
Yasuno Takekazu 安野毅一
Ye Dengzhong 叶澄衷
Yeqin 业勤
Yisheng 义生
Yingchang 荧昌
yizhan yangzhan 以战养战
Yong'an fangzhi gongsi 永安纺织公司
Yong'an renshou baoxian gongsi 永安人寿保险公司
Yong'an shachang 永安纱厂
Yong'an shuihuo baoxian gongsi 永安水火保险公司
Yongfeng qiye gongsi 永丰企业公司
Yonghe gongsi 永和公司
Yongli huaxue gongye gongsi 永利化学工业公司
Yongli jian gongsi 永利碱公司
Yongli liusuan yachang 永利硫酸錏厂
Yongni gongsi 永泥公司
Yongtai 永泰
You Jusun 尤菊荪

Yu Hongjun 俞鸿钧
Yu Xiaqing 虞洽卿
Yu Zhiqing 余芝卿
Yu Zuoting 俞佐庭
Yuan Ludeng 袁履登
Yuan Yuquan 袁愈佺
Yuchang 裕昌
Yue Songsheng 乐松生
Yūhō bōseki kabushiki kaisha 裕豐紡績株式會社
Yuhua 裕华
Yunli 允利
Yusheng huochai chang 裕生火柴厂
Zhabei 闸北
Zhang Jianhui 章剑慧
Zhang Naiqi 张乃器
Zhang Sumin 张素民
Zhang Yifei 张一飞
Zhang Yuanji 张元济
Zhang Zhipeng 张志彭
Zhanghua mao fangzhi chang 章华毛绒纺织公司
Zhaoshang ju 招商局
Zhaoxin 肇新
Zhejiang xingye yinhang 浙江兴业银行
Zhenhua fangzhi gongsi 振华纺织公司
Zhenhuan shachang 震寰纱厂
Zhenjiang zizhi weiyuan hui 镇江自治委员会
Zhengtai 正泰
Zhenxin 振新
Zhenxing zhuzhai zuhe 振兴住宅组合
Zhenye 振业
Zhi'en lu 支恩路
Zhonggu fangzhi jianshe gongsi 中国纺织建设公司
Zhongguo guohuo yinhang 中国国货银行
Zhongguo guoji xintuo zi gongsi 中国国际信托资公司
Zhongguo huochai yuanliao gongsi 中国火柴原料公司
Zhongguo jianshe yin gongsi 中国建设銀公司
Zhongguo lianhe zhunbei yinhang 中国联合準备银行
Zhongguo mao fangzhi gongsi 中国毛纺织公司
Zhongguo mianye gongsi 中国棉业公司
Zhongguo qiye yinhang 中国企业银行
Zhongguo shuini gongsi 中国水泥公司
Zhonghua gongye huaxue yanjiu suo 中华工业化学研究所
Zhonghua huaxue gongye hui 中华化学工业会
Zhonghua lunchuan gufen youxian gongsi 中华轮船股份有限公司
Zhonghua matou gongsi 中华码头公司
Zhonghua minguo linshi zhengfu 中华民国临时政府
Zhonghua niantong chang 中华辗铜厂

Zhongnan yinhang 中南银行
Zhongyang chubei yinhang 中央储备银行
Zhongyang huaxue boli chang 中央化学玻璃厂
Zhongyang huaxue gongye gufen youxian gongsi 中央化学工业股有限公司
Zhongyi 中一
ZhongYi lunchuan gongsi 中意轮船公司
Zhou Jimei 周继美
Zhou Jue 周珏
Zhou Shunqing 周舜卿
Zhou Xuexi 周学熙
Zhou Yangqiao 周仰乔
Zhou Zhaofu 周肇甫
Zhou Zhijun 周志俊
Zhou Zongliang 周宗良
Zhou Zuomin 周作民
Zhu Baosan 朱葆三
Zhu Boquan 朱博泉
Zhu Wenxiong 朱文熊
zuguo 族国

Index

Compositor: Integrated Composition Systems
Text and display: Sabon
Printer and binder: Thomson-Shore